CONGRESS VOLUME

COPENHAGEN 1953

SUPPLEMENTS

TO

VETUS TESTAMENTUM

EDITED BY

THE BOARD OF THE QUARTERLY

G. W. ANDERSON
AAGE BENTZEN †
P. A. H. DE BOER
MILLAR BURROWS
HENRI CAZELLES
MARTIN NOTH

VOLUME I

LEIDEN
E. J. BRILL
1953

CONGRESS VOLUME

COPENHAGEN

1953

LEIDEN
E. J. BRILL
1953

PRINTED IN THE NETHERLANDS

CONTENTS

In memoriam Professor AAGE BENTZEN VII
Bibliography of AAGE BENTZEN IX
Editor's Note XV
AUERBACH, ELIAS, Die grosse Überarbeitung der biblischen Bücher 1
BIČ, MILOŠ, Zur Problematik des Buches Obadjah 11
DRIVER, G. R., Hebrew poetic diction 26
DUPONT-SOMMER, A., Sur les débuts de l'histoire araméenne .. 40
GEMSER, B., The importance of the motive clause in Old Testament law 50
JOHNSON, A. R., The primary meaning of √גאל 67
LINDBLOM, JOH., The political background of the Shiloh oracle 78
MOWINCKEL, SIGMUND, The Hebrew equivalent of Taxo in Ass. Mos. ix 88
MUILENBURG, JAMES, A study in Hebrew rhetoric: repetition and style 97
PARROT, ANDRÉ, Autels et installations cultuelles à Mari 112
VON RAD, GERHARD, Josephsgeschichte und ältere Chokma 120
ROBINSON, T. H., Hebrew poetic form: the English tradition 128
SEELIGMANN, I. L., Voraussetzungen der Midraschexegese .. 150
DE VAUX, R., A propos du second centenaire d'Astruc—réflexions sur l'état actuel de la critique du Pentateuque ... 182
VRIEZEN, TH. C., Prophecy and Eschatology 199

AAGE BENTZEN

IN MEMORIAM PROFESSOR AAGE BENTZEN

When Professor AAGE BENTZEN was elected President of the newly-founded "International Organization of Old Testament Scholars" three years ago in Leyden, he said that he regarded his election as an acknowledgement of Danish research of the Old Testament, and he promised to do everything in his power to prove worthy of the honour. Everybody who knew him well, knows how much time and energy he expended on the arrangement of the Congress in Copenhagen at the end of August, and when his sudden death occurred on 4th June 1953 in the midst of these preparations it was felt by those who had to make the decision that they owed it to Professor BENTZEN's memory to carry out the Congress as planned.

At the time of his death Professor BENTZEN was only 58 years old, but he had been teaching at the University for a great many years. After taking part, in 1923, in a preceding competition, he was appointed lecturer in Old Testament exegesis at the University of Copenhagen, and in 1929 he became professor ordinarius. The result of the competition, for which the participants had only 2 months for preparation, was BENTZEN's first published work: *Den israelitiske Sabbats Oprindelse og Historie indtil Jerusalems Erobring 70 e.K.* [The Origin and History of the Israelite Sabbath until the Conquest of Jerusalem, 70 A.D. (157 pages)].

During his studies in Copenhagen BENTZEN had Fr. BUHL, J. C. JACOBSEN and JOHANNES PEDERSEN as teachers, and each of them exercised an influence which lasted all BENTZEN's life. BUHL and JACOBSEN, in their youth, had introduced the WELLHAUSEN theories into Denmark, and to the end BENTZEN continued to support their conception of the sources of the Pentateuch. Through JOH. PEDERSEN BENTZEN acquired an understanding of the religious-historical school, the works of which were just beginning to be acknowledged at this period. In this way BENTZEN also became a close follower of S. MOWINCKEL who published the 1st volume of his *Psalmenstudien* in 1921 (a year after the publishing of JOHANNES PEDERSEN's *Israel* I-II).

Before BENTZEN obtained an appointment in Copenhagen he had spent several months studying in Germany and England. In Germany he studied in 1921—22 under GUSTAV HÖLSCHER and under PAUL KAHLE in Giessen and here he came under an influence which definitely affected his view of the Massoretic text. The year after his appointment to the University of Copenhagen he undertook a journey to Palestine for the purpose of studying, as a member of "Deutsches evangelisches Institut für Altertumswissenschaft des Heiligen Landes". This journey is the source of his thorough knowledge of the geography of Palestine, and also of his appreciation of the importance of archaeology to old Testament research. Also his *Israels Historie* (1930) and *Bibelatlas* (1938) and his contribution on the Archaeology of the Old Testament in *Haandbog i Kristendomskundskab* vol. II (1943) are fruits of this journey.

During his first years as lecturer at the University BENTZEN devoted much attention to the Psalms, and he knew how to arouse his students interest in the new view of the Psalms which was especially expressed in MOWINCKEL's *Psalmenstudien*. His own little study *Jahves Gæst* bears witness of this. The same year he also published *Die josianische Reform und ihre Voraussetzungen* in which he attempted to prove the influence of the country priests in the reform of 622 B.C. The same question is dealt with in a somewhat different connection in his *Studier over det zadokidiske Præstedømmes Historie* [Studies on the History of the Zadokite Priesthood] (1931).

As University lecturer BENTZEN attached much importance to writing books for his students which acquainted them with the results of modern research. In 1932 he published an introduction to the Psalms, followed by a commentary on the Psalms in 1939. Of other commentaries may be mentioned the commentary on Daniel, in *Handbuch zum Alten Testament*, herausg. von O. EISSFELDT, (1937, second edition 1952), on the *Preacher* (1942) and *Isaiah* (1943-44). During the war he published an *Introduction to the Old Testament* in Danish and later a re-edited edition in English (1948-49, second edition 1952).

Characteristic for BENTZEN as a scholar was his unusually extensive reading and his power of being able to make himself familiar with the latest developments and weigh them in the balance. When he found something new which he could acknowledge, he was not afraid to reject his former ideas. This can be observed in his two works *Det sakrale Kongedømme* (1945) and *Messias—Moses redivivus—Menschensohn* (1948) in which he attempted to estimate both the English and the Swedish form for "Myth and Ritual" research.

BENTZEN's capacity for work was immense and he worked quickly, so that his scientific production — see the bibliography below —

is considerably more extensive than generally. In 1950 the University of Basel honoured him with a degree of Doctor of Theology, and in 1953 he became honorary member of the British Society for Old Testament Study.

At the time of his death BENTZEN was engaged on a new edition of his History of Israel and a Commentary on Deuteronomy, and he had begun work in collaboration with Egyptologists on a edition of the Coptic Septuaginta.

BENTZEN will be missed as an indefatigable investigator and a good and loyal colleague.

E. HAMMERSHAIMB

BIBLIOGRAPHY OF AAGE BENTZEN

a. BOOKS

Den israelitiske Sabbats Oprindelse og Historie indtil Jerusalems Erobring Aar 70 e. Kr. Arbejde, indleveret under Konkurrencen om Universitetets Docentur i det gamle Testamente. J. H. Schultz, Copenhagen 1923. 160 pp.

Die josianische Reform und ihre Voraussetzungen. P. Haase, Copenhagen 1926. 122 pp.

Jahves Gæst. Studier i israelitisk Salmedigtning. Haase, Copenhagen 1926. 72 pp.

Jahves Tjener. Haase, Copenhagen 1928. 64 pp.

Det gamle Testamente. Tre Foredrag. Haase, Copenhagen 1929. 62 pp.

Israels Historie, Haases Haandbøger, vols. 18-19, Copenhagen 1930. 372 pp.

Studier over det Zadokidiske Præsteskabs Historie, in Festschrift Københavns Universitet, November 1931, Copenhagen 1931. 3-114 pp.

Forelæsninger over Indledning til de gammeltestamentlige Salmer, holdt i Efteraarssemestret 1931. G. E. C. Gad, Copenhagen 1932. 180 pp.

Omkring Bibelhistorien. Seks Foredrag. Haase, Copenhagen 1933. 108 pp.

Anti-Kaper. Et fredsvenligt Svar. Haase, Copenhagen 1933. 40 pp.

Israels Folk, in Den bibelske Historie bearbejdet for Mellemskolen, Aschehoug, Copenhagen 1934. 102 pp. 2nd ed. 1939. 3rd ed. 1941. 4th ed. 1947.

Daniel, in Handbuch zum A.T., Tübingen 1937, ix + 53 pp. 2nd revised ed. 1952. 87 pp.

Danielsbogens Aktualitet. Forelæsninger holdt paa det videnskabelige Præstekursus i København, Oktober 1938. Gad, Copenhagen 1938. 40 pp.

Det Danske Bibelselskabs Bibelatlas. Haase, Copenhagen 1938. 16 pp.

Finder vi Kristus i det gamle Testamente? Et Foredrag. Gad, Copenhagen 1938. 24 pp.

Fortolkning til de gammeltestamentlige Salmer. Gad, Copenhagen 1939. xi + 690 pp.

Indledning til det gamle Testamente. I 1. Skrifterne. I 2. Literaturformerne. II. Skriften. Gad, Copenhagen 1941. 454 pp.

Tillæg til Israels Folk og Jesus og hans Apostle, in Den bibelske Historie bearbejdet for Mellemskolen, Aschehoug, Copenhagen 1941. 12 pp.

Prædikerens Bog, fortolket. Gad, Copenhagen 1942. 138 pp.

Jesaja, fortolket. Vol. I, Jes. 1-39; Vol. II, Jes. 40-66. Gad, Copenhagen 1943. 336 and 169 pp.

Hverdagsliv og Gudstjeneste. Gammeltestamentlig Arkæologi. In: Haandbog i Kristendomskundskab. E. Munksgaard, Copenhagen 1943, pp. 72-203.

Helgen eller Højforræder? Jeremias og hans Folk. Gad, Copenhagen 1943. 103 pp.

Det har slet ingen Hast for den, som tror —. Fire Foredrag og en Prædiken. Gad, Copenhagen 1944. 52 pp.

Loven, Profeterne, Skrifterne. Aschehoug, Copenhagen 1944. 48 pp.

Det sakrale Kongedømme. Bemærkninger i en løbende Diskussion om de gammeltestamentlige Salmer. In: Festskrift Københavns Universitet, November 1945. Copenhagen 1945. 3-127 pp.

Introduction to the Old Testament. Vol. I The Canon of the O.T. The Text of the O.T. The Forms of O.T. Literature. Vol. II. The Books of the O.T. Gad, Copenhagen 1948. 268 and 300 pp. 2nd ed., revised and with a supplement, 1952. 268 and 332 pp.

Messias—Moses redivivus—Menschensohn. Skizzen zum Thema Weissagung und Erfüllung. Zwingli-Verlag, Zürich 1948. 80 pp.

b. ARTICLES

Ezra-Nehemia, in *Teologisk Tidsskrift for den danske Folkekirke* (*Teol. Ts.*) iv, 1, 1920. pp. 177-205.

Ezrakildens Slutning, in *Teol. Ts.* iv, 2, 1921. pp. 15-48.

De aramaiske Dokumenter i Ezra—nogle Bemærkninger, in *Teol. Ts.* iv, 4, 1923. pp. 97-127.

Om Dekalogen, in *Teol. Ts.* iv, 5, 1924. pp. 306-343.

Salme 27—et Par Bemærkninger, in *Festschrift Fr. Buhl*, V. Pios Boghandel, Copenhagen 1925. pp. 14-23.

Deuteronomiumproblemerne. Et Referat og en Thesis, in *Teol. Ts.* iv, 7, 1926. pp. 34-43.

Formodninger angaaende Dateringen af Salme 110 og 2, in *Teol. Ts.* iv, 8, 1927. pp. 50-53.

Zur Erläuterung von Jesaja 5, 1-7, in *Archiv für Orientforschung* iv, 1927, pp. 209-210.

I Anledning af Gunkels Kommentar og Indledning til Salmerne, in *Teol. Ts.* iv, 9, 1928. pp. 99-122, and *ib.* iv, 10, 1929. pp. 177-203.

Davids Salmer, in *Frem* iv, 1, 1928. pp. 432-440.

Israels Ordsprogsdigtning, in *Frem* iv, 1, 1928. pp. 818-823.

Udtrykket mischpath katub i Salme 149, 9, in *Teol. Ts.* iv, 10, 1929. pp. 60-63.

Det gamle Testamente i ny Oversættelse, in *Nationaltidende*, May 14, 1929.

Priesterschaft und Laien in der jüdischen Gemeinde des fünften Jahrhunderts, in *A.f.O.* vi, 1930-31. pp. 280-286.

Quelques remarques sur le mouvement messianique parmi les Juifs aux environs de l'an 500 av. J.-C., in *Revue d'hist. et de philos. rel.* x, 1930, pp. 493-503.

Ved Valg af Fagstudium. De aandelige Kaar under Studiet af 1. Teologi, in *Studenten*, Akademisk Ugeblad for Studerende ved Københavns Universitet 2, Sept. 10, 1930.

Frants Buhl, in *Berlingske Tidende*, Sept. 9, 1930.

„De stille i Landet", in *Teol. Ts.* v, 3, 1932, pp. 196-204.

Lidt Materiale til Forstaaelse af Kingos Oversættelse af „Poenitendse-Psalmerne" i Aandeligt Sjungekors Første Part, in *Teol. Ts.* v, 3, 1932, pp. 241-294.

Det gamle Testamente historisk og filologisk belyst, in *Akademisk Tidende*, 3, 1932, pp. 495-497.

Biographies of Old Testament scholars etc., in *Dansk Biografisk Leksikon*, vols. 1-27. Schultz, Copenhagen 1933-1944.
Kingos Poenitendse Psalmer. En Efterskrift, in *Teol. Ts.* v, 4, 1933, pp. 24-36.
Niels Pedersens hebraiske Metrik—et 300 Aars Jubilæum, in *Teol. Ts.* v, 4, 1933, pp. 81-106.
Zur Geschichte der Sadokiden, in *Z.A.W.*, N.F. 10, 1933, pp. 173-176.
De ti Bud, in *Berlingske Tidende*, Dec. 15, 1933.
Palæstinesiske Grave i Oldtiden, in *Dansk Ligbrændingsforening*, Copenhagen 1934, pp. 119-154.
Gammel og ny Bibelhistorie, in *Vor Ungdom* 1934, pp. 298-306.
En engelsk "Skolebogsbetærkning", in *Gymnasieskolen* 17, 1934, pp. 167-172.
To arkæologiske Opdagelser, som er af Vigtighed for Forstaaelsen af det gamle Testamente, in *Teol. Ts.* v 8, 1937, pp. 18-40.
Övergången över havet, in *Svensk Exegetisk Årsbok*, 2, 1937, pp. 93-106.
Missionstanker hos Profeterne. Foredrag, in *Nordisk Missions Tidsskrift*, 48, 1937, pp. 49-66 and 100-111.
Om kristologisk exegese, in *Dansk Teol. Ts.* i, 1938, pp. 65-93.
1913-1938, og derefter —, in *Studenterne 1913*, Haase, Copenhagen 1938, pp. vii-xiv.
Die Schwindsucht in Ps. 106, 15b, in *Z.A.W.*, N.F. 16, 1939, p. 152.
Missionstankens baggrund i de gammeltestamentlige salmer, in *Nordisk Missions-Tidsskrift* 51, 1940, pp. 236-242.
Lakisj Brevene—en arkæologisk Sæbeoble? in *Gads danske Magasin* 34, 1940, pp. 491-500.
Gud er til, saa er der intet at frygte! Om det gamle Testamentes Salmebog, in *Nationaltidende*, Sept. 22, 1940.
Nyere synspunkter vedrørende Israels indvandring i Palæstina, in *Dansk Teol. Ts.* iv, 1941, pp. 1-26.
Israels gudstjeneste—strejflys ud fra salmerne, in *Gads danske Magasin* 35, 1941, pp. 469-480.
Skolen og Kristendommen, in *Berlingske Aftenavis*, Aug. 22, 1941.
Det gamle Testamente og Krigen, in *Kirken og Tiden* 18, 1942, pp. 33-39 and 65-71.
Et Fags Forvandling, in *Nationaltidende*, Jan. 16, 1942.
Faget "Bibelkundskab" ved teologisk Forprøve, in *Kristeligt Dagblad*, Febr. 7, 1942.
Professor Dr theol. J. C. Jacobsen 80 Aar, in *Berlingske Aftenavis*, March 5, 1942.
Ny dansk Udgave af Oversættelsen af det gamle Testamente, in *Berlingske Aftenavis*, Aug. 1, 1942.
Det israelitiske historiesyn, in *Dansk Teol. Ts.* vii, 1944, pp. 155-172.
Om Sigmund Mowinckels indsats i den gammeltestamentlige forskning, in Acta Mowinckeliana, *Norsk Teol. Ts.* xlv, 3, 1944, pp. 3-15.
Forklaringer til udvalgte Tekster fra det gamle Testamente: Gen. xxii 1-14; 1 Sam. xv 22-23; 1 Reg. xvii; Ps li; Is. lii 13-liii 12; Jer. vii 1-15 and 21-24, in *Haandbog i Kristendomskundskab*, Vol. viii Forklaringer til Lidelseshistorien, Opstandelses- og Himmelfartshistorien samt udvalgte Tekster fra det gamle Testamente, Munksgaard, Copenhagen 1945, pp. 142-146; 154-161; 171-175; 195-207.
Syndens sold er døden, in *Dansk Teol. Ts.* viii, 1945, pp. 65-82.
Palæstina, in *Ledetraad ved folkelig Universitetsundervisning*, Munksgaard, Copenhagen 1946. 4 pp.
Professor Holger Mosbech 60 Aar, in *Nationaltidende*, March 18, 1946.
Egon Johannesens Testamente, in *Berlingske Aftenavis*, July 19, 1946.

On the Idea of "the old" and "the new" in Deutero-Isaiah, in *Studia Theol. cura ordinum theologorum Scandinavorum edita*, i, 1947, pp. 183-187. Cp. Actes du XXIe Congrès internat. des Orientalistes, Paris 1948 (Paris 1949, p. 115).
Der Tod des Beters in den Psalmen. Randbemerkungen zur Diskussion zwischen Mowinckel und Widengren, in *Festschrift Eissfeldt*, Halle 1947, pp. 57-60.
Kan ordet "Messiansk" anvendes om Salmernes kongeforestillinger?, in *Svensk Exeg. Årsbok* xii, 1947, pp. 36-50.
De ti bud og tidens moral, in *Ledetraad ved folkelig Universitetsundervisning*, Nr. 207, Munksgaard, Copenhagen 1947. 4 pp.
Skal Religions-Undervisningen i Gymnasiet afskaffes?, in *Kristeligt Dagblad*, Nov. 11, 1947.
The Cultic Use of the Story of the Ark in Samuel, in *J.B.L.* 67, 1948, pp. 37-53.
Ezras Persönlichkeit, in *Studia Theol. etc.*, ii, 1948, pp. 95-97.
Skandinavische Literatur zum Alten Testament 1939-1948, in *Theol. Rundschau*, N.F. 17, 1948-1949, pp. 273-328.
J. C. Jacobsen, in *Stud. Theol.* x, 5, Nov. 1948, pp. 3-5.
Many articles on O.T. etc. in *Illustreret Religionsleksikon*, Vol. I, Skandinavisk Bogforlag, Odense 1949; Vols. II and III, 1950.
King Ideology—"Urmensch"—"Troonsbestijgingsfeest", in *Studia Theol. etc.* iii, 1949, pp. 143-157.
Sirach, der Chronist, und Nehemia, in *Studia Theol. etc.* iii, 1949, pp. 158-161.
Poznámky k Novějším Řešením Otázky Pentateuchu (translated by M. Bič), in *Theol. Evangelica*, Ročník ii, 1949, Čislo 4.
J. C. Jacobsen, 6. marts 1862-10. september 1948, in Festskrift København Universitet, Nov. 1949, pp. 165-170.
Ud af Tyskland, in *Berlingske Aftenavis*, Jan. 8, 1949.
D. G. Monrad og Profeterne, in *Berlingske Aftenavis*, May 12, 1949.
Daniel 6. Ein Versuch zur Vorgeschichte der Märtyrerlegende, in *Festschrift Bertholet*, Tübingen 1950, pp. 58-67.
Der Hedammu-Mythus, das Judithbuch und ähnliches, in *Festschrift Hrozny, Archiv Orientalní* xviii, 1950, pp. 1-2.
The ritual Background of Amos i 2-ii 16, in *O.T.S.* vii, 1950, pp. 85-99.
Der böse Fürst, in *Studia Theol. etc.* iv, 1950, pp. 109-119.
The Old Testament and the New Covenant, in *Herv. Teol. Stud.* (Pretoria) vii, 1950, pp. 1-15.
De nye hebraiske haandskrifter fra Palæstina, in *Gads danske Magasin*, 44, 1950, pp. 349-356.
En akt af den jødiske tragedie, in *Gads danske Magasin* 44, 1950, pp. 201-204.
"Vi, der er onde". Tidens moral og dens forhold til kristendommen, in *Våbenhuset* i, 1950, pp. 42-49.
Det gamle Testamente og Den nye Pagt, in *Bibelsyn*, A. Busch, Copenhagen, 1951, pp. 192-210.
Den gammeltestamentlige profetisme—"det enestaaende"? Foredrag under den tredje konferanse av de nordiske teologiske fakulteters lærere, Oslo 30. august-1. september, in *Norsk Teol. Ts.* lii, 1951, pp. 209-226.
"Adam" og "menneskene", in *Svensk Teol. Kvartalskrift* xxvii, 1951, pp. 166-168.
Patriarchal "Benediction" and Prophetic Book, in Gemser Jubileumnummer, *Herv. Teol. Stud.* vii, 1951, pp. 106-109.
Biblical Criticism, History of Israel, and O.T. Theology, in *The Evangelical Quarterly* xxiii, 1951, pp. 85-88.
Bemerkungen über neuere Entwicklungen in der Pentateuchfrage, in *Archiv Orientalní* xix, 1951, pp. 226-232.

The Weeping of Jacob, Hos. xii 5b, in *V.T.* i, 1951, pp. 58-59.
Der Sichel, in *V.T.* i 1951, pp. 216-217.
Universitetets Stilling i den tyske Østzone, in *Nationaltidende*, Aug. 29, 1951.
'Επύρωσεν, Judith 8, 27, in *Bibliotheca Orientalis* ix, 1952, pp. 174-175.
Hvor gammel blev Moses?, in *Nationaltidende*, July 11, 1952.

c. REVIEWS [1])

Aalen, Die Begriffe "Licht" und "Finsternis" im A.T., im Spätjudentum und im Rabbinismus, 1951, in *V.T.* ii 2, 1952, pp. 382-384.
Abrahams, Bevan and Singer, The Legacy of Israel, 1948, in *Dansk Teol. Ts.* xiii, 1950, pp. 49-51.
Allwohn, Die Ehe des Propheten Hosea in psycho-analytischer Beleuchtung, 1926, in *Theol. Ts.* iv, 8, 1927, pp. 295-299.
Baumgärtel, Hebräisches Wörterbuch zur Genesis, 1926, in *A.f.O.* iv, 1927, p. 167.
Beer, Kurze Uebersicht über den Inhalt der Alttest. Schriften, 1926, in *A.f.O.* iv, 1927, p. 167.
Beer u. Galling, Exodus, 1939, in *Th. L. Z.* 1940, p. 13.
Bendixon, Israels historia från äldsta tider til Herodes Tronbestigning, 1948, in *Dansk Teol. Ts.* xiii, 1950, p. 47.
Boström, Proverbiastudien, 1928, in *Teol. Ts.* v, 7, 1937, pp. 258-259.
Brunner, Die Unentbehrlichkeit des A.T.s für die missionierende Kirche, 1934, in *Teol. Ts.* v, 6, 1935, pp. 76-77.
Bruno, Das hebräische Epos, 1935, in *Acta Or.* xv, 1936-1937, pp. 329-331.
Coppens, Les harmonies des deux Testaments, 1949, in *Dansk Teol. Ts.* xiii, 1950, pp. 44-46.
Daniélou, Sacramentum futuri, 1950, in *Erasmus* iv, 1951, pp. 213-215.
Dietrich, שוב שבות, 1925, in *Teol. Ts.* v, 1, 1930, pp. 267-270.
Dietze, Ussia, 1929, in *Deutsche Lit. zeit.* 1930, p. 1011.
Edelkoort, Nahum, Habakuk, Zefanja, 1937, in *Acta Or.* xvi, 1937-38, p. 245.
Eichrodt, Hoffnung d. ewigen Friedens, 1920, in *Teol. Ts.* iv, 2, 1921, pp. 165-170.
Eichrodt, Theologie des A.T.s, I, 1933, in *Teol. Ts.* v, 5, 1934, pp. 288-307; II, 1935, *ib.* v, 7, 1937, pp. 259-260; III, 1939, in *Dansk Teol. Ts.* iii, 1940, pp. 116-117.
Eichrodt, Das Menschenverständnis, 1944, in *Præsteforeningens Blad* 36, 1946, pp. 177-178.
Engberg and Shipton, Notes on the Chalcolitic and Early Bronze Age Pottery of Megiddo, 1934, in *Acta Or.* xv, 1936-37, p. 329.
Fischer, Zur Septuaginta-Vorlage im Pentateuch, 1926, in *Teol. Ts.* iv, 8, 1927, pp. 295-299.
Fog, Kirkelige Brydninger i Danmark i Nutiden, 1935, in *Berlingske Tidende*, Dec. 29, 1935.
Friediger, Grundtræk af Jødedommens Etik, 1938, in *Berlingske Tidende*, July 10, 1938.
Fries, Vår kärleks historia, 1945, in *Berlingske Aftenavis*, April 12, 1946.
Gadd, The Fall of Nineve, 1923, in *Teol. Ts.* iv, 7, 1926, pp. 160-163.
Galling, Die Erwählungstraditionen Israels, 1928, in *Teol. Ts.* iv, 10, 1929, pp. 189-191.
Gunkel, Einleitung in den Psalmen, 2, 1933, in *Teol. Ts.* v, 5, 1934, pp. 208-209.

[1]) This alphabetical list is incomplete.

Hempel, A.T. und Geschichte, 1930, in *Teol. Ts.* v, 2, 1931, pp. 73-84.
Herner, Gamle Testamentets Religion, 1927, in *Teol. Ts.* v, 2, 1931, pp. 335-337.
Hertzberg, Prophet und Gott, 1923, in *Teol. Ts.* iv, 8, 1927, pp. 63-64.
Hjerl-Hansen, Emmaus, 1947, in *Præsteforeningens Blad* 38, 1948, pp. 35-36.
Høyer, Fra Sinai til Sion, 1930, in *Teol. Ts.* v, 3, 1932, pp. 60-67.
Hulst, Het karakter van den cultus in Deuteronomium, 1938, in *Theol. Lit. zeit.* lxv, 1939, pp. 168-169.
Hylmö, De s. k. vallfartssångerna i psaltaren, 1925, in *Teol. Ts.* iv, 8, 1927, pp. 66-67.
Johannesen, Studier over Esras og Nehemjas Historie, 1946, in *Theol. Lit. zeit.* lxxiii, 1948, p. 348; cp. too *Nationaltidende*, March 25, 1946.
Jørgensen, Bibelhistorie og Kirkehistorie, 1936, in *Berlingske Tidende*, Dec. 20, 1936.
Kegel, Die Kultusreformation des Esra, 1921, in *Teol. Ts.* iv, 3, 1922, pp. 152-153.
Kittel, Die Religion des Volkes Israel, 1921, in *Teol. Ts.* iv, 2, 1921, pp. 165-170.
Kittel, Die alttest. Wissenschaft, [4]1921, in *Teol. Ts.* iv, 2, 1921, pp. 165-170.
Kuhl, Die drei Männer im Feuer, 1930, in *Teol. Ts.* v, 3, 1931, p. 150.
Kuhn, Erklärung des Buches Koheleth, 1926, in *Teol. Ts.* iv, 8, 1927, pp. 295-299.
Laqueur, Josephus, 1920, in *Teol. Ts.* iv, 3, 1922, pp. 153-159.
Lerch, Isaaks Opferung christlich gedeutet, 1950, in *Erasmus* iv, 1951, pp. 345-349.
Lindblom, Die literarische Gattung der prophetischen Literatur, 1924, in *Teol. Ts.* iv, 8, 1927, pp. 63-66.
Lindblom, Hosea literarisch untersucht, 1927, in *Teol. Ts.* v, 10, 1930, pp. 339-341.
Lindblom, Micha literarisch untersucht, 1929, in *Teol. Ts.* v, 2, 1931, pp. 330-335.
Lindblom, Profetismen i Israel, 1934, in *Teol. Ts.* v, 6, 1935, pp. 143-155.
Lindblom, Den gammeltestamentlige Religionens egenart, 1935, in *Teol. Ts.* v, 7, 1937, pp. 156-158.
Lurje, Studien zur Geschichte der wirtschaftlichen und sozialen Verhältnisse, 1927, in *Teol. Ts.* iv, 9, 1928, p. 55.
Lüthi, Den kommende Kirke, 1938, in *Berlingske Tidende*, July 17, 1938.
Melchior, "Man siger, at Jøderne", 1936, in *Berlingske Tidende*, Oct. 18, 1936.
Möbius, Die Aktualität der Eschatologie bei den alttestamentlichen Propheten, 1940, in *Theol. Lit. zeit.* lxxiii, 1948, p. 416.
Mowinckel, Profeten Jesaja, 1925, in *Teol. Ts.* iv, 6, 1925, pp. 340-343.
Mowinckel, Religion og kultus, 1950, in *Dansk Teol. Ts.* xiii, 1950, pp. 113-114.
Mowinckel, Han, som kommer, 1950, in *Dansk Teol. Ts.* xiv, 1951, pp. 112-124; cp. too *Politiken*, March 1, 1951.
Mowinckel, Offersang og sangoffer, 1951, in *Dansk Teol. Ts.* xv, 1952, pp. 234-238.
Glueck, Das Wort *ḥesed*, 1927, in *Teol. Ts.* iv, 9, 1928, pp. 338-339.
Noth, Geschichte Israels, 1950, in *Dansk Teol. Ts.* xiv, 1951, pp. 58-61.
Nowack, Schabbat, 1924; 'Erubin, 1926; Windfuhr, Baba batra, 1925, in *Teol. Ts.* iv, 9, 1928, p. 55.
Oestreicher, Reichstempel und Ortsheiligtümer in Israel, 1930, in *Teol. Ts.* v, 2, 1931, pp. 252-257.
Pfeiffer, History of New Testament Times, 1949, in *Dansk Teol. Ts.* xiii, 1950, pp. 46-47.
Price, The Ancestry of our English Bible, 2nd ed. 1949, in *Dansk Teol. Ts.* xiii, 1950, pp. 42-44.
Quell, Das kultische Problem der Psalmen, 1926, in *A.f.O.* iv, 1927, pp. 98-99.
Robinson, The Genius of Hebrew Grammar, 1927, in *A.f.O.* vii, 1931, p. 51.
Rowley, Recent Discovery and the Patriarchal Age, 1949, in *Dansk Teol. Ts.* xiii, 1950, pp. 47-49.
Rowley, ed., The Old Testament and Modern Study, 1951, in *Dansk Teol. Ts.* xvi, 1953, pp. 63-64.

Sellin, Alttestamentliche Theologie, 1933, in *Teol. Ts.* v, 5, 1934, pp. 288-307.
de Senarclens, Le mystère de l'histoire, 1949, in *Dansk Teol. Ts.* xv, 1952, pp. 117-118; cp. too in *Erasmus* iv, 1951, pp. 15-16.
Schmidt-Phieseldeck, Sproglige Noter til den hebræiske Genesis, 1936, in *O.L.Z.* 1936, pp. 230-231.
Stave, Israels Profeter (Jesaja), 1926, in *Teol. Ts.* iv, 9, 1928, pp. 54-55.
Stave, Samhällsliv, egendom och arbete i Bibelns ljus, 1927, in *Teol. Ts.* v, 3, 1931, pp. 148-150.
Thiele, The Mysterious Numbers of the Hebrew Kings, 1951, in *Dansk Teol. Ts.* xv, 1952, pp. 250-252.
Vischer, Das Christuszeugnis des A.T.s I, 1933, in *Dansk Teol. Ts.* i, 1938, pp. 65 sq.
Vriezen, Palestina en Israël, n.y., in *Præsteforeningens Blad* 41, 1951, pp. 510-512.
Weiser, Die Prophetie des Amos, 1929, in *Teol. Ts.* v, 1, 1930, pp. 337-338.
Welsh, Jeremiah, 1928, in *A.f.O.* vii, 1931, pp. 50-51.
Winquist, Paul Nicolay och kretsen kring honom, 1944, in *Berlingske Aftenavis*, Aug. 19, 1946.
Wischnitzer, The Messianic Theme in the Paintings of the Dura Synagogue, 1948, in *Dansk Teol. Ts.* xi, 1948, pp. 186-188.
Young, The Prophecy of Daniel, 1949, in *Præsteforeningens Blad* 41, 1951, pp. 425-429.

EDITORS' NOTE

This Congress Volume has become at the same time a Memorial to AAGE BENTZEN who was born December 13, 1894 in Ordrup and died June 4, 1953 in Copenhagen. He was President of the International Organization of Old Testament Scholars and a member of the Editorial Board of *Vetus Testamentum* from 1950 until his death.

The Organization is much indebted to Mrs E. A. BENTZEN-SMITH who has finished her husband's work on the congress with great devotion and ability.

The editors are indebted to Professor HAMMERSHAIMB, Aarhus, for the article in commemoration of Professor BENTZEN; to Professor JANSMA, Leyden, for reading most of the proofs; and to Mr F. WILLESEN, stud. theol., Hellerup, for assisting in the preparation of the bibliography of Professor BENTZEN.

DIE GROSSE ÜBERARBEITUNG DER BIBLISCHEN BÜCHER

von

Dr Elias Auerbach
Haifa

Wer tiefer in den Aufbau der hebräischen Bibel eindringt, hat ein in der Welt-Literatur wohl einzigartiges Phänomen vor sich: Es sind eigentlich zwei Bibeln. Die eine ist die Bibel der ursprünglichen historischen und sagenhaften Erzählungen und der originalen prophetischen Schriften; die andere ist das Werk, das ich „die grosse Überarbeitung der Bibel" nennen möchte. Zu einer bestimmtem, gut definierbaren Zeit hat eine grosse Überarbeitung der gesamten bis dahin vorhandenen „heiligen Schriften" stattgefunden, und diese bestimmt Aufbau, Inhalt und Wirkung der uns heute vorliegenden Bibel in entscheidender Weise, da sie in gewissem Sinne etwas ganz Neuartiges entstehen liess.

Diese Veränderung umfasst den Pentateuch, sämtliche historischen Bücher und den weitaus grössten Teil der prophetischen Schriften. Frei von dieser Bearbeitung sind alle Schriften, die im Exil oder nach dem Exil entstanden sind, also im wesentlichen der dritte Hauptteil der Bibel und die letzten Propheten von Ezechiel an.

Die volle Bedeutung dieser Überarbeitung wird durch eine einfache Feststellung klar: *Bis heute ist die Auffassung des Bibellesers von wichtigen Entwicklungen der äusseren und geistigen Geschichte Israels stärker durch die Überarbeitung geprägt als durch die originalen Traditionen und Berichte der älteren ursprünglichen Quellen.*

Dafür ein paar Beispiele. Wir sehen die Schöpfung als das Sechs-Tage-Werk des Schöpfers in Gen. 1 und nicht als die ältere einfache Schöpfungs-Geschichte des Jahwisten in Gen. 2. Unser Bild von der Sintflut ist durch die jüngere Darstellung geprägt. Der wundersame Durchzug des Volkes zwischen den Wassermauern des Schilfmeeres hat einen älteren natürlicheren Bericht völlig verdrängt. Moses darf das Gelobte Land nicht betreten, weil er ein Vergehen begangen hat, von dem die Älteren nichts wissen. Die Eroberung Canaans erfolgt in raschem Ansturm, unter Ausrottung der Canaanäer, im Gegensatz zum wirklichen Gang der Dinge im alten Bericht, der langsamen Durchdringung unter Verschmelzung beider Völker. Saul wird König durch einen gottgewollten Zufall, nicht durch eigene Leistung, und wird sofort verworfen. Fast alle Könige sind Bösewichter, das Volk fällt fortwährend zu fremden Göttern ab und führt dadurch alles Unglück herbei. So ist das Bild, das der Bibelleser seit mehr als 2000 Jahren sieht, weil die Bearbeitung es so malt.

Eine so grundlegende Neu-Bearbeitung einer umfangreichen Literatur wird nicht an *einem* Tage gemacht und nicht von *einer* Hand; gewiss haben ganze Generation an ihr gearbeitet. Wichtig aber ist vor allem, ihren *zeitlichen Ansatz* zu finden, also ihren „Sitz im Leben" zu bestimmen. Gelingt das auch nur für einzelne Teile, so können wir an diesen ihre Besonderheit in Form und Inhalt, in Motiven und Zielen studieren und andere Teile an ihrer Verwandtschaft in diesen Zügen erkennen.

Diese Möglichkeit ist jetzt mit grosser Sicherheit durch die „babylonische Datierung" im Pentateuch gegeben. So lässt sich erweisen, dass die Arbeit an der Neugestaltung der Überlieferung *in den* 50 *Jahren des babylonischen Exils und in den ihm folgenden Generationen* geleistet worden ist. Alles, was zur Überarbeitung der Bibel gehört, ist nach 605 geschrieben. Der Bruch in der äusseren Geschichte des Volkes ist zugleich auch der Bruch in der Geschichte der Traditions-Gestaltung.

Dieser zeitliche Ansatz erklärt sofort zwei Dinge; wir verstehen ohne weiteres, warum ein Teil der biblischen Bücher von der Überarbeitung nicht erfasst worden ist: es sind die Bücher, die mit dem Geist der Überarbeiter übereinstimmen oder erst nach der Überarbeitung entstanden sind; wir verstehen zweitens sofort die Motive der grossen Überarbeitung. Für die Zeit des Exils ist es verständlich, dass sie nach einer inneren Ursache für das nationale Unglück sucht und sie in einer Schuld der Väter, in einem Abfall von den Geboten Jahwes, findet. Das wird zum Leitgedanken der Bearbeitung der alten Geschichte und zur allgemein anerkannten „richtigen" Deutung dieser Geschichte.

Zweck der Bearbeitung der Bibel ist die Anpassung der alten heiligen Schriften an den Geist einer neuen Zeit. Wir werden dies alsbald im einzelnen zeigen.

Wer waren die *Bearbeiter*?

Wenn wir von der heute wieder allgemein acceptierten Anschauung ausgehen, dass das unter Josia aufgefundene Gesetzbuch der Kern des Deuteronomiums war, müssen wir die langen Einleitungen (Dt i-xi) und die Schlussbetrachtungen (xxviii-xxxi) als das Werk etwas späterer „deuteronomistischer" Kreise ansehen, die in die Zeit des Exils zu setzen sind. Dafür sprechen die wiederholten Hinweise auf das Exil und das Versprechen der Rückkehr bei Befolgung der göttlichen Gebote. Charakteristisch für diese Einleitungs- und Schluss-Reden zum Gesetzbuch sind zwei Rede-Formen: die Ermahnung zum Halten der Gebote und die geschichtlichen Überblicke mit Aufzählung der Grosstaten Jahwes an Israel.

Beide sind nun bezeichnend für eine Reihe von Stücken im Buche Josua, und diese hat man darum mit Recht als „deuteronomistisch" bezeichnet. Man vergleiche etwa Dt xi 3-6 mit Jos xxiii 3-9.

Wichtiger aber ist hier die Erkenntnis, dass Jos xxiv in den Kreis der „deuteronomistischen Bearbeitung" ebenfalls gehört. Dieses Kapitel spielt eine erhebliche Rolle in zahlreichen neueren Publikationen. Man sieht in ihm eine historische Quelle für einen „Sichem-Bund der Zwölf Stämme" und hat darauf weitreichende Theorien aufgebaut. Es muss mit aller Schärfe gesagt werden, dass *hier von einer historischen Quelle gar keine Rede sein kann.*

Das ganze Kapitel (ausser 30-33) ist vielmehr eine typische deuteronomistische Konstruktion exilischer Herkunft. Die Darstellung Sichems als eines alt-israelitischen Zentral-Heiligtums hat nicht die geringste historische Basis. Sichem ist noch bis auf Abimelech (um 1100) eine canaanäische Enklave geblieben und in seiner Zeit zum ersten Mal erobert worden. Hier stand noch in Abimelechs Tagen nicht ein *israelitisches* Heiligtum, sondern ein *canaanäisches* des „baʿal brit" (Jud ix 4 und 27; in ix 46 ist nach Erweis von LXX und Lat. Lugd. „baʿal" erst in „ēl" korrigiert worden). Die künstliche Konstruktion des Verfassers von Jos xxiv verrät sich durch die Erwähnung des Gottesbaumes in 26. Wann ist diese Eiche gewachsen? In den wenigen Jahren der Landeseroberung durch Josua? Die Idee, dass die Israeliten schon zur Zeit Josuas, wenige Jahre nach dem Tode Moše's, fremde Götterbilder besassen (xxiv 23), ist ebenso ungeheuerlich wie charakteristisch für die unhistorische Auffassung der Exilszeit. Das Ganze hat nichts mit Geschichte zu tun, und die Theorien, die darauf aufgebaut worden sind, sind damit hinfällig. — Das genaue Gegenstück zur Rede Josuas findet sich in Neh ix und hier passt sie durchaus in den Geist ihrer Zeit.

Ganz allgemein gesprochen *müssen* diese Reden mit den historischen Reminiszenzen jung sein. Als wirkliche Reden an Miterlebende könnten sie *einmal* gehalten werden; in ihrer immer wiederkehrenden Wiederholung sind sie nicht nur wirkungslos, sondern unmöglich.

Eine Anzahl solcher Stücke kann man als „deuteronomistisch" bezeichnen; aber es ist eine bekannte Erfahrung, dass man bei vielen ebenso geneigt sein kann, sie P zuzurechnen. Denn P ist die zweite und weit umfangreichere Schicht der „grossen Überarbeitung" und dem D in vieler Beziehung sehr ähnlich. Diese Erscheinung ist von grosser Bedeutung. Beide Schichten gehören der gleichen Zeit und den gleichen Gedanken-Kreisen an. Aber es ist auch nicht besonders wichtig, sie überall von einander zu scheiden, und deshalb wähle ich für beide den gemeinsamen Namen „die grosse Überarbeitung". Sie haben beide das gleiche Ziel: die Anpassung der überlieferten Texte an die Bedürfnisse ihrer Zeit.

Aber die Überarbeitung durch P, da wo sie sicher als ihm zugehörig zu erkennen ist, ist nach Umfang und Wirkung so viel bedeutender, dass wir sie gesondert betrachten müssen.

Sehr klar tritt die *Überarbeitung des P* in den *Sagen des Pentateuchs* hervor, an der D gar nicht beteiligt ist.

Der Unterschied gegen J ist frappant in der Schöpfungsgeschichte. J erzählt schöne Märchen mit individuellen Zügen: die Formung des Menschen aus Lehm, die Schaffung der Frau aus der Rippe des Mannes, die Benennung der Tiere, die Pflanzung des Gartens. P(Gen i) erzählt systematisch, „wissenschaftlich", und nach religiösem Plan. Gott ist eine kosmische Kraft, er befiehlt und alles wird. Ein 6-Tage-Werk, am siebenten der Sabbat. An die Stelle des Märchens tritt das Wunder. Das Märchen ist religiös indifferent, das Wunder ist ein religiöser Begriff.

P begleitet weiter die Erzählungen des J mit seinen Korrekturen. Die Sintflut ist bei J eine Naturkatastrophe, ein 40-tägiger Regen mit Überschwemmung; bei P eine mythische Katastrophe, die „Schleusen des Himmels" öffnen sich, sodass obere und untere Wasser sich wieder vereinigen, die „Quellen der Tehom" brechen auf. Aber auch hier verläuft das Wunder systematisch, genaue Daten (nach babylonischer Datierung!) regeln das Steigen und Fallen der Wasser. — Der gleiche Unterschied zeigt sich im Stammbaum der Urväter vor der Sintflut.

Ein anderes klares Beispiel liefert der Durchzug durch das Schilfmeer. Der Bericht des J weiss nichts von einem Zug des Volkes durch das Wasser; die Katastrophe der Ägypter erfolgt zwar durch göttliche Fügung, aber durch natürliche Kräfte, durch einen Ostwind. Im Bericht des P teilt sich das Meer, die Wasser stehen als Mauern zu beiden Seiten, das Volk zieht zwischen ihnen hindurch. — Das Manna ist bei J ein einmaliges Wunder (Ex xvi 13-15): am Abend kommen die Wachteln, am Morgen mit dem Tau das Manna; P macht daraus die 40 Jahre dauernde, regelmässige Speisung der Israeliten.

Besonders kennzeichnend für die Überarbeitungs-Tendenz des P ist seine Umformung der Quellsage von Kadeš in Num xx 1-13. In ihrer ursprünglichen Gestalt (J) ist sie völlig parallel einer anderen Quellsage (Ex xvii 1-7): Moše schlägt den Felsen mit seinem Stab und es springt eine reiche Quelle hervor. Der P aber, der die Version des J fast Zeile für Zeile begleitet, bringt ein ganz neues Motiv hinein: Moše erhält den Auftrag, zum Felsen zu *sprechen*, dass er sein Wasser gebe. Er ist ungehorsam und *schlägt* den Felsen. Für diesen Ungehorsam, der nachweislich nur der Version des P angehört, wird er verurteilt, das Gelobte Land nicht zu betreten, sondern vorher zu sterben. Aus einer typischen Quellsage zum Ruhm des Moše macht P eine religiöse Erzählung von Schuld und Strafe, die unser Bild vom Schicksal Moše's bis heute formt.

Es ist eine merkwürdige Tatsache, dass P im Pentateuch nur die Erzählungen des J überarbeitet und verändert, nicht aber die des E. Warum nicht? Hier liegt ein Problem vor, dessen Lösung von grosser Bedeutung für unser Verständnis der Schichtungen im Pentateuch sein könnte.

Aber die Überarbeitung älterer Texte durch die Schicht, die wir D oder P oder neutraler einfach die „Schicht der grossen Überarbeitung" nennen, reicht weit über den Pentateuch hinaus. Sie erfasst die *gesamten geschichtlichen Bücher*, Richterbuch, beide Bücher Samuel und beide Königsbücher, mit einer einheitlichen und vollkommen klaren Tendenz. Sie bringt keinerlei eigenes neues Quellenmaterial; für sie sind die älteren Quellen nur Stoff, den sie mit einer Rahmen-Erzählung ordnet und mit einer Kritik begleitet.

Hier sind wir in der glücklichen Lage, dass die Verfasser der Überarbeitung die Tendenz, die sie leitet, als eine Art Einleitung ganz klar und in programmatischer Form zum Ausdruck bringen. Dieser rote Faden durch das Labyrinth der Texte findet sich in Jud ii 7-23.

Es ist ein klares Schema. Die Israeliten fallen immer wieder von Jahwe ab und dienen fremden Göttern. Gottgesandte Männer, hier „Richter" genannt, führen sie auf den rechten Weg zurück, aber nach ihrem Tode wendet sich das Volk wieder dem Götzendienst zu. Das Schicksal des Volkes, Glück und Unglück, entspricht genau dem religiösen Verhalten. — Das ist nicht eine Darstellung der Ereignisse, denn diese gehen einen ganz anderen Gang, sondern es ist eine religiöse Geschichts-Philosophie. Wo Strafe ist, muss Schuld sein.

Wann und wie konnte sich diese Geschichts-Auffassung bilden? Sie ist entstanden durch das erschütternde Ereignis der Zerstörung Jerusalems und das Exil. Die führenden Geister des Exils fragen sich: Wie war das möglich? Und die einzige Antwort, die ihre religiöse Selbstbehauptung ermöglicht, ist: Es ist die Strafe Gottes für die Schuld der Väter.

Diese Deutung der Geschichte hat zu einer umfassenden Überarbeitung aller geschichtlichen Bücher geführt. Der grösste Teil des Buches Josua trägt das Signum dieser Schicht. In ihm haben wir nur einzelne Spuren historischer Nachrichten, aber auch nur ganz wenige echte Sagen (Einnahme Jerichos; der Heeresoberst Jahwes; das Sonnenwunder von Gibeon). Alles Übrige — mit Ausnahme der geographischen Listen — ist eine eigentümliche literarische Gattung, die wir „Pseudo-Geschichtsschreibung" nennen können, weil sie vorgibt, Historie zu erzählen, ohne dabei auf irgendwelchen geschichtlichen Quellen zu beruhen.

Das ganze Richterbuch, das eine Reihe hervorragender alter Geschichtserzählungen enthält, ist in den Rahmen der Überarbeitung eingespannt (ii ganz; iii 1-11; iv 1-3, vi 1. 7-10; viii 23. 33-35); ix 56-57; x 6-8. 10-16; xiii 1; xvi 31b; K. xx-xxi zum grössten Teil).

Die charakteristische Überarbeitung der alten Quellen setzt sich in I Sam. fort. Sie beginnt in vii 2-17 mit einem angeblichen Philistersieg Samuels („Pseudo-Geschichtsschreibung") und der Verderbnis seiner Söhne (viii 1-3). An die Stelle der historischen Quelle über den Aufstieg Sauls (K. xi) und der sagenhaften über die Suche nach den Eselinnen (K. ix) tritt eine pseudo-historische Erzählung viii 4-22; x 17-27; weiter K. xii mit der typischen Geschichts-Übersicht xii 6-12. Überarbeitet ist der Bericht über den Amalek-Krieg (xv) und Teile der Goliat-Geschichte (xvii).

Mit dem Einsetzen des grossen Geschichtswerks über Sauls und Davids Regierung tritt die Überarbeitung zurück (IS xviii-IR ii), mit

Ausnahme des ganz in D-Stil gehaltenen Natan-Orakels II S vii.

Aber in den Königsbüchern ist die Überarbeitung überall zu spüren. Schon I R viii 15-53 gehören ihr an, weiter ix 2-9; xi 1-13. 29-39; xii, 26-33. — Dann erhält jeder König eine „Zensur" nach seinem religiösen Verhalten, meist eine schlechte. Wichtige Nachrichten, die nicht gefehlt haben können, werden ausgeschieden, so der Anteil Ahabs an der Schlacht bei Karḳar, und von den bedeutenden Königen 'Omri, Ahab, Jerobeam II., Manasse und Josia wird kaum etwas ausser ihrem religiösen Verhalten berichtet, weil nur dies die Bearbeiter interessiert.

Noch der letzte König von Juda, Zedekia, erhält diese Zensur in typischer Form (II R xxiv 18), ein Beweis, dass diese Bearbeitung erst im Exil stattgefunden hat. Das erweisen in allen Teilen auch die babylonische Datierung, der Gebrauch typischer später Worte und die Anschauungen der Exilszeit und der nachexilischen Zeit.

Die Überarbeitung der Sagen und der geschichtlichen Bücher macht auch nicht vor den *Gesetzen* halt, wo es ihr notwendig erscheint. Dafür einige Beispiele, vor allem aus den Festgesetzen.

Für das Passah-Opfer hat das Dt zwei Neuerungen durchgeführt: 1) Das Opfer darf nur am Tempel, nicht im Hause dargebracht werden (Dt xvi 2 und bes. 5-6). II R xxiii 21-23 lässt keinen Zweifel daran, dass hier eine Neuerung vorliegt. 2) Das Opferfleisch soll *gekocht* werden. — In beiden Punkten bringt Ex xii 1-10 eine Veränderung des Gesetzes, und dieser Abschnitt gehört sicher dem P an (bab. Datierung; „'edah"): 1) Das Opfer soll im *Hause* dargebracht werden (xii 6 u. bes. 7). 2) Das Opferfleisch soll *geröstet* werden (8-9), und hier wird scharf der Gegensatz gegen das Dt hervorgehoben. P stellt damit alten Brauch wieder her.

Eine wirkliche Neuerung wird vom P beim *Herbstfest* durchgeführt. In alter Zeit ein Erntefest (ḥag hā-āsif) heisst es in Dt xvi 13 sukkot-Fest nach den Hütten, in denen um diese Jahreszeit (noch heute!) der Bauer wohnte, um seine Wein- und Oel-Ernte zu bewachen. Das wird im Exil unverständlich, da es in Babylon keine Weinberge und Oelbäume zu bewachen gab. Darum deutet der P das Fest in ein Erinnerungsfest an den Wüstenzug um, bei dem angeblich das Volk in Laubhütten wohnte (Lev xxiii 43), obwohl das in der Wüste ganz unmöglich ist. Und er befiehlt *als Neuerung*, sieben Tage in Hütten zu wohnen. Diese Bestimmung ist erst nach dem Abschluss der Festgesetze (xxiii 37) als Novelle hinzugefügt (xxiii 39-43). Das Fest ist in dieser Form nach dem klaren Bericht Neh viii 7 *zum ersten Mal* im Jahre 445 gefeiert worden.

Zwei *ganz neue Feste* sind erst vom P eingeführt worden: das Neujahrsfest am 1. tišrē und der Versöhnungstag am 10. tišrē. Beide kommen in den alten Listen der Feste (Ex xxiii, Ex xxxiv, Dt xvi nicht vor, sondern zum ersten Mal im P (Lev xxiii 24 und 27). *Im alten Israel gab es überhaupt kein besonderes Neujahrsfest.* Seine Deutung als „Thronbesteigungs-Fest Jahwes" könnte also höchstens für die nachexilische Zeit zutreffen, und sie hat in der Tat in Texten der Königszeit nicht die geringste Basis. Im alt-israelitischen Kalender begann zudem das neue Jahr nicht am 1. tišrē, sondern, wie ich gezeigt habe, am 1. ḥešwan. Diese beiden Feste sind sogar, wie aus dem Bericht über den Verlauf des Monats tišrē 445 im Buch Nehemia hervorgeht, auch im Jahre 445 noch nicht gefeiert worden.

Die „grosse Überarbeitung" erfasst schliesslich auch den grössten Teil der *prophetischen Literatur*. Der Grund dafür ist klar. Die Propheten sind, wie DUHM es ausgedrückt hat, die „Sturmvögel des Unheils"; das ist ihre Aufgabe. Erst bei vollendetem Unheil werden sie Tröster, wie wir an den beiden Propheten sehen, die die Zerstörung Jerusalems erlebt haben, Jeremia (xxxi 2-6.15-21; xxxii 1-14) und Ezechiel (von Kap. xxxiv an). Das liefert das Motiv der Überarbeitung. Im Exil sind die Drohreden nicht mehr „aktuell", die Strafe ist verhängt, jetzt gilt es, das Volk zu trösten und seinen Mut aufrechtzuerhalten.

Jetzt werden den Prophetenbüchern ganze Teile tröstlichen Inhalts angehängt. Dem Buch Jesaja von Kap. xl an die Bücher des „Deutero-" und des „Trito-Jesaja", dem Buch Jeremia xlvi-li, dem Amos ix 8-14, dem Hosea xiv, dem Micha iv 5-5, 8; vii 7-20.

Aber es ist methodisch nicht richtig, zu sagen, dass nach einem festen Schema bei den Propheten den Drohreden die Tröstungen folgen, denn die Tröstungen gehören nicht zum originalen Bestand der Prophetenbücher. Was hätte es auch für einen Sinn gehabt, wenn die Propheten erst drohen und tadeln, um gleich hinterher zu versichern, dass schliesslich alles gut werden würde? Sie hätten sich damit um alle Wirkung gebracht.

Der Inhalt der Hinzufügungen zeigt zwei verschiedene Tendenzen: 1) Weissagungen der Rückkehr und Tröstung, 2) Ankündigung eines Schreckens-Gerichtes über die Völker und herrschende Macht Israels. Ihr Unterschied ist am besten illustriert durch den Unterschied zwischen Deutero-Jesaja und Trito-Jesaja. Wir werden kaum fehlgehen, wenn wir die erste Tendenz der Zeit des Exils zurechnen, die zweite der Zeit nach dem Exil mit ihrem Gefühl der Enttäuschung und der politischen Ohnmacht.

Neben diesen Zusätzen finden sich zahlreiche andere, die meist erbaulichen oder psalmartigen Charakter tragen; andere sprechen, wie in den historischen Büchern, von „Abfall von Jahwe" und von „Götzendienst", für die geschichtlich nicht die geringsten Beweise vorliegen.

Alle Aussprüche der vorexilischen Propheten sind in strengem Metrum geschrieben, und darum heben sich alle Zusätze deutlich ab, da sie entweder in Prosa oder in abweichendem Metrum geschrieben sind.

Im Buch des Amos sind mit grosser Sicherheit als Zusätze zu erkennen: iii 1. 7; 9-11; iv 7-12; v 6-15; vi 12-14; viii 11-12; ix 5-14. Das ist etwa ein Fünftel des ganzen Buches.

Bei Jeremia umfassen die Zusätze fast genau die *Hälfte des heutigen Buches*, bei Jesaja die *Hälfte von Jes* i-xxxv. Diese Bücher sind also sehr stark überarbeitet worden. Zwei Drittel der Zusätze befassen sich mit den typischen Themen: Abfall von Jahwe, Exil und Rückkehr, Gericht über die Völker; ein Drittel sind Predigten, Belehrungen und Psalmen.

Es bedarf nicht vieler Worte, um klarzumachen, dass diese Bearbeitung von grundlegender Bedeutung für das wirkliche Verständnis der Propheten ist. Die Persönlichkeit und das Wirken des Propheten tritt erst nach Ausscheidung der Zusätze hervor.

Sehr verständlich ist jetzt die Erscheinung, dass die exilischen und nachexilischen Prophetenbücher *keine Spur einer Überarbeitung* zeigen. Das sind die Bücher Ezechiel, Deuterojesaja, Tritojesaja, Jona, Haggai, Secharja, Maleachi. Der Grund ist einfach, dass sie in ihrer Haltung dem Geist der Zeit angehören, die die Zeit der Überarbeitung ist. (Eine interessante Ausnahme ist Sach vi 9-15, wo der hier ursprünglich mit Sicherheit genannte Serubabel durch den Hohepriester Jehošua ersetzt worden ist).

Die „grosse Überarbeitung", die im 6. und 5. Jahrhundert stattgefunden hat, ist von entscheidender Bedeutung für das wirkliche Verständnis des A. T. Sie hat nicht nur den Text verändert, sondern auch grossen Teilen des Inhalts eine neue Richtung gegeben und einen neuen Sinn untergelegt. Die Veränderung ist fast so, als hätten wir etwa für die Königs-Geschichte anstelle der Bücher Samuel nur die Fassung der Chronik.

Von einem „Geschichtswerk des Deuteronomisten" oder des Priesterkodex zu sprechen, ist unmöglich. Beide sind keine Geschichtswerke. Sie haben keine eigenen Quellen und bieten keinerlei eigenes neues Material. Ihr geschichtlicher Wert (mit Ausnahme der Chronik) ist fast gleich Null. Echte Sagen und echte Geschichte bietet nur J und seine Fortsetzung, die Geschichte Sauls, Davids und der Könige; das Überarbeitungs-Werk bietet nur eine *Deutung* der Geschichte. Es begnügt sich damit, „Pseudo-Geschichte" zu schreiben, das heisst, künstliche Legenden in geschichtlichem Gewande.

Das Geschichtsbild, das die Überarbeitung zeichnet, ist ein völlig irreales. Nicht Geschichte, wie sie geschehen ist, sondern wie sie hätte geschehen sollen. Der grosse *geschichtliche* Wert der Überarbeitung liegt vielmehr darin, dass sie uns einen Einblick in die geistigen Strömungen gibt, die zu ihrer Entstehung geführt haben. Aber das darf uns nicht darüber hinwegtäuschen, dass das sachliche Verständnis der Bibel durch diese Überarbeitung ausserordentlich erschwert worden ist.

Erst die Überarbeitung und nur sie hat den Begriff einer „Heils-Geschichte" geschaffen; die alte Quelle J weiss davon nichts, wenn man die Zusätze ausscheidet. — Ebenso wenig hat der Begriff der „Theokratie" eine Basis in den alten Quellen; er ist ein Produkt der Nach-Königs-Zeit (gegen Buber). — Wenn es in der älteren Zeit ein Zentral-Heiligtum überhaupt gegeben hat, so war es Siloh mit der Lade; in Sichem hat die Lade nie gestanden.

Von älteren Schriften hat den Überarbeitern J mit Sicherheit vorgelegen; ob auch E, ist nicht sicher.

Nur die vorexilischen Prophetenbücher sind überarbeitet worden, diese aber gründlich. In ihnen sind, mit Ausnahme einiger Jeremia-Stücke, Exils-, Tröstungs- und Heils-Weissagungen Eigentum der „grossen Überarbeitung".

ZUR PROBLEMATIK DES BUCHES OBADJAH

von

MILOŠ BIČ
Praha

1. Vorbemerkungen:

Welche Einleitung in das A. T. wir auch immer in die Hand nehmen, überall stossen wir auf Ratlosigkeit betreffs des Buches *Obadjah*. Deutlich drückte es schon z.B. SELLIN aus: „So klein das Büchlein ist, so verwickelt ist die kritische Frage, die sich an dasselbe knüpft" [1]). Besonders klar wird die Unverbürgtheit der Schlussfolgerungen durch die Datierung bewiesen. Mehr als ein halbes Jahrtausend liegt zwischen den Grenzdaten, von der Zeit des judäischen Jehorams (circa 849-842) bis in die der Ptolemäer (nach 323) [2]), innerhalb deren entweder das Büchlein als Ganzes oder seine Einzelteile sollen entstanden sein.

Dabei drängen sich einige Fragen auf. Vor allem die, um welches historische Ereignis es sich da handeln kann. Eben die Uneinmütigkeit der Kommentatoren zeugt dafür, dass man zu keiner unbestreitbaren Deutung gelangt ist, ja ich wage es direkt zu behaupten, dass alles nur unbegründete Historisierungsversuche sind. Hat es denn überhaupt je eine solche Situation in der Geschichte Israels oder Judas gegeben, die den Schilderungen des Ob. entspräche? Wir besitzen jedenfalls nicht die geringste Nachricht darüber, wenn man nicht direkt das in Frage gestellte Buch Ob. als eine solche betrachten will. Aber in dem Fall ist es von grösster Wichtigkeit, dass seine erste Hälfte in Jer. xlix 7-22 wiederkehrt — und dazu nicht wörtlich! Über das gegenseitige Verhältnis soll noch näher gesprochen werden (sub 2 u. 3), es ist jedoch unvermeidlich jetzt schon darauf hinzuweisen, dass man das Problem Ob.s nicht isoliert lösen kann, möge man nun den einen oder den anderen Text für den ursprünglicheren halten oder lieber eine gemeinsame Vorlage voraussetzen.

---

[1]) E. SELLIN: *Einleitung in das A. T.*, 5. Aufl., Leipzig 1929, S. 112.

[2]) Vgl. die Übersicht, dargeboten in Dre Bartholomaeo KUTAL *Libri Prophetarum Amos et Abdiae* . . ., Olomucii 1933, S. 183 f.

Damit hängt allerdings eine weitere Frage zusammen: Welchem Zwecke verdankt Ob. seinen Ursprung? Ohne eine klare Antwort darauf zu haben sollte man nicht allzu schlagfertig nationalistische Momente als leitendes Motif geltend machen [1]). Die wissenschaftliche Arbeit muss jedenfalls selbst der Bibel gegenüber ihre Freiheit bewahren, aber andererseits darf sie nicht übersehen, dass die biblischen Bücher nicht nur aus antiquarischem Interesse entstanden sind, um eine Volkschronik oder ein Weisheitskompendium den Nachkommen darzubieten. Das erste und grundlegende Interesse war das religiöse, oder noch konkreter ausgedrückt: nicht selten das kultisch-religiöse. Wir werden der Problematik der einzelnen Bücher des A.T.s nicht gerecht bleiben, wenn wir nicht eben diesen Tatbestand klar sehen und unsere ganze Forschung danach einstellen. Demnach können wir aber schon *a priori* nationalistische Motive im heutigen Sinne des Wortes ohne weiteres ausschliessen. Mögen sie sich in der ausserkanonischen Literatur noch so stark geltend machen, für das A.T. halte ich sie nicht für angebracht.

Schliesslich kann nun die dritte Frage gestellt werden, nämlich nach dem literarkritischen Sachverhalt. Klar ist dabei nur eine Tatsache, die nämlich, dass das Buch Ob. uns als eine literarische Einheit übergeben wurde. Dass es auch theologisch gesehen eine untrennbare Einheit bildet, soll nachgewiesen werden (sub 3 u. 4). Eine nur halbwegs wahrscheinliche Datierung ist nur für das Ganze denkbar, vorausgesetzt, dass wir zuerst den Zweck des Buches richtig erkannt haben und ebenso sein Verhältnis zum Parallelabschnitt in Jer. xlix. Ob bei der Niederschreibung des Buches ältere Bestandteile eingearbeitet wurden, ist jedenfalls nicht einfach nachweisbar, wenn auch theoretisch die Möglichkeit anzunehmen ist (vgl. Jer. xlix). Inwiefern mit mündlicher Tradition zu rechnen ist, ist ebenfalls unmöglich festzustellen, aber diese Frage ist letzten Endes belanglos, insofern wir das Buch als Ganzes vor den Augen haben, denn ob mündlich oder schriftlich weitergegeben spielt in diesem Falle keine Rolle — und von einer „Vorgeschichte" der einzelnen Worte sprechen zu wollen, entbehrt jede Grundlage.

Nach diesen Vorbemerkungen gehen wir nun zu den Grundproblemen über!

---

[1]) Z. B.: R. H. PFEIFFER: *Introduction to the O.T.*, 5. ed., New York-London 1941, S. 586.

2. Grundprobleme:

Gleich die *Überschrift* des Buches beweist, dass bereits im Altertum schon Ob. missdeutet wurde. Das griechische *Abdiū* lässt sich neben dem hebräischen *ʿōbadjâ* nämlich nicht nur durch den Hinweis auf eine vielleicht üblichere Aussprache, deren Abweichung nichts zu bedeuten hätte, abtun. Wenngleich gewöhnlich aus diesem Unterschiede keine Schlüsse gezogen werden, wird doch grösstenteils mindestens der eigenartige Charakter des Buches hervorgehoben. So lesen wir neuerlich bei A. Bentzen: „As Pfeiffer rightly observes, his (= Ob.s) passionate cry for vengeance is diametrically opposed to the spirit of self-sacrifice for the benefit of mankind. ʿObadjahu is no ʿEbed Yahweh in the sense of Is. liii" [1]). Das ist richtig gesehen!

In der kirchlichen Terminologie könnten wir es so ausdrücken: Der ʿEbed Jahwä ist ein Vorbild des Messias, also ein christologischer Typus. Der *ʿObadjah* unseres Buches ist dagegen durch die palestinensisch-jüdische Tradition von jenem scharf abgetrennt, will auch wahrscheinlich überhaupt nicht als Eigennamen aufgefasst werden. Die anderen ʿObadjahs im A.T. müssen deswegen noch nicht als Gegenbeweis dienen. Der Text würde demnach ursprünglich nur von einem namenlosen Verehrer Jahwäs (*ʿōbēd jahvę̂*) gesprochen haben, der gleichzeitig das Kollektivum der Gläubigen, Israel, vorstellt. So erklärt sich u.a. am ehesten die im solchen Zusammenhange ungewöhnliche Pluralform des Verbums *šåmaʿnū* Ob. 1. Diese Erkenntnis öffnet uns aber ganz neue Ausblicke, die mit der historisierenden Tendenz des Septuagintatextes diametral differieren! Mit der Namenänderung geht nämlich dringend in der griechischen Version Hand in Hand auch die Veränderung des Numerus (*ēkūsa*!), offensichtlich unter Einwirkung der Parallelstelle in Jer. xlix 14.

Durch das Ändern eines einzigen Wortes wird also leicht der Sinn des ganzen Kontextes geändert, wodurch dann eine Reihe weiterer Eingriffe sich notwendig erweist. So auch im gegebenen Fall. Es ist doch nicht gleichgültig, ob der hebräische Text *ʾedōm* und der griechische *Idūmaia* liest. Zwar bietet das Femininum *ʿålęhå* Ob. 1 gewisse exegetische Schwierigkeiten, die beseitigt würden, handle es sich um das Land Edom. So fasste offenbar die Septuaginta

---

[1]) A. Bentzen: *Introduction to the O. T.*, II., Kopenhagen (1. Aufl. 1949, 2. 1952), S. 144. — Cf. Pfeiffer, op. cit. 586.

die Sachlage auf und unter ihrem Einflusse die meisten christlichen Theologen der ältesten wie der neuesten Zeit.

Ist es aber wirklich so einwandfrei festgestellt, dass vom Lande Edom die Rede ist? Im hebräischen Text folgen weiter maskuline Suffixe und nicht ein einzigesmal kommt das Wort *'ęręṣ* vor. Dagegen wechselt aber Edom (1a 8b) mit Esau (6a), bzw. *har 'eśâv* (8b 9b 19a 21a) und *bēt 'eśâv* (18b c), wobei die beiden letztgenannten Verbindungen keinesfalls geographische oder ethnographische Grössen vorstellen müssen (s. sub 4).

Der Lösung kommen wir näher, wenn wir sehen, dass es Jahwä ist, der zum Kampf aufruft. Er und Edom stehen also im Streit. Wenn dabei ein Legat unter die *gōjīm* gesandt wird (1), um von dort die Auserwählten zum Schauspiele zu versammeln, bis Edom vernichtet wird, folgt nur ein Resultat, dass nämlich Edom hier eine ganz eigenartige Stellung einnimt. Wenn Hesychios Edom geradezu mit dem *diabolos* gleichsetzt [1]), ist es, theologisch gesehen, vollkommen in Ordnung. Hier darf ganz einfach Edom „keinesfalls in einem historisch oder geographisch verengten Sinne aufgefasst werden, sondern nur in seiner theologischen Wertung als Vertreter alles Widergöttlichen. Zwei Motive durchflechten sich dabei: das leiblich-menschliche (*'-d-m*) und das widerspenstig-dämonische (*ś-'-r*[1])" [2]).

Und plötzlich ergibt sich uns von hier aus die Antwort, weshalb das Suffix in *'ālęhā* in Femininum steht. Edom wird mit der *Tiâmat*, der Urfeindin des Schöpfergottes, verglichen. Die Alten mussten eine solche Anspielung gut verstanden haben, besonders wenn das betreffende Wort unter ganz bestimmten Umständen, während der Kultfeier, vorgetragen wurde. Es ist also überhaupt nicht notwendig den Text zu „verbessern", sondern vielmehr die Erklärung zu suchen, wie man ihn einstens verstanden hat. Dass weiterhin Edom als Masculinum angeführt wird, ist begreiflich. So forderte es der normale Sprachgebrauch und zur Charakteristik Edoms genügte das einmalige Femininum.

Nun kompliziert sich jedoch die Problematik durch die Wiederholung Ob. 1-10 bei Jer. xlix 7 ff, wobei eben die Unterschiede höchst aufschlussreich sind. Notieren wir wenigstens die wichtigsten! Gegen die Mehrzahl „wir" Ob. 1 steht die Einzahl „ich" Jer. xlix 14. Der Kampfaufruf bei Ob. 1 setzt schon die Kämpfer versammelt

1) Migne, *Patrologia graeca* 93/1353.

2) M. Bič: *Ein verkanntes Thronbesteigungsfestorakel im A. T.*, in: Archiv Orientální XIX. No 3-4, Praha 1952, S. 568-578, Zitat S. 572 f.

voraus, Jer. xlix 14 lässt sie dagegen erst in der Zukunft versammeln. Ebenso in den folgenden Versen finden wir Abweichungen, die nicht belanglos sind, hier jedoch übergangen werden können. Dagegen die schroffe Formulierung Jer. xlix 9 gegenüber Ob. 5 lehnt ausdrücklich jeden Vergleich mit Lev. xix 9 f oder Dt xxiv 19-22 ab, offenbar darum, weil man den alten Spruch in einer Zeit nach der Josianischen Reform nicht in seiner Fülle aufgefasst hätte. Aber noch wichtiger ist der Vergleich zwischen Ob. 6 und Jer. xlix 10a. Von den fünf Worten des Obadjah'schen Textes sind nur zwei allgemeiner bekannt (Esau und *'ajik*, *'ēk*), beide Verba sind im Nif'al nur hier bezeugt und *maṣpūnīm* ist überhaupt ein *hapax legomenon*. Weicht nun bei Jer. der Wortlaut von diesem ab, folgt daraus, dass wir es bei Ob. mit einem uralten Orakel zu tun haben, das Ausdrücke verwendet hat, die nicht der Alltagssprache entstammten und deshalb wahrscheinlich nicht mehr ganz klar verstanden wurden.

So könnten wir fortsetzen und immer neue Belege dafür aufbringen, dass Jer. absichtlich ein altes Orakel zitiert, sich aber gezwungen sieht es den neuen Umständen anzupassen und neu formulieren. Warum benützt er es aber überhaupt, wenn er es nicht wörtlich übergibt? Warum lässt er sich es so darauf anliegen, dass er den Sinn, den Geist jener Sprüche aufs genaueste reproduziere? Dass das Verhältnis etwa umgekehrt sein könnte, halte ich für volkommen ausgeschlossen und hoffe es im weiteren (sub 3 u. 4) restlos nachzuweisen.

Die *Autorenfrage* des Jeremiahtextes ist mir völlig gleichgültig, da das Buch Jer. eine literarische Komposition sowieso ist und kein Spruch von seinem Autor unterschrieben ist. Letzten Endes spielen die leitende Rolle auch hier die religiösen Motive und nur von diesem Standpunkte aus erhalten wir befriedigende Antworten auf die soeben aufgeworfenen Fragen.

3. Thesis:

Bevor wir nun auf weitere Einzelheiten eingehen, wollen wir unsere Thesis klar formulieren.

Ich halte Ob. für ganz ahistorisch. Jedenfalls lässt es sich nicht nachweisen, dass oder ob ein geschichtliches Ereignis den Hintergrund des Buches bildet. Dagegen bietet der Text ein höchst gegenwärtiges Gebilde, wie es nur aus einem Kultdrama erklärlich ist. Dieser Auffassung entspricht auch das früher gesagte. Schon die Überschrift des Buches (*ḥ*ª*zōn 'ōbadjâ*) deutet an, dass es sich um eine Verehrung (*ʿ-b-d*) Jahwäs handelt, der bei dem betreffenden Feste seinen Urfeind Edom niederschmettert und vernichtet.

Jahwä selbst wird dabei ausser mit seinem Namen (1b 4b 8a 15a 18c 21b) gleich in der Ueberschrift als *ʾadōnåj jhvh* (1a) angesprochen, was mit dem Schlusswort: „Denn Jahwäs wird das Königtum sein" (21) ganz deutlich auf einen Inthronisationsritus hinweist. Mit anderen Worten: Wir fassen den Text Ob. als ein liturgisch erweitertes Thronbesteigungsfestorakel auf [1]).

Bei der Benennung Gottes als *ʾadōnåj jhvh* handelt es sich unstreitbar um einen Königstitel Jahwäs. Dazu bietet die Konkordanz schwerwiegendes Beweismaterial.

Im A.T. kommt er 280mal vor [2]). Davon befinden sich 211 Stellen bei Hesekiel, gerade in jenem Buche, wo die irdischen Könige ihre Rolle ausgespielt haben. Das Buch selbst ist durch den Uebergang von der Geschichte zur Eschatologie gekennzeichnet. Durch den Fall Jerusalems ist die Geschichte des konkreten Israels zu Ende (darum fordert das Buch im Gegensatze zu Ps cxxxvii 6 auf zu vergessen!), zwischen der Geschichte und Eschatologie gibt es keinen Uebergang. Dort das Ende, hier ein neuer Anfang, mit einem neuen Jerusalem und einem neuen Tempel, wo nach vollbrachtem Gerichte Gott alles in Allen (cf 1. Kor. xv 28) sein wird, alleiniger Herrscher mit einem Fürsten (*nåśîʾ*, Hes. xxxiv 24, xxxvii 25 u.a.) als Vertreter, nichtmehr aber mit einem König [3]). — Zahlenmässig folgt dann das Buch Amos mit 20 Stellen, eben das Buch, das

---

[1]) Angedeutet schon im Bericht des Unterzeichneten zum Orientalistenkongress in Prag und Dobříš 1949: *Le champ de travail des études bibliques en Tchécoslovaquie*, in: Archiv Orientální XIX. No 1-2, Praha 1951, S. 233-242, Zitat S. 242. Die dort angesagte Studie erschien daselbst, wie näher angegeben hier in Anm. 2 S. 14). Nach der Einsendung des Manuscripts der vorliegenden Abhandlung zur Drucklegung, teilt mir Prof. A. BENTZEN-København brieflich (9. III. 1953) mit, dass I. ENGNELL-Uppsala in Svenskt Bibliskt Uppslagsverk II (1952) ähnlich das Buch Ob. auffasst, als „eine Nachdichtung einer Liturgie über den Tag Jahwes". Möchte auch an dieser Stelle Prof. BENTZEN meinen Dank aussprechen für seine Mitteilung und den Hinweis auf das mir unzugängliche schwedische Werk, ebenso wie meine Freude darüber ausdrücken, dass meine Untersuchungen auch andererseits, und zwar völlig unabhängig, unterstützt werden.

[2]) L. KOEHLER: *Lexicon in Veteris Testamenti libros*, Leiden 1948 ff., 1. Lieferung, S. 11.

[3]) S. DANĚK, *Fakultätsvorlesungen*, Prag 1932-33, s. M. BIČ: *Palestina od pravěku ke křesťanství* (= Palestina von der Urzeit zum Christentum), Bd. III., Praha 1950, S. 214.

gegen dem nordisraelitischen Kultus im „Königsheiligtum" von Bethel (Am. vii 13) so scharf auftritt [1]). — Weiter folgt Jesaja mit 17 Stellen im logischen Anschluss an die Theofanieschilderung im Kap. vi. Und schliesslich Jeremia mit 9 Stellen und mit dem Bericht vom Ende des irdischen Königtums in Israel (Juda).

Haben wir das Buch Ob. einmal als ein liturgisch erweitertes Thronbesteigungsfestorakel aufgefasst, scheiden alle „nationalistischen" Momente gänzlich aus (vgl. oben sub 1). Die Sache Jahwäs ist im Spiele. Das Volk — oder wohl besser gesagt: die Gemeinde (es handelt sich doch um eine geistige Grösse!) — wird zwar aufgefordert am Kampfe teilzunehmen (V. 1), rührt jedoch weiter nicht den Finger, da Gott seine Heilstaten allein vollbringt. Ja der Text führt uns schon in den Augenblick des Festes hinein, wo der rituelle Kampf bereits zu Ende ist und Jahwä als Gebieter (*'adōnåj*) zum Gericht übergeht.

Von hier aus wäre es schon möglich einen Datierungsversuch zu unternehmen. Alles spielt sich höchst gegenwärtig ab, von eschatologischen Erwartungen findet sich nicht die leiseste Spur. Inhaltlich also im schroffen Gegensatz zu Amos, dessen eschatologische Aussicht des *jōm jahvę̂* gut als Ansatzpunkt dienen kann. Obwohl uns z.B. Jes. vi in eine etwas jüngere Zeit führt, wo das alte Fest noch im vollen Umfange gefeiert wurde [2]), glaube ich, dürfen wir Ob. mit Recht vor Amos einsetzen in Uebereinstimmung mit der alten jüdischen und einem Teil der christlichen Tradition, die allerdings den richtigen Sachverhalt nicht gesehen haben. Eine besondere Stütze dieser Auffassung sehe ich im Paralleltext Jer. xlix, 7ff [3]).

Die Frage, ob Jer. xlix vom Propheten selbst herkommt oder „sekundär" ist, zeugt von falscher Fragestellung. Ueber die *ipsissima verba* der Propheten wurde schon viel geschrieben und polemisiert [4]),

---

[1]) Vgl. M. Bič: *Bet'el — le sanctuaire du roi.* In: Symbolae Hrozný, Archiv Orientální XVII., Praha 1949, S. 46-63.

[2]) Ausführlich bei S. Mowinckel: *Psalmenstudien II. Das Thronbesteigungsfest Jahwäs und der Ursprung der Eschatologie*, Kristiania 1922.

[3]) Gegen Bentzen's Standpunkt, dass "at all events, the relationship with Jer. xlix is quite irrelevant for a dating of Ob., because it is not sure that Jer. xlix comes from the mouth of Jeremiah (Pfeiffer)"; Bentzen, op. cit. II. 144.

[4]) Nur beispielsweise: S. Mowinckel: *Prophecy and Tradition*, Oslo 1946, besonders S. 88 u. Anm. 130! G. Widengren: *Literary and Psychological Aspects of the Hebrew Prophets*, Uppsala-Leipzig 1948.

aber es muss doch einmal anerkannt werden, dass die Propheten nicht aus eigenem Willen gesprochen und eigene Einfälle vorgetragen haben, sondern im Auftrage einer höheren Autorität ihr Werk taten. Die Anonymität der einzelnen Sprüche ist also ganz natürlich und es wäre unbegreiflich, wäre es anders. Damit sollen nicht die grossen Meistergestalten unter den Propheten bestritten, weder der Einfluss ihrer „Schulen" negiert werden. Ausschlaggebend ist jedoch die Grundtendenz des ganzen Buches, das wir einfach als literarische Grösse aufzufassen haben. Denn eben diese Tendenz hat letzten Endes über die Auswahl und Zusammenstellung einzelner Worte entschieden. Das Buch Jeremia ist durch die Katastrophe von 586 gekennzeichnet. Alles menschliche Werk ist zu Grunde gegangen, ja selbst der Tempel liegt in Trümmern. Wo bleiben nun die Hoffnungen, die sich an Jahwäs Thronbesteigung knüpften? Wurde nicht Jahwä durch Marduk geschlagen?

Das ist keine rednerische Frage, sondern ein todernstes Problem, das wie die Exilierten, so auch die Zurückgebliebenen tief beschäftigen musste. Und eben aus dieser Lage heraus verstehen wir, dass im Buche Jer. dringend das uralte Orakel wiederholt werden musste, um zu beweisen, dass das Wort Gottes zu ihm nicht leer zurückkehrt (Jes. lv 11). Gerade dort, wo menschlich gesehen alles verloren war und jede Hoffnung als Wahn erscheinen musste, war an Ort und Stelle zu betonen, dass doch Jahwä König ist und bleibt.

Von hier aus verstehen wir nun auch die Unterschiede zwischen beiden Paralleltexten. Bei Ob. hört die versammelte Gemeinde das Wort ihres Gebieters (deshalb *šâmaʿnû*), bei Jer. sind die Treuen jedoch zerstreut. Nur der namenlose Prophet steht auf den Trümmern menschlicher Hoffnungen und Bestrebungen. Und da, eben da, wo alles so leer und vergebens erschien, hört er die Stimme seines Gottes und die Aeusserung seines königlichen Willens. Was er hört (Singular *šâmaʿtî!*), verkündet er weiter. Bei Ob. konnte der Aufruf zum Kampfe unvermittelt folgen, die Kämpfer waren ja versammelt, bei Jer. müssen sie sich erst versammeln, denn sie sind zerstreut. Trotzdem bleibt der Wille Jahwäs derselbe; niemandem hat er seine Macht übergeben. Und wiederum handelt es sich um jenen übermenschlichen Edom wie bei Ob. (oben sub 2), unter dessen Namen eventuell auch Babel gemeint sein konnte [1]).

Das ursprünglich ahistorische Obadjahorakel kehrt also bei Jer.

---

[1]) So offenbar auch Ps. cxxxvii 7 cf. 8.

in aktualisierter (historisierter) Form zurück. Dass seine Wiederholung gerade in diesem neuen Zusammenhang die Folge eines sehr durchdringenden theologischen Denkens ist, sollte keinem Zweifel unterliegen. Denn nur von hier aus erklären sich in befriedigender Weise alle Unterschiede zwischen beiden Texten und ebenso würde sich auch manches weitere Problem im A.T. lösen.

Die Septuaginta hat hier manches Uebel angestifftet, indem sie die at. Texte oft als historische Berichte aufgefasst hat. So gerade auch in unserem Falle, wofür besonders massive Belege die griechische Patristik in Fülle bietet. Die moderne Wissenschaft hat leider allzu bereit diese falsche Auffassung weiterverbreitet und noch durch anderswärtige Konjekturen zu stützen versucht [1]), anstatt die Texte von innen heraus zu begreifen und erklären.

4. Hauptlinien:

Versuchen wir nun zu Ende kurz die Hauptlinien des Buches Ob. zu skizzieren! Von Einzelheiten sehen wir ab.

Gleich im ersten Vers erfahren wir eine merkwürdige Tatsache, dass nämlich zu den *gōjīm*, oder unter, in die *gōjīm*, genauer ausgedrückt, ein Legat gesandt wurde. Da weiter (15) auch über die *gōjīm* das Gericht kommen wird, nach 19f man jedoch schliessen kann, dass Reste von ihnen erlöst werden, möchte man bereits schon bei 1 an eine solche Scheidung denken, wenngleich wahrscheinlich erst das Gericht über Edom, bei dem die *gōjīm* vielleicht als Zuschauer beiwohnen sollen, zur endgültigen Trennung der Erlösten von den Verdammten führen wird.

2 geht zur direkten Ansprache Edoms über. Die Urfeindin (1, s. oben sub 2) nimmt anthropomorphe Züge an. Das Perfektum besagt, dass der Schöpferkampf vorbei ist und nun nur noch der Rechtsspruch mit folgender Vollstreckung des Urteils bevorsteht. Jer. erweitert und glättet teilweise die Aussagen. Der unerwartete zweifache Uebergang zur 3. Person (3) bei Ob. scheint auf einen konkreten Vorsteller Edoms zu zielen, wobei der „Adler", *nęšęr*, möglicherweise an das ägyptische *neṯer* = Gottheit assonieren will [2]), und der Text sonst in Einzelheiten stark an Jes. xiv 13f erinnert.

---

[1]) Z.B. *ʾᵉdōm* statt *ʾᵃrâm* 2. Kön. xxiv 2.

[2]) Nach S. Daněk: *Krise kritiky, tři filologické vykřičniky* (= Die Krisis der Kritik, drei philologische Ausrufungszeichen), Praha 1935, S. 26 f. (allerdings da in anderem Zusammenhange, zu Hes. xvii 7 ff.); näheres bei M. Bič, op. cit. (s. oben Anm. 2, S. 14), S. 574.

In diesem „Adler" einen Phönix zu sehen, der alljährlich stirbt und immer wieder neuerwacht, wäre im Lichte von Ps ciii 5 nicht ausgeschlossen, wobei das *hapax legomenon tiplęṣęt* Jer. xlix 16 mit dem *bis legomenon miplęṣęt*, das die Vulgata mit *simulacrum Priapi* wiedergibt, ganz nahe verwandt sein wird und uns so wieder in den Umkreis der vegetativen, ba'alischen, Kulte führt, mit denen eben Jahwä in Kanaan unvermeidlich im Konflikt stehen musste.

5-7 schildern die bevorstehende totale Vernichtung Edoms. Zu 5 bietet Jer. xlix 9 eine klare Deutung: Nichts bleibt übrig! Die Gesetzesvorschriften (Lev. xix 9f Dt xxiv 19ff) sind hier ausser Geltung. Nur einen Sieger kann es geben, nur einen König: Jahwä oder Edom. Hier ist die Königsherrschaft Gottes im Spiel, es können also keine Humanitätsideale entscheiden. — Zu 6 bietet die Parallelstelle in Jer. xlix 10a sehr aufschlussreiches Material. Wenn man hinter den *maṣpūnīm* Ob. 6 nur „verborgene Dinge" (Gesenius-Buhl) oder „versteckte Güter" (Köhler) sieht, versteht man eben die Sache nicht! An Kriegsbeute denken bedeutet den Text seines tiefsten Inhaltes zu entleeren. Jer. sagt doch ausdrücklich, dass Edom selbst für sich kein Schlupfwinkel findet (gemeint: bis der Tag Jahwäs hereinbricht; vgl. auch Jes. ii 10ff) und *maṣpūnīm* (Ob.) hängt doch so offensichtlich mit *ṣåpōn* = Norden zusammen, dass einem der Götterberg sofort vor den Augen auftaucht, besonders wo schon Ob. 3f so deutlich die Richtung angibt!

7 schliesst das Bild ab und will überhaupt nichts von politischen Bündnissen Edoms und der dem Könige Nebukadnezar von ihm angeblich gegen Juda geleisteten Hilfe wissen. Haben wir bis jetzt eher von der übermenschlichen Natur Edoms gesprochen, zeigt sich die Notwendigkeit zu betonen, dass wir uns auf dieser Erde befinden und Edom sich eben im Alltagsleben äussert. Die göttlichen Mächte bedeuten nichts ohne menschliche Helfer, was längst bekannt ist [1]). Für den Menschen sind aber ebenso seine Bündnisse mit jenen göttlichen Mächten von grösster Wichtigkeit und nur die mit ihnen abgeschlossene *b^erīt* kann *šålōm* und *lęḥęm* garantieren. Aber wehe! Edoms Verbündete stehen da machtlos, ja sie werden ihm zum Verderbnis werden. — „Es ist keine Vernunft in ihm", d.h. in Edom, wenn er so kurzsichtig handeln kann, endet der Vers.

Die Weisheit der Weisen und die Macht der Mächtigen wird an

---

[1]) S. für die Psalmen A. Bentzen: *Messias — Moses redivivus — Menschensohn*, Zürich 1948 (tschechische Übersetzung, Praha 1953).

jenem Tag zu Schanden werden (8f) — "wegen des Mordes (9), wegen der Gewalttat an deinem Bruder Jaakob" (10). Mit Vorliebe wird in Ob. der Name Jaakob gebraucht (neben „das Haus Jaakob", 17f) offenbar in Anspielung an die Urvätergeschichten, mit denen das Buch auch sonstige linguistischen Zusammenhänge aufweist.

> So sei hier schon auf das rätselhafte *pęręḳ* Ob. 14 hingewiesen, das nur noch Nah. iii 1 vorkommt und durch die Wörterbücher ruhig grundverschieden übersetzt wird, als ob es so selbstverständlich wäre, dass kein Zusammenhang möglich sei. Bei Ob. wirkte jedenfalls die Historifikation der Septuaginta mit, die jedoch eher ein *pęręṣ* voraussetzen würde. Unbeachtet blieb dabei in den Kommentaren vollkommen, dass die Wurzel *p-r-ḳ* merkwürdigerweise in Gen. xxvii 40 in den Worten des blinden Isaak zu Esau erscheint. Ja, es ist höchst wahrscheinlich, dass auch die eben daselbst vorkommende Wurzel *r-v-d* im verdächtigen „Proprium" *sᵉpårad* Ob. 20, das die Alten aber als Appellativum „das Ende der Herrschaft" (*s-v-p* + *r-d-j*[1]) verstanden haben [1]), vorauszusetzen ist, wobei an das „Ende des Herumirrens" während der Entfernung und Verborgenheit des Gottes (vgl. Jes. liv 7) zu denken wäre.

Jer. xlix bietet keine direkte Parallele zu diesen Versen, aber man könnte eventuell. 7f zum Vergleich heranziehen und erhält darin einen teilweisen Beleg, dass Edom auch da als ein bestimmter geistiger Typus, nicht als ethnologische Grösse auftritt — und ebenso auch sonst in analogen Prophetensprüchen. Fragen wir nun, wie denn eigentlich die Weisen Edoms und die Helden Temans (Ob. 8f) den Mord, bezw. die Gewalttat an Jaakob begangen haben, scheint uns Elifaz aus Teman, einer der „Freunde" Hiobs, mit seiner „Weisheit" den Weg zu weisen.

> Sein selbstbewusstes „Ich" (Hi xv 17), das sich auf irgendeine alte Weisheit stützt, die jedoch nicht vom Allerhöchsten stammt (18), ja geradezu mit Zauberei zusammenhängt (iv 12f), wird als Mordanschlag vom Leidenden abgewiesen (vi 27) und von Gott als Narrheit verworfen (xlii 7f), Narrheit, die durch das

---

[1]) So z.B. die „Kralicer" Übersetzung der Bibel durch die böhmisch-mährische Unitas fratrum, 1579-1593; vgl. aber auch die *Synopsis criticorum aliorumque Sacrae Scripturae interpretum et commentatorum*, (III. Prophetae), a Matthaeo Polo Londinensi, Francofurti ad Moenum M DC XCIV, ad l.

Herausreissen aus der Gemeinschaft mit Gott ins ewige Verderben den Menschen wirft.

Dabei können wir gleich noch ein anderes Problem erörtern. Nach Ob. 15 heisst es: „Wie du gehandelt, wird mit dir gehandelt, was du getan, kehrt auf dein Haupt zurück". Allzu leicht ist man bereit im israelitischen Recht babylonische, hethitische und wer weiss was für noch andere Einflüsse zu suchen und sieht nicht die religiöse Motivierung der zwei grundlegenden Rechtsgrundsätze im A.T.: einerseits des im Vergleich mit dem babylonischen Recht sehr milden Grundsatzes der Entschädigung da, wo der Mensch irgendwie beschädigt wurde, andererseits des unerbittlich harten Grundsatzes der *retaliation* besonders dort (wenn nicht ausschliesslich dort!), wo Gottes Recht verletzt wurde. Das ist die logische Folge der religiösen Einstellung Israels. Nur Gott gilt als Quell des Lebens. Sich von ihm trennen heisst sich ins (ewige) Verderben stürzen. Der Frevler, der sich trotzig gegen den Herrn stellt und mutwillig seine eigenen Wege gehen will, darf mit keinem Erbarmen rechnen. Wenn er dabei noch andere dem Herrn entführen und so ins Verderben bringen will, ist sein Los versiegelt: Tod hast du verursacht, der Tod wird dich treffen.

Nur nebenbei sei darauf hingewiesen, dass von diesem Standpunkt aus erst manche Psalmen richtig verstanden werden und man darin deutlich Königspsalmen, wahrscheinlich aus der Neujahrsliturgie, anstatt Gebeten von Kranken oder Angeklagten [1]) sehen wird. Besonders wenn man erkannt hat, dass die Psalmen nicht willkürlich zusammengestellt wurden, sondern grössere Zusammenhänge nach der vorauszusetzenden ursprünglichen Festliturgie bilden. Für das erste Buch des Psalters glaube ich es gut nachweisen zu können, was allerdings in diesem Zusammenhange nicht möglich ist.

Die Feindseligkeit Edoms seinem Bruder Jaakob gegenüber hat sich besonders an jenem Tag krass geäussert, als Fremdlinge ins Tor [2]) eingedrungen sind um die Mannschaft wegzuführen (Ob. 11) und gegen Jerusalem das Los zu werfen. Da hat sich Esau als Erbfeind erwiesen und kaum anders ist das Femininum *'al tišlaḥnâ* (13) zu verstehen, als durch eine neue Betonung seines tiâmatischen Cha-

---

[1]) Im Gegensatz zu H. Schmidt: *Die Psalmen*, Tübingen 1934.

[2]) Singular mit Ketib zu lesen, in Einklang mit 13.

rakters (s. oben sub 2), wobei die Mehrzahl gut begründet ist im Gegensatz zu 1, da hier eben noch von den Fremdlingen, also eigentlich dem Gefolge der Tiâmat die Rede ist. Unter *ḥajil* (11.13) ist dabei wohl die Mannschaft des *ḥēl* (20) zu verstehen, die nun weggeführt wird, dann jedoch wieder zurückkehrt um das Gefolge des neuinthronisierten Gottes zu bilden [1]. Von da aus wird sich wohl richtig auch der *jōm ḥēlᵉkå* Ps cx 3, ebenso wie das viel umdisputierte *ḥelkåh* bzw. *ḥelkå'īm* Ps x 8.10.14 erklären.

Bei der betreffenden Kultszene kam offensichtlich ein bestimmtes Tor in Frage; so richtig das Ketib Ob. 11 (cf 13), wogegen das Qere eher auf ein Kriegsereignis zu weisen scheint, in Einstimmung mit der Septuaginta, aber inkonsequent im Vergleich mit 13. — Das Loswerfen als Bestandteil des Neujahrsfestes braucht keine nähere Erklärung. Hier wird es zwar dem Feind zugeschrieben, aber das bedeutet einen weiteren Beweis, dass es sich um einen übermenschlichen Feind handelt, der sich das Recht aneignen kann, an Gottes Stelle zu entscheiden — allerdings nur solange es ihm Jahwä gewährt.

Dieser Tag der Bedrängnis, Not und Angst, *jōm ṣårå̂* (Ob. 12ff), den Jaakob mitmachen muss, ausgeliefert den Fremdlingen und ganz besonders bedroht durch Edom (14), hätte schon längst vor dem Vorwurf nationalistischen Hasses (oben sub 1) warnen sollen, auch wenn der kultische Hintergrund nicht erkannt wurde. Wir dürfen darin ein Merkmal voramosischer Tradition sehen. Bis der eigentliche *jōm jahvę̂* einbricht, kann er nur die Feinde betreffen (15ff), Jaakob hat seinen Kelch schon getrunken (16, cf Jer. xlix 12). Dass sich dabei die Anrede Gottes gegen alle *gōjīm* plötzlich wendet, darf nicht verwundern. Nur dann kann die selige Zeit einbrechen, wenn alle Feinde vernichtet sind. Es sollen ja schliesslich nur die Feinde vernichtet werden, während die Auserwählten dem Volke Gottes zum Erbteil fallen werden (19f).

Nun stehen wir aber noch vor zwei schwierigen Fragen. Erstens, wer ist als das „Haus Josef" (18) bezeichnet, das neben dem „Haus Jaakob" (17f) erscheint? Nach SELLIN [2] soll das nördliche Israel damit gemeint sein. Dagegen TH. H. ROBINSON [3] fasst beide Ausdrücke als Synonyma für Juda auf, was ihm gleichzeitig

[1] Vgl. eine ähnliche Situation Nah. ii 6 (mit *ḥōmå* anstatt *ḥēl*) bei A. HALDAR: *Studies in the Book of Nahum*, Uppsala-Leipzig 1947, S. 125 f.

[2] E. SELLIN: *Das Zwölfprophetenbuch*, Leipzig-Erlangen 1922, S. 235.

[3] TH. H. ROBINSON: *Die Zwölf Kleinen Propheten*, Tübingen 1936, S. 115.

zum Beweis für den angeblich späten Ursprung des Abschnittes Ob. 16-18 dient. In Wirklichkeit haben beide teilweise Recht. Die doppelte Bezeichnung — Haus Jaakob und Haus Josef — will die Einheit ganz Israels betonen. Denn als Volk Gottes kommt nur ganz Israel in Frage, wenngleich unter Umständen die Aufgabe auch nur auf einen einzelnen Stamm (Juda) übertragen werden konnte, ja sogar auf einen alleinstehenden Propheten (Jer. xlix 14, cf oben sub 3). Der zur Frage stehende Abschnitt will durch die Doppelbezeichnung (auf die wir noch 19f zurückkommen) also nichts anderes betonen, als dass es sich um das wahre Israel als Ganzes und nicht blos um eine irdische Grösse handelt. Dabei tritt als sichtbarer Vertreter des Hauses Josef sein Bruder Benjamin auf, der wohl geeignet war den Segen Josefs (Gen. xlviii 22, xlix 22-26, Dt. xxxiii 13-17) zu übernehmen und mit dem Segen Judas (Gen. xlix 8-12 Dt. xxxiii 7) vereinigen, denn das Wort Gottes kehrt nicht leer zu ihm zurück (Jes. lv 11) und sein Segen kann nicht vereitelt werden.

Die zweite Frage ist nun aber schwieriger. Wen meint der Text mit den Deportierten (20)? Und was soll mit ihnen geschehen? Die beiden angeblichen Propria sind sehr zweifelhaft. Die Stadt Sarepta kennen wir zwar aus der Elialegende und ihrer neutestamentlichen Zitation. Ist aber wirklich diese phönizische Stadt gemeint? Warum gerade sie, wenn wir doch von keiner Deportierung der Israeliten dorthin wissen!? Der Zweifel wird aber noch gestärkt, wenn es sich feststellt, dass das zweite „Proprium", Sefarad, wenigstens von einem Teil der Tradition überhaupt nicht proprie verstanden wurde (s. oben), während der andere Teil der Tradition vergebens von Medien über Kleinasien und Griechenland bis nach Spanien einen geeigneten Ort zur Identifikation sucht. Wäre auch dies Bestreben berechtigt, müsste es nicht auffallen, dass die eine Gruppe der Deportierten knapp hinter der Landesgrenze sitzen bleibt, während die andere bis an das Ende der damals bekannten Welt vertrieben wird? Die Frage bleibt auch dann bestehen, wenn es sich um keine Deportierung dorthin handelt, sondern um eine Beerbung der genannten Gebiete. Historisch lässt sich dies Problem nicht lösen!

Und im Kultus kommen solche Reisen nicht in Frage. Einfacher ist es, Appellativa anzunehmen. So für Sefarad etwas wie „das Ende (*s-v-p*) des Herumirrens (*r-v-d*)" in Hinblick auf Gen. xxvii 40, wie oben bereits angedeutet, wogegen das verdächtige Sarepta wahrscheinlich mit „prüfen und bewähren" (*ṣ-r-p*) etwas zu tun haben wird. Das würde gut zu dem passen, was wir von *ḥajil* (11.13) feststellen konnten und lässt annehmbar die Tatsache erscheinen, dass eben diese Bewährten zu Erben werden sollen von allem, was dem Feind, ja genauer ausgedrückt allen *gōjīm*, gehört hat. Dass da ausdrücklich das Gebiet der abtrünnigen 10 Stämme Israels darunter genannt wird, lässt sich wohl in dem Sinne begreifen, dass die Erinnerung an das früher einige Reich noch stark nachwirkte; ein weiterer Beweis für das hohe Alter des Ob.

Der letzte Vers (21) lässt nun die Befreier (nicht die Befreiten, wie Septuaginta meint) den Berg Zion besteigen, von dem vorher (17) schon die Rede war, dass dort das Heil sein wird und dass der Berg heilig sein wird (ib.), nachdem dort das Vernichtungsurteil über die Feinde vollbracht sein wird (16). Die Feier naht dem Kulminationspunkt. Der Berg Esau soll endgültig gerichtet werden (21). Auf der einen Seite der Berg Zion, Jahwä, die Erlösten, auf der anderen der Berg Esau, die geschlagenen Helden und beschämten Weisen. Man spürt, dass es sich hier um ein Gegenstück zu den Bergen Ebal und Gerizzim (Dt. xxvii) handelt, um zwei Grössen, die im Kult, nicht aber in der Geographie ihren Gewichtspunkt haben.

„Und Jahwäs wird das Königtum sein". Auch dies Schlusswort hebt den religiösen Charakter des ganzen Buches, das inhaltlich eine fest aufgebaute Einheit bildet, deutlich hervor. Wie und wann die einzelnen Sprüche zum erstenmal ausgesprochen wurden, werden wir kaum einmal erfahren, jedenfalls sind sie dem Ganzen untrennbar einverleibt, haben sie überhaupt je isoliert existiert! Dass Jer. xlix nur einen Teil von ihnen benutzt, hängt mit dem Ziel, das das Buch verfolgt, zusammen und ist keinesfalls ein Beweis für die jüngere Herkunft von Ob. 11ff.

HEBREW POETIC DICTION

BY

G. R. DRIVER

Oxford

I here take up a hint, dropped some years ago in a letter to Prof. BENTZEN [1]), that the diction of Hebrew poetry owes much of its distinctive colouring to the Aramaic language; for, where two synonyms are in use, one in prose and the other in poetry, whatever the linguistic affinities of the word current in prose may be, that used in poetry can often be traced to one or other of the Aramaic dialects, whether it is found only there or also in some other of the cognate languages.

Such an enquiry is fraught with difficulties, and no one will be surprised that hardly anyone but KAUTZSCH [2]) has attempted it. The initial problem is to discover what is and what is not in general terms an Aramaism. The original group or groups of Hebrews who came in at various periods from the desert would certainly have included Aramaeans, since they were in all probability a very mixed body; Aramaeans invaded Israel in war and Aramaean traders would often have travelled through it, and indeed there was an Aramaean quarter in Samaria under the monarchy [3]). Aramaic, too, was the language of diplomacy and was understood by the upper classes of Judah in the 8th century B.C. [4]). At the same time it was already beginning to displace the sister languages in the neighbouring countries. In fact, its influence was all-pervading. Further, Aramaic stands very close to Hebrew, and words in the two languages may often have been indistinguishable except when marked by a typical

---

[1]) Noted in his *Introduction to the Old Testament* [2]) II 168 [4]).

[2]) In *Die Aramaismen im Alten Testament* (1902); cp. HÄVERNICK, *Einleitung in das Alte Testament* [1849] I 172-6, BÖTTCHER & MUHLAU, *Ausführliches Lehrbuch der Hebräischen Sprache* [1866] I §§ 50-58, KÖNIG, *Stylistik Rhetorik Poetik* [1900] 282-7, KAUTZSCH & COWLEY *Hebrew Grammar* § 2 s, v, DRIVER *Problems of the Hebrew Verbal System* [1936] 98-107 (s. KAUTZSCH *op. cit.* 1-4 for other references).

[3]) I Ki. xx 34.

[4]) II Ki. xviii 26.

inflection, and the process of adapting a word from Aramaic will often have obliterated any difference that may have previously existed. Further, words of genuine Hebrew stock may have fallen into disuse but have been re-introduced subsequently from an Aramaic dialect (for example *sāḇal* 'bore, carried', which after occurring in an early poem disappears from use only to come back in the exilic or post-exilic period); ought such words to be treated as Aramaisms or not? Lastly, are words which are known to have been current in the literature of the northern kingdom (for example *ša-* 'which') properly regarded as Aramaisms when they are found in other works?

KAUTZSCH [1]) defines Aramaisms as (i) words which appear in a recognizably Aramaic form; (ii) words which can be traced to the West-Aramaic vocabulary but are not found in the Canaanite and South-Aramaic dialects; (iii) words which do not occur in pre-exilic literature or, if occurring there, have a different sense from that which they afterwards bear but which become common in exilic and post-exilic literature.

Words in the first class are easily recognized if they contain consonants which are not the same in Aramaic and Hebrew or vowels which the Massoretes have not obscured. Such are *tinnāh* 'praised' in the Song of Deborah, which has extended its range into other branches of literature, [2]) *ḥāraṯ* 'engraved' and *ṭāʿan* 'loaded', which the Elohist uses once each. Such words were probably endemic in the northern dialect and, wherever they were used, were perhaps often not felt to be foreign. So too *ʾessaq* 'I go up' exhibits an Aramaistic form. After the exile Aramaic forms of this sort became increasingly numerous (for example *rāḇaʿ* for *rāḇaṣ* 'lay down' and *maddāʿ* for *dēʿāh* 'knowledge') but were probably long regarded, except the commonest, as loan-words by educated persons, especially when verb and noun came to represent different types of formation. Loan-words distinguished by the vocalization are not so easy to detect, since that of those which came early into the language has been hebraized (for example *ʾĕnôš* from *ʾĕnāš* 'man'); but examples can still be recognized (for example *keṯāḇ* beside *keṯôḇeṯ* 'writing'). Words of the second class are extremely difficult to identify in consequence of the extraordinarily small number of Canaanite and South-

[1]) In *Aramaismsn* 15.

[2]) Jud. v 11 xi 40; possibly also Ps. viii 2 (*tunnāh*) and Prov. xxxi 31 (*tannû*).

Arabic words available for comparison; they can indeed hardly be used except when helped out by other tests. The third class offers not a few examples (for example *ṭerep̱* 'prey' and also 'leaves', *'ātaq* 'advanced' and also 'grew old' and *pāraq* 'snatched away' and also 'rescued'); it is however open to the objection that such secondary meanings, though extant only in late Hebrew, may in fact have been current long before their first appearance. This objection, indeed, is more or less applicable to the use of all three classes in the present enquiry. Granted the existence, however, of Aramaisms for the sake of argument, to what extent had those in the second and third, and indeed in the first, class become so fully naturalized that they were no longer regarded as foreign? That some post-exilic works are almost if not quite free from Aramaisms suggests a conscious effort by educated people to write a pure classical Hebrew due to an uneasy feeling that such words were not genuinely Hebrew; but the test is not one that can be applied with exactitude or to individual words. If only those words which the Hebrews themselves may be thought to have regarded as foreign are listed as Aramaisms, the number will probably be very small: if all those words and roots which can be traced solely to an Aramaic dialect are included, it will become considerable. This is a dilemma which can hardly be resolved in view of the small amount of matter available for study.

Another test may be found in the existence of synonyms, of which there is a very large number in Hebrew due to the parallelistic nature of Hebrew poetry; for many of these can be traced to an Aramaic source.

This part of the enquiry, too, is full of uncertainty; for parallelism brings together many words which at first sight seem synonymous but are shown by examination to be only roughly so. The same difficulty recurs in the case of words used in pairs; they may be mere synonyms used to re-inforce one another but they may describe different aspects of the same action or state or varieties of the same object. For example, are *gyl* - *ḥdh* - *śyś* - *śmḥ*, all denoting some form of rejoicing, or *gwr* - *ẓḥl* - *ygr* - *yr'* - *pḥd*, all denoting fear, true synonyms derived from different linguistic stocks or do they refer to different aspects respectively of the same emotion? Further, the small bulk and narrow range of the surviving literature has the result that an unduly high proportion of words is exceedingly rare, so that their precise sense can hardly be determined, and many which are found only in poetry may once have been in common use also in prose, in which by a mere chance they do not happen now to be recorded. [1])

In any such discussion, then, the following synonyms or apparent synonyms must be used with caution if not entirely excluded:

(i) inexact synonyms, such as *nāṭa'* 'planted' and *šāṯal* 'transplanted', which are really distinct even though they may be confused in usage;

(ii) by-forms, such as *mā'as* = *māsāh* = *māsas* 'melted', even though one or other has only been traced otherwise in Aramaic, since all will or may have existed side by side in Hebrew [2]);

(iii) ephemeral loan-words introduced at a late date but not found in post-Biblical literature, such as *māḥā'* for *māḥaṣ* 'struck' [3]);

(iv) synonyms described as Aramaic solely on the strength of Judaeo-Aramaean sources, which may well be aramaized Hebrew words;

(v) merely descriptive terms used as substitutes for the proper word, such as *rahaḇ* 'boisterousness' for 'ocean', or occurring merely as proper names, such as *yᵉmîmāh* for *yônāh* 'dove;'

(vi) special words introduced for the purpose of the story, such as *mān* for *mah* 'what' and *śāhᵉḏû* for *'êḏāh* 'testimony'.

An attempt may now be made to see how far the thesis here put forward can be supported by an examination, however superficial and uncertain if the safe-guards first mentioned are borne in mind, of samples of the actual vocabulary of the Old Testament and a comparison of the Hebrew roots found in it with those of the cognate languages. [4])

(i) Words regularly used in prose with poetical synonyms (i) drawn solely from an Aramaic sense:

bḥn	(3)	*bḥr*	(3)	'tested' [5])
g'l	(3)	*ṭnp*	(3)	'soiled'

[1]) In the following lists words are counted as poetical if they are cited mostly from poetry.

[2]) Allowance must by made also for variations of dialect and colloquialisms within the pure or classical speech.

[3]) An early Aramaic by-form is *māḥaq* 'struck', which would seem to have become so completely naturalized that it could be used beside *māḥaṣ* 'struck,' unless it it represents a different root or the text is incorrect (Jud. v. 26).

[4]) The various Semitic languages are cited by the following numbers: 1. Babylonian and Assyrian; 2. Ugaritic and Phoenician; 3. Aramaic and Syriac; 4. Arabic and Ethiopic.

[5]) Is. xlviii 10 Jb. xxxiv 33 (?)

dbr	(2)	*mll*	(3)	'spoke'
ḥgr	(3)	*ḥzq*	(3)	'girded' [1]
ḥkh		*śbr*	(3)	'hoped'
ḥrp	(3)	*ḥsd*	(3)	'reproached'
yrd	(1, 2, 4)	*nḥt*	(3)	'went down'
mšl	(1, 3, 4)	*dmh*	(3)	'was like'
npḥ	(1, 3, 4)	*nšb*	(3)	'blew'
ngd	(4)	*ḥwh*	(3)	'told'
spd	(1)	*ʾlh*	(3)	'wailed'
ʿlh	(1, 4)	*slq*	(3)	'went up'
pṭr	(4) [2]	*plḥ*	(3)	'came to birth' [3]
rʾh	(4)	*ḥzh*	(3)	'saw'
tʿh		*ṭʿh*	(3)	'strayed'
ʾdmh		*rbʿ*	(3)	'soil' [4]
ʾwr	(1)	*nhrh*	(3)	'light' [5]
kbwd		*yqr*	(3)	'honour'
mlḥmh		*qrb*	(3)	'war'
mʿśh		*mʿbd*	(3)	'deed'
ʿzr	(3, 4)	*ʾyl*	(3)	'help'
ʿlh		*ʿpy*	(3)	'leafage'
ʿnn	(3, 4)	*ʿb*	(3)	'clouds'
ʿpr	(3, 4)	*nḥl*	(3)	'dust' [6]
pgr	(1, 2)	*gwph*	(3)	'corpse'
rʿb	(4)	*kpn*	(3)	'hunger'
šḥt		*gwmṣ*	(3)	'pit'
yph		*pʾh*	(3)	'fair' [7]
ʾm		*hn*	(3)	'if'

(ii) drawn from an Aramaic dialect and one or other of the cognate languages:

ʾhb	(2)	*ḥbb*	(3, 4)	'loved'
ʾrb	(4)	*ṣdh*	(3, 4)	'lay in wait'
bwʾ	(1, 4, 5)	*ʾth*	(3, 4)	'came'

---

1) Is. xxii 21.
2) In *peṭer* 'what opens the womb' compared with *faṭara* 'created.'
3) Jb. xxxix 3 (s. Targ. Jer. II on Exod. xxxiv 19).
4) Numb. xxiii 18.
5) Arab. *nahâru(n)* 'daylight' apparently an Aramaic loan-word.
6) Jb. xxi 33.
7) Am. iii 12 (MAAG).

bwš	(1)	*ḥpr*	(3, 4)	'was ashamed'
bkh	(1, 3, 4)	*dmʿ*	(3, 4)	'wept'
hdp	(4)	*dkh*	(3, 4)	'thrust'
hrg	(4)	*qṭl*	(3, 4)	'killed'
ḥzh	(4)	*qbl*	(1, 3, 4)	'was opposite'
yʿṣ	(3, 4)	*mlk*	(1, 3)	'counselled'
yph	(3, 4)	*špr*	(3, 4)	'was fair'
yṣq	(2)	*nsk*	(2, 3)	'poured out'
lmd	(1, 3)	*ʾlp*	(3, 4)	'learnt'
mlṭ		*plṭ*	(3, 4)	'escaped'
šmr	(1)	*nṣr*	(1, 3, 4)	'watched'
mšš	(3, 4)	*gšš*	(3, 4)	'felt'
nʾṣ		*gdp*	(3, 4)	'reviled'
swr		*ʿṭp*	(3, 4)	'turned aside'
ʿwp	(2, 3, 4)	*ṭwś*	(3, 4)	'flew'
ʿkr	(4)	*dlḥ*	(1, 3)	'troubled'
ʿlm		*str*	(3, 4)	'hid'
ʿśh		*pʿl*	(2, 3, 4)	'did'
ptḥ	(1,2,3,4)	*pqḥ*	(3, 4)	'opened'
qdd	(1)	*sgd*	(3, 4)	'bowed down'
rʿb	(4)	*kpn*	(3, 4)	'hungered'
šʾp		*nšm*	(3, 4)	'panted'
škḥ		*nšh*	(1, 3, 4)	'forgot'
šlw	(3, 4)	*šʾn*	(3, 5)	'was at ease'
gʾh	(3)	*yhyr*	(3, 4)	'proud'
drk	(3, 4)	*ʾrḥ*	(1, 3)	'way'
yyn[1]	(2, 4)	*ḥmr*	(3, 4)	'wine'
lhb	(1, 3, 4)	*lhṭ*	(1, 3)	'flame'

(iii) drawn from a non-Aramaic source:

ʾkl	(1, 3, 4)	*lḥm*	(1)	'ate'
ʾsp	(1)	*qbṣ*	(4)	'gathered'
ʾml	(4)	*mll*	(4)	'wilted'
bʾš	(1, 3)	*znḥ*	(1, 4)	'stank'
bws		*rms*	(4)	'trampled'
bzz	(3, 4)	*šll*	(1, 4)	'despoiled'
blʿ	(3, 4, 5)	*lhm*	(4)	'swallowed'

[1]) Probably a non-Semitic loan-word.

brʾ	(2, 3, 4)	*ḥlq*	(4)	'created' [1])
yrʾ	(4)	*ygr*	(4)	'feared'
lʾh	(1, 4)	*yʿp*	(4)	'was weary'
śyb	(1, 3, 4)	*zrq*	(4)	'was [2]) gray'
ʿml	(1, 3, 4)	*ygʿ*	(1, 4)	'toiled'
qll	(1,3,4,5)	*ḥzh*	(4)	'was [3]) vile'
qṣp	(3)	*znh*	(1)	'was [4]) angry'
špṭ	(1, 2)	*dyn*	(1, 4)	'judged'
ʾryh	(1, 3)	*lyš*	(1)	'lion'
gwrl	(4)	*ḥṣ*	(4)	'lot' [5])
zhb	(3, 4)	*ḥrwṣ*	(1, 2)	'gold'
ʿdy	(3)	*ḥly*	(4)	'ornament'
ʿd		*śhd*	(3, 4)	'witness'
ʿm	(3, 4)	*lʾm*	(2)	'people'
pgr	(1, 3)	*nblh*	(1, 3)	'corpse'
rʾš	(1,2,3,4)	*qdqd*	(1, 2)	'head'
škr	(1, 3, 4)	*sbʾ*	(1, 4)	'liquor'
šmš	(1,2,3,4)	*ḥrs*	(?)	'sun'
tmr	(4)	*nḥl*	(4)	'palm'

II. Words used mostly in prose with synonyms used also chiefly in prose (i) drawn from an Aramaic source alone:

hlk	(1, 3, 4)	*ʾzl*	(3)	'went'
sḥr	(1, 3)	*rkl*	(3)	'trader'
plḥ	(3, 4)	*bqʿ*	(3)	'clave'
qṣ	(1)	*swp*	(3)	'end'

(ii) drawn from an Aramaic dialect and one or other cognate language:

ʾrr	(1)	*qbb*	(3, 5)	'cursed'
dšn	(4)	*šmn*	(1, 3, 4)	'was fat'
ḥbh	(1, 3, 4)	*str*	(3, 4)	'hid'
ḥkh	(4)	*yḥl*	(3, 4)	'waited'
zrr		*ʿṭš*	(3, 4)	'sneezed'
yṣt		*yqd*	(3, 4)	'burned'

[1]) J.b. Sir. xxxi 13,27 xxxiii 13 xxxviii 1; cp. Is. lvii 6.
[2]) Hos. vii 9 (Ruben).
[3]) S.p. 14.
[4]) Jud. xix 2 (DRIVER in *Eph. Theol. Lov.* XXVI 348-9).
[5]) Jb. xxxiv 6.

lqḥ	(1, 2, 4)	*ʾḥz*	(1,2,3,4))	'took'
šth	(1, 2, 3)	[*šqh*]	(1, 2, 3, 4)	'drank'
mdd	(1, 4)	*mšḥ*	(1, 3)	'measured'
sbb	(2, 4)	*sḥr*	(1, 3)	'went round'
spr	(4)	*mnh*	(1, 3, 4)	'counted'
pwṣ	(3, 4)	*pzr*	(3, 4)	'scattered'
šlm	(1,2,3,4)	*tmm*	(2, 3, 4)	'was complete'
šqr	(1, 2)	*kzb*	(3, 4)	'lied' [1])
šyt		*śym*	(1, 3, 4)	'put'
hryq		*šlp*	(1, 3)	'drew (a sword)'
ʾbr	(1)	*knp*	(1, 2, 3, 4)	'wing'
ʾl	(1, 2)	*ʾlh*	(3, 4)	'God'
ḥbl	(1, 3)	*qw*	(1, 3)	'cord'
ḥdš	(2)	*yrḥ*	(1, 3)	'month'
ḥlh	(1, 3)	*dwh*	(3, 4)	'was sick'
mṭh	(1)	*šbṭ*	(1, 3)	'staff'
špḥh		*ʾmh*	(1, 2, 3, 4)	'slave-girl'
ʿyr	(2)	*qryh*	(2, 3, 4)	'city'
ʿṣm	(1,2,3,4)	*grm*	(3, 4)	'bone'
ʿt	(1, 2, 3)	*zmn*	(3, 4)	'time'
śdh	(1, 2)	*br*	(3, 4)	'open country'
šʾr	(1)	*bśr*	(3, 4)	'flesh'
škm	(2)	*ktp*	(3, 4)	'shoulder'
ʾnky	(1, 2)	*ʾny*	(3, 4)	'I'
ʾt		*ʿm*	(2, 3)	'with'

(iii) words drawn from a non-Aramaic source:

bgd	(2, 4)	*mʿl*	(4)	'was treacherous'
ḥrš	(1, 3, 4)	*ptḥ*	(1)	'engraved'
mwt	(1,2,3,4)	*gwʿ*	(4)	'died'
ntṣ		*hrs*	(4)	'tore down'

KAUTZSCH [2]) too, has compiled a list of Aramaisms, from which the following words are added, whether found otherwise only in an Aramaic dialect or also in any cognate language, as occurring mainly though not necessarily solely in poetry:

[1]) The Acc. *kuzbu* 'luxuriance', found also in Hebrew names such as *Kôzᵉḇâ* and *Kozbî* (persons) or *Kᵉzîḇ* and *ʾAkzîḇ* (places) is a different root, apparently not found in the other cognate languages (s. STAMM, *Akk. Namengeb.* 226-7).

[2]) In *Aramaismen* 93-99.

zqp	‘set up’	*mwq*	‘to mock’	*šbḥ*	‘praised’
tpl	‘smeared’	*swg*	‘to fence in’	*šlṭ*	‘domineered’
ktr	‘waited’	*slh*	‘despised’	*šrh*	‘loosed’
l‘z	‘spoke barbarously’	*‘kb*	‘checked’ [1]	*twh*	‘rued’
mgr	‘hurled down’	*psq*	‘bestrode’	*tqp*	‘overpowered’
		rgš	‘was in turmoil’		
’mn	‘craftsman’	*kšyl*	‘axe’	*swq*	‘lane’
zwyt	‘corner’	*kwšrh*	‘prosperity’	*štw*	‘winter’
ḥp	‘clean’	*ktl*	‘wall’	*‘štwn*	‘thought’
kp	‘rock’	*mzg*	‘mixed drink’	*r‘*	‘purpose’
		mḥwz	‘haven’		

Some words, commonly confined to prose, have several, chiefly poetical, synonyms derived from various sources of which one is almost always an Aramaic dialect:

b’š (1, 3, 4) — *znḥ* (4) and *ḥnn* (3, 4) ‘stank’
ṭyṭ (1) — *ywn* and *š’n* [2] (3) ‘mire’
’šr (1, 2) and *š-* (1, 2) — *zh* (3, 4) ‘who(m), which’
’dm (2, 3) and *’yš* (2) — *’nwš* (3, 4) ‘man’
’wyl (4) and *ksyl* (4) — *skl* (1, 3) ‘fool’
’sr (1, 3, 4) and *ḥbš* (1, 4) — *šq‘* (3) [3] ‘tied’
’rg (2) and *nsk* — *šth* (3) ‘wove’
n’d (1, 3) and *ḥmt* (Eg.) — *rqb* (3) [4] ‘skin-bottle’
nṣl (3, 4) — *ḥlṣ* [5] (2) and *pṣh* (3, 4) and *prq* (3, 4) ‘rescued’
’zr (4) and *ḥgr* (3) — *’sr* [6] (3) and *ḥzq* [7] (3) ‘girded’
ybš (3, 4) and *ḥrb* (3) — *’bl* [8] (1, 4) and *nšt* ‘dried up’
zqn (4) and *yšn* — *yšyš* and *‘tyq* (3) ‘old’.

These lists of synonyms yield the following figures for synonyms used in poetry and found

[1]) Jb. xxxvii 4.
[2]) Ps. xl 3 (Gaster).
[3]) Jb. xl 25.
[4]) Jb. xiii 28.
[5]) Ps. vii 5.
[6]) Jb. xii 18 Neh. iv 12.
[7]) Is. xxii 21.
[8]) Driver in *Occident and Orient* 73-75.

(i) only in Aramaic dialects 29
(ii) in Aramaic and cognate languages 34
(iii) only in non-Aramaic sources 25

and for synonyms used in prose and found

(i) only in Aramaic dialects 4
(ii) in Aramaic and cognate languages 31
(iii) only in non-Aramaic sources 4

These figures, though based only on samples and therefore not exhaustive, show that (i) the Aramaic is by far the largest single extraneous element in the Hebrew language and (ii) the percentage of words found otherwise only in Aramaic is far higher in poetry than in prose.

The use of words derived from an Aramaic source is characteristic also of certain authors. For example, the *Elohist* amongst historical writers has several such words, whether found otherwise only in an Aramaic dialect (such as *zbd*, *ḥdh*, *ḥydh*, *ḥrb*, *ḥrt*, *ṭʿn*, *mzwn*, *mll*, *pqʿ*, *ptr*, *ṣnm*, *qwṣ*) or shared with the cognate languages (such as *ʾmh*, *ʾlh*, *ʾny*, *ḥzq*, *ḥzy*, *ḥlṣ*, *nkry*), and *Hosea* among the prophets uses a high proportion of Aramaic words (such as *drk*, *ḥwh*, *ysr*, *yrb*, *ʿlwh*, *šḥt*, *tnh*). In the same way the *Priestly Code* contains a small number of Aramaisms, some of them shared with poetry (such as *gwʿ*, *yšn*, *šgh*). The reasons, however, for this peculiarity are not the same. *Hosea* and the *Elohist*, on the one hand, living in the northern kingdom which was always subject to strong Aramaean influence, naturally used Aramaisms; they were proper to their own dialect and were presumably part of their daily speech. The *Priestly writer* or writers, on the other hand, living at a time when the Aramaic language was overrunning the whole Semitic world and the distinction between the Hebrew and Aramaic vocabularies was fading, employed Aramaisms because they were becoming part of the stock of the Hebrew language, which required then to be enriched because of its growing inadequacy to the needs of daily life.

KAUTZSCH counts 153 Aramaisms in the whole Old Testament. [1]) Some however are clearly such only through the chance of having

---

[1]) These include 21 (not 23) in the Pentateuch; of these J has three (*hn*, *ḥdh*, *šhdw*) and E has six (*ḥydh*, *ṭʿn*, *mll*, *ptr*, *ptrwn*, *šlyṭ*), while D has one (*šryzwt*) and P has eleven (*bqr*, *hn*, *ḥsd*, *kpr*, *ktbt*, *mwk*, *mḥh*, *mn*, *qbl*, *qnyn*, *rbʿ*).

survived once or twice in late texts (for example *kōṯel* 'wall' and *sûq* 'lane, which are almost *gemeinsemitisch* and must have been in regular use at every period of Hebrew history). Others, though Aramaic in form, must have been naturalized in Hebrew at a very early date (for example *seṯāw* 'winter', for which no Hebrew word is known, although its form is Aramaic). At the same time, not a few Aramaisms have escaped his notice. In fact, his list shows only too well the difficulty of bringing such an enquiry to a satisfactory conclusion.

In considering this problem, KAUTZSCH [1]) draws attention to two points, which have already been noted; these are the high incidence of words of Aramaic origin in the poetical books of the Old Testament and the large number of synonyms required to meet the needs of parallelism in Hebrew poetry. He thinks that the Hebrew vocabulary itself was too poor to meet this need, which could only be made good by borrowing from the stores of the Aramaic language. He thinks also that this borrowing was increased by a feeling which some authors had that such Aramaic words as they borrowed had some connection with the old Hebrew speech and that an *aerugo vetustatis*, especially dear to poets, was imparted to their language by the use of them. The idea of such conscious borrowing on any extensive scale may be doubted. The bulk of Hebrew literature which has survived is slight and is restricted to very few subjects, and the Hebrew vocabulary reflected in it is correspondingly small. Many if not most of the supposed Aramaisms, at any rate of those found in the pre-exilic literature, possibly or probably descended from the old common Semitic stock on which the vocabularies of the several languages were based. They may be called 'Aramaisms' only in the sense that they cannot otherwise be traced except in Aramaic; if a more extensive Hebrew literature of the early period could be recovered, they would certainly be far fewer. [2]) The bulk of these so-called Aramaisms are found in poetry only because poets normally employ an extensive and recondite vocabulary which naturally makes considerable use of archaisms. The earliest loan-words, whether of Aramaic or any other origin, must have been for so long a time and so completely naturalized that they are no longer instantly recognized unless the grammatical form is non-Hebraic; the two

---

[1]) In *Aramaismen* 103-4.

[2]) Not every word which Hebrew shares with Aramaic must necessarily be regarded as an Aramaism (STADE, *Hebr. Gramm.* 12).

stocks are as indissolubly and indistinguishably merged as the Scandinavian and Teutonic elements in the English language of to-day. Further, there was a continuous infiltration of Aramaic into Hebrew, new words coming in and old words coming back, just as American is affecting English at the present time; some of these words are genuinely old English [1]) but others are purely American coinages but, if properly formed, indistinguishable from English words. Occasionally a poet may have introduced an Aramaic word consciously to suit his own purpose, but he will surely have adopted most unconsciously from the speech of his own time and neighbourhood; others will have come from proverbs and gnomic sayings reflecting now ancient wisdom and now contemporary wit expressed in the popular idiom of the day. Lastly, as time went on, other Aramaic words would be adopted to express concepts for which Hebrew had no word; and the influence of Aramaic would increase as it conquered new fields, while Hebrew was pushed into the background of school and synagogue; it had neither the richness of vocabulary nor the simplicity of grammar and syntax of its successful rival.

In conclusion, many if not most of the supposed Aramaisms, though now found only in Aramaic dialects, might be proved *gemeinsemitisch* if the sources were available for tracking them down; but whether such words came into Hebrew directly or through Aramaic would be an insoluble problem in the majority of instances unless their form betrayed them. The residue of real Aramaisms would consist of such words as were consciously borrowed by poets or writers for the purpose of enriching their vocabulary, an incalculable number of terms peculiar to certain trades or professions which would but rarely find their way into the surviving literature of the Bible, and words which when taken over from Aramaic into Hebrew preserved their original form [2]); these would come in for the most part directly from the north but after a long period of acclimatisation had probably ceased to be regarded as foreign. Only

---

[1]) So 'hiked' is an old English verb which, having become obsolete, has been re-introduced as an Americanism into modern English speech.

[2]) Words of the type of *tinnâ* 'praised', which might easily have come to be regarded by the ordinary person and even by a poet as truly Hebrew, must be distinguished from strictly Aramaic grammatical forms such as occur in North-Palestinian stories (s. BURNEY, *Kings* 208-9) and late Psalms (*e.g.* Ps. ciii 3-5), which would probably always be felt strange.

extreme purists would recognize any but those in the last class as loan-words and perhaps also object to their use. They would too have little means of distinguishing Aramaic words derived from the old Semitic stock and those coined within the language since its separation from that stock, unless they wore a distinctly Aramaic form. The description of most of these words, except the last, as Aramaisms therefore is rather a philological convenience than a demonstrable fact; yet it is a yardstick for measuring the development of the Hebrew language.

NOTE

The recognition of Aramaisms in specific authors may throw light on the interpretation of prose as well as poetry. For example, when Moses was summoned to go up onto Mt. Sinai with Aaron, Nadab and Abihu and seventy elders of Israel, God told him that he was to come near unto Him while the others worshipped Him afar off. Accordingly they went up 'and they saw (*wayyir'û*)' the God of Israel with a platform of sapphire beneath his feet; but 'He did not stretch out his hand unto' (*'el . . . lō' šālaḥ yāḏô*) the leaders of Israel, *i.e.* he did not beckon to them to advance up to His throne [1]), 'and they beheld (*wayyeḥĕzû*) God' and took a meal, (Exod. xxiv 11, J). Meanwhile Moses advanced to converse with God. The sudden introduction of *ḥāzāh* 'beheld' in this passage is in itself surprising enough; for it occurs elsewhere in the O.T. almost exclusively in poetry [2]), and *rā'āh* 'saw', the usual verb in prose, has just been used in precisely the same sense. Further, there is no need to repeat that these persons have seen God; that has already been said immediately before. The purpose of the verse is clearly to differentiate the course followed by them from that taken by Moses. The verb therefore must be thus misinterpreted; it is not I *ḥāzāh* (Arab. *ḥazâ*) 'beheld' but II *ḥāzāh* (Arab. *ḥaḏâ*) 'stood over against, opposite to', which has already been detected in three other places [3]). The meaning

[1]) Cp. II Sam. xv 5 Esth. iv 11 v 2 viii 4 for the gesture. That the phrase means that God does not put out His hand to injure them is most unlikely; for they have been commanded to ascend the mount and approach Him and have made no attempt to exceed any limit set by Him on their movements. If that were its sense, it would have no point.

[2]) Only once again in prose (Exod. xviii 21, E).

[3]) Ps. xlii 3 (Hitzig; s. Driver in J.T.S. XL 391) and Jb. viii 7 (s. Driver *ibid.* XXXIV 381 XL 391); so also *ḥôzeh* and *ḥāzûṯ* 'agreement' (Is. xxviii 15, 18)

of the verse then is that Aaron, Nadab and Abihu and the seventy elders, having come so far as to see God, were not invited to come close up to Him but 'they stood over against' Him, *i.e.* stayed where they were at a distance and had a meal (a human touch) while Moses went forward to converse face to face with God.

When Elihu asks: "For hath any said unto God: 'I have borne (chastisement), I will not offend (any more); '(That which) I see not do Thou teach me; if I have done iniquity, I will do so no more?"' (Jb. xxxiv 31-2; R.V.), he is made by the translators to talk very dubious sense; for 'I have borne (chastisement)' is not parallel with 'that which I see not', neither clause as thus translated has much point in the context, and several words have to be added even to obtain this poor sense. Both *nś'ty* and *'ḥzh* must describe actions or states *eiusdem generis*, and these must be some offence which the speaker has committed and the state in which he is before being taught by God. The Vulg.'s *erravi* for *'ḥzh* shows some recognition of this fact, but the actual sense suggested by it cannot be extracted from the verb; the other versions throw not light on the passage. I suggest, however, that with but slight alteration of the text the two verses may be translated 'Does a man say [1]) to God: I have presumed, I will do no more [2]) harm; 'I am vile, do Thou teach me; if I have done injustice, I will do so no more?'

In this translation I take *nś'ty* as standing elliptically for *nś'ty r'šy* 'I have lifted up my head', used in a bad sense here as elsewhere [3]), and I explain *'ḥzh* as coming from a Hebr. *ḥāzāh* = Arab. *ḫaziya* I 'became' or 'was base, vile, despicable, ignominious; was disgraced, perplexed by reason of disgrace' (Lane).

On this supposition I *ḥāzāh* = *ḥazâ* 'saw' and II *ḥāzāh* = *ḥaḏâ* 'was opposite' and III *ḥāzāh* = *ḫaziya* 'was .... vile, disgraced' must be recognized as three distinct verbs in the Hebrew dictionary.

---

after S. Arab. *ḥḏyt* 'congruent things' (Ehrlich; s. Driver in J.T.S. XXXVIII 44); cp. I Chron. xxv 5, where the LXX's ἀνακρούεσθαι 'to start back, stop short' seems to reflect this verb.

1) Reading *hky 'mr 'l-'l* (cp. Gen. xxvii 36 Jb. vi 22).

2) So Duhm, deleting *bl* as a dittograph.

3) Cp. Jud. viii 28 and Ps. lxxxiii 2; also in מָדוֹן יִשָּׂא 'strife lifts up (its head)' (Hab. i 3; s. J.T.S. XXXIX 394) and נשׂאו > נשׂא 'they have lifted up (their heads)' (Ps. cxxxix 20; Olshausen).

SUR LES DÉBUTS DE L'HISTOIRE ARAMÉENNE

PAR

A. DUPONT-SOMMER

Paris

Les débuts de l'histoire araméenne sont particulièrement obscurs. C'est seulement dans les inscriptions de Téglatphalasar I (1116-1090) qu'apparaît pour la première fois la mention de peuplades belliqueuses portant expressément le nom d'„Araméens". Voici un premier passage, se rapportant à la campagne de 1112: „Sous la protection du dieu Assour mon maître, je pris mes chars et mes braves, je marchai contre les Aḫlamu-Araméens (*Aḫ-la-mi-ia* *mât**Ar-ma-a-ia*), ennemis du dieu Assour mon maître. Depuis le pays de Sûḫi jusqu'à la ville de Karkémiš qui est au pays des Hittites, en un jour je ravageai. Je les massacrai, je ramenai leur butin, leur avoir, leurs biens sans nombre. Le reste de leurs troupes, en présence des armes terribles du dieu Assour mon maître, s'était enfui et avait passé l'Euphrate; derrière elles je passai l'Euphrate sur des bateaux de cuir. Je conquis six de leurs villes qui sont au pied du mont Bišri, je les brûlai par le feu, les détruisis, les anéantis. J'emmenai à ma ville d'Assour leur butin, leur avoir et leurs biens." [1]) Vers la fin de son règne, le même souverain déclare: „Vingt-huit fois derrière les Aḫlamu-Araméens, j'ai traversé l'Euphrate à raison de deux fois par an. Depuis la ville de Tadmor (Palmyre) qui est au pays d'Amurru, depuis la ville de Anat qui est au pays de Sûḫi et jusqu'à la ville de Rapiqu qui est au pays de Karduniaš, je réalisai leur défaite, j'emmenai à ma ville d'Assour leur butin, leur avoir, leurs biens." [2])

Il ressort clairement de ces deux textes que, vers la fin du XIIe siècle, les Araméens sont solidement accrochés sur les rives du Moyen-Euphrate, depuis Rapiqu, à l'est, jusqu'à Karkémiš, a l'ouest. Ils occupent notamment six villes dans la région du mont Bišri, près de l'embouchure du Baliḫ. Il faut les traquer jusqu'à Palmyre, en plein coeur du désert syrien.

Ces Araméens, on l'a remarqué, sont désignés sous le double nom d'„Aḫlamu-Araméens"; cette double désignation se rencontre

1) LUCKENBILL, *Ancient Records of Assyria and Babylonia*, I, § 239.
2) *Ibid.*, § 308.

encore dans quelques textes ultérieurs, notamment dans une inscription d'Assur-nirari II (911-890), qui les qualifie de „gens de la steppe" [1]), et dans une inscription d'Assur-naṣir-pal II (884-859), qui déclare avoir déporté 15.000 Aḫlamu-Araméens du Bît-Zamani (sur le Haut-Tigre) au pays d'Assour [2]). Mais, le plus souvent, ils sont désormais nommés tout simplement „Araméens", tandis que, d'autre part, les textes mentionnent encore quelquefois les „Aḫlamu".

Le rapport exact existant entre les deux mots n'est pas clair [3]). Rappelons seulement que les Aḫlamu sont déjà mentionnés, au XIVe siècle, dans une lettre d'El-Amarna [4]). Un peu plus tard, un texte assyrien nous fait savoir que le roi d'Assour Arik-dên-ilu (environ 1325-1311) lutta victorieusement contre „la troupe des Aḫlamu et des Sutu" [5]). Au siècle suivant, une lettre du roi hittite Ḫattušil III au roi de Babylone Kadašman-enlil III (vers 1275) nous apprend que les Aḫlamu rendent les routes peu sûres entre leurs deux royaumes [6]). Salmamasar I (environ 1280-1256), lors d'une campagne contre le roi de Ḫanigalbat (région du Ḫabur), doit combattre en même temps Hittites et Aḫlamu, qui, profitant de la décadence du Mitanni, cherchaient sans doute à s'emparer eux aussi de cette riche région [7]). Tikulti-ninurta I (environ 1255-1218) déclare avoir conquis, tout le long du Moyen-Euphrate, „le pays de Mari, le pays de Ḫana (Anat), le pays de Rapiqu et les montagnes des Aḫlamu." [8]) Puis, quand l'Empire hittite, vers 1200, se fut écroulé, Assur-reš-iši (environ 1149-1117), le père de Téglatphalasar I, rencontre encore ces redoutables ennemis; il se vante d'avoir massacré „les troupes considérables des Aḫlamu". [9])

---

[1]) *Ibid.*, § 362.

[2]) *Ibid.*, § 502.

[3]) Plusieurs ont proposé de reconnaître dans Aḫlamu un appellatif et dans Araméens un gentilice dérivé d'un nom de lieu; les Aḫlamu-Araméens seraient les Aḫlamu du pays d'Aram.

[4]) Edition Knudtzon, n° 200, 1.7-11. Cette lettre, malheureusement très mutilée, fait état de certaines rumeurs concernant les Aḫlamu; ceux-ci se trouvaient, semble-t-il, du côté de l'Euphrate, puisque la même lettre fait mention en même temps que du roi de Karduniaš (Babylonie). — Ajoutons qu'au XIVe siècle encore, deux lettres provenant de Dilmun (Bahrein) signalent dans cette région la présence d'Aḫlamu pillards; cf. *J.C.S.*, VI (1952), p. 137-145.

[5]) Inscription de son fils Adad-nirari I; Luck., I, § 73. — Les Sutu, ici associés aux Aḫlamu, apparaissent dans les textes à partir de l'époque de la première dynastie babylonienne Cf. R. O'Callaghan, *Aram Naharaim* (1948), p. 93 ss.

[6]) *Keilschrifttexte aus Boghazköi*, I, n° 10, l. 36 ss.

[7]) Luck., I, § 116.

[8]) *Ibid.*, § 166.

[9]) *Ibid.*, § 209.

Du XIVe au XIIe siècle, ces divers textes, on le voit, signalent la présence continue des Aḫlamu du côté de la Mésopotamie; quant aux Aḫlamu-Araméens, ils ne commencent à apparaître qu'à la fin du XIIe siècle, sous Téglatphalasar I. Antérieurement à l'époque d'El-Amarna, existe-t-il quelque trace des Araméens ou des Aḫlamu?

Récemment, N. Schneider a attiré l'attention sur un texte de la IIIe Dynastie d'Ur: l'inscription Wengler 22 [1]). Cette inscription fut publiée en transcription par A. Deimel [2]). Elle figure sur une tablette provenant de Puzurišdagan (Drehem), près de Nippur, et datée de l'an 46 du roi Šulgi (environ 2006). En voici le texte, au recto:

6 gud, 40 udu, 20 máš-gal, erín Áš-nun^{ki}
6 gud, 52 udu, 8 máš-gal, erín A-ra-mi^{ki}
6 gud, 42 udu, 18 máš-gal, erín Kaš-da-dun^{ki}
ugula A-ḫu-ni
„6 boeufs, 40 brebis, 20 boucs, (offerts par) les colons d'Áš-nun^{ki}.
6 boeufs, 52 brebis, 8 boucs, (offerts par) les colons d'A-ra-mi^{ki}.
6 boeufs, 42 brebis, 18 boucs, (offerts par) les colons de Kaš-da-dun^{ki}.
Conducteur: A-ḫu-ni."

Il s'agit d'animaux offerts en vue des sacrifices par des colons militaires de divers districts. Au verso de la tablette sont indiquées les offrandes de chacun: les donateurs (à une exception près) portent des noms akkadiens, tout comme cet A-ḫu-ni chargé d'amener les bêtes dans le parc. Le district d'Áš-nun^{ki} est à identifier avec Ešnunna (dans la vallée de la Diyala). Celui d'A-ra-mi^{ki} se trouvait sans doute non loin de là. Il est difficile de ne pas reconnaître dans A-ra-mi le nom même d'Aram; la désinence *-i* se rencontre en d'autres toponymes de la région [3]). Cet Aram pourrait se situer sur le Bas-Tigre.

De ce texte, S. Moscati a proposé tout récemment d'en rapprocher un autre, provenant également de Puzurišdagan, et publié par C. E. Keiser [4]). La tablette sur laquelle il figure est datée du

---

[1]) *Aram und Aramäer in der Ur III-Zeit*, dans *Biblica*, XXX (1949), p. 109-111.

[2]) *Orientalia*, II (1920), p. 62. La tablette appartient à la collection privée Wengler.

[3]) Schneider, *art. cit.*, p. 110. — Le district de Kaš-da-dun^{ki}, note Schneider, ne peut être pour le moment identifié.

[4]) *Cuneiform Bullae of the Third Millenium B.C.* (*Babylonian Records in the Library of J. Pierpont Morgan* edited by A. T. Clay, Part III, New York, 1914), pl. 45, n° 159. Keiser y donne seulement une copie du texte. Schneider, en signalant ce texte (*art. cit.*, p. 111), reste réservé sur la portée exacte du nom propre A-ra-mu, vu le mauvais état du document. Voir l'étude de S. Moscati, *Sulle origini degli Aramei*, dans *Rivista degli Studi Orientali*, XXVI (1951), p. 16-22.

règne de Šu-Sin (environ 1994-1985); elle est donc de quelques années postérieure à la précédente. C'est un document du même ordre, où sont décomptés les animaux offerts et indiqués les noms des offrants. Malgré le mauvais état de la tablette, on comprend que, sur un total de 260 têtes de bétail, 33 brebis ont été prises en charge par un certain A-ra-mu; les mots: A-ra-mu ì-KU „A-ra-mu a pris en charge", se lisent clairement. Moscati propose de traduire ce nom de personne „Araméen"; cette traduction nous semble extrêmement plausible.

Rappelons qu'en 1083, c'est un chef araméen, Adad-apal-iddin, qui s'empare du trône de Babylone, après avoir renversé Marduk-šapik-zer-mati; le nouveau roi est reconnu par le roi d'Assour, Assur-bel-kala, qui épouse même la fille de l'usurpateur. Les tribus araméennes accentuent alors leur pénétration et leur main-mise sur la région du Bas-Tigre [1]). Mais la présence des Araméens en cette région a toute chance d'être plus ancienne: nous voici invités à remonter jusqu'aux environs de 2000 av. J.-C., s'il est vrai qu'un district (ou une ville) y portait dès cette époque le nom d'„Aram" et qu'un certain „Aramu" conduisait de là jusque près de Nippur les troupeaux voués aux sacrifices.

A ces deux textes, si heureusement mis en lumière par SCHNEIDER et MOSCATI, nous croyons pouvoir en ajouter plusieurs autres, qui constituent de précieux jalons pour les débuts de l'histoire araméenne. Les uns proviennent de Mari (tell Hariri), sur le Moyen-Euphrate; les autres, d'Ugarit (Ras Shamra), dans la Syrie du Nord.

A Mari, une liste de rationnaires, sur une tablette de Zimrilim (contemporain de Hammurabi, roi de Babylone), présente le groupe de noms suivants: A-ra-mu, Belí-an-dúl-li, La-ba (?)-an, Ia-at-nu, [d]Šamaš-a-bi, A-bi-E-ra-aḫ, Bur-[d]Ma-ma, Ì-lí-[d]Addu, Sú-mu-ḫu-um, I-din-Ka-ak-ka. Le premier nom est „Aramu", comme sur la tablette de Drehem [2]).

---

[1]) Cf. A. DUPONT-SOMMER, *Les Araméens* (Paris, Adrien-Maisonneuve, 1949), p. 22, 24.

[2]) Le troisième nom: La-ba(?)-an (= Laban), bien que de lecture un peu incertaine, est ici fort suggestif; cf. „Laban l'Araméen" dans Genèse xxxi 20, 24. — Ce texte m'a été signalé et communiqué par Monsieur M. BIROT, qui doit le publier dans un article intitulé *Trois textes économiques de Mari* (à paraître prochainement dans la *Revue d'Assyriologie*). Les trois textes suivants mentionnant „Aḫlamu" m'ont été également communiqués par ce jeune et très distingué savant, que je remercie très vivement; ils prendront place dans un tome prochain des *Archives royales de Mari*.

En outre, à Mari encore, trois tablettes, de la même époque de Zimrilim, livrent le nom d'un personnage nommé „Aḫlamu", qui était un officier de la cour attaché au service de la table royale. Voici le texte de ces trois tablettes, qui sont de simple reçus:

I

11 qa šamnim	11 qa d'huile
^{I}Aḫ-la-mu	(moi) Aḫlamu
am-ḫu-ur	j'ai reçu
a-na NÍG-DU šarrim	pour le repas du roi.
Waraḫ U-ra-ḫi-im	Mois d'Uraḫim,
UD 16 KAM	le 16e jour,
šanat Zi-im-ri-li-im	l'année où Zimrilim
ṣalam ^{d}Ḫa-ta	la statue du dieu Ḫata
ú-še-lu	a élevé.

II

6 qa šamnim	6 qa d'huile
^{I}Aḫ-la-mu	(moi) Aḫlamu
am-ḫu-ur	j'ai reçu
a-na NÍG-DU šarrim	pour le repas du roi.
Waraḫ ^{d}Belet-bi-ri	Mois de Bêlet-biri,
UD 30 KAM	le 30e jour,
šanat Zi-im-ri-li-im	l'année où Zimrilim
ṣalam ^{d}Ḫa-ta	la statue du dieu Ḫata
ú-še-lu	a élevé.

III

40 šamnin	40 (qa d') huile
^{I}Aḫ-la-mu	(moi) Aḫlamu
am-ḫu-ur	j'ai reçu
a-na NÍG-DU šarrim	pour le repas du roi.
Warah ^{d}Belet-bi-ri	Mois de Belet-biri,
UD 20 KAM	le 20e jour,
šanat Zi-im-ri-li-im	l'année où Zimrilim
Dûr-Ia-aḫ-du-li-im	(la ville de) Dûr-Iaḫdulim
i-pu-šu	a construit.

La présence des noms de personne Aramu et Aḫlamu dans ces tablettes de Mari semble bien être l'indice qu'Araméens et Aḫlamu avaient alors réussi à s'infiltrer dans la population de Mari et même à pénétrer jusque dans les services et dans la cour même du roi. Cette infiltration, bien que nous n'en puissions préciser l'importance à l'époque de Zimrilim, invite du moins à penser qu'Araméens et Aḫlamu devaient être alors répandus en assez grand nombre dans la région avoisinante. Ils n'en disparurent point durant les siècles suivants; nous avons rappelé plus haut que Salmanasar I et Tikultininurta I, au XIIIe siècle, eurent affaire aux Aḫlamu dans la région du Ḫabur et celle du Moyen-Euphrate. Quant à Téglatphalasar I, sur la fin du XIIe siècle, nous avons vu qu'il dut traquer les Aḫlamu-Araméens „depuis le pays de Sûḫi jusqu'à la ville de Karkémiš", „depuis la ville de Tadmor ..., depuis la ville de Anat ... et jusqu'à la ville de Rapiqu": de Karkémiš à Rapiqu, sur une longueur d'environ 700 kilomètres, — en amont et en aval de Mari —, tout le Moyen-Euphrate est infesté de ces dangereux Aḫlamu-Araméens. Six siècles déjà avant Téglatphalasar I, à Mari même, il est intéressant de constater la présence d'un nommé „Aramu" et celle d'un nommé „Aḫlamu". [1])

De l'Euphrate, de la Mésopotamie, passons à la côte syrienne. Dans les textes d'Ugarit, au XIVe siècle, figurent également plusieurs attestations qui semblent bien être en rapport avec les Araméens.

Voici d'abord une tablette sur laquelle est inscrit en cunéiforme alphabétique un état des armes (arcs et frondes) existant en diverses villes du royaume. Cet inventaire, établi sans doute pour le cas de

---

[1]) Concernant la présence et la turbulence des tribus araméennes en Haute-Mésopotamie avant Téglatphalasar I, signalons ici un texte d'époque kassite récemment publié par O. R. GURNEY, *Texts from Dur-Kurigalzu*, dans *Iraq*, XI (1949), p. 139-141 (texte n° 10). C'est une lettre adressée au roi kassite par un certain Zikir-ilišu, qui pouvait être, selon GURNEY, l'ambassadeur kassite à la cour assyrienne, apparemment au temps d'Adad-nirari I (environ 1311-1280). Zikir-ilišu y informe son maître que „500 guerriers des Ḫiranu", associés „aux guerriers des Ḫasmu", ont été poursuivis par un certain Ki-pî-Assur, un fonctionnaire assyrien, et aussi que „la bande armée de Ḫirana — [la moitié de] celle-ci est installée dans le pays de Subartu parmi les villes [que le roi d']Assur a prises, [et l'autre moi]tié est installée dans le pays de Suḫi et le pays de Mari (?) ...". Le nom de Ḫiranu, comme le fait observer GURNEY, est connu plus tard comme celui d'une tribu araméenne (cf. *MVAG*, 1906, 3, p. 25); et Ḫasmu est à rapprocher de Ḫasame/u, nom qui désigne une ville ou une région dans le nord de la Mésopotamie (cf. ^{âl}Ḫa-sa-me, dans JOHNS, *Doomsday Book*, n° 1, II, 32; ^{mât}Ḫa-sa-mu, dans l'inscription du Monolithe de Salmanasar III = LUCK., I, § 599, 601, 602.

mobilisation, indique, ville par ville, les noms de ceux qui détiennent des armes, ainsi que la nature et le nombre de celles-ci [1]); les totaux sont inscrits en akkadien. Sur cette tablette (col. III l. 22), on lit ceci: bn . army . ṯt . qštm . wq[lʿ] „Fils-de-Army: deux arcs et une fr[onde]". Le mot *army* est un ethnique; il est tout indiqué de comprendre „Araméen", ainsi que l'a fait THUREAU-DANGIN [2]).

En second lieu, il faut signaler une tablette en cunéiforme akkadien trouvée en 1951 (RS 15, 37) et encore inédite. C'est un contrat privé portant sur l'achat d'une vigne pour le prix de 57 sicles d'argent; l'acheteur est un nommé Bu-lu-zi-nu, le vendeur un nommé Aḫ-li-ia-nu: tous les deux sont vraisemblablement d'origine hourrite. Les quatre témoins se nomment: Te-ša-ma-nu, En-ta-ša-lu, Be-ia-nu(?), Ar-me-ya. Il est assurément fort tentant de reconnaître dans cet Ar-me-ya (l.13), tout comme dans le mot *army* de la tablette précédente, le nom propre „Araméen".

En troisième lieu, voici une autre tablette en cunéiforme akkadien trouvée en 1952 (RS 16, 178) et également encore inédite [3]): c'est un acte de donation royale sur laquelle figure (l. 10) un lieu-dit: eqlêt^{meš} a-ra-mi-ma. Le mot a-ra-mi-ma semble bien être la transcription du pluriel oblique proprement ougaritique de *army* [4]). On

---

1) Voir F. THUREAU-DANGIN, *Une tablette bilingue de Ras Shamra*, dans *Revue d'Assyriologie*, XXXVII (1940-1941), p. 97-118 (= C. H. GORDON, *Ugaritic Handbook*, II, p. 172-174, texte n° 321).

2) *Art. cit.*, p. 115 n. 6. Comme le fait observer THUREAU-DANGIN, le même mot se retrouve dans une inscription phénicienne d'Abydos: *ʿbd'smn bn 'rmy* (*C.I.S.*, I, 109; LIDZBARSKI, *Altsemitische Texte*, n° 41).

3) Les informations relatives aux deux textes RS 15 37 et RS 16, 178 m'ont été communiquées par mon éminent collègue et ami Monsieur J. NOUGAYROL, directeur d'études à l'Ecole des Hautes Etudes, qui doit les publier prochainement dans un ouvrage collectif intitulé *Le Palais d'Ugarit*. Qu'il veuille bien trouver ici mes meilleurs remerciements. C'est à lui, ainsi qu'à Monsieur M. BIROT, que la présente communication doit son originalité. — Monsieur J. NOUGAYROL m'a signalé, en outre, que, sur une autre tablette trouvée en 1952 (RS 16, 257), — c'est une liste de fonctionnaires —, figurent deux personnages nommés "Ar-mu-nu": l'un comme père d'un certain SIG_5-nu (probablement Naʿmânu), l'autre comme père de fonctionnaires nommés Gi-im-ra-nu (?), Ga-mi-ru-su (?) et ^{il}Baʿali^{il}-ya. Ce nom Ar-mu-nu serait-il l'équivalent de *army* „Araméen"? La finale -unu (au lieu de -anu) fait difficulté et nous oblige à rester sur la réserve. — Signalons encore que plusieurs noms de personnes hourrites, dans des textes du XVe siècle environ, présentent un élément aram-: arampate, aramsuni, aramuzni (cf. I. J. GELB, P. M. PURVES et A. A. MACRAE, *Nuzi Personal Names*, p. 203 b). Cet élément aram- est-il un nom divin? Y a-t-il un rapport quelconque avec les Araméens?

4) Sur ce pluriel oblique en -îma, cf. C. H. GORDON, *Ugaritic Handbook*, I, p. 42, § 8, 6.

traduirait alors „Champs-des-Araméens", — toponyme qui rappellerait que le territoire en question avait appartenu jadis à des Araméens ou que des Araméens y avaient campé.

Si ces diverses interprétations sont recevables, on voit que les textes de Ras Shamra, tout comme ceux de Drehem et de tell Hariri, fournissent un précieux apport à la protohistoire araméenne. Cet élargissement de notre documentation concernant les Araméens au second millénaire invite sans doute à examiner à nouveau — ainsi que le fait MOSCATI [1]) — un autre texte, connu depuis une quarantaine d'années, mais demeuré assez énigmatique. Il s'agit d'une inscription du roi Narâm-Sin publiée en 1911 par F. THUREAU-DANGIN [2]). Cette inscription avait été gravée sur une statue du roi dans le temple d'Enlil à Nippur; le texte en est conservé sur une tablette d'argile où il fut anciennement recopié. Voici le début de ce texte: „Narâm-Sin, roi des quatre régions, lorsqu'il combattit Ḫaršamatki, seigneur d'A-ra-am et d'Am: dans Ti-ba-ar, la montagne, lui-même le terrassa."

THUREAU-DANGIN ne proposa aucune explication des noms propres contenus dans ce texte; il nota seulement: „Les informations nous manquent sur Aram et Am. Il est probable que cet Aram n'a rien à voir avec les Araméens. „Telle ne fut point l'opinion de DHORME [3]). L'éminent orientaliste identifie d'abord Ti-ba-ar avec le Tabal des textes cunéiformes ultérieurs (hébreu Tubal), entre la Cilicie et la Mélitène: le mot Tibar, explique-t-il, „pourrait être un des sommets de la chaîne du Taurus qu'atteignait Salmanasar III après avoir reçu le tribut des rois de Tabal." Quant à Aram, ce serait l'Aram des deux fleuves (Aram-Naharaïm), c'est-à-dire la région de Ḫarran. Ḫaršamatki, le roi vaincu, aurait été poursuivi au-delà de l'Euphrate et finalement défait dans le Taurus. Am serait un pays limitrophe de l'Aram des deux fleuves; le nom serait à comparer à Ham mentionné dans Genèse xiv 5 comme habitat des Zouzim.

B. HROZNY [4]) se rallia à l'opinion de DHORME concernant Tibar et Aram. Quant au mot Am, il proposa de l'identifier avec l'égyptien

---

[1]) *Art. cit.*, p. 16-19.

[2]) *Une inscription de Narâm-Sin*, dans *Revue d'Assyriologie*, VIII (1911), p. 199-200.

[3]) *Revue Biblique*, 1928, p. 487-488 (= *Recueil Edouard Dhorme*, p. 219-220).

[4]) *Narâm-Sin et ses ennemis d'après un texte hittite*, dans *Archiv Orientální*, (1929), p. 75-76.

'*Am*, désignant dès les inscriptions de l'Ancien Empire les Sémites asiatiques, les Cananéens, etc. Ce mot Am reste reste mystérieux [1]). Mais l'identification de Aram avec le peuple araméen ou quelque pays araméen, de même que celle de Tibar avec Tabal, nous semblent des plus probables. Hrozny a judicieusement noté: „Il semble étrange de rencontrer ce peuple (araméen) dans notre texte à peu près un millénaire avant l'époque de Tell el-Amarna. Mais aujourd'hui où de même d'autres peuples, qu'on ne connaissait que des temps postérieurs, paraissent déjà dans le troisième millénaire av. J.-C., ... cet argument ne peut pas avoir la même valeur comme auparavant. Il n'est pas impossible d'après mon opinion que les Araméens, un peuple parent avec les Assyro-Babyloniens et les Hébreux, commençaient de pénétrer *sporadiquement* déjà dans le troisième millénaire av. J.-C. en Syrie et en Mésopotamie dans les territoires qu'ils devaient habiter plus tard et où ils rencontraient naturellement une résistance violente de l'empire accadien."

Entre la mention d'Aram dans l'inscription de Narâm-Sin et celle des Araméens dans les textes de Téglatphalasar I, s'intercale désormais une série de témoignages qui jalonnent tout le second millénaire. Le saut à franchir était autrefois de douze siècles; il n'est plus maintenant que de deux ou trois siècles, puisque les plus anciens de ces témoignages, semble-t-il, remontent aux environs de 2000.

Remarquons, pour conclure, que cette protohistoire araméenne, telle qu'elle s'esquisse à présent, n'est pas sans offrir quelque analogie avec notre documentation relative aux Ḫabiru ou Ḫapiru (idéogramme SA-GAZ) [2]). Ceux-ci se trouvent déjà mentionnés dans l'„Epopée de Narâm-Sin", dont la rédaction, toutefois, est postérieure à Narâm-Sin. Un texte, en tout cas, les signale dès le temps de la IIIe Dynastie d'Ur. Au XIXe siècle, on saisit leur trace en Asie Mineure, puis au XVIIIe siècle, en Basse-Mésopotamie. Un peu plus tard, il en est question dans les lettres de l'époque de Hammurabi, et aussi dans les textes de Mari. Au XVe siècle, ils sont mentionnés dans les tablettes de Nuzi. Aux XVe et XIVe siècles, les lettres d'El-Amarna décrivent leurs agissements en Syrie et en

---

[1]) I. J. Gelb, *Inscriptions from Alishar and Vicinity* (*The University of Chicago Oriental Institute Publications*, XXVII, 1935), p. 6, a proposé d'y reconnaître une forme brève archaïque du mot Amânum (les monts Amanus).

[2]) Bon résumé de cette documentation, avec références précises, dans R. de Vaux, *Revue Biblique*, 1948, p. 338 ss.

Palestine. Au XIVe siècle, dans les textes de Ras Shamra, apparaît une ville appelée $^{\hat{a}l}$Ḫal-bi $^{am\hat{e}l\hat{u}ti}$SAG-GAZ dans les listes en écriture akkadienne, *Ḫlb ʿprm* dans les listes en écriture alphabétique: la graphie *ʿprm* (= ʿApirîm) [1]) semble bien nous livrer ici la forme sémitique exacte du mot akkadien Ḫabiru/Ḫapiru. Enfin, aux XIVe et XIIIe siècles, les textes hittites présentent encore plusieurs mentions de ces Ḫapiru [2]). On voit que ces divers témoignages jalonnent tout le second millénaire, tout comme ceux que nous avons relevés concernant Aram et les Araméens: la série araméenne est évidemment beaucoup moins riche; mais, telle quelle, elle éclaire quelque peu une période restée jusqu'ici extrêmement obscure.

Les Hébreux de la Bible (ʿIbrîm) sont-ils à rattacher aux fameux Ḫapiru — ʿApirîm? Nous ne saurions ici aborder ce problème. Ce qui est sûr, c'est que la tradition biblique rapprochait des Araméens les ancêtres d'Israël. Cette tradition s'exprime crûment dans la phrase bien connue (Deut. xxvi 5): „Mon père était un Araméen errant." Elle se reflète aussi en divers passages de la Genèse qui montrent la famille d'Abraham fixée en Paddan-Aram ou dans l'Aram-Naharaïm; Laban, petit-neveu d'Abraham, est appelé „l'Araméen"; et c'est dans ce groupe araméen que les patriarches hébreux vont chercher des épouses: Rébecca, Lia, Rachel. L'historien du peuple hébreu ne peut donc que porter intérêt à toute recherche tendant à éclairer les débuts de l'histoire araméenne; et c'est pourquoi nous nous sommes permis de proposer la présente étude à ce Congrès „of Old Testament Scholars".

---

1) Plus précisément, en ougaritique, ʿApirûma (nom.), ʿApirîma (gén.-acc.)

2) Quant aux ʿApiru qui figurent en divers textes égyptiens allant du XVe au XIIe siècle, sont-ils à identifier avec les Ḫapiru/ʿApirîm, ainsi que l'ont déjà proposé de nombreux auteurs? Une telle identification semble très probable.

THE IMPORTANCE OF THE MOTIVE CLAUSE IN OLD TESTAMENT LAW

BY

B. GEMSER

Pretoria

In the so-called Elohistic or ethical Decalogue the third commandment reads (Ex. xx 7): *lô tissā ʾet-šēm-Jahwè ʾᵉlôhèkâ laššāw, kî lô jᵉnaqqè Jahwè ʾēt ʾᵃšer-jissā ʾet-šᵉmô laššāw*, probably a rhythmic verse of the double-six scheme. The so-called Yahwistic or cultic Decalogue has as the equivalent of the first commandment the four-three-three verse: *lô tištaḥᵃwè lᵉʾēl ʾaḥēr, kî Jahwè qannâ šᵉmô, ʾēl qannâ hû* (Ex. xxxiv 14). In the Book of the Covenant we read the double-four verse: *wᵉgēr lô tônè wᵉlô tilḥaṣènnû, kî gērîm hᵉjîtèm bᵉʾèreṣ miṣrājim* (Ex. xxii 20). "No man shall take a mill or an upper millstone in pledge; for he would be taking a life in pledge"[1]) says Deuteronomy[2]). "You shall not uncover the nakedness of your mother's sister, for she is your mother's near kinswoman", commands the Law of Holiness in one of its oldest constituent parts[3]). And further-on in the same law-corpus is said with as motive clause the well-known refrain of this collection: "You shall have one law for the sojourner and for the native; for I am the Lord your God"[4]).

These six examples of motive clauses, taken from the five most easily discernible law-collections of the Old Testament, make it sufficiently clear what is meant by the designation: motive clauses. They are the grammatically subordinate sentences in which the motivation for the commandment is given. The German designation would be: "Begründungssätze" or "Begründungsklauseln". They are by no means scarce in the Old Testament laws, although their

---

[1]) In the English translation I follow mostly the new American Revised Standard Version of 1952.

[2]) Ch. xxiv 6, in a four-three or double-three verse: *lô-jaḥᵃbōl rēḥàjim wārākeb, kî-nèfeš hû ḥôbēl*; perhaps better: *lô taḥabōl* "You shall not".

[3]) Lev. xviii 13, in Hebrew *ʿerwatʾ ᵃḥôt-ʾimmᵉkā lô tᵉgallē, kî šᵉʾēr ʾimmᵉkā hī*, probably a four-three verse.

[4]) In Hebrew again in rhytmic form: *mišpaṭ ʾeḥād jihjè lākèm, kaggēr kāʾezrāḥ iihjè, kî ʾᵃnî Jahwè ʾᵉlôhēkèm* (Lev. xxiv 22).

frequency differs in the separate collections. In the Exodus-version of the Decalogue there are 3 cases [1]), in the Deuteronomy-version 4 [2]), in the so-called Yahwistic Decalogue again 3 [3]), and in that other Decalogue in which as in a mantle or cloak the Book of the Covenant has been inserted, Ex. xx 23-26 plus xxiii 10-19, there occur 3 or 4 cases [4]). The percentage in these four Decalogues thus appears to be 33 or 25. In the Book of the Covenant as well as in the other two larger collections, it is not so easy to determine the proportion of the clauses with motive sentences over against those without. The difficulty arises out of the question how many verses the separate law paragraph comprises, and whether the subdivisions of a law statement (e.g. in the casuistic laws the subordinate *ʾim-* sentences after the *kî*-clause which opens the case) must be reckoned as a new paragraph. In the Law of Holiness several short commandments often are strung together by the motive refrain *kī ʾanī Jahwè ʾelôhêkèm* and its variant readings. All this taken into consideration, I have counted about 59 paragraphs in the Book of the Covenant together with its "mantle" [5]) of which 9 are provided with a motive clause [6]); this means a percentage of 17 [7]). The Laws of Deuteronomy give the following picture: on about 99 paragraphs (subjects or cases) there are 61 motive clauses which provide the high percentage of 60 [8]). In the Law of Holiness the frequency of the motive clause is even higher. On the 122 subjects or cases stated in this law-collection there is a total of 77 motive clauses (made up of 45 times the well-known motive refrain plus 32 other forms of motivation), providing a percentage as high as 65 [9]).

By taking into account the relative dating of the Old Testament law collections a clear and very considerable increase in the frequency of motive clauses is perceivable from the Book of the Covenant with its 17 per cent until the Laws of Deuteronomy with their 60 and the

---

1) Ex. xx 5, 7, 11.
2) Dt. v 9, 11, 14 sq., 16.
3) Ex. xxxiv 14, 18, 24.
4) Cp. xx 25, 26, xxiii 12, 15.
5) Or 88 the subclauses included.
6) Ex. xx 25, xxi 8, 21, xxii 20, 25 sq., xxiii 7, 8, 9, 15.
7) Or according to the less pertinent reckoning of the subclauses as separate items, a percentage of 8.
8) Or when subcases are included and less certain motivations counted in, a total of 129 cases on which there are 71 motivations, which means 55 percent.
9) By a less probable counting of 136 items and 95 motivations the percentage would be almost 70.

Law of Holiness with its 65 per cent. The four decalogues with their 25 or 33 per cent stand formally in this respect in between the Book of the Covenant and Deuteronomy; in these decalogues the motivations mostly occur in the younger enlargements of the original lapidary conceptions of the commandments. It may be asked however in view of the above-mentioned form of the first commandment in the Yahwistic decalogue and of the rhythmic form of the third commandment, if we do not have to assume the possibility of some kind of motivation already in the earlier versions of the Decalogue. And although the percentage of motive clauses in the Book of the Covenant is considerably lower than in Deuteronomy and in the Law of Holiness, its 17 per cent is remarkable enough and some of these motive clauses belong, as we shall see later on, probably already to the oldest conception of this law book.

The strongest emphasis, however, is laid upon this phenomenon of motivation in law clauses by a comparison of the laws of the Old Testament with the law collections and codices of Israel's "Umwelt", the Ancient Near East. The material for comparison fortunately is already abundant. Eight collections are extant, this means about double the number of those of Israel. Perhaps it would even be better to speak of ten collections, by reckoning the Sumerian Family Laws [1]) as two and also the Hittite Laws as two, by distinguishing their original conception, probably from the times of Hattušiliš I and onwards, from their subsequent reform by the incorporated statute laws of Telipinuš (c. 1500) [2]). For our purpose the exact chronological order of these collections is not so important. They are 1. and 2. The Sumerian Family Laws, 3. The Sumerian Lawcode of Lipit-Ishtar, 4. The Old-Akkadian Lawbook of Bilalama of Eshnunna, 5. The Code of Hammurabi, 6. The Old-Assyrian Laws, 7. The Middle-Assyrian Laws, 8. and 9. The Hittite Lawbook, 10. The New-Babylonian Laws [3]). In absolutely none of these lawbooks or-codes or-collections can one single instance of motive clauses be discovered. The motive clause is clearly and definitely a peculiarity of Israel's or Old Testament law. The famous and

---

[1]) Cp. A. T. Clay, *Miscellaneous Inscriptions in the Yale Babylonian Collection*, New Haven, 1915, Tabl. 28, p. 20 sqq., and H. F. Lutz, *Selected Sumerian and Babylonian Texts UMBS*, I, 2, Philadelphia, 1919, Nr. 100-102.

[2]) Cp. e.g. E. Neufeld, *The Hittite Laws*, London 1951, p. 100-115.

[3]) Cp. F. E. Peiser, *Sitz. Preuss. Akad. d. Wiss.*, 1889, S. 823 ff.

fortunate distinction by A. Alt of casuistic and apodictic laws [1]) does not explain this conspicuous difference between the legal forms of the Ancient Near East and of Israel. Apart from the above-mentioned decalogues with their apodictic form the motive clause occurs in the Book of the Covenant in four casuistic laws [2]) over against five apodictic ones. In Deuteronomy and in the Law of Holiness apodictic laws alternate with casuistic ones, as already a cursory turning of their pages shows, and motive clauses occur in both types indiscriminately.

Formally the motive clauses are not all of one and the same type. The most frequent is the type which commences with the motivating or causal conjunction *kî*; examples have been given in the first paragraph of this article.

Once in the Book of the Covenant the preposition *bᵉ* with the infinitive construct occurs [3]). In a related case in Deuteronomy the double conjunction *taḥat ʾᵃšer* is used [4]). Twice the composite conjunction *ʿal dᵉbar ʾᵃšer* is found [5]). The motive clause can also start with the conjunction *wᵉ* in the sense of a *Wāw explicativum* or *epexegeticum*, as in Ex. xxiii 9 in the double-four rhythmic verse: "You shall not oppress a stranger *wᵉʾattèm jᵉdaʿtèm ʾet nèfeš haggēr kî-gērîm hᵉjîtèm bᵉʾèreṣ miṣrājim* [6]).

---

1) Cp. his *Die Ursprünge des israelitischen Rechts*, Verh. Sächs. Akad. d. Wiss., Phil.-hist. Klasse, 86,1. Leipzig 1934. (Cf. now *Kleine Schriften zur Geschichte des Volkes Israel* I (1953), pp. 278 ff.).

2) Cp. Ex. xx 25, xxi 8, 21, xxii 25 sq.).

3) Where it is said of a Hebrew female slave: "If she does not please her master, who has designated her for himself (or: so that he has not designated her for himself), then he shall let her be redeemed; he shall have no right to sell her to a foreign people *bebigdôbāh*, since he has dealt faithlessly with her" (Ex. xxi 8).

4) Deut. xxi 14 on the treatment of a captive woman who has become the wife of an Israelite: "Then, if you have no delight in her, you shall let her go where she will; but you shall not sell her for money, you shall not trade with her *taḥat ʾᵃšer ʿinnîtāh* since you have humiliated her". For the meaning of *hitʿammēr* see M. David, *V. T.* I, 3, p. 219-221.

5) Deut. xxii 24 when a man lies with a betrothed virgin in a city, both of them shall be stoned to death, the young woman *ʿal dᵉbar ʾᵃšer* because she did not cry for help though she was in the city, and the man *ʿal dᵉbar ʾᵃšer* because he violated his neighbour's wife". The same conjunction is used in Deut. xxiii 3 sq. where the Ammonites and Moabites are prohibited from entering the assembly of the Lord for even *ʿal dᵉbar ʾᵃšer* they did not meet you with bread and with water on the way when you came forth out of Egypt"; the second reason is introduced by *ʾᵃšer* alone: "and because they hired against you Balaam the son of Be'or".

6) The same construction occurs in the Deuteronomic version of the Decalogue in the Sabbath-commandment *wᵉzākartā kî ʿèbed hājîtā bᵉʾèreç miçrajim* etdc. "an so you shall remember that you were a servant in the land of Egypt etc." (Deut. v 15; compare also Deut. xvi 12 and xix 10). In the paragraph on false witness

In the Deuteronomic Sabbath-commandment the motivation is taken up again and strengthened by the composite conjunction *ʿal kēn*: *ʿal-kēn ṣiwwᵉkâ Jahwè ʾᵉlôhèkâ laʿᵃśôt ʾet-jôm haššabbāt* [1]). The motive clause of a dehortative, dissuasive character commences with the conjunction *pen*, e.g. the cities of refuge are instituted *pen jirdōf gôʾēl haddām ʾaḥᵃrê hārôṣēaḥ kî jēḥam lᵉbābô* [2]). Another form of the dissuasive clause is found in Deut. xvi 22 *wᵉlô tāqîm lᵉkâ maṣṣēbâ ʾᵃšer sānē Jahwè ʾᵉlôhèkâ* "which the Lord your God hates" [3]).

The opposite of such dehortative phrases are the clauses beginning with the conjunction *lᵉmaʿan* "in order that", which are of a promissory nature, of which the best known is the fourth commandment in the Deuteronomy version. [4]) In Deut. xxv 15 sq. the promise is connected with and strengthened by the strong *tôʿēbâ*- warning [5]). Double motivations occur often in the Law of Holiness where the motive refrain or sanction clause *kî ʾᵃnî Jahwè ʾᵉlôhèkâ* or one of its variations frequently follow or precede another motivation, especially a reference to Israel's own experience in and deliverance from Egypt, e.g. after the commandment to love the stranger *kî gērîm hᵉjîtèm bᵉʾèreṣ miṣrajim, ʾᵃnî Jahwè ʾᵉlôhēkèm* [6]). But already in the Book of the

---

Deut. xix 15-21 the wâw is more of a final, consecutive kind, when it is said vs. 20: "*wᵉhannišʾārîm jišmᵉʿû wᵉjîreʾû wᵉlôʾ jôsīfû laʿᵃśôth ʿôd kaddābār hārāʿ hazzè bᵉʾqirbèkâ*" so that the rest shall hear and fear and shall never again commit any such evil among you".

[1]) The same construction in other wording shows this commandment in the Exodus-version: *ʿal-kēn bērak Jahwè ʾet-jôm haššabbāt wîqaddᵉšēhû* (Ex. xx 11; cp. also in the paragraph on the cities of refuge Deut. xix 4-10, verse 7).

[2]) Deut. xix 6. Not more than forty stripes may be given *pen-jôsîf lᵉhakkôtô ʿal-ʾēllè makkâ rabbâ wᵉniqlâ ʾāḥîkâ lᵉʿênèkâ* "lest, if one should go on to beat him with more stripes than these, your brother be degraded in in your sight". (Deut. xxv 3). In the human war laws of Deuteronomy xx the four exemptions from military service are three times motivated by a clause with the conjunction *pen* and once with *welô* (vss. 5-9).

[3]) Apparently a very strong disapproval as it occurs in ch. xii 31 and Prov. vi 16 parallel with *tôʿēbâ* "an abomination".

[4]) "Honour your father and your mother as the Lord your God commanded you, *lᵉmaʿan jaʾᵃrîkûn jāmèkâ ûlᵉmaʿan jîṭab lᵉkâ ʿal hāʾadāmā ʾᵃšer Jahwè ʾᵉlôhèkâ nôtēn lāk* (Deut. v 16, which St. Paul calls "the first commandment with a promise", Eph. vi 1-3). Already the preceding verse in the third commandment contains a *lᵉmaʿan*-clause as it reads *lᵉmaʿan jānûaḥ ʿabdᵉkâ waʾᵃmātᵉkâ kāmôkâ* (cp. furthermore Deut. xii 28, xiv 29, xvi 20, xxii 7, xxiii 21, Lev. xxiii 43).

[5]) In the pericope against dishonesty in trade: "A full and just weight and measure you shall have *lᵉmaʿan jaʾᵃrîkû jāmèkâ ʿal hāʾᵃdāmâ ʾᵃšer Jahwè ʾᵉlôhèkâ nôtēn lāk, kî tôʿᵃbat Jahwè ʾᵉlôhèkâ kol-ʿôśé ʾēllè kōl ʿôśē ʿāwel*".

[6]) Lev. xix 33 sq.; and the prohibition of taking interest from the impoverished Israelite is motivated by the clause *ʾᵃnî Jahwè ʾᵉlôhēkèm ʾᵃšer hôṣētî ʾetkem mēʾèreṣ miṣrajim* etc. (Lev. xxv 35-38; cp. similar cases in Lev. xix 35 sq., xxii 32 sq., xxiii 43, xxv 55, xxvi 13, 44 sq.).

covenant we find a two-fold motivation, the one on a rational, human principle, the other on a religious basis, when in the prohibition from keeping the garment as a pledge until after sunset [1]), it is argued: firstly: *kî hî kesûtô lebaddô, hî simlatô le'ôrô, bammè jiškāb*, secondly: *wehājā kî jiṣ'aq 'ēlaj wešāma'tî kî-ḥannûn 'ānî* (Ex. xxii 25 sq.) [2]).

Quite opposite to these double motivations are the cases of asyndetic connection, where the motive clause follows the commandment or prohibition without a conjunction. The motive refrain in the Law of Holiness, which occurs about 45 or 47 times, is mostly added asyndetically [3]). Inside this Law of Holiness there is the small corpus of chastity- and incest-laws, ch. xviii vs. 6 sqq.; the reason why one is prohibited from approaching any one near of kin is given ten times in a sentence which asserts a kind of proprietory right, e.g. "You shall not uncover the nakedness of your father's wife; it is your father's nakedness" (vs. 8). Nine of these ten motive clauses are added asyndetically, only once the conjunction *kî* is being used (vs. 13). Other forms of motivation in these and similar laws (cp. Lev. xx 10-21) are also given without a conjunction, when it is said that something would be a *tô'ēbâ* [4]), or a *tèbel* ("perversion") [5]), or a *zimmâ* ("wickedness, a foul crime") [6]), or a *niddâ* ("an impure act") [7]), or a *ḥèsed* ("a shameful thing") [8]).

While the formal aspects of the motive clauses in their variety are interesting, still more important are their contents. One can discern four or five kinds of motivation: 1) the motive clauses of a simply

---

[1]) The three times occurring stipulation in the Bilalama Code, parg. 3 (A, 4 (A) and 10 (A): "in the evening he shall give it back", cp. Sir John Miles and O. R. Gurney, *The Laws of Eshnunna*, in *Symbolae Hrozny dedicatae*, Archiv Orientalni xviii, Praga 1950, and F. M. Th. de Liagre Böhl, *Het Wetboek van Bilalama*, Jaarbericht No. 11, Ex Oriente Lux, 149-50, p. 95 vv., is not a motive clause.

[2]) Again in the Deuteronomy law against destroying the fruit-trees around a besieged city it is said as a first utilistic ground *kî mimmènnû tōkēl* "for you may eat of them" and as a second reason in the chocmatic form of a question: *kî ha'ādām 'ēṣ haṣṣādè lābô mippānèkâ bammāṣôr.* "Are the trees of the field human beings that they should be besieged by you?" (Deut. xx 19).

[3]) I found only 13 times the conjunction *kî* being used; of course these 13 times are important as giving the right meaning of the added sanction-clause.

[4]) Lev. xviii 22, xx 13; in the *tô'ēbâ*-laws of Deuteronomy the conjunction *kî* is always used.

[5]) Lev. xviii 23, xx 12.

[6]) Lev. xviii 17.

[7]) Lev. xx 21.

[8]) Lev. xx 17.

explanatory character, 2) those of ethical contents, 3) those of a religious kind, cultic as well as theological, and 4) those of religious-historical contents. Of all four or five groups some of the more striking examples will be given.

The explanatory motive clause is represented by the already mentioned stipulations concerning the fruit-trees of a besieged city (Deut. xx 19) and especially in the exemptions from military service (Deut. xx 5-8), where each case is separately motivated with the conjunction *pen*: "lest", e.g.: "lest another man dedicate the new house", "lest another man enjoy the fruit of the new vineyard", "lest another man take the betrothed wife" etc. In the paragraph on the rape of a betrothed virgin in the city we encounter a similar explanatory clause (Deut. xxii 24, 26): "the young woman shall be stoned because she did not cry for help, the man because he violated his neighbour's wife". In the Book of the Covenant the law stipulates that, when a man strikes his slave but the slave survives a day or two, the master is not to be punished *kî kaspô hû* "for the slave is his money" (Ex. xxi 21). In the "mantle" of this lawbook the altar-regulation says: "You shall not go up by steps to my altar, that your nakedness be not exposed on it" (Ex. xx 26). In Deuteronomy is decreed that a man with two wives is not allowed to treat the son of the favourite wife as the first-born in preference to the really first-born son of the disliked; "but he shall acknowledge the first-born, the son of the disliked, by giving him a double portion of all that he has *kî hû rēšît 'ônô, lô mišpaṭ habbekôrâ*" (xxi 17). In the Law of Holiness we read: If a man lies carnally with a woman who is a slave, betrothed to another man and not yet ransomed of given her freedom, an inquiry (*biqqôret*) shall be held. They shall not be put to death *kî lô ḥuppāšâ* "because she was not (yet) free", but he shall bring a guilt offering, etc. (Lev. xix 20 sq.). All ten motivations in the above-mentioned chastity laws Lev. xviii 6 sqq. are of this nature. This kind of motive clauses of which I counted about 20 [1]) are an appeal to the common sense, to the *ratio*, whereby the sense of justice and the moral sense are neither excluded nor explicitly brought to the foreground.

In another group of clauses the ethical contents are more clearly discernible. Mention has been made already of the Deutero-

---

[1]) Or 29 when the chastity-laws are reckoned separately; the other cases are Deut. xii 23, xv 11, xvi 3,6, xix 6 sq., 10, xxiii 8, xxiv 6, xxv 6, Lev. xvii 11, 14, xx 9-16 the clause *dâmâ bô* or *demēhèm bām*, xxiii 28, xxv 8-12 and 16.

nomic version of the Sabbath-commandment (Deut. v 14 sq. "that your manservant and your maidservant may rest as well as you"), the stipulation about the captive woman (Deut. xxi 14), the prohibition from taking the millstone as a pledge (Deut. xxiv 6) and of giving more than forty strikes (Deut. xxv 3). In the law on witnesses the punishment is urged by reference to the principle of *talio*: "Your eye shall not pity; it shall be life for life, eye for eye, tooth for tooth, hand for hand, foot for foot" (Deut. xix 21). The prohibition from reaping to the very boundary of the land or to gather the gleanings is ethically motivated by the clause; "You shall leave them for the poor and the stranger" [1]). An appeal to the sense of national honour and pride resounds in the law against a husband charging his wife with not being a virgin, where the punishment is introduced by the motive clause *kî hôṣî šēm rāʿ ʿal beṭûlat jisrāʾēl* (Deut. xxii 19), and in the same law the punishment of the wife by the sentence: *kî ʿāsetā nebâlâ bejisrāʾēl* (vs. 21). Already in the Book of the Covenant three ethical motivations are found among its nine motive clauses, of which we mentioned above the commandment not to keep the garment of the poor as a pledge during the night (Ex. xxii 25 sq.), and in the *speculum judicis* the commandment not to oppress the stranger for: "You know the heart (*nèfeš*) of the stranger, etc." (Ex. xxiii 9, cp. xxii 20). In this same small collection occurs the very interesting motivation by means of a proverb of classical rhythmic form in the commandment against bribery: *wešōḥad lô tiqqāḥ kî haššōḥad jeʿawwēr piqeḥîm wîsallēf dibrê ṣaddîqîm* [2]). In all there are about 11 or 12 of this kind of motive clauses with their direct appeal to the ethical sentiments or to the conscience. The 3 of them in the Book of the Covenant represent an important percentage.

A third kind of motivation is that on r e l i g i o u s grounds. Under this heading fall the wellknown *tôʿēbâ*-laws from Deuteronomy and some verses from the Law of Holiness. The motive clause can be as short as only the statement *tôʿēbâ hî* (Lev. xviii 22), or more often and more explicit like *kî tôʿabat Jahwè hû* (Deut. xvii 1) and *kî tôʿabat Jahwè ʾelôhèkâ kolʿôsē ʾēllè* (Deut. xxii 5). The subject matter in Deuteronomy is preponderantly idolatry, cult of images, Canaanite

[1]) Lev. xxiii 22, strengthened here by the motive refrain: "I am the Lord your God".

[2]) Ex. xxiii 8. To this connection of law and wisdom, *ḥokmâ* we hope to come back at the end of this essay.

cults and cultic usages (vii 26, xii 31, xiii 15, xvii 4), child-offering, all kinds of divination (xviii 9-12, xx 18), temple-prostitution (xxiii 18 sq.) and wearing of men's clothes by women and vice versa (xxii 5). It is interesting that already in the Dodecalogue of Curses of Deut. xxvii in the first cursing the image-cult is prohibited as *tôʿᵃbat Jahwè* (vs. 15). Under the *tôʿēbôt* fall furthermore the sacrifice with a blemish (xvii 1), the taking back of a divorced, remarried woman (xxiv 4), and even the use of double weights and measures (xxv 13-16). In the Law of Holiness homosexuality (Lev. xviii 22, xx 13) is condemned as an abomination [1]). Here the similarity with the Hittite laws is very remarkable, where in the paragraphs 189, 190, 191 and 195 eight cases of incest or impurity are mentioned in the wellknown casuistic form, and every time they are comdemned as *ḥurkel*, a Hittite word which NEUFELD in his Hebrew translation of these laws rightly expresses with *tôʿēbâ* [2]). In Lev. xx 13 the *tôʿēbâ*-crime is punished with the death penalty, and NEUFELD will be right in assuming that the *ḥurkel*-stipulations in the Hittite laws as well as the *tôʿēbâ*-laws in the Bible imply the death penalty. The difference between the Hittite and Biblical laws is as remarkable as their similarity in so far as in the Old Testament always, with only a single exception (Lev. xviii 22), the name of God is connected with the word *tôʿēbâ*; this means that a religious sanction underlies the commandment, and that the real motive force of the commandment has to be sought not in abhorrence or in fear of the legal penalty, but in the nature and will of God.

The undoubtedly very ancient ban on the eating of flesh with its lifeblood, which has found its most stringent and rhythmic expression in Lev. xvii 14 *dam kol-bāsār lô tôkēlû, kî nèfeš kol-bāsār dāmô hû* [3]) is by its context in Deuteronomy and in the Law of Holiness clearly put under the sanction of the divine right and holiness. God's holy presence in the midst of the camp of his people motivates the order to keep it clean (Deut. xxiii 15), and the archaically-sounding

---

[1]) Other forms of unchastity or incest by synonymous expressions as mentioned above (p. 55).

[2]) E. NEUFELD, *The Hittite Laws translated into English and Hebrew with Commentary*, London, Luzac, 1951, p. 189; cp. also his *Ancient Hebrew Marriage Laws, with special references to General Semitic Laws and Customs*, Longmans, London 1944. p. 197 sqq.

[3]) Or *baddām hû* xvii 11, or *kî haddâm hû hannèfeš* Deut. xii 23; cp. other references Gen. 9 : 4, Deut. xii 16, xv 23 Lev. xvii 11, iii 17, vii 26, xix 26, Ez. xxxiii 25, Acts xv 29.

wording of the motive clause in the commandment not to let remain the executed man all night upon the tree *kî qilᵉlat ʾᵉlôhîm* (not *Jahwè*!) *tālûj* is still strengthened by the more purely Israelitic motivation: "You shall not defile your land which the Lord your God gives you for an inheritance" (Deut. xxi 22 sq.). All the, partly very old, commandments and prohibitions of the Law of Holiness, are separately or in small groups but also in their totality, placed under and sanctioned by the acknowledgement and confession of a holy God who created and who demands a holy people [1]). Already the chapter on clean and unclean animals in Deuteronomy xiv is placed under this sanction of Israel as the *ʿam qādôš* [2]).

The character of Yahwe as a jealous God is, as previously mentioned, the motive basis of the first commandment in the so-called Yahwistic decalogue (Ex. xxxiv 14) and in the enlarged second commandment (perhaps meant as including the first commandment as well) in the Elohistic version. The same motive basis is meant in the third commandment, in the *kî lô jᵉnaqqē* Ex. xx 7. Well-known is the genuinely theological foundation of the *mimèsis theou* in the Elohistic version of the Sabbath-commandment with its reference to the creation (xx 11). God's graciousness serves in the Book of Covenant as the incentive to return the pledged garment to its owner before nightfall (Ex. xxii 26). In the same lawbook the justice of God enjoins not to pervert the justice in law cases: *nāqî wᵉṣaddîq ʾal tahᵃrog kî lô ʾaṣdîq rāšāʿ* [3]). Yahwe's ownership of the land is the sanction which should prohibit the Israelite from selling his portion of the land for always: "The land shall not be sold in perpetuity, for the land is mine; for you are strangers and sojourners with me" (Lev. xxv 17).

The number of motivations of this religious and theological

---

[1]) Cp. Lev. xviii 2, 4, xix 37, xx 7 sq. and the variant readings of the motive refrain *kî qādôš ʾᵃnî Jahwè* (*ʾᵉlôhēkèm*), xix 2, xx 26, and *kî qādôš ʾᵃnî Jahwè mᵉqaddiškèm* xxi 8, or shorter *ʾᵃnî Jahwè mᵉqaddiškèm* xx 8, or *mᵉqaddᵉšām* xx 9, or *kî ʾᵃnî Jahwè mᵉqaddᵉšām* xxi 23, xxii 16, or *mᵉqaddᵉšô* xxi 5. The right meaning of the expression *qaddēš* is indicated by the addition of *hibdîl* in xx 26: *wîhᵉjîtèm lî qᵉdôšîm kî qādôš ʾᵃnî Jahwè wāʾabdîl ʾetkem min-hāʿammîm lihᵉjôt lî.*

[2]) In its second and last verses, while the first verse reads: *bānîm ʾattèm lᵉJahwè ʾᵉlôhekèm, lô titgôdᵉdû wᵉlô tāsîmû qorḥâ bên ʿênêkèm lāmēt.*

[3]) Ex. xxiii 7; this Masoretic reading is supported by the ancient rhythmic "elohistic" formulation of the motive clause in a passage from the first discourse of Moses in Deuteronomy (i 17): *lô-takkîrû phānîm bammišpat, kaqqātôn kaggādôl tišmāʿûn, lô tāgûrû mippᵉnê ʾîš, kî hammišpāt lēlôhîm hû.*

character amounts, inclusively about 12 *tô'ēbâ*-laws, to more or less 25 in Deuteronomy [1]), about 6 in the Book of the Covenant and the Decalogue, whereas the Book of Holiness with its very frequent refrain (about 45 times) and some other forms of religious motivation reaches the high mark of certainly more than 50 cases [2]).

A fourth group of motive clauses can be defined as of h i s t o r i c o-r e l i g i o u s character. They could be called soteriological or rather, in the German expression, "heilsgeschichtlich". They urge the fulfilling of the commandment by reference to and on the ground of "die grossen Heilstaten Jahwes in der Geschichte", especially the deliverance from Egypt and the granting of the land of Canaan as heritage. Classical in form and well-known is the second motivation of the Sabbath-commandment in the Deuteronomic version of the Decalogue: *wezākartā kî 'ebed hājîtâ be'èreṣ miṣràjim wajjôṣî'akâ Jahwè 'elôhèkâ miššām bejad ḥazāqâ ûbizerôa' neṭûjâ; 'al- kēn ṣiwwekâ Jahwè 'elohèkâ la'asôt 'et-jôm haššabbāt* (Deut. v 15); in the next commandment, concerning the honouring of the parents the second "Heilstat" is referred to, namely the giving of the land (vs. 16). In the book of the Covenant the two already mentioned prohibitions from oppressing the stranger (Ex. xxii 20, xxiii 9) are both motivated by the reference to the people's own experience in Egypt, and implicitly to their deliverance from there (cp. xxii 22). The sanction of the commandment to eat only unleavend bread sounds almost identical in the Book of the Covenant and in the Yahvistic decalogue (Ex. xxiii 15, xxxiv 18): *ka'ašer ṣiwwîtîkâ lemô'ēd ḥodeš hā'ābîb kî beḥodeš hā'ābîb* (var. *bô*) *jāṣā'tâ mimmiṣrājim*. The same motivation reads in Deuteronomy in the Pesah-commandment: *kî beḥōdeš hā'ābîb jôṣî'akâ Jahwè 'elôhèkâ mimmiṣràjim lājlâ* (Deut. xvi 1); in the Massôt-paragraph *kî beḥippāzôn jāṣā'tâ mē'èreṣ miṣràjim* (vs. 3); in the specially Deuteronomic stipulation to celebrate the Passover at the central sanctuary the time is fixed as *bā'èreb kebô haššèmeš mô'ēd ṣētekâ mimmiṣrājim* (vs. 6), and in the equally typical Deuteronomic law of the Feast of Weeks the joyful celebration is motivated by the clause *wezākartâ kî 'èbed hājîtâ bemiṣrājim* (vs. 12). This same phrase occurs

1) Cp. except the above-mentioned loci also Deut. xvi 15, 22, xviii 2, xix 14, xx 16-18, xxi 5, xxiii 22, xxiv 13.

2) Cp. especially Lev. xxiv 22, xxv 17, xxvi 1 sq. and the 14 times occurrence of the refrain in ch. xix, and 11 motivations in the chapters xxi and xxii on priests and holy things.

four times in Deuteronomy in several laws protecting the underprivileged. [1])

The motive refrain of the Law of Holiness is four times expanded with a reference to the deliverance out of Egypt (Lev. xix 36, xxv 38, xxvi 13, 14), the first time in so unexpected and unrelated a connection as with the law against false weights and measures. In the law against the oppression of the stranger the motive clause of the Book of the Covenant reappears verbatim (Lev. xix 33 sq.), in those against the keeping of Israelites as slaves for debts and as slaves by strangers again the reference to the deliverance from Egypt is mentioned: *kî ʿabādaj hēm ʾ^{a}šer hôṣētî ʾôtām mēʾèreṣ miṣrājim* (Lev. xxv 42, 55). The closing sentence of this Law of Holiness explicitly refers to this fundamental act of Israel's history (Lev. xxvi 44 sq.).

Other references to the great acts of God in Israel's past occur in the king's law Deut. xvii 16: *w^{e}Jahwè ʾāmar lô tôsîfûn lāšûb baddèrek hazzè ʿôd*, and where Israel is reminded of its election as a people holy to Yahwe, as his sons (Deut. xiv 1 sq., Lev. xx 26); or the reserving of the first fruits for the Levitical priests is motivated by their election to the priesthood (Deut. xviii 4 sq.). Events during the trek in the desert are taken as justifications for the laws against Moabites (Deut. xxiii 4 sq.) and Amalekites (Deut. xxv 17-19); the directions of the Levitical priests about leprosy are to be carefully kept, for: "Remember what the Lord your God did to Mirjam on the way as you came forth out of Egypt" (Deut. xxiv 8 sq.). In the Law of Holiness in the chapter on the great Festivals the dwelling in booths on Sukkoth is decreed *l^{e}maʿan jēd^{e}ʿû dôrôtêkèm kî bassukkôt hôšabtî ʾet b^{e}nê jisrāʾēl b^{e}hôṣîʾî ʾôtām mēʾèreç miṣrājim* (Lev. xxiii 43). And the prohibition of all kinds of cultic and moral customs is sanctioned in Deuteronomy as well as in the Law of Holiness by their stigmatisation as *tôʿebôt* committed by the peoples which Yahwe drove out before Israel (Deut. xviii 9-14, Lev. xviii 24, 27, 29). Of these about 30 cases of historico-religious motivation the greater half is found in Deuteronomy, about 10 in the Law of Holiness, while this kind of motivation is not absent in the older laws, the Book of the Covenant and the Yahwistic decalogue.

---

[1]) Namely in the law of letting free of the Hebrew slave in the seventh year (xv 15; with the addition of *wajjifd^{e}kâ Jahwè ʾ^{e}lôhèkâ*), of not perverting the justice due to the sojourner or to the fatherless nor to take a widow's garment in pledge (xxiv 17 sq.), and of leaving the gleanings to the stranger and the poor (ib. vs. 21 sq.), while in the law of the admitting of Egyptians to the *q^{e}hal Jahwè* (xxiii 8) the motivation of the Book of the Covenant returns: *kî gēr hājîtâ b^{e}ʾarṣô.*

This abundance of motive clauses of various contents and forms so conspicuously contrasting with their total absence in the lawcodes of the Ancient Near East requires explanation. The reason could be sought in a more primitive, less developed technique of lawmaking in Israel. One could compare the Syrian-Roman Laws of the fifth century A.D., in the 127 paragraphs of the Syriac version of which in the London Manuscript I found 19 cases of motive clauses. [1]) The lack of order and the loose, unjuristic wording and reasoning of many of these laws are caused, according to the jurist-editor, by its origin in ecclesiastical circles and its destination for the legal practice of the bishop and for the instruction of the clergy and the people (l.c. p. 330). A similar explanation for the Old Testament laws would overlook the fact that in the younger and more developed laws the frequency of the motive clauses increases enormously.

Rather than in their primitiveness the explanation has to be sought in the nature and character of the Old Testament law-collections. They direct themselves not so much to the official instances, the judges and the jurists, as to the people, collectively and individually. Just as the sacrificial laws in Leviticus, especially the first five chapters and the whole of the Law of Holiness are laws for the laymen and not specifically for the priests, so the great law-collections of the Old Testament are not judges' laws, but people's laws.

The "Sitz im Leben" of these lawcodes probably also has to be taken into consideration here. Their intrinsic connection with the cultic life of the people must be kept in mind. The big gatherings of the people or of the amphictyony of a group of tribes at the sanctuaries undoubtedly were the occasions of their promulgation and of their recitation and reenactment. There is certainly historical truth in the tradition which connects all the principal lawcodes with one or other general assembly of the people at a place of epiphany, revelation or guidance of God [2]).

---

[1]) Cp. K. G. BRUNS u. ED. SACHAU, *Syrisch-römisches Rechtsbuch aus dem fünften Jahrhundert*, Leipzig 1880, parg. 1 (3 times), 9, 41, 44, 46, 53, 64, 75, 84, 86, 89, 94, 98, 99, 102, 108, 112; e.g. parg. 53: "it is permitted for a slave to buy a thing, for what the slave buys, belongs to his master, and what they buy is binding"; parg. 99: when a man gives his slave-girl as a pledge and she begets children, they belong to her master, who has become surety for the money; "for a daughter of man is not like the earth, for God's goodness lets the fruit sprout forth from the earth for man".

[2]) At Mount Horeb, in the desert, at Kadesh, before the entry into the Holy Land in the plains of Mo'ab, and at Sichem.

But above all it is the spirit imbued by the leaders and lawgivers of Israel, ultimately by its divine Leader and Lawgiver, which provides the best explanation for this remarkable phenomenon of motivated law in Israel, and in Israel alone among all the peoples of the Ancient Orient as far as we can see at present. [1])

The motive clauses with their appeal to the common sense and to the conscience of the people disclose the truly democratic character of their laws, just as those of the religious kind testify the deep religious sense and concentrated theological thinking of their formulators. The organic connection of Israel's history and religion finds one of its most striking expressions in the historico-religious motivations of its laws.

A comparison of the law stipulations with and without motive clauses teaches that in the Book of the Covenant those for the protection of the underprivileged, the female slave, the poor, the stranger and for unpartial judgement are sanctioned by motive clauses, and also the one for the celebration of the Massôt-festival. In Deuteronomy the same applies to the laws in favour of the underprivileged and for impartial justice, but the motivation is expanded to several other subjects like the blood-taboo, the exemption from military service, marriage-laws, the purity of the *qᵉhal Jahwè*, and in the *tôʿēbâ*-laws to several cultic, religious and moral prohibitions. The same applies to the Law of Holiness, where moreover all the stipulations are sanctioned by the motive refrain *kî ʾᵃnî Jahwè ʾᵉlôhēkèm* and its variations. This refrain can better be understood as a kind of antiphon to the recital of the laws by the priest at the assembly in the sanctuary or like the response Amen to the *ʾārûr* of the Dodecalogue of Curses (Deut. xxvii), than as an insertion of a scribe and redactor. However this may be, the motive clauses constitute an instructive compendium of the religion, theology, ethics and democratic, humanitarian outlook of the people of Israel as represented in the Old Testament laws.

The antiquity of this tendency of appealing to the moral and religious sense of the people is proved by its occurrence already in the Book of the Covenant, in the so-called Yahwistic Decalogue

---

[1]) The motivations of explanatory and ethical contents in the Hittite Instructions for Temple Officials, cp. E. H. STURTEVANT and G. BECHTEL, *A Hittite Chrestomathy*, Philadelphia, 1935, p. 148-167, and the translation by A. GOETZE in *Ancient Near Eastern Texts relating to the Old Testament*, ed. by JAMES B. PRITCHARD, Princeton, 1950, p. 207 sqq., §§ 2, 3, 4, 7, 8, 9, 10, 13, 14, 16, 18, 19, hardly come in for comparison on account of their very specific destination.

and perhaps already also in the Elohistic Decalogue. The commentaries of the literary-critical school usually refer the motive clauses in the Book of the Covenant in their totality or partially to a later redactor [1]. The rhythmic form of so many of the motive clauses to which we drew attention, rather points to an archaic, traditional element in the formulation of the laws. In this connection I would refer to the well-known phrasing of the blood sanction in Gen. ix: 6 *šôfēk dam hāʾādām, bāʾādām dāmô jiššāfēk, kî beṣèlem ʾelôhîm ʿāsā ʾet-hāʾādām* of which already H. GUNKEL said "Er mag ein alter Rechtsspruch sein" [2]; I do not even see an insurmountable difficulty in assuming that the motive clause here is an integral part of the stipulation.

Most interesting is, in the question of an early date of the motive clause, the occurrence in Ex. xxiii 8 of the proverb (*kî*) *haššōḥad jeʿawwēr piqeḥîm wîsallēf dibrê ṣaddîqîm*, with only little and apparently younger, less rhythmic variation reoccuring in Deuteronomy xvi 19 (*kî*) *haššōḥad jeʿawwēr ʿênê ḥakāmîm wîsallēf dibrê ṣaddîqîm*. Here we find a striking example of the intrinsic coherence of legal practice and wisdom or proverbs, so characteristic for a certain stage of development in the administration of justice and so well-known among the native peoples of e.g. East, Southern and West Africa. "Many an angry dispute has been silenced, many an inhospitable chief has been rebuked into generosity, many a forward beggar has been reduced to shame, and many a long diffuse argument has been clinched by the apt quotation of one of these proverbs", write the Rev. EDWIN W. SMITH and Captain ANDREW MURRAY DALE in the chapter on Proverbs, Riddles and Conundrums of their famous two volumes study on *The Ila-speaking Peoples of Northern Rhodesia.* [3]) Experts on Bantuology and African folklore have assured me that in most legal cases administered along the old traditional lines, the plaintiff as well as the accused, the judges as well as the witnesses

[1]) E.g. H. HOLZINGER in E. KAUTZSCH-A. BERTHOLET, *Die Heilige Schrift des Alten Testaments*, Tübingen, 1922, 4te Aufl. and BRUNO BAENTSCH in *Handkommentar zum Alten Testament her.* v. W. NOWACK, Göttingen, 1903. The transition from the singular to the plural in the prohibitions to oppress the stranger (E. xxii 20, xxiii 9) can hardly serve as an argument, where in the same law in Lev. xix 33 sq, this alternation occurs two times.

[2]) H. GUNKEL, *Genesis, Göttinger Handkommentar z.A.T., her. v.* W. NOWACK, 1917, 4te Aufl., S. 149 and *Die Schriften d. A. T. f. d. Gegenwart erklärt*, Göttingen, 1921, 2te Aufl., S. 129; also J. SKINNER, *Genesis, I. C. C.*, Edinburgh, 1930, 2nd ed., p. 171.

[3]) London 1920, Vol. 11, p. 311.

conclude their addresses with the quotation of a proverb; proverbs have the force of legal maxims [1]). Therefore such studies could have been written as "*Das Leben der Schambala beleuchtet durch ihre Sprichwörter*" [2]) in which a chapter on "Der Schambala und seine Prozesse" occurs, and even a study as by BRUNO GUTMANN, *Das Rechtsleben der Wadschagga im Spiegel ihrer Sprichwörter* [3]). JOHANSSEN and DÖRING rightly stress the significance of proverbs for our knowledge of peoples in the preliterary stage (l.c., p. 137). SMITH and DALE state that the so-called prophets or inspired men of the Ba-ila are actually the law-givers of the community, and that proverbs are taken largely as a rule of life (l.c., I, p. 345, II, p. 141, 311), and HENRI A. JUNOD in what generally is considered as one of if not the best of monographs on African tribal life declares: "We might also consider as proverbs, and include under this heading, the figurative terminology used to express the principles of right and justice, which are, as it were, a first codification of the common law". [4])

This connection of legal practice and wisdom deserves a specific and more extensive research also on the field of Old Testament studies. Here I only refer to the occurrence of the *tôʿēbâ*-sanction against the use of double weights and measures in the Law of holiness (Lev. xix 35 sq.) and similarly in the Book of Proverbs—here even three times (Prov. xi 1, xx 10, 23)—and to the resemblance of the stipulation in the Book of the Covenant *nāqî wᵉṣaddîq ʾal tahᵃrōg kî lô ʾaṣdîq rāšā* (Ex. xxiii 7) with the verse in Proverbs (xvii 15): *maṣdîq rāšāʿ ûmaršîaʿ ṣaddîq tôʿabat Jahwè gam-šᵉnêhèm.* [5])

---

[1]) Striking examples are quoted by Dr. N. J. VAN WARMELO, Government Ethnologist of the Union of South Africa, in his collections *Venda Law*, Part 3 (Divorce), paragr. 1056 and note, 1144, 1151, 1186, 1174, 1188, 1404, 1503, 1574, 1600, 1601, and Part 4 (Inheritance), paragr. 1999 & 2113, 1920, 2178, 2224, 2370, 2400, 2401, 2402, 2409 and 2565 in the Series: Ethnological Publications of the Department of Native Affairs of the Union of South Africa, No. 23, Pretoria 1948, 1949.

[2]) Von den Missionaren ERNST JOHANSSEN & PAUL DÖRING, *Zeitschrift für Kolonialsprachen*, her. v. CARL MEINHOF, Band V, Heft 2 u. 3, Berlin 1914.

[3]) *Zeitschrift für Eingeborenensprachen*, her. v. CARL MEINHOF, Band XIV, Heft 1, Berlin 1924. S. 44 ff.

[4]) HENRI A. JUNOD, *The Life of a South African Tribe*, Neuchatel 1913, Vol. II, p. 159, n. 1, where the author gives as in Vol. I, p. 215 a striking example of the use of the proverbial saying: "A cow which has calved is not used to pay a debt" as the formula by which the family of a deceased wife remembers the husband who in the mean time has received another wife from this family, after she has given birth to a child, of his duty to pay the full *lobola* or brides-price for her.

[5]) Other *tôʿēbâ*-proverbs Prov. vi 16-19, xv 8, xxi 27, xxviii 9.

Thus the occurrence in the Book of the Covenant of a proverb could be considered not as a late gloss but rather as a survival of ancient legal procedure [1]).

I am well aware of not having exhausted the subject of motivating sentences in Israel's legal collections, and certainly of not having exhausted that of the connection of wisdom and legal practice. I may, however, have thrown some fresh light upon the relevant problems and in a way have succeeded in proving the importance of the remarkable phenomenon of the motive clause in the laws of the Old Testament.

---

[1]) Geo Widengren, *Literary and Psychological Aspects of the Hebrew Prophets*, Uppsala 1948, p. 21 quotes five instances from pre-Islamic and early Islamic times which prove that proverbs are among the first forms of literature which have been transmitted in writing in the Arab world.

THE PRIMARY MEANING OF √גאל [1]

BY

A. R. JOHNSON
Cardiff

I

While the nucleus of the social unit in ancient Israel was the household, which in itself was regarded as a psychical whole representing the extended personality of the man at its head [2]), kinship was, of course, found to reach far beyond its borders; and wherever such kinship was recognized there was the further recognition of a psychical whole [3]) or what has been described as a corporate personality [4]). Accordingly kinship, however widely conceived, was idiomatically expressed as a totality of "bone and flesh". Abimelech, for example, concludes his appeal, addressed not simply to his mother's brothers but to the whole circle of kinsfolk on his mother's side, by saying, "Remember, too, that I am your bone and your flesh." [5]) Similarly, after Absalom's abortive rebellion, David can appeal both for loyalty on the part of the people of Judah and for mutual confidence between his near relative Amasa (the leader of Absalom's forces) and himself on the ground that they are one and all of the same "bone and flesh." [6]) Indeed in the story of David's election to the kingship of Israel at Hebron all the tribes are represented as stressing their kinship with

---

[1]) The greater part of the following paper has been taken from the author's promised sequel to *The Vitality of the Individual in the Thought of Ancient Israel* (1949), as referred to, *op. cit.*, p. 84, n. 1. Accordingly the annotation is here reduced to a minimum; and the reader must be referred to the larger work for fuller notice of the relevant literature on the subject.

[2]) Cf. the writer's monograph, *The One and the Many in the Israelite Conception of God* (1942), pp. 5 ff.

[3]) Cf. J. PEDERSEN, *Israel: its Life and Culture I-II* (1926), pp. 263 ff.

[4]) i.e. by H. W. ROBINSON, e.g. "The Hebrew Conception of Corporate Personality", in *Werden und Wesen des Alten Testaments*, ed. J. HEMPEL, *Beihefte zur Zeitschrift für die alttestamentliche Wissenschaft* 66 (1936), pp. 49-62.

[5]) Judges ix 1 f.

[6]) 2 Sam. xix 11 ff.: see also 2 Sam. xvii 25 and 1 Chron. ii 15 f.

him by saying, "We are thy bone and thy flesh". [1]) Moreover, in the legal codes kinship is similarly expressed as a community of flesh, the term used being שְׁאֵר [2]), either separately or in combination with בָּשָׂר [3]). Accordingly "the near (*or* next) of kin" is expressed by saying "the near (*or* next) of flesh" [4]).

The use of the term שְׁאֵר in this connexion, however, is doubly interesting in that, as distinct from the term בָּשָׂר, it as much suggests totality of blood as totality of flesh; for comparison with the Arabic ثَأْر as denoting "blood-revenge" suggests that it denotes flesh as the seat of blood. In so far as this is the case the term שְׁאֵר serves to show that the Israelite denomination of kinship conforms to that current amongst the Arabs; for in the latter case the emphasis falls consistently upon community of blood [5]). Amongst the Israelites as amongst the Arabs [6]), however, this emphasis upon community or totality of blood finds most vivid expression in the fore-mentioned practice of blood-revenge. When a man's life has been taken, it is the blood of the kin-group, even more than its bone and flesh, which has been made to suffer, for the blood is the real bearer of its common life; indeed its blood *is* its life [7]). Accordingly the restoration of order is a matter for the kin-group. There is a collective responsibility; and, originally at least, this applies equally to the kin-group of the slayer and that of the slain. Thus the Gibeonites can claim and can secure the execution of seven of Saul's descendants as compensation for the blood which he shed in an effort to exterminate them [8]). With the death of these his kinsmen the breach is healed, and

---

[1]) 2 Sam. v 1: cf. 1 Chron. xi 1. See further Gen. xxix 14 (J); also Gen. xxxvii 27 (J); Neh. v 5; Isa. lviii 7.

[2]) e.g. Lev. xviii 12 (H).

[3]) e.g. Lev. xxv 49 (H).

[4]) e.g. Lev. xxi 2 (H).

[5]) Cf. W. R. Smith, *Kinship and Marriage in Early Arabia*, 2nd edit. by S. A. Cook (1903), and *The Religion of the Semites*, 3rd edit. with notes by S. A. Cook (1927), *passim*.

[6]) Cf. W. R. Smith, *Kinship and Marriage in Early Arabia*, pp. 25 ff., 55 ff., 66 ff.; J. A. Jaussen, *Coutumes des Arabes au pays de Moab* (1908), pp. 144 f., 158 ff., 185 ff., 211 ff. and esp. 220 ff.

[7]) Cf. Gen. ix 4 (P); Lev. xvii 11, 14 (H); Deut. xii 23: and see further *The Vitality of the Individual in the Thought of Ancient Israel*, pp. 71 ff.

[8]) 2 Sam. xxi 1-14: cf. Gen. iv 14 f., 23 f. (J).

balance is restored. In the historical period, however, such collective responsibility on the part of the aggressor's kin-group is perhaps to be regarded as somewhat abnormal; the exceptional state of famine at the time of the fore-mentioned incident may have demanded an exceptional explanation and equally exceptional measures for relief. In any case the legal codes, as represented by that of the Book of the Covenant as well as those of D and P, draw a distinction between manslaughter and murder; and even so it is only the murderer and not just any one of his kinsmen, apparently, whose blood may be shed in return [1]. Nevertheless something of the collective responsibility on the part of the victim's kin-group is still to be seen in the fact that, as in the case of the Gibeonites, the actual execution remains the obligation of his kinsmen. It forms but one aspect of that collective responsibility on the part of the kin-group which is covered by the term גְּאֻלָּה, which is commonly rendered, inasmuch as it involves, "redemption" [2]. That is to say, the kinsman in question acts as a גֹּאֵל, traditionally rendered for the most part by "redeemer"; and in this particular instance he is further defined as the גֹּאֵל of blood or, as this expression is rendered in the standard English versions, "the avenger (*or* revenger) of blood" [3].

A closely analogous situation is that created by any form of premature death which involves a man's dying and leaving behind no male descendant to carry on his name, for this involves a break in the genealogical line represented by the "fathers' house" [4]; and in such a case the need of male offspring to preserve the father's name and safeguard the continuity of the line of descent is met by the provision which is made for a levirate marriage as preserved, for example, by the D code, which lays down that, if a man should die childless, his wife [5] "shall not marry without unto a stranger: her husband's brother shall go in unto her and take her to him for a wife and enter into a levirate marriage with her; and the first male child she beareth

---

[1]) Exod. xxi 12-14 (E); Deut. xix 1-13 (cf. iv 41-3); Num. xxxv 9-29 (P) (cf. Joshua xx (P)).

[2]) Cf. Lev. xxv 26, 29, 31, 32, 48, 51, 52 (H); Ruth iv 6; Jer. xxxii 7, 8; Ezek. xi 15.

[3]) Cf. Deut. xix 6, 12; Num. xxxv 19 ff. (P); Joshua xx 3 ff. (P). See also Num. v 8 (P); 2 Sam. xiv 7, 11; 1 Kings xvi 11.

[4]) Cf., for example, Num. i 2 ff. (P); 1 Chron. v 13 ff.

[5]) Deut. xxv 5 f.

shall maintain the name of his dead brother, so that his name may not be wiped out of Israel." What is more, the brother of the deceased, in filling this role, is evidently regarded as performing the function of a גֹּאֵל, as we may infer from the Book of Ruth, which reveals an added awareness that the responsibility in such a case was felt to extend beyond the close ties of immediate brotherhood [1]). Once again there is a collective responsibility to see that the breach in the life of the kin-group is healed and its balance restored.

Further this common responsibility of the kin-group reappears in the fact that under the idealistic provisions of the law of Jubilee, when a man's circumstances have become so reduced that he has had to sell himself into servitude, he may claim the right to another form of גְּאֻלָּה, in this case involving a literal "redemption", on the part of his kinsmen [2]). Moreover, in keeping with the normal conception of the individual, whose personality is thought to reach far beyond the mere contour of the body [3]), the responsibility of the גֹּאֵל extends not merely to a kinsman's person but also to his possessions. Accordingly a man who through straitened circumstances finds himself compelled to sell any of his property is again in a position to claim the right of גְּאֻלָּה; and indeed Jeremiah happily supplies an illustration of this particular form of "redemption", for upon one occasion he was called upon to fill the role of a גֹּאֵל in connexion with land belonging to a kinsman [4]). This procedure, however, implies something more than an interest in the household of a kinsman conceived as his extended personality. As in the case of the levirate marriage, it reflects an interest in the "fathers' house" or ancestral line of kinsmen who are the predecessors of the גֹּאֵל within the wider sphere of the kin-group. The soil, quite as much as the bones, flesh and blood belonging to a man, forms a vital link with both his ancestors and his descendants; so that this form of גְּאֻלָּה merely emphasizes

---

[1]) Cf. Gen. xxxviii (J); and see further H. H. Rowley, "The Marriage of Ruth", in *The Servant of the Lord and Other Essays on the Old Testament* (1952), pp. 161-86.

[2]) Lev. xxv 47 ff. (H).

[3]) Cf. p. 67, n. 2.

[4]) Lev. xxv 25 ff. (H); Jer. xxxii 6-11. Cf. Lev. xxvii 1-34 (P); and esp. Ruth iv 3 ff., as discussed by Rowley, *op. cit.*, pp. 172 ff.

what is implicit throughout, i.e. the fact that the responsibility of the גֹּאֵל is primarily a responsibility towards the kin-group as an extension in time as well as space. The soil, like the man himself, is to be kept within the kin-group and is not to be sold unreservedly to an outsider. It is this thought, apparently, which lies behind Naboth's refusal to sell his vineyard to Ahab despite the latter's seemingly generous offer. His reply is prompt and emphatic, "Yahweh forbid that I should let thee have the inheritance of my fathers!" [1]) A certain continuity of interest is obviously recognized, and, as already observed, this particular form of גְּאֻלָּה closely corresponds to the further role of the גֹּאֵל in carrying out a levirate marriage and thus preserving the name of his kinsman. In each case the גֹּאֵל is helping to ensure the temporal extension of the "fathers' house"; and this in turn contributes to the temporal extension of that wider sphere of the kin-group, conceived as an extension in both time and space, of which a "fathers' house", as representing but one line of descent, is but a single factor.

Now, to sum up, when in the language of the standard English versions a man acts as an "avenger of blood" in a case of murder, or plays "the kinsman's part" in what approximates to a levirate marriage, or "redeems" the person or property of someone, even if it be only himself [2]), who has been in straitened circumstances, he is doing something which, even though the varying activities may require different renderings, must stem from one common underlying principle; and the basic idea in question seems to be that of "protection". When a kinsman is slain or dies childless, or when he is forced to sell himself into servitude or to part with his property, there is a breach of continuity, and the normal life of both individual and society is upset. Disorder has been introduced into the life of each, and in the case of the corporate unit as in that of the ordinary individual, any weakness or disorder, whether brought about by actual physical death or not, involves a certain loss of vitality [3]); and it is the function of the גֹּאֵל to "protect" the life or vitality of both the individual and the kin-group and thus preserve their standing

[1]) 1 Kings xxi 3.

[2]) Cf. Lev. xxv 26 f., 49 (H); also the extension of this principle in Lev. xxvii 13, 15, 19 f., 31 (P).

[3]) See *The Vitality of the Individual in the Thought of Ancient Israel*, pp. 94 ff.

in society by keeping intact their essential unity or integrity. At one extreme, as when the ordinary individual "redeems" his own person or property, he may be doing little more than "protecting" himself and his own immediate interests. On the other hand, however, this principle is so far-reaching that, at the other extreme, the responsibility of the reigning house towards the nation as a whole may be summed up in the same terms, as when it is said of the ideal king [1]):

He will have pity upon the weak and needy;
Yea, the lives of the needy will he save.
He will *protect* their life from oppression and violence,
And their blood will be precious in his eyes.

II

As a result of the foregoing discussion two points emerge which may be of importance for our understanding of √ גאל (a) on the philological side, and (b) from the theological standpoint. In the first place, the evidence afforded by the use of √ גאל with its peculiarly social implication appears to substantiate the view that this root may not be divorced, as is commonly [2]) done, from √ גאל, which is found in various forms with the implication of "defilement" and is usually regarded as etymologically akin to גָּעַל, "to abhor"; for it seems likely that in both cases the basic idea is one of "covering (up)" an object [3]). So far as the use of this root in a protective sense is concerned, it is possible that we ought not to put too narrow a construction upon the fact that, as is clear from the account of Ruth's nocturnal visit to Boaz [4]), the promise of a גֹּאֵל to exercise his right or responsibility towards the widow of a kinsman was expressed in ancient Israel, as amongst the Arabs [5]), by covering her symbolically with his mantle and thus, in a very real sense, taking her under his "wing" (כָּנָף). What is more, it seems likely that the original force of this root is preserved in the vivid metaphor employed

[1]) Ps. lxxii 13 f.

[2]) E.g., most recently, in L. Koehler and W. Baumgartner, *Lexicon in Veteris Testamenti Libros*, Lieferung III (1949), s.v.

[3]) Cf. M. Jastrow, *A Dictionary of the Targumim, the Talmud Babli and Yerushalmi, and the Midrashic Literature* (1903), s.v.

[4]) Ruth iii 9: cf. Ezek. xvi 8.

[5]) Cf., for example, G. A. Cooke, *The Book of Ruth, Cambridge Bible for Schools and Colleges* (1918), in loc.

by Job when, thinking back to the day of his birth and its issue in his current misery, he is represented as saying, in the language of the English Revised Version following the Septuagint, Theodotion and Symmachus [1]),

> Let darkness and the shadow of death *claim it for their own*;
> Let a cloud dwell upon it;
> Let all that maketh black the day terrify it.

While at first sight, as this rendering suggests, the Hebrew may seem to imply the thought that what has proved a dark day for Job is to be given its rightful place along with that to which it is akin, this interpretation is belied by the last stichos; for the action of a גֹּאֵל in restoring one to where one belongs is the rendering of a service and should bring pleasure rather than terror. Nor is the situation eased by following the lead of Aquila and the Targum and vocalizing the form under discussion as the verb *Piʿēl* from √ גאל with its notion of "defilement", i.e., in the language of the English Authorized Version,

> Let darkness and the shadow of death *stain it*;
> let a cloud dwell upon it; let the blackness of
> day terrify it.

Such a rendering is equally unjustifiable; for it, too, introduces an idea which fails to do justice to the context, dominated as this is by the thought that the day in question should be completely blotted out of existence. In fact, as may be seen in the translations offered by the Peshiṭta Syriac [2]) and Latin Vulgate [3]), even though they look very much like consciously free renderings so far as the translators themselves were concerned [4]), the meaning required by the context is simply that of "covering", i.e.

> Let darkness, let utter blackness *cover it*;
> Let a cloud settle upon it;
> Let the o'er-shadowings of day bring terror to it.

All in all, therefore, there is good reason to believe that the idea of offering or obtaining "cover" is the one which is original to

---

[1]) iii 5.

[2]) ܢܟܣܘܗܝ.

[3]) *obscurent eum.*

[4]) In the case of the Peshiṭta, for example, the same form is used again in the following verse to render the verb לָקַח.

√ גאל in so far as it was used with the special connotation and in the restricted sense which we have had under discussion; for this obviously carries with it the notion of "protection", the verb *Qal* yielding the meaning "to protect", the verb *Niph'al* meaning "to be protected", and the noun גְּאֻלָּה denoting "protection". What is more, if we seek a modern parallel, we have what appears to be a perfect analogy close at hand, if we think of the way in which, in the case of, say, accident, fire or theft, we lose no time in finding out if we have the proper "cover" (or are duly "covered") so far as the appropriate insurance policy is concerned!

Such being the case, it seems reasonable to take the further step of considering the possibility that the somewhat late use of √ גאל to denote "defilement" should also be traced back to this use of √ גאל in its primary sense of "covering". In other words, it may well be that the verb *Niph'al* came to be used, not merely of being "covered" in the sense of being "protected", but also with the force of being, as we say in English, "coated over" and so, in certain circumstances as when we speak of an object as being "covered with dirt" or "coated with rust", of being "stained" or "defiled" and thus, in the light of the actual use of this supposedly independent root, of being "degraded." [1]) Indeed the analogy may be reinforced by noting that the English expression need not be defined in every instance by referring to the particular form of defilement under consideration. For example, some of my English colleagues, if they know anything of the responsibilities of parenthood, have probably had occasion to exclaim at some time or another, "Look at that child! Where has she been? She's *covered* from head to foot!"! If the verb *Niph'al* came to be used in such a way, the use of the *Pi'ēl* [2]) and its associated forms in the *Pu'al* [3]) and *Hithpa'ēl* [4]) to express the thought of "defilement" or "degradation" would follow naturally from this; and the likelihood that we have here the actual line of development is heightened by the fact that √ גאל is not found in the verb *Qal* in

---

[1]) Isa. lix 3; Lam. iv 14; Zeph. iii 1. For the vocalization of the consonantal text in the first two instances, see GESENIUS-KAUTZSCH, *Hebrew Grammar*, 2nd English edition, revised by A. E. COWLEY (1910), § 51h.

[2]) Mal. i 7; Isa. lxiii 3. For what was probably the original reading in the latter case, see, for example, GESENIUS-KAUTZSCH, *op. cit.*, § 53p, N. 1, and A. B. EHRLICH, *Randglossen zur hebräischen Bibel*, iv (1922), p. 222.

[3]) Ezra ii 62; Neh. vii 64; Mal. i 7, 12.

[4]) Dan. i 8.

this sense. In the same way a nominal form such as גֹּאֶל would denote "defilement" or "degradation" by being connected with the thought of what was originally an offensive "covering" or "coating" of some kind [1]). Here, then, we may indeed have the explanation of the fact that this root, which appears to have no exact parallel in the cognate languages, could be employed in order (a) to describe the "degradation" of the holy city and its inhabitants, including even their religious leaders, who by their repeated acts of injustice had become "stained" (i.e., originally, as being "covered") with blood [2]); (b) to condemn the Jews of the post-exilic period for the poor quality of their offerings and the resultant "degrading" treatment of Yahweh and His altar [3]); (c) to tell how a priest, whose genealogy was uncertain, came to be "degraded" from office [4]); and (d) to describe how Daniel avoided the risk of "degradation" which might have been involved in his accepting food from Nebuchadrezzar's table. [5]) Moreover, if this be so, we seem to have here what may be described as a form of semantic polarization, whereby √גאל, as originally conveying the thought of "covering", came to be used (a) of protecting from harm or degradation, and (b) of suffering or causing degradation [6]).

Finally, from the theological standpoint, this basic idea of "protection" should be borne in mind when, as commonly happens, this root is used in its wider application to the corporate unit in order to describe the way in which, at the two critical periods in Israel's history marked by the Exodus and the Return, Yahweh came to the rescue of His chosen people. The deliverance from Egypt was one of the great lessons of their history which successive generations of Israelites had to learn, and we need not doubt that it was found proper from time to time that they should praise Yahweh and pay tribute to Him as their Guardian and Guide in the words of the so-called "Song of Moses" [7]),

In Thy devotion Thou hast led the people whom Thou didst *protect*;
Thou hast guided them by Thy strength to Thine own sacred domain.

---

[1]) Cf. Neh. xiii 29.
[2]) Isa. lix 3; Lam. iv 14; Zeph. iii 1: as above, p. 74, n. 1.
[3]) Mal. i 7, 12: cf. Neh. xiii 29.
[4]) Ezra ii 62; Neh. vii 64.
[5]) Dan. i 8.
[6]) Cf. *The Vitality of the Individual in the Thought of Ancient Israel*, p. 73, n. 4.
[7]) Exod. xv 13. Cf. Exod. vi 6 (P); Pss. lxxiv 2, lxxvii 16 (EVV. 15), cvi 10.

In this way, like their forefathers under the discipline of the Wandering [1]),

They remembered that God was their Rock,
That God Most High was their *Protector*.

Moreover, as the great prophet of the Exile so triumphantly proclaimed, with the new "Exodus" which was marked by the deliverance from Babylon the God of Israel actually proved Himself to be not only the one true God but also the true guardian King of this privileged people [2]).

Now thus saith Yahweh,
Who created thee, O Jacob, and formed thee, O Israel.
Fear not, for I am thy *Protector*.
I gave thee thy name; thou art Mine.

Thus saith Yahweh, Israel's King.
His *Protector*, Yahweh of Hosts.
I am both first and last;
There is no god apart from Me.

This, in turn, corresponds to the way in which the individual Israelite may be found pleading with Yahweh for support and praying that he may be protected from the destructive forces of the Underworld which have been brought near by the relentless animosity of his enemies [3]).

Draw near to me, *protect* me;
In reply to mine enemies, ransom me!

Conduct my case and *protect* me;
In accordance with Thy promise, extend my life (חַיֵּנִי).

Bearing in mind, then, that this particular connotation of √ גאל is normally used of the ties of kinship, we may say that the underlying thought throughout is (a) that, ideally at least, Yahweh and His covenant people are one, and, this being the case, He is their proper Protector and they are properly His *protégés*; and (b), as the correlative to this, that it is He who has the power to safeguard the integrity of the individual and that of society in however material a way

[1]) Ps. lxxviii 35.

[2]) (a) Isa. xliii 1; (b) Isa. xliv 6. Cf., in general, Isa. xxxv 9, xli 14, xliii 14, xliv 22 ff., xlvii 4, xlviii 17, 20, xlix 7, 26, li 10, lii 9, liv 5, 8, lix 20, lx1 6, lxii 12, lxiii 4 (?), 9, 16: also Ps. cvii 2; Jer. xxxi 11, l 34; Mic. iv 10.

[3]) (a) Ps. lxix 19 (EVV. 18); cf. Hos. xiii 14: (b) Ps. cxix 154; cf. Prov. xxiii 11; Lam. iii 58.

this may be contemplated or however spiritually it may be viewed. That is to say, if we may end on this deeper note, it is Yahweh, as one psalmist reminds himself with such evident feeling [1]),

> Who forgiveth thine iniquity,
> Who healeth all thy diseases,
> Who *protecteth* thy life (חַיִּים) from the Pit, [2]),
>
> Who surroundeth thee with yearning devotion.

Accordingly it may not be altogether inappropriate to bring this paper to a close by recalling the words of yet another psalmist who, like his forefathers in the wilderness, turns to Yahweh as to some great guardian Rock which offers shelter from all the storm and stress of life, and thus ends his plea for deliverance from all errant thoughts arising from the perils of self-conceit [3]):

> Prevent Thy servant from joining the arrogant;
> Let me not be governed by them.
> Then I shall be free from fault, and guiltless
> Of a widespread apostasy.
> May the words of my mouth be pleasing,
> And the thoughts of my heart be acceptable to Thee [4]),
> O Yahweh, my guardian Rock
> (O Yahweh, my Rock and my *Protector*)!

---

[1]) Ps. ciii 3 f. Cf. Gen. xlviii 16 (E); Job xix 25.

[2]) Cf., *The Vitality of the Individual in the Thought of Ancient Israel*, p. 91, where the context makes it clear that the alternative rendering, "destruction", is at least perfectly apposite.

[3]) Ps. xix 14 f. (EVV. 13 f.).

[4]) I.e. "in accordance with Thy will". Cf., *The Vitality of the Individual in the Thought of Ancient Israel*, p. 45, n. 3.

THE POLITICAL BACKGROUND OF THE SHILOH ORACLE

BY

JOH. LINDBLOM

Lund

The famous passage in "the Blessing of Jacob" (Gen. xlix) about the sceptre that shall not depart from Judah "until he comes to Shiloh" (or "until Shiloh comes") belongs to the most discussed passages in the Old Testament. Dozens of explanations have been brought forward, but none of them has been able satisfactorily to dispel the obscureness that covers the extraordinarily ambiguous words.

The space I have at my disposal in this volume does not allow me to give a report of the various explanations. I presume that all the scholars who are going to read this article are well acquainted with them.[1] Without spending many introductory words, I shall go directly *in medias res*, presenting an attempt of my own to solve the problem connected with the curious Judah oracle v. 10, which has vexed so many generations of biblical scholars. I venture to do that although I have slight hopes that the debate will thereby be settled.

In the ancient Hebrew poetry *the tribe poem* is a clearly distinguishable species though there are very scanty remnants of it in the Bible. The tribe poem aimed at celebrating or blaming, from various points of view, the different tribes belonging to the group of tribes which reckoned Jacob as their ancestor and, after the occupation of the promised land, were comprised under the name of "Israel". Of this literature we have only two distinct examples in the Old Testament: "the Blessing of Jacob" and "the Blessing of Moses" (Deut. xxxiii).

The Song of Deborah in Judges v is partly composed after the pattern of a tribe poem. The same is true of the benedictions of

---

[1]) For earlier explanations of the Judah oracle see particularly the commentaries by SKINNER, DILLMANN, and PROCKSCH. Further A. POSNANSKI, *Schiloh. Ein Beitrag zur Geschichte der Messiaslehre*, I (Leipzig 1904). E. BURROWS, *The Oracles of Jacob and Balaam* (London 1939), attempts to explain the Blessing of Jacob in the light of Babylonian uranography.

Shem and Japheth and the curse of Canaan in Gen. ix 25-27, the lays of Balaam in Num. xxii-xxiv and, perhaps, in a wider sense, with the series of oracles against foreign nations in Amos and other prophetic books.

It seems that there were two types of the tribe poem: the epigrammatic tribe poem and the prophetic tribe poem. In the former type the different tribes were briefly and pregnantly characterized with regard to their distinguishing features, customs, and dwelling places, often with a humorous or satiric sting. Word-plays of various sorts, alluding to the proper names, were highly appreciated. The prophetic tribe poems again were composed of oracles containing curses and blessings in a more or less explicit form. In the tribe poems of the Old Testament the two types are not preserved in their pure and original form. Both "the Blessing of Jacob" and "the Blessing of Moses" present mixed forms. Epigrams and oracles are jumbled together, but the epigrams and the oracles alike are quite distinguishable. In "the Blessing of Jacob" the sayings on Zebulun, Issachar, Dan, Gad, Asher, Naphtali and Benjamin have the form of epigrams (examples: "Dan shall judge his people as one of the tribes of Israel."—"Dan shall be a serpent in the way, an adder in the path, that bites the horse's heels, so that his rider falls backward."—"Benjamin is a ravening wolf; in the morning he devours prey, and in the evening he divides spoil" [1]). On the other hand, the verses which deal with Reuben, Simeon and Levi, Judah and Joseph are typical oracles. In "the Blessing of Moses" we have one typical epigram, that on the tribe of Dan ("Dan is a lion's whelp, that leaps forth from Bashan"). All the other sayings are oracles in a more or less characteristic form.

The epigrammatic tribe poems were originally popular songs composed by poets aiming only at entertaining and amusing a listening crowd. [2]) Skilfulness in characterisation and in the invention of sallies of wit were demanded and appreciated. This species of poetry had no religious object in view, but was of a purely secular interest. Quite different was the case with the prophetic tribe poems. They were composed of oracles and, as oracles, they were regarded as

---

[1]) The future form of the verbs is due to the predictive character of the Blessing. Originally the epigrams contained descriptions of facts.—The Dan epigram seems to have been composed of two originally independent epigrams.

[2]) Of course, the single epigrams may have circulated isolated before being combined into continuous poems.

divinely inspired. Behind them stood prophets, and as prophetic utterances they were of great significance and severe effect. Their place in practical life was the sanctuary, where the tribes assembled, or the court, where the oracles, in the mouths of the court seers, served a practical purpose, possibly of a political nature.

"The Blessing of Jacob" is a mixed composition. Epigrams and oracles alternate with one another. The poet formulated a series of oracles, but he added numbers of epigrams, certainly taken from the popular epigrammatic poetry. In this species of literature the dependence of the tradition was generally very strong. This fact clearly appears through a comparison between "the Blessing of Jacob" and "the Blessing of Moses", which, as we know, have some elements in common. [1]) The oracles in "the Blessing of Jacob" prove that the poem has at any rate been composed by a prophet. There are reasons to suppose that the poem is the work of a single person, who composed it for a given object and, according to a common custom and for greater authority, laid it in the mouth of the dying patriarch.

Everybody who wants to explain the poem must take into consideration both that the sayings are thought of as predictions and that the poem as a whole was composed in a certain historical situation and occasioned by concrete historical circumstances. It is to be expected that the sayings, though formally referring to future events, contain allusions to and descriptions of facts belonging to the very epoch of the poet who composed the song. To unveil these facts a careful exegetical analysis is indispensable.

From the oracle about Simeon and Levi we get nothing of value for the dating of "the Blessing of Jacob". The oracle presupposes that Simeon and Levi did not exist any more as independent tribes in the Israelite amphictyony. They were "divided in Jacob and scattered in Israel". The dispersion of these tribes belonged to a very early epoch in the history of Israel. In the tradition this tragic fact was occasioned by a deed of violence committed in old times (cf. Gen. xxxiv).

The case is different with the oracle about Reuben. The tribe of Reuben is assigned an unexpectedly high position. The poet lays emphasis upon the fact that Reuben is the firstborn and the firstfruit of the strength of his father. He is further distinguished by *yether* *s*ᵉ*'ēth* and *yether ʿāz*. The word *yether* means "superiority". Reuben

---

[1]) See especially the oracles about Joseph.

is superior to the other tribes. *s*ᵉ*'ēth* signifies "highness", "majesty" (cf. Job xiii 11. xxxi 23. Hab. i 7. Ps. lxii 5); *'ōẓ* combined with *s*ᵉ*'ēth* is power and mightiness (cf. Ps. xc 6. cxxxii 8. Hab. iii 4. ii Chr. vi 41 etc.). What is said of Reuben is that, in relation to the other tribes, he occupies a position of highness, dignity, and power, comparable with that of a ruler, a king. Reuben exercising such a force and might is impressively compared to water that boils over. However, he will not keep his might for ever; he will fall down from his high position. He bears a guilt from olden times: once he defiled his father's bed (allusion to the notice in Gen. xxxv 22).

The Joseph oracle begins with an epigrammatic fragment pointing out the fertility of the territory of the Joseph tribes. Then follows, in historical tenses, a description of the skilfulness and bravery in warfare that characterized these tribes. [1]) Joseph had had to fight against archers, but he had battled bravely and successfully. His strength came from his God. The oracle ends in a benediction: blessed be Joseph with blessings of heaven and blessings of the deep, blessings of the breasts and blessings of the womb etc.

The historical tenses in vv. 23-24 are astonishing in a prophecy referring to the future. They show that the poet has forgotten his rôle as a prophetic foreteller and suddenly appears as a narrator of historical facts. Archers were the Midianites and other tribes from the desert who assailed the Israelites in the epoch of the judges, archers were also the Philistines against whom the Israelites had to fight in the time of Saul (1 Sam. xxxi 3). On both these occasions the central tribes were engaged in hot battles, but in the latter combats the Israelites seem to have reaped no great praise.

The expressions in v. 24 are somewhat obscure owing to the prophetical style. The meaning of the phrase: "His bow stayed firm (cf. Num. xxiv 21: *'ēthān mōshābhekhā*) and his arms were agile", can only be this: he resisted in the battles with valour and vigour. The expressions are to be explained as figurative, the "bow" symbolizing the military force of Joseph (cf. Hos. i 5. Jer. xlix 35) [2]). In the fol-

---

[1]) Most commentators object to the form *wā-robbū*. But the perfect with *wāw* is not seldom used—even after imperf. cons.—to indicate a circumstance connected with the main action. Examples: Judges iii 23. vii 13. 1 Sam. XVII 38. 1 Kings xx 21 etc. See the Hebrew grammar by H. S. NYBERG recently published in Swedish: *Hebreisk grammatik* (Uppsala 1952), § 86 kk. The initial words of v. 23 should, consequently, be translated: And they irritated him in shooting. BURROWS thinks of a consecutive perfect with frequentative value; op. cit., p. 35.

[2]) In *b*ᵉ*'ēthān* the preposition is to be conceived of as *bēth essentiae*: GESENIUS-

lowing phrases the poet tells us from where the resisting power of Joseph came. First we meet the old divine name *ʾ^{a}bhīr yaʿ^{a}qōbh* (cf. Is. i 24. xlix 26. lx 16. Ps. cxxxii 2, 5); then *rōʿeh*, the Shepherd, which must likewise have been an old name of the Israelite God (cf. Gen. xlviii 15 and Ps. lxxx 2, where the name likewise occurs in connexion with Joseph). "The stone of Israel", alludes to the sacred stone of Bethel (Gen. xxviii), an important cult object in the territory of the Joseph tribes, and is here used as an epithet of God the Shepherd. [1]) Finally the God of Joseph is called *shadday*, a name the origin of which is unknown, but which was probably connected with a primitive sanctuary in Palestine. [2]) What the poet lays stress upon is that the tribe of Joseph had a source of strength and perseverance in its paternal religion and venerable cult. In the light of this the remarkable description of Joseph as *n^{e}zīr ʾeḥāw*, v. 26, becomes intelligible. *nāzīr* is one who is dedicated to holy service, devoted to God. Joseph is a *nāzīr* among his brother tribes because there existed in the territory of Joseph cult places, especially Bethel, to which there was nothing comparable in the other tribes.

Now we pass over to the oracle about Judah. It is formulated on

---

Kautzsch, *Hebräische Grammatik*, § 119 i; cf. Nyberg, § 98 j. For the meaning of *ʾēthān* cf. further Jer. v 15 (*gōy ʾēthān*) and Job xxxiii 19. — The expression *z^{e}rōʿē yādhāw* has given trouble to the interpreters. It is, however, to be observed that in Hebrew *yādh* often signifies the forearm with the hand. See for instance Gen. xxvii 16 (LXX βραχίονας), 23. Ex. xvii 11 f. xxvi 17. xxxvi 22. Lev. xxi 19. Judges xv 14 (LXX βραχιόνων; *z^{e}rōʿōthāw* and *yādhāw* synonyms). 1 Sam. xv 12. 1 Kings vi 32 ff. x 19. 2 Kings xix 26. Is. xxxvii 27. lvii 8 (= phallos) Prov. vi 10. xxiv 33. Zech xiii 6. Cant. v 14. In the early Phoenician alphabet the sign for *yōdh* was a hand with the forearm. The same is true of the corresponding ideogram in the oldest form of the Sumero-Akkadian script. Thus, in our passage the words *z^{e}rōʿīm* and *yādhayim* are to be regarded as synonyms. The peculiarity of the expression is due to the poetical style.

[1]) The vocalization *mish-shām* (LXX ἐκεῖθεν) shows that the massoretes were dependent on a settled tradition. The change into *mish-shēm* is to be rejected. The significance of *mish-shām* approaches to that of the simple *shām* (see f. i. Num. xiii 23. Is. lxv 20. Jer. xxxvii 12. Hos. ii 17; cf. *mimm^{e}qōmō* Ez. iii 12). The phrase: "There is the Shepherd, the Stone of Israel", is parenthetical (or the sentence has the value of a relative clause: "From the place (Bethel) where the Shepherd dwells" cf. Ges.-Kautzsch, § 155 n; Nyberg, § 94 o).

[2]) Nyberg, *Archiv für Religionswissenschaft*, 35, 1938, pp. 350 f., rightly maintains that *El Shadday* was a pre-Israelite God of Palestine. He thinks that the name was a parallel to *El Elyon* and that the God *Shadday* belonged to the type of the great "Landesgötter" in Palestine. From our passage, it seems to me, it can be concluded that *El Shadday* had a sanctuary in the territory of Joseph, just as God the Shepherd seems to have had a special connexion with the Joseph tribes.

the basis of an old epigram, where Judah is likened to a lion's whelp that after having taken its prey, has started to return to his dwelling place. At the moment he is couched and nobody dares to rouse him. At the end the poet proceeds with a new series of figures denoting the fertility of the land of Judah; he binds his ass to the vine and his foal to the choicest vine; he washes his garments in wine and his clothes in the blood of grapes. His eyes are dull (?) with wine and his teeth white with milk.

The oracle proper begins with a word-play upon the name Judah: *yᵉhūdhāh yōdhūkhā*: "Judah, thee shall thy brethren praise", and then: "thy father's children shall bow down before thee". This means to say that the tribe of Judah shall have a position of superiority over the other tribes. That is not all. Judah's hand shall be on the neck of his enemies: a political power is foreseen for Judah, comprising foreign nations too.

A sequel to this prophecy follows in v. 10 containing the famous saying: "The sceptre shall not depart from Judah, nor the commanders staff from between his feet" etc. The sceptre and the staff are symbols of royai power. What the poet wants to say is this: the kingship of which the tribe of Judah actually is in possession will not cease, but continue till something happens that is expressed by the enigmatic words *yābhō' shīlōh*.

It is to be observed that it is not said that some time in the future Judah will be in possession of a king, it is said that the kingship that Judah actually is in possession of will continue till a certain goal has been reached. The utterance is formulated not from the point of view of the dying patriarch, but from the point of view of the prophet-poet. Of course, the words *ʿad kī* do not signify that the kingship will come to an end at the very moment when the event occurs that is expressed by the words *yābhō' shīlōh*; the words indicate, here as often elsewhere, not the end but the climax [1]). At the end of the oracle the promise of a political dominion over foreign nations is repeated: the obedience of the nations shall fall to his share.

Before attempting to explain the debated words, a summing up of the main ideas of the oracles in "the Blessing of Jacob" would be expedient.

---

[1]) Of this meaning of *ʿad kī* or *ʿad ʾᵃsher* there are many examples: Gen. xxvi 13. xli 49. Num. xi 20. Judges iv 24. 2 Sam. xxiii 10. 1 Kings xvii 17. 2 Kings xvii 20. Ez. xxxiv 21. After negative phrases: Gen. xxviii 15. Ps. cxii 8.

1. Among the Israelite tribes there are three which are given particular precedence: Reuben, Joseph, and Judah.

2. The tribe of Judah is the seat of a kingdom. The king is promised hegemony over the other Israelite tribes. In addition, an empire including foreign nations is foreseen for him.

3. Reuben actually occupies a glorious and powerful position among the Israelite tribes; but he will not be able to maintain his high position. The loss of his accidental superiority is prophetically foretold.

4. Joseph is described as supereminent in fertility and wealth of all kinds. He is praised for valour and resisting power in battle. He is in possession of old and venerable cult places, and thus superior in religious respects, but there is no mention at all of a kingdom in his territory.

5. Finally it is to be observed that all the tribes are thought of as dwelling in Palestine. Their territories are only referred to in general terms, but in certain cases we notice a correspondence to what we know from other historical sources.

Now the question arises into which epoch of the history of Israel this state of things fits. The first thing that can be said is that the poem in its actual form must have been composed after the occupation of the promised land and at a time when the system of the twelve tribes was still living. There are biblical scholars who have suggested the time of the judges; but the mention of a king in the tribe of Judah makes such a dating impossible, namely if the oracles, as we regard as evident, contain *vaticinia ex eventu*, and the poem as a whole is a coherent composition, though making use of rich traditional material. Since there is no mention of a king in the northern tribes, we must think of the time of the undivided kingdom; and since the king resides in Judah, only the epoch of David or Solomon is acceptable.

However, we can go a step further. My thesis is *that the poem was composed during the seven years and six months that David was king in Judah and resided in Hebron.*

The historical circumstances at that time are well-known. After the defeat of Saul and his army in mount Gilboa and the death of Saul and his three sons, the Philistines occupied the northern parts of the country. Meanwhile David seized the opportunity of getting a firm position with the people. He went with his men to Hebron. Then the men of Judah came and anointed David king over the tribe of

Judah. Simultaneously Abner, one of Saul's superior officers, took Ishbaal, the still living son of Saul, and brought him to Mahanaim, on the other side of Jordan, making him king over the Transjordanian territory and formally also over Israel as a whole. In consequence of this war broke out between David and Ishbaal. After varying fortunes David prevailed, and with the murder of Ishbaal his chance came.

It is told in 2 Sam. v that all the tribes of Israel came to David to Hebron to make him king over all Israel. David made a pact with them and was then anointed king of Israel. This was brought about in a wholly peaceful manner. According to tradition, already in the time of Saul the northern tribes had felt sympathy for David, and after the death of Saul, David consistently endeavoured to obtain favour with the northern tribes and maintain a friendly and conciliatory attitude to the high-spirited central tribes. [1]) Particularly after the loss of the assistance of Abner, weak Ishbaal was not able to gain confidence in his capability to liberate the country from the Philistine invaders. Moreover, a prophetic oracle was current that designated David future king of all Israel and its saviour from the hands of the Philistines. [2])

Seen in the light of this historical situation, the characteristic details of "the Blessing of Jacob" become intelligible.

In the tribe of Judah a king reigns. The Joseph tribe is spoken of with the greatest sympathy, but there is no hint of a kingdom in that territory. On the other hand, the emphasis laid upon the prominence of Joseph in a cultic respect is quite natural in a time when Jerusalem had not yet been made a cult place of unique significance. That only occurred after the end of David's kingship at Hebron. The high position ascribed to Reuben is accounted for by the fact that at that time the territory east of Jordan was the seat of a kingdom, that of Ishbaal. Reuben, having got his territory on the other side of Jordan and being often accorded first place among the Transjordanian tribes, is quite suitably given prominence as a representative of the country east of Jordan. The prediction in the Reuben oracle of the downfall of Reuben and the loss of his glory and power

---

[1]) See passages such as 2 Sam. ii 4-7. iii 17-19, 27-28.

[2]) 2 Sam. iii 9. v 2. The commentators think of the notice in 1 Sam. xxii 10, 13 that Ahimelek, the priest in Nob, inquired the Lord for David. But there nothing is said about the future kingship of David over Israel, nor about his victory over his enemies.

refers to the expected dethroning of Ishbaal and the cessation of his kingdom. [1])

If I am right in establishing the historical situation of "the Jacob Blessing" in this way the explanation of the words *ʿad kī yābhōʾ shīlōh* becomes a matter of course. They must be taken as they stand and are to be translated in this way: till he, viz. Judah, comes to Shiloh. The sense of the expression is that the kingdom which has been established in Juda through the election of David will not be limited to the tribe of Judah, but extended to comprise the northern tribes too. Shiloh appears as a representative of these tribes just as Reuben appeared as a representative of the kingdom of Ishbaal. The use of such "representative names" is, as we know, very common in the Old Testament. In the epigram on Zebulun (v. 13) Zidon stands for Phoenicia. Other examples are Zion, Ephraim, Joseph, Jezreel (Hos. ii 24) etc. representing kingdoms, territories, and peoples. It cannot be denied that Shiloh could be very appropriately used as such a "representative name". Shiloh was one of the oldest and most prominent places in the territory of Ephraim. The Ark of the Covenant for one century or two was installed here, and thus Shiloh was a cult place of central significance. At Shiloh the Israelite tribes gathered in the time of the judges; there the common affairs of the amphictyony were settled. Thus Shiloh in the pre-monarchic time was a sort of metropolis or capital of Israel. Shiloh was destroyed during the earlier wars with the Philistines but not laid totally waste. In any case the memory of the place was preserved for centuries, even after it had lost its original importance.

---

[1]) For the settlement of the Reubenites together with the tribe of Gad and other tribes or fragments of tribes in the Transjordanian territory see M. NOTH, *Geschichte Israels* (Göttingen 1950), pp. 54 f., 60. At times it is said that on the division of the land, the Reubenites got their dwelling places in the land of Gilead. The extent of Gilead varies in the Old Testament, but, at any rate, there exists a firm tradition that Reuben belonged to the Transjordanian tribes, or fragments of tribes, among which, at times, he is mentioned in the first place (Num. xxxii. Josh. xiii. xxii). See further NOTH, *Beiträge zur Geschichte des Ostjordanlandes, Palästinajahrbuch*, 37, 1941, pp. 50-101, and *Israelitische Stämme zwischen Ammon und Moab, ZAW*, 60, 1944, pp. 11-57. Thus, Reuben belonged to the territory of Ishbaal in a narrower sense and could appropriately be mentioned as a representative of his kingdom. The reason for the prominence of Reuben among the Transjordanian tribes, and the Israelite tribes in general, is not clear. It must be due to pre-historic circumstances unknown to us.—Of course, the interpretation of the Reuben oracle here presented does not exclude that, in an earlier form and in earlier times, it may have referred to other historical facts no longer distinguishable.

Just in a prophetic oracle with its mysterious mode of expression—"Prophetenwort ist Rätselwort" (Gunkel)—Shiloh could appropriately serve as a symbol for the territory where the city was in fact one of the most venerated places, rich as it was in historical associations and sacred memories. [1])

We are told that David had prophets and seers about him. We know the names of two of them: Gad and Nathan. There might have existed more than these two. One court prophet of king David's at Hebron composed the so called "Blessing of Jacob", foretelling a great future for David and his kingdom, and at the same time aiming at gaining for David the sympathy of the northern tribes.

According to tradition the extension of the kingdom of David to all Israel was really foreseen by a prophetic oracle (see p. 83 and 84). Perhaps this oracle was just the oracle about the sceptre of Judah and his coming to Shiloh in "the Blessing of Jacob".

---

[1]) Ever since the Danish excavations at *chirbet seilūn*, it must be taken as proved that Shiloh was levelled with the ground about 1050 B.C. See further *Palestine Exploration Fund.* Quarterly Statement 1927, pp. 202 ff., 157 f.; 1931, pp. 71 ff., and H. KJAER, *I det Hellige Land. De danske Udgravninger i Shilo* (Köbenhavn 1931). The prophet Ahia lived in Shiloh (1 Kings xiv). Even in the time of Jeremiah the memory of Shiloh was living (ch. vii and xxvi; cf. xli 5).

THE HEBREW EQUIVALENT OF TAXO IN ASS. MOS. ix

BY

SIGMUND MOWINCKEL

Oslo

In the apocalyptic book Assumptio Mosis, or more correctly: The Testament of Moses, from the age of the sons of Herodes, in the 9th chapter we read as follows:

"Then in that day [i.e. the days of the ungodly king of the end time, chp. vii-viii] there shall be a man of the tribe of Levi, whose name shall be Taxo, who having seven sons shall speak to them exhorting (them): 'Observe, my sons, behold a second ruthless and unclean visitation has come upon the people, and a punishment merciless and far exceeding the first. For what nation and region or what people of those who are impious towards the Lord, who have done many abominations, have suffered as great calamities as have befallen us? Now, therefore, my sons, hear me, for observe and know, that neither did the fathers nor did their forefathers tempt God so as to transgress His commands. And ye know that this is our strength, and thus we will do. Let us fast for a space of three days, and on the fourth let us go into a cave which is in the field, and let us die rather than transgress the commands of the Lord of Lords, the God of our fathers. For if we do this and die, our blood shall be avenged before the Lord.

And then His kingdom shall appear throughout all His creation, and then Satan shall be no more, and sorrow shall depart with him ..." etc. (translation of the Latin text in R. H. CHARLES's *Apocrypha and Pseudepigrapha of the Old Testament* II, Oxford 1913, p. 421) [1]).

This figure of Taxo does only occur here. He is obviously neither the Messiah, as he does none of the Messianic deeds, nor a forerunner of Messiah, in as far as the "Assumptio" mentions no Messiah at all; the voluntary death of Taxo and his seven sons will have the effect that the Lord will do mercy towards his oppressed people and

[1]) In the following abbreviated as *APOT*.

rise to avenge their blood, crush the tyrant king and the heathen peoples and let the eschatological salvation come.—Taxo has no Messianic character at all; but as will be seen below, the conception is influenced by, or have one of its roots in the idea of the Messianic forerunners.

In the structure of the book Taxo belongs to the future, but it may very well be assumed that some historical person of the time of the author, or a somewhat earlier time, has served as a model to this figure.

"The identification of the figure of Taxo has provided the most vexed question associated with the Assumption of Moses", says Professor Rowley [1]). The discussion has in the first place been concerned with the interpretation of the name Taxo [2]). As Clemen and Rowley and others have demonstrated, all explanations of the name as some sort of Gematria or of cipher symbolism—as e.g. the cipher 666 in the Apocalypse of John—have failed.

The only probable explanation as yet is that of Schmidt-Merx and Clemen: Taxo is the Latin form of the Greek τάξων = the "Orderer". As well known the Latin "Assumptio" is a translation, and a rather poor one, of a Greek text [3]). The translator has taken "Taxo" as the "name" of the person in question, and that means that he has had before him a Greek word which he could understand thus, and that means again, that he found a similar "name" in his Greek text, which he has not translated but only transliterated, eventually adapting its grammatical form to the corresponding Latin form; a Greek τάξων would then normally become Taxo; cp. Platon > Plato, Zenon > Zeno, and the other way Nero > Neron. Other such transliterations have been pointed out by Charles: *chedrio* i 17 from κεδρόω, *heremus* iii 11 from ἐρῆμος, *acrobistia* viii 3 from ἀκροβυστία [4]).

Now it is agreed by nearly all scholars that the Greek text itself was a translation of a Semitic original, either Hebrew or Aramaic. There can in my opinion be no doubt that Charles and others are

---

[1]) H. H. Rowley, *The Relevance of Apocalyptic*, Lutterworth Press 1944, p. 128.

[2]) A short review of the different theories gives C. Clemen in E. Kautzsch, *Apokryphen und Pseudepigraphen des Alten Testaments* [APAT] II, Tübingen 1900 p. 326. Cp. also C. Lattey in *Cath. Bibl. Quarterly*, 1942; C. C. Torrey in *JBL* 62, 1943, pp. 1 ff.; 64, 1945, pp. 547 ff.; Rowley, *Relevance of Apocalyptic* pp. 128 ff.; *JBL* 64, pp. 141 ff.

[3]) See on this question Charles, *APOT*, p. 409 f.

[4]) See Charles, *op. cit.*, p. 409.

right in assuming a Hebrew original [1]).—In this original text the corresponding Hebrew expression, N.N. ושמו must not have meant what we should call the "Christian name" of the person in question; the "name" may equally well have been meant as a title, a honorary name which he was to obtain through his vicarious deed; cp. Jer. xxiii 6. If, then, we have to presuppose a τάξων in the Greek text, this means that the translator has found in the Hebrew original a word that he has *translated* with this Greek participle. The question, then, is: which Semitic word? The weak point of SCHMIDT-MERX's and CLEMEN's explanation was that they have not been able to point out any such Hebrew (or Aramaic) word, which the Greek may have translated in this way.

The question to be put is: which ideas and conceptions have the Greek speaking and Greek writing Jews connected with the words τάξις and ταξων?

Now dr. AALEN, in an other connexion, has pointed out that there in the Jewish-Greek religious philosophy exists a near connection between the Hebrew חק, חקה and the Greek τάξις [2]).

In O.T. *ḥoq* and *ḥuqqå* also are used about the laws of nature, of the world order; as the law of the shifting seasons of the year, with their different rainperiods Jer. v 24; the laws of day and night and of the celestial bodies Ps. cxlviii 3-6; the established limits of the ocean, which it can not transgress Jer. xxxi 35 f.; Job xxxviii 10; the laws of the universe ("heaven and earth") Jer. xxxiii 25; the laws of the heavens and the constellations (sun, moon, *mazzålot̲*) Job xxxviii 33. The meaning of the words in these cases may oscillate between "law" and "(imposed) limit" [3]).—The same meaning the words also have in later Judaism, see Sir. xliii 7 10; cp. also xvi 26, where the last word of the verse, exactly the word in question is lacking in the fragmentary Hebrew text, but where a comparison between the Greek and the Syriac texts clearly shows that the original word was *ḥoq* or *ḥuqqå*, as already RYSSEL has seen [4]) and AALEN demonstrated more in detail [5]). The difference between O.T. and

---

[1]) CHARLES, *op. cit.*, p. 410.

[2]) SVERRE AALEN, *Die Begriffe 'Licht' und 'Finsternis' im Alten Testament, im Spätjudentum und im Rabbinismus* [Skrifter utgitt av Det Norske Videnskaps-Akademi i Oslo II. Hist.-Filos. Klasse. 1951. No 1], Oslo 1951, pp. 159 f.

[3]) Cp. AALEN, *op. cit.*, p. 28.

[4]) V. RYSSEL, *Die Weisheit Jesus Sirachs*, in KAUTZSCH, *APAT* I, p. 312.

[5]) AALEN, *op. cit.*, p. 159.

later Judaism is only that in the latter the more philosophical conception of a universal "world order" stands behind or over the definite single "laws" and "limits", and the technical Greek-Jewish word for this world "order" is τάξις [1]).

The Septuagint translation (G) of the above mentioned places differs: πρόσταγμα Jer. v 24; Ps. cxlviii 6 [2]); ὅρια Job xxxviii 10; τροπάι Job xxxviii 33. In Sir. xliii 10 G has κρίμα = (world) order, cosmic law; in xvi 26 μερίδαι = limits, limited parts, whereas the Syriac version (P) has "laws".

τάξις renders in G i.a. *tôrå* (Prov. xxxi 24); the verb τάσσειν i.a. *ṣiwwå* (2 Sam. vii 11; 1 Ch. xvii 10; Is. xxxviii 1). But what is important in this connection is that there in G is a tendency to use τάξις where in the translators' opinion the natural or cosmic law and order are mentioned or hinted at. So in Jud. v 10: the stars fought ἐκ τῆς τάξεως αὔτών; the moon was standing on his τάξις Hab. iii 11 (*zĕḇulo*); the τάξις of the morning flush Job xxxviii 12 (*måqom*); the τάξις of the wild asses Job xxiv 5 (var. πράξεις, Hebr. *på'ålåm*); the τάξις of the darkness Job xxxiii 3 (*qeṣ*); the τάξις of conception and birth Job xxxvi 28b (the distich is wanting in Hebr.); cp. words without τάξις Job xvi 3.

Also in the Greek Book of Enoch we find "law", both as cosmic and ethic entity, and "order", τάξις, as parallel words and ideas; see 1 En. lxxii 1. 35; lxxiv 1; lxxix 1; lxxx 4.7; the phenomena on the heaven "all rise and set in order each in its season, and transgress not against their appointed order" — τάξις —, 1. En. ii 1, and the same is the case with the (divine) "works on the earth", summer, winter, and so on, 1 En. ii 2-v 3. In parallelism to the "law" or the "commandments" of God appears the τάξις of the stars Test. Naphth. iii 2; 1 En. ii 1; v 4 [3]).

In the above mentioned places different words for the "law" and the "commandments" are used, but at all events there is a close connection between this conception and that of the "order", τάξις. And the word that in itself includes both these ideas and the meaning of which, therefore, always more or less oscillates between "(divine) law" and "(divine and cosmic) order" is *ḥoq* or *ḥuqqå*.

We may, thus, take for granted that in the ideology of later Greek

---

[1]) Cp. AALEN, *op. cit.*, pp. 158 ff.

[2]) Jer. xxxi 36 is misunderstood by G; xxxiii 14 ff. is wanting in G.

[3]) See AALEN, *op. cit.*, p. 160.

speaking and Greek writing Judaism there was a close correspondence between the idea of *ḥoq* (*ḥuqqâ*) and that of τάξις.

An other word for "order", used in the Cairo Manuscripts of the Damascus Covenanters (*CDC*) is *særæḵ* סרך, vii 6.8; x 4; xii 19, 22; xiii 7; xiv 3.12; to *sarḵê hâ'âræṣ* in vii 8 correspond *ḥuqqê hâ'âræs* in xix 2 f.; in xii 19-23 the *særæḵ* of the congregation is also called its *ḥuqqim*. — To *særæḵ* corresponds the Greek τάξις; "*særæḵ* is found in vv. 29, 30 of the Aramaic fragments of an original source to the Test. Twelve Patr. In the Greek, which is here happily preserved, τάξις appears as the equivalent of *særæḵ*" [1]); cp. Dan. vi 3-5.7, where Theod. renders *sarĕḵin* with τακτικόι.

Our thesis now is that in the light of the above observations it seems very probable to explain the Taxon of the Greek "Assumptio" as a translation of the Hebrew term מְחֹקֵק, *mĕḥoqeq*.

In O.T. we meet this word in two meanings: a) commander, Jud. v (9) 14; Is. xxxiii 22; (Dt. xxxiii 12); Sir. x 5; b) commander's staff Gen. xlix 10; Num, xxi 18; Ps. lx 9; cviii 9. The "commander" is not only the commander in war, but the "orderer" of all important things in the life of the people. In most of these places, G has taken the word in the first meaning: ἡγούμενος Gen. xlix 10; ἄρχων Dtn. xxxiii 12; Is. xxxiii 22; βασιλευς Ps. lx 9; cviii 9; γραμματέυς (!) Sir. x 5; in Num. xxi 18 G translates *bimĕḥoqeq* ἐκ τῇ βασιλείᾳ (ἀυτῶν) and *ḥoqĕqê* Jud. v 9 τὰ διατεταγμένα.

Of special interest is here the translation in Sir. x 5, γραμματευς [2]), which indicates that the translator (and his circle) has related the word to the spiritual leadership of the learned and pious men. It is obvious that the translator, the grandson of Jesus Sirach, has derived *mĕḥoqeq* from *ḥoq* or *ḥuqqa* and understood it as: one who is concerned with the divine *ḥuqqim* (*ḥuqqot*), having studied and practised them and thus having got the ability and right — and the duty— to lead and "order" the life of the congregation in accordance with those *ḥuqqim*. Just what the Judaism meant by a γραμματέυς and νομοδιδάσκαλος, "a scribe instructed unto the kingdom of Heaven" (Mt. xiii 52).

In a meaning very like this we meet *mĕḥoqeq* in CDC. In CDC p. vii 1. 18 we are told that the sect migrated to Damascus under the leadership of one called "the Star", with reference to Num. xxiv

---

1) Charles in *APOT*, II, p. 815.
2) Cp. γράφειν as G translation of *ḥqq* Is. x 1.

17. "The Star" is called "he who studies the Law", *doreš hat-tôrå*, just what the translator of Sirach means with γραμματεύς. But "He who studies the Law" is not any γραμματεύς, but a unique such, a definite man of a special authority in the sect. In vi 7 we read that the *mĕḥoqeq* is "he who studies the Law", *doreš hat-tôrå*; accordingly "the Star" and "the *mĕḥoqeq*" are the same person. It is expressly said (vi 2 ff.) that the title *mĕḥoqeq* is taken from Num. xxi 18; the sect has found a prophecy about their leader at the time of the migration both in "the Star" in Num. xxiv 17 and in the *mĕḥoqeq* in Num. xxi 18; the connecting link between the two Bible inferences is the expression "staff" which occurs in both of them, in Num. xxiv 17 *šebæṯ* // *koḵåb*, in xxi 18 *miš'ån* // *mĕḥoqeq*.

This word CHARLES in *Apocrypha and Pseudepigrapha* II translates "lawgiver", but as CHARLES says himself (*op. cit.* p. 792): "he was not a lawgiver in the sense of Moses, but rather an interpreter of the Law". His rôle is explained in this way:

"God remembered the covenant with the forefathers, and he raised up from Aaron men of understanding and from Israel wise men. And he made them to hearken, and they digged a well: 'A well the princes digged, the nobles of the people delved it by the order of (or: through, ב) the *mĕḥoqeq*'. The well is the Law, and they who digged it are the penitents of Israel who went forth out of the land of Judah and sojourned in the land of Damascus, all of whom God called princes ... And the *mĕḥoqeq* is he who studies the Law, in regard to whom Isaiah said: 'He bringeth forth an instrument for his work' (Is. liv 16). And the nobles of the people are those who came to dig the well by the precepts which the *mĕḥoqeq* ordained that they should walk throughout the full period of wickedness. And save them they shall get nothing until there arises the Teacher of Righteousness in the end of the days".

The *mĕḥoqeq* is the leader of the sect, who has studied the Law and given its authoritative explanation and the halakoth, the right ordinances, which the members of the sect have to obey until the Teacher of Righteousness returns at the end of the days. The *mĕḥoqeq* is the "orderer", who has established the right order within the congregation of the covenanters. They should follow him until the highest and last authority of the sect, the "Teacher" himself comes. In so far the idea of the *mĕḥoqeq* has been influenced by the conception of the "forerunner".

To sum up: the Damascus covenanters have found the reorganizor and "Orderer" of their sect prophezied in Num. xxi 18 and xxiv 17 just because he was an "Orderer" and thus "the Orderer" mentioned in xxi 18. I do not believe that *mĕḥoqeq* has been a title that was in ordinary use to design a learned leader of a congregation of some sort, although the γραμματέυς in Sir. x 5 might be taken as an indicium of such an usage. I find it more probable that the covenanters have applied the mysterious Biblical word *mĕḥoqeq* to their reorganizer, just because he became the "orderer" after the disasters in connection with the death of the "Teacher of Righteousness", and because he did it as a "student of the Law" and an expert in the *ḥuqqim* of the Lord.

When, thus, the title *mĕḥoqeq* has been known in certain religious circles as the characteristic title of an "Orderer", of a τάξων, then there seems to be very good reasons to think that it is just this word that lies behind the translation τάξων in Assumptio ch. ix. This is corroborated by the fact that Taxo(n) is said to come from the tribe of Levi, which is in full accordance with CDC VI 2: "He raised up from Aaron men of understanding", and among them the *mĕḥoqeq*.

When the translator has chosen the future participle for his translation this is in accordance with the fact, that this "Orderer" still belongs to the future. — One might perhaps object that a classic Greek should have said ὁ τάξων, with article. To this is to answer that John in his Apocalypse ix, 11 translates the Hebrew Abaddon by 'Απολλύων without article.

Here arises the question about the relations between the circles from which the "Assumptio" originated, and the Damascus covenanters. It can now be taken for granted that these covenanters are identic with the "sectarians" of the Dead Sea scrolls, or perhaps more correctly: that the first represent a somewhat later stage in the history of the latter [1]). We cannot take up this whole problem here. But so much can be taken for granted, that the apocalyptic and pseudepigraphic literature has been much appreciated among the covenanters, and that there accordingly may have been rather close historical connections between these and the circles behind the "Assumptio". Among the Dead Sea Manuscripts are also fragments

[1]) It suffices here to refer to H. H. Rowley, *The Zadokite Fragments and the Dead Sea Scrolls*, Oxford 1952.

of the Hebrew Book of Jubilees, a scroll probably containing the lost Apocalypse of Lamech, and a fragment of an unknown apocryptical book with references to the Book of Jubilees, 1. Enoch and the Testaments of the Twelve Patriarchs [1]).

But there are good reasons to believe that the "Assumptio" itself originated from these same "sectarian" circles. That its spirit and "theology" are very closely related to the spirit and the ideas of the Book of Jubilees is quite obvious. But it is also obvious that it has originated from a circle or a "congregation" which is not identical with the people of Israel as such, although it claims to represent the true Israel. When Taxo says to his sons: "Neither did the fathers nor their forefathers tempt God so as to transgress His commands" ix 4, this can not be referred to the forefathers of Israel in general; on the contrary the "Assumptio" has much to say about the sinfulness of the forefathers of Israel, cp. iii 13; v 2 ff.; vi 1.

Of special interest is here v 2 ff., where Moses in the form of a prophecy describes the ways of the people in its later history: "And they themselves (i.e. the Jews) shall be *divided as to the truth*, because it has come (which has been prophezied): 'They shall turn aside from righteousness and approach iniquity, and they shall defile with pollutions the house of their worship', and 'they shall go a-whoring after stange gods'. For they shall not follow the truth of God, but some shall pollute the altar with the (very) gifts they offer to the Lord, *who are not priests*, but slaves, sons of slaves. And many in those times shall have respect unto desirable persons and receive gifts and pervert judgement. And on this account the colony and the borders of their habitation shall be filled with lawless deeds and iniquities: those who wickedly depart from the Lord shall be judges: they shall be ready to judge for money as each may wish. Then kings shall arise over them bearing rule, and they shall *call themselves priests* of the most High (or: high priests): they shall assuredly *work iniquity in the Holy of Holies*".

That sounds very much like the accusations of the Damascus covenanters and the "sectarians" of the Dead Sea Scrolls against the "wicked priest" and "the man of the lie" and their followers, for whose sake the congregation has been "divided as to the truth". Taxo does not speak of the fathers and the forefathers of the apostate

---

1) Cp. W. Baumgartner, *Der palästinische Handschriftenfund*, in *Theol. Rundschau*, N. F., 19, 1951, pp. 123, 126.

majority of the people, but of those of the just minority, the forefathers of the "sect" to which he himself belongs.

It thus seems very probable that the "Assumptio" has been written within the same circles as are represented by the Damascus covenanters and the sect of the Dead Sea Scrolls—or shall we say: by a man who belonged to this sect.

So we can more easily understand that the author of the „Assumptio", and perhaps already the tradition within the circle which represents, has taken up the religious title of the historical figure of the "Orderer" as the apocalyptic "name" of the "forerunner" before the days of the end, whom he and his circle expected and hoped for, and who through his voluntary "sacrifice" should make the Lord let salvation come. — This does not mean that he expected a return of the definite "Orderer" of the covenanters, only that he has taken some features from this figure for his picture of the last "Orderer". Also in other respects the author of the "Assumptio" has drawn his picture of the "Orderer" after the model of earlier historical events. CLEMEN has pointed out that important traits of the description of the work and fate of the "Orderer" in ix 1 ff. "obviously have been taken from certain events in the age of the Maccabees", and refers to 1 Macc. ii 29 f.; 2 Macc. vi 18 ff., 4 Macc. v 4 ff. [1]). This seems very probable.

---

[1]) Cp. KAUTZSCH, *APAT*, II, p. 326.

A STUDY IN HEBREW RHETORIC: REPETITION AND STYLE

BY

JAMES MUILENBURG

New York

In 1741, at the age of thirty, RICHARD LOWTH was appointed Professor of Poetry at Oxford University, and it was in that capacity that he delivered his famous lectures on the poetry of ancient Israel. In 1753 these lectures were published under the title *de sacra poesi Hebraeorum praelectiones academicae*. The importance and value of this work transcends any of the specific theories or literary judgments which are expressed in it. For LOWTH was something of a poet, and he read biblical poetry with the mind of a poet. For one thing he recognized the wide range of poetic utterance in the Old Testament, and drew the consequences of this literary form for the interpretation of the sacred records. He was aware, too, that poetry has its special techniques: thus he sought to discern its cadences and rhythms, its lineaments and configurations. But he was more than a technician or craftsman. He had an acute sensitivity to the connotations which words possess beyond all the precision of their denotations, and he perceived the ever-changing nuances which words achieve in fresh contexts. His description of the sententious quality of Hebrew speech has never been surpassed; his feelings for imagery and the effects that imagery produces upon the reader gives his work an aesthetic authenticity rivalled in our day only by the work of HERMANN GUNKEL; his openness to the spontaneity, immediacy, concreteness, and primitive vitality of the Hebrew mind classes him among the peers of Old Testament study.

That LOWTH was in many respects a representative of his own age goes without saying. It would be easy to mark the defects of his work or to show the many ways in which his work has been superseded. Not least of all the theory by which he is best known has required restatement and reformulation. For it is now obvious to most students that the theory of *parallelismus membrorum* is far more complicated and involved than LOWTH supposed although he did seek to guard himself on this matter, especially in his preliminary dissertation in the commentary on Isaiah [1]). The first major type of parallelism to which LOWTH called attention was the synonymous. But if one inspects his examples either in the lectures or in the Isaiah commentary, it will be seen that the parallelism is in reality very seldom precisely synonymous. The parallel line does not simply repeat what has been said, but enriches it, deepens it, transforms it by adding fresh nuances and bringing in new elements, renders it more concrete and vivid and telling. One example must suffice [2]):

> Arise, shine, for thy light has come,
>   and the glory of Yahweh has dawned upon thee;
> For, behold, darkness shall cover the earth,
>   and deep gloom the peoples;
> But upon thee Yahweh dawns forth,
>   on thee his glory appears,
> And nations shall come to thy light,
>   and kings to the brightness of thy dawning. (Isa. lx 1-3)

It is clear that there is repetition in the parallel lines. But almost invariably something is added, and it is precisely the combination of what is repeated and what is added that makes of parallelism the artistic form that it is. This intimate relation between old and new elements is an important feature of Hebrew composition and Hebrew thought. On the one hand we observe form and pattern; on the other form and pattern are radically altered. Here, as elsewhere, there is a native resistance to stereotype or fixity, and yet form is clearly present and registers its effect upon the mind. In our modern study of Old Testament poetry synonymous speech has been recognized in the criticism of literary types (*Gattungkritik*), above all, of course, in the studies of HERMANN GUNKEL, and especially in his commentary on the Psalms. In the hymn, the lament, the song of thanksgiving,

---

1) *Isaiah: a New Translation with Preliminary Dissertation* (Cambridge, 1834), p. xx: "Sometimes the parallelism is more, sometimes less exact; sometimes hardly at all apparent. It requires indeed particular attention, much study of the genius of the language, much habitude in the analysis of the construction, to be able in all cases to see and to distinguish the nice rests and pauses which ought to be made, in order to give the period or the sentence its intended turn and cadence and to each part its due proportion." The influence of LOWTH's classical studies in Greek and Latin is apparent here as elsewhere in his work and is one of the features which the discovery of the other literatures of the ancient Near East has in large measure corrected. See also LOWTH, *Lectures on the Sacred Poetry of the Hebrews* (Andover, 1829), p. 35 for a cautious statement of parallelism.

2) Compare also Ps. cxiv; Is. liii 1-5; Nah. i 2; Ps. xciii 3 f.; Dt. xxxii 42.

and other literary types synonymous speech plays a major role; indeed, it is not too much to say that the dominant impression that these poetic compositions make upon us is to be explained by the profuse employment of synonymous words, phrases, and lines. The studies of GUNKEL are yet to be extended into a more detailed consideration of literary structure, but even a cursory examination of biblical poetry will show that the appearance of synonymity is seldom fortuitous or capricious. In the present discussion we shall endeavour to survey in a very general fashion the phenomenon of repetition in ancient Hebrew literature as a major feature of Hebrew rhetoric and style. For the most part we shall confine ourselves to actual repetition, i.e., where the same words and sentences are repeated.

Repetition plays a diverse role in the Old Testament. It serves, for one thing, to center the thought, to rescue it from disparateness and diffuseness, to focus the richness of varied predication upon the poet's controlling concern. The synthetic character of biblical mentality, its sense for totality, is as apparent in Israel's rhetoric as in her psychology. Repetition serves, too, to give continuity to the writer's thought; the repeated word or phrase is often strategically located, thus providing a clue to the movement and stress of the poem. Sometimes the repeated word or line indicates the structure of the poem, pointing to the separate divisions; at other times it may guide us in determining the extent of the literary unit. Our commentaries contain numerous instances where words and phrases have been deleted as mere repetition. It is a highly precarious procedure, one which violates the character of biblical writing, both prose and poetry, and is refuted quite decisively by the other extant literatures of the Near East, above all, perhaps, by the Ugaritic epics, which cast a strong light on the method and mentality of ancient Semitic thinking and literary composition. Finally, repetition provides us with an open avenue to the character of biblical thinking [1]).

---

[1]) See especially JOHANNES PEDERSEN, *Israel: its Life and Culture*, Vol. I-II (London, 1926), p. 123: "The very language shows how Israelite thought is dominated by two things: *striving after totality* and *movement*. Properly speaking it only expresses that the whole soul takes part in the thinking and creates out of its own essence. The thought is charged with the feeling of the soul and the striving of its will after action. This characterizes the Hebrew manner of argumentation. We try to persuade by means of abstract reasoning, the Hebrew by directly influencing the will. In expressing a thought he makes the souls of his listeners receive his mind-image, and thus the matter itself; but at the same time

This iterative propensity of ancient Israel extends beyond its expression in poetry. In narrative, the literary genre most characteristic of her life and thought, repetition appears as a major stylistic feature. In such accounts, for example, as the wooing of Rebecca [1]), or the Elijah stories [2]), it is used with a high degree of artistic skill, both because of its great variety and because of its power to relate speaker and hearer in the immediacy and concreteness of dialog or to bring them into participation with common words. It is an eloquent witness to the literary genius of ancient Israel that this constant resort to iterative discourse so seldom palls or wearies the reader. In the cult, too, repetition rendered a special service. In the annual festivals commemorating the unique historical events of the sacred past, Israel recited year after year her memorabilia: the theophanic accounts of the holy places, the stories of the Fathers, the epic events associated with the Exodus and with the covenant at Sinai, and the *toroth* that were incumbent upon her. The various rituals and liturgies were themselves filled with numerous repetitions as we can see most readily in such books as Deuteronomy and Ezekiel, some of the Psalms, and the Priestly Code and history. In the instruction of the young, too, iteration proved an effecuve device for stamping the mind with the things that must be remembered [3]). Psalm cxxxvi, where every alternate line reads, "For his steadfast love endures forever", is reminiscent of the endless repetitions in the Near Eastern liturgies, but there is evidence that it was not only one of the best loved but also one of the most familiar of all of Israel's liturgies [4]).

---

he produces an effect by the feeling and will which he puts into the words. His argumentation therefore consists in assurance and repetition. The "*parallelismus membrorum*" has become his natural manner of expression; he expresses his thought twice in a different manner, the result of which is a totality with a double accent: "Therefore the wicked shall not stand in the judgment, nor sinners in the congregation of the righteous" (Ps. i 5). When the Preacher wants the reader to see that "to everything there is a season" then he proves it by constantly repeating first one thing, then another (Eccles. iii). Upon the whole the book of the Preacher is characteristic of Israelite argumentation. He repeats and repeats, and it seems to us that he practically ends where he began." Also J. G. HERDER, *The Spirit of Hebrew Poetry* (Burlington, 1833), pp. 39 ff.; S. A. COOK, "The Semites", *Cambridge Ancient History*, Vol. I, pp. 195-197; AUBREY R. JOHNSON, *The Vitality of the Individual in the Thought of Ancient Israel* (Cardiff, 1949).

1) Gen. xxiv.

2) I Kings xvii-xix, xxi; II Kings i-ii.

3) Deut. iv 9 ff.; xi 18 ff.; Exod. xii 14; xiii 9-10, 16.

4) It is significant that the Chronicler quotes this line in connection with the establishment of the ark in Jerusalem (I Chron. xvi 41), with the response of the

The fact that the refrain appears in other liturgies is not surprising; we encounter the same circumstance again and again in the Ugaritic poems.

The roots of repetition lie deeply embedded in the language and literature of Israel [1]). An examination of the various modes of reduplication in Hebrew syntax or of the repetition of single words in elemental contexts of unreflected speech will reveal very clearly how the primitive spirit of the language continues to be preserved and lends to it an intensity, a spontaneity and freshness, a directness and immediacy which would be difficult to achieve in any other fashion [2]). Thus in such stems as the *Peʿalʿal*, *Pilpel*, and *Hithpalpel* the verb is given a special energy or movement. The verb פחר, e.g., in the *peʿalʿal* may describe the palpitation of the heart or "to go about quickly" or the *Pilpel* גלגל from the root גלל meaning "to roll". This repetition of the root to denote rapidity of movement is also characteristic of other languages, modern as well as ancient [3]). It is only to be expected that this same primitive survival should express the superlative: *ṣedeq ṣedeq tirdoph*, "justice, only justice you shall pursue" (Deut. xvi 20), or *ʿamok ʿamok*, "deep, very deep" (Eccles. vii 24), or *rʿa rʿa*, "it is bad, bad" (Prov. xx 14), or *meʾod meʾod*, "exceedingly great" (Ezek. ix 9; xvi 13), or *qadosh*, *qadosh*, *qadosh* — "utterly" or "supremely holy" (Isa. vi 3). The same intensity is implied in such expressions as *ʿebed ʿebadim*, "servant of servants" (Gen. ix 25), *qodesh ha-qodashim*, "holy of holies" (Exod. xxvi 23), or "God of gods" (Deut. x 17; Josh. xxii 22; Dan. ii 47) or "Lord of lords" (Deut. x 17; Ps. cxxxvi 3). Similarly a word is frequently

---

people upon the descent of the holy fire after Solomon's dedicatory prayer (II Chron. vii 3), and with the preparation for battle against Moab and Ammon in Jehoshaphat's reign (II Chron. xx 21). It is probable that in all three of these cases the line is simply an incipit for the entire psalm. The view of H. Wheeler Robinson (*Inspiration and Revelation in the Old Testament*, p. 115, nt. 17) that the repetition of the refrain is accidental has nothing to commend it.

[1]) See Israel Eitan, "La Repetition de la Racine en Hebreu", *Journal of the Palestine Oriental Society*, 1921, pp. 171-186.

[2]) Cf. Eitan, *ibid.*, p. 172: "Se différenciant en plusieurs procédés grammaticaux ou syntaxiques, ou en séries-types d'expressions idiomatiques, la *répétition de la racine* a fourni à la langue hébraïque, par voie de formation *spontanée*, souvent même *populaire* et sous l'influence de l'action *analogique*, des ressources précieuses pour rendre d'une façon plus vive et intense, surtout plus *concrète et intuitive*, certaines nuances d'expression sur lesquelles on tient à insister sans les affaiblir par un langage abstrait."

[3]) Gesenius-Kautzsch-Cowley, *Hebrew Grammar*, Sec. 55 d-g and 84^b k-p.

repeated to express urgency as in the Song of Deborah, the great classic of the iterative style, *'uri 'uri*:

> Awake, awake, Deborah!
> Awake, awake, utter a song! (Ju v 12)

To this is to be compared the similarly passionate outcry in Second Isaiah:

> Awake, awake, put on thy strength,
> O arm of Yahweh;
> Awake as in primeval days,
> the generations long ago. (Isa. li 9. cf. lii 1)

Other examples of almost equal interest are *naph^{e}lah naph^{e}lah Babel*, "fallen, fallen is Babylon" (Isa. xxi 9) or "I pine away, I pine away" (Isa. xxiv 16), "comfort, O comfort" (Isa. xl 1) or "for my sake, for my sake" (Isa. xlviii 11) or *shalom shalom* (Jer. vi 4; viii 11) or *'amen 'amen* (Pss. lxxii 19; lxxxix 53). Emphatic vocatives are expressed in the same manner, thus "Abraham, Abraham" in the crisis of the story of Isaac's sacrifice (Gen. xxii 11) or "Moses, Moses" as he is about to violate the divine holiness (Exod. iii 4) or David's heartbroken apostrophe, *b^{e}ni Abshalom b^{e}ni b^{e}ni* (II Sam. xviii 33; Heb. xix 1) or *'abi 'abi*, Elisha's cry at the ascent of Elijah in a chariot of fire (II Kings ii 12) or the forlorn words *'eli 'eli* of Ps. xxii. Interjections are repeated as in Amos' *ho ho*, "alas, alas!" (v 16), or Ezekiel's *'oi 'oi*, "woe, woe!" (xvi 23), or the psalmist's *he'ah he'ah*, "aha, aha!" (lxx 4). Not unrelated to the foregoing discussion is the vast area of assonance in its many varied forms, of euphony and cacophony, of alliteration and the prevalence of single sounds throughout a context to express the mood and temper of the passage [1]). An outstanding example is the confessional lament of Isa. liii 1-9, another classic of iterative composition.

The foregoing discussion has dealt with what we may call elemental or primitive iteration, the kind of language which is used spontaneously in moments of excitement or urgency. Many other types might be adduced, but we shall now turn to an aspect of repetition which has so far received less than sufficient observation. We refer to the relation of repetition to the literary forms of the Old

---

1 IGNAZ GABOR, *Der Hebräische Urrhythmus*, BZAW 52 (1929). GABOR believes that the masoretic accentuation has obscured the original stresses, that originally the tone fell not on the last but the first syllable. For an assessment of this view, see O. S. RANKIN, "*Alliteration in Hebrew Poetry*", JTS 31 (1930), pp. 285-291.

Testament. If we were to include within our inquiry words, phrases, and sentences which are synonymous, the evidence for the relationship would be very impressive indeed. But we restrict ourselves almost exclusively to repetition in the narrower sense. A good example, though not necessarily the most felicitous, is the acrostic poem as it is found in the Book of Lamentations. The alphabetic arrangement of the successive verses would naturally encourage repetition, but the phenomenon penetrates much more deeply. And here we are confronted with a characteristic of Hebrew literature in general: wherever the writer shows any inclination to employ the iterative style he does so in a variety of ways, i.e., he uses repetition as a creative literary device. This is especially true of *Lamentations* where the repetitions are abundant and varied. Condamin suggested some years ago that the first two acrostic poems form a kind of concentric setting in such a manner that the same key-words appear in the first and last strophe, in the second and the second from the last, in the third and the third from the last, and so on. He encountered several exceptions to this form, but, interestingly enough, scholars had detected textual confusion in precisely those instances which did not conform to the rule [1]). What is notable about this ancient poetry is that such an artificial contrivance does not stand in the way of producing literature of a high order, in which the emotions find full expression and the language bodies forth the intensity and passion of the poet.

The Old Testament provides a number of instances where the verbal structure of a poem is completely conditioned by repetition. Most notable, of course, are Jotham's fable [2]) and Amos' oracles against the foreign nations [3]), but Job's great apologia [4]), and many of the passages in Ezekiel [5]), illustrate the same phenomenon. Jotham's fable has an interesting parallel in *Baal and Anath* where the general context appears to have many elements in common with the setting of *Judges* (e.g. Lebanon with its trees, the fire, food and drink for men and gods, etc.) [6]). It is worth observing that the pattern of

[1]) ALBERT CONDAMIN, "Symmetrical Repetitions in *Lamentations* Chapters I and II", JTS 7 (1906), pp. 137-140.

[2]) Judges ix 8-15. [3]) Amos i-ii. [4]) Job xxxi.

[5]) For example, Ezek. xiv 12-30; xviii 5 ff.; 25. Note also the elaborate "because ... therefore" constructions.

[6]) H. L. GINSBERG (JAMES B. PRITCHARD, *Ancient Near Eastern Texts Relating to the Old Testament*, p. 140a) renders the inscription, unfortunately only partially preserved, as follows:

the Ugaritic poem is similarly determined by repetition, as, to be sure, are many other contexts in the Ugaritic literature. Jotham's fable is the most perfect and detailed of all biblical iterative poems.

The presence of refrains sometimes serves to articulate the structure of a poem, most notably in such instances as Pss. xlii-xliii, xlvi, cvii, cxxxvi, Isa. ix 8-x 4, v 25-30; Amos iv 6-11 [1]). Sometimes the last line of the poem repeats the opening as in the eighth psalm. Similarly the last line of the Nikkal poem from Ugarit practically repeats the beginning [2]). In many instances the key-word of the opening line or introduction is repeated at the close [3]). More important is the repetition of central key-words throughout a poem. There are many examples of this phenomenon. A noteworthy example is the poem contained in Jer. iii 1-iv 4. After the prose additions,

---

"Hark, Lady A(sherah of the S)ea
Give one of thy s(ons I'll make king."
Quoth Lady Asherah of the Sea:
"Why, let's make Yadi' Yalhan king."
Answered kindly One EL Benign:
"Too weakly, He can't race with Baal,
Throw jav'lin with Dagon's Son Glory-Crown!"

Replied Lady Asherah of the Sea:
"Well, let's make it Ashtar the Tyrant;
Let Ashtar the Tyrant be king."
Straightway Ashtar the Tyrant
Goes up to the *Fastness* of Zaphon
(And) sits on Baal Puissant's throne.
(But) his feet reach not down to the footstool,
Nor his head reaches up to the top.
So Ashtar the Tyrant declares:
"I'll not reign in Zaphon's *Fastness*!"
Down goes Ashtar the Tyrant,
Down from the throne of Baal Puissant,
And reigns in El's Earth, all of it.

[1]) Note also the use of refrains in Pss. xxxix 5d and 11c (Heb. 6 and 12); xlix 12 and 20 (Heb. 13 and 21); lvii 5 and 11 (Heb. 6 and 12); lxvii 3 and 5 (Heb. 4 and 6).

[2]) ALBRECHT GOETZE, "The Nikkal Poem from Ras Shamra", *JBL* LX, pp. 353-373. Observe the characteristic hymnic opening, common both in ancient Near Eastern and Western poetry:

"Let me praise and exalt Hirihbi."

For other discussions of the poem, see C. H. GORDON in *BASOR*, 65 (1937), pp. 29-33; H. L. GINSBERG in *Orientalia*, N. F. viii (1939), pp. 317-327.

[3]) Compare Pss. i 1bc and 6b; xx 1a and 10b; lxvii 1a and 7a; xcvii 1 and 12; ciii 1-2 and 20-22; cvi 1a and 48d; cxi 1a and 9c (cf. cvi supra and also cxvii; cxlvi-cl); cxviii 1 and 29; cxxxv 1-2 and 19-21; cxxxvi 1 and 26; cxxxix 1-3 and 23-24; cxlv 1 and 26.

generally recognized as secondary, have been excised, we have ten strophes, three series of three strophes each (iii 1, 2-3b, 3c-5; 12b-13, 19-20, 21-22; 23-24, 25-26, iv 1-2) followed by a most impressive climax to the whole (iv 3-4). The strophic construction here is especially well marked by the characteristic opening and concluding formules. But what gives the poem its unity and determines its progress is the verb שׁוּב and the noun מְשֻׁבָה. Thus the first three strophes open with a dual reference: *shall return to her again* (ld) *and would you return to me* ? (lh), the second three open with the appeal, *Return*, *apostate Israel* (12b) שֻׁבָה מְשֻׁבָה and end, *Return*, *apostate sons*, *I will heal your apostasies* (22a) שׁוּבוּ בָנִים שׁוֹבָבִים אֶרְפָּה מְשׁוּבֹתֵיכֶם, while the third strophe of the third series reads, *If thou return*, *O Israel*, *oracle of Yahweh*, *return to me* (iv 1ab). The poem is fused into a whole by the repetition of other words also, above all perhaps by the iteration of Yahweh, Yahweh our God, Yahweh thy God, but others also. Psalm cxxxix is another excellent example where the verb ידע dominates the opening and closing lines. Psalm lxxxix is rich in many key-words: *steadfast love* (lxxxix 1a, 2a, 14b, 24a, 28a, 33a, 49a), *faithfulness* (1b, 2b, 5b, 8c, 33b, 49b. cf. 28b), *the throne of David* (4b, 14a, 29, 36, 44), *David my servant* (3b, 20a. cf. 35b, 49b and 50a), *anoint* (20a, 38b, 51b), *covenant* (3a, 28b, 34a, 39a), the reference to the primeval sea (9-10, 25).

Perhaps no poem in the whole Old Testament more rewards examination from the point of view of the art of repetition than the Song of Deborah [1]). Here the primitive characteristics of repetition, which arise from the depths of the soul deeply aroused and completely liberated in an outburst of uninhibited emotion, come to superb expression; yet it must be recognized that, despite its exultancy and passion, it is nevertheless a masterpiece of literary form and structure [2]). Other Hebrew poems achieve great elevation and

---

[1]) The literature on the subject is vast. See *inter alia* JULIAN MORGENSTERN, *JQR*, IX (1919), pp. 359-369; C. F. BURNEY, *The Book of Judges* (London, 1920), pp. 78 ff.; W. F. ALBRIGHT, *JPOS* I (1922), pp. 68-83; *BASOR*. No 62, pp. 26-31, esp. 30-31; DUNCAN BLACK MACDONALD, *The Hebrew Literary Genius* (Princeton, 1933), pp. 16-19; ERNST SELLIN, "Das Deboralied", *Festschrift Otto Procksch* (Leipzig, 1934), pp. 148-166; MARTIN BUBER, *The Prophetic Faith* (New York, 1949), pp. 8-12; GILLIS GERLEMAN, "The Song of Deborah in the Light of Stylistics", *Vetus Testamentum*, I, No. 3 (July, 1951), pp. 168-180.

[2]) Cf. DUNCAN BLACK MACDONALD, *ibid.*, p. 18: "This song may seem to us disjointed, but it was not, is not so in reality." In the light of the many Canaanite parallels in Ugaritic literature, however, the structure is now susceptible of

power through the art of repetition. The twenty-ninth psalm is all repetition, the seven-fold *qol Yahweh* as well as the impressive opening with its three-fold *habu la-Yahweh*, and its moving finale raising it to the level of sublimity. Equally impressive, though in quite a different manner, is Jeremiah's vision of chaos in iv 23-26.

The one word used above all others in biblical poetry is the divine name. As we should expect it appears most frequently at the beginning and end of poems, but in other cases it is repeated frequently throughout the whole of the composition. In such a short psalm as the sixth, Yahweh appears eight times; in the seventh the divine name occurs thirteen times but in a variety of usages: my God, thou righteous God, Yahweh Elyon, Yahweh my God (*bis*), Yahweh (four times), God (four times). This diversity of usage is characteristic of scores of Old Testament poems, especially of those literary types like the hymn and lament where the mood is impassioned and intense. The poet exhausts every resource of speech to address his God. As a true Israelite, he lives in a name relation to his God. Yahweh has communicated his name to his people, and he has given Israel her name. The interior psychic reality of dialog in which the egocentric boundaries are overcome are concretized in the name relationship [1]). So it is not surprising that in many poems *Yahweh* and *Israel* become not only the central key-words but also determine the structural patterns of the poem, as, for example, in the Song of Deborah [2]) and Ps. cxxxv [3]). This psychic rapport embodied in names is illustrated in Ps. cxxxii by the proper names, Yahweh and David.

In recent years we have come to recognize the place of repetitive parallelism. Attention has been drawn particularly to its presence in the tristich or tricola [4]). But this repetitive parallelism is much

---

better understanding. Note also MACDONALD, p. 19: "Hebrew poetry was all under impulse and the Hebrew poet could not rule and control his form." On the contrary, it is the genius of much biblical poetry that with all the spontaneity and excitement of mood which characterizes it the presence of form is perceptible. See especially ALBRIGHT's rendering in *JPOS* I, pp. 68-83, where the structural features of the poem are clearly evident.

1) JOHANNES PEDERSEN, *Israel, its Life and Culture*, I-II, pp. 244-259.

2) MARTIN BUBER, *The Prophetic Faith*, pp. 9-10.

3) Compare *inter alia* Ps. cxxx.

4) H. L. GINSBERG, "The Rebellion and Death of Ba'lu", *Orientalia* V (1936), pp. 161-198; W. F. ALBRIGHT, "The Psalm of Habakkuk", *Studies in Old Testament Prophecy*, edited by H. H. ROWLEY (Edinburgh, 1950), pp. 1-18; JOHN HASTINGS PATTON, *Canaanite Parallels in the Book of Psalms* (Baltimore, 1944), pp. 5-11.

more extensive and diverse. The profuse employment of this literary device and its great variety mark it as a major stylistic feature of biblical poetry. The following patterns are illustrative:

a b / a c	Exod. xv 3
a b c d / a b e f	xv 6
a b c / a b d	xv 6cd, cf. Ps. lxvii 3 (Heb. 4); lxvii 5 (Heb. 6)
	Ps. lxxvii 17; xcii 10; xiv 1
a b a / a c a	Ps. xlvii 6 (Heb. 7)
a b c / d e f	Ps. ciii 1. Cf. also Ps. cxxiv 1bc, 2ab.
a b c / g h i	
a b c	Ps. ciii 20a
a b d	21a
a b e	22a
a f b	22c
a b c d / a b e f	Ps. xcvi 1-2
a b c d / a b e f / a b e g	Ps. xcvi 7-8. Cf. xxix.
a b c d / a f c d / a g c d	Ps. cxxxv 19-20.

Of the many stylistic comments that emerge from a scrutiny of these and other examples, we confine ourselves to these two: (1) the members of the series tend to focus upon the final member, (2) often the member which follows the series and breaks the repetitive sequence gives point and force to the whole series. The most obvious example, of course, is the last psalm, where the effect is almost overwhelming in its climax, "Let everything that has breath praise Yahweh!"

We turn now to the place of repetition in the strophic structure of Hebrew poetry. There are a number of examples where successive strophes begin with the same emphatic construction such as the imperative in Ps. xxxvii 1, 3, 5, 7, 8: *fret*, *trust*, *commit*, *be still*, *refrain* or the same key-word is repeated:

Thy steadfast love, O Yahweh, extends to the heavens xxxvi 5a
How precious is thy steadfast love, O God 7a
O continue thy steadfast love to those who know thee 10a

Or strophes may end in similar fashion as we have seen in the refrains, but it must also be recognized that the same key-words sometimes appear at the close of successive strophes. Again, beginning and end sometimes show correspondence [1]). Very interesting are the

[1]) E.g. Gen. xlix 22a and 26d; Pss. lxvi 2 and 4bc; cxxxiv 1a, 2b; Amos v 18 and 20; viii 9a and 10 f.; ix 5 and 6.

numerous instances where a new strophe takes up the major key-word of the previous strophe, as, for example, when the first line repeats the key-word of the last line before. Note the following [1]):

> Our feet have been standing
> within your gates, O Jerusalem!
> Jerusalem, built as a city ... Ps. cxxii 2b and 3a
> Blessed are those who dwell in thy house
> Blessed are the men whose strength is in thee. Ps. lxxxiv 4a, 5a.

We have a number of cases where strophes are connected with the presence of a single key-word or expression in successive or nearly successive strophes: *ḥesed* "steadfast love" (xxxvi 5-6, 7-9, 10-12) or *rashʿa* or *rᵉshaʿim* "the wicked" (xxxvii 10-11, 12-13, 14-15, 16-17, 20, 21-22, 32-33, 35-36, 39-40). But the most impressive and interesting of all is the repetition of single words or phrases within the strophe, usually three times in which the third member characteristically receives the stress, thus preserving the emphasis and intensity so characteristic of repetition in its primitive forms [2]). The most familiar example is Ps. cxxi 7-8:

> Yahweh will keep you from all evil;
> he will keep your life.
> Yahweh will keep your going out and your coming in
> from now and forevermore.

A stylistically superior example is Ps. cxxxix 11-12:

> If I say, "Let only darkness cover me
> and light about me be night,"
> Even darkness is not too dark to thee,
> the night is light like the day,
> as the darkness, so the light.

One more example notable for its rhetorical felicity:

> O mighty mountain (lit. "mountain of God"), O mount Bashan!
> O many-peaked mountain, O mount of Bashan!
> Why, O many-peaked mountain, do you envy
> the mountain God desired for his abode,
> yea, where Yahweh will dwell forever? Ps. lxviii 15-16, Heb. 16-17)

---

[1]) See also Pss. cxxviii 4, 5; cxxxii 10, 11; Isa. xliv 28d and xlv 1a.

[2]) Gen xlix 22-26 (the blessing of Joseph, a model of Hebrew repetitive style); Is. xli 41-43; xlii 1-4 (note the strong emphasis on *mishpat*); lx 1-3 (three-fold repetition of "dawn" and "light" noun and verb forms); 4-5, 19-20 ("your light, your everlasting light, your everlasting light" cf. lx 1-3); Zeph. i 7, 14-16 (*yom* repeated ten times); Pss. lxviii 1-3 (Heb. 2-4), 19-21 (Heb. 20-22); lxxxii 1-4; cxxiii 1-2; cxxxiv; cxxxv 19-21.

Perhaps a more convincing approach to an examination and evaluation of the repetitive style in ancient Hebrew rhetoric would be to subject the individual poems to analysis. Such an undertaking would reveal the importance of this literary method not only for an evaluation of the Hebrew temperament and literary manner but also for hermeneutics. The words must be allowed to have their own way with the reader. The supreme exemplar of the Hebrew repetitive style is Second Isaiah, and nowhere is the sheer artistry of this style exhibited more happily and impressively than in his great poems. The first two poems (xl 1-11 and xl 12-31) are masterpieces of iterative utterance [1]). The third poem, too, achieves the same high level, but in a somewhat different fashion. The finale of the poem reads: למשפט נקרבה יחדו. Then Yahweh presents the content of his *rib* with the nations (vss. 2-4). The nations *fear* and *tremble*; each man *helps* his neighbor in making an image, and says to his neighbor, "Be strong" (חֲזָק) or, as usually rendered, "take courage". So the craftsman *encourages* (וַיְחַזֵּק) the goldsmith, and they *fasten* (וַיְחַזְּקֵהוּ) it with nails so that it cannot be moved. Thus the three verbs which are given great stress are ירא, חזק, עזר. Then comes the finale to the first triad of strophes, and it is precisely these three verbs which receive the burden of the poet's thought:

> But thou, Israel, my servant,
>   Jacob, whom I have chosen,
>   offspring of Abraham, my friend;
> whom I took (הֶחֱזַקְתִּיךָ) from the ends of the earth,
>   and called from its remote regions;
>   to whom I said, "You are my servant,

---

[1]) SIGMUND MOWINCKEL ("*Die Komposition des deuterojesanischen Buches*", *ZAW* 49 [1931], pp. 87-112, 242-260) views the present ordering of the book as the work of the compiler of the poems. The *Stichworte* are understood by him to provide the clue for the ordering. "Der Sammler kann selbstverständlich nach einem gewissen Plan gearbeitet und gewisse Gesichtspunkte für die Ordnung der Einzelstücke gehabt haben. — Es soll daher der Versuch gemacht werden, das Sammlungs- oder vielleicht besser: Anreihungsprinzip des Sammlers aufzuzeigen." The difficulty with this view of an external ordering is that it does not recognize the genuine lines of continuity which persist from poem to poem nor the ordered structure of the whole. Moreover, the reduction of the poems to a collection of small pieces or fragments ignores the strophic structure of the poems and the relation of key-words to the literary structure. To be sure, these key-words sometimes pass beyond the limits of the individual poems, but in each case it is apparent that they are employed as a transitional device explicable only on the assumption that it is the work of the original writer and not the compiler.

I have chosen you and not cast you off";
fear not (אַל תִּירָא), for I am with you,
be not dismayed, for I am your God;
I will strengthen you, I will help you (עֲזַרְתִּיךָ),
I will uphold you with my victorious right hand. xli 8-10.

The second triad of strophes (vss. 11-13, 14-16, 17-20) develops these three verbs, by repetition, by solemn and climactic divine self-asseveration [1]), by a lyrical song (vss. 17-20), vivid imagery (e.g. the threshing sledge), and by various emphatic particles. But then, quite remarkably, the trial scene is repeated, repeated with greater urgency and intensity, but the issue is, of course, precisely the same, i.e., the nations' response to Yahweh's historical *rib*, and the outcome is the same. It is to be noted that the sequence of the first two triads is exactly the same, and this is also true of the third except that the chapter ends with the judgment of the nations in the second member of the third division of the poem. But is this likely? If we assume this to be the case, the structure is destroyed, for we naturally expect a third strophe to compare with the other triads (and there are other poems in the Old Testament of three triads of three strophes each!). Moreover, content also demands a reference to the Servant of the Lord as in the climax of vss. 8-11.

Again, a purely literary examination of xlii 1-4 reveals that it has essentially the same style as xli 8-10, but more important it brings the whole motif of judgment, perfectly stated in the opening strophe, to a triumphant culmination. It opens with the climactic *hen* (cf. 24a and 29a), then continues, line upon inevitable line, to describe the judgment in language which is now recognized as coming from the court of law [2]). Observe how every climax of the strophe falls on *mishpat*, thus the end links with the beginning to make of the poem the magnificently ordered composition that it is:

---

[1]) Cf. e.g. vs. 13. כי אני יהוה אלהיך מחזיק ימינך
האמר לך אל-תירא אני עזרתיך

[2]) Joachim Begrich, *Studien zu Deuterojesaja*, pp. 134-137; Sidney Smith, *Isaiah Chapters XL-LV*, pp. 54-57, 164 and note 25-32; Joh. Lindblom, *The Servant Songs in Deutero-Isaiah* (Lund, 1951), pp. 14-18. See also Ludwig Köhler, *Die hebräische Rechtsgemeinde*. Jahresbericht der Universität Zurich, 1930/1931. Compare also Duhm's words in his commentary (1922), p. 312 where he points out that *mishpat* like the Arabic *din* is the judicial authority and exercise of justice of the people of God, the sum of the beneficent institutions of the people of Yahweh. *Mishpat*, he says, is related to the *mishpatim* of Deut. xxi as *ha-torah* is to *torah*.

Behold, my servant, whom I uphold,
  my chosen, in whom I delight,
I have put my spirit upon him,
  he will bring forth *mishpat* to the nations.
He will not cry or lift his voice,
  or make it heard in the street;
A bruised reed he will not break,
  and a dimly burning wick he will not quench;
  he will faithfully bring forth *mishpat*.
He will not fail or be discouraged
  till he has established *mishpat* in the earth;
  and the coastlands wait for his law.

The significance and function of xlii 1-4 thus become crucial. They become even more crucial when it is understood, as it usually is not, that by every canon of literary form xlii 5 must begin a new poem. The usual arguments for the excision of the so-called Servant song are familiar and well worn, but recent scholarly inquiry has made it more and more likely that all the Servant songs are related to their contexts. Excision raises more difficulties than it solves as the history of Second Isaiah study makes eloquently clear. The only plausible solution, then, on the basis of literary form, in which the repetitive style has been of major service, is that xlii 1-4 belongs inextricably with the whole of chapter xli. It need only be added that when this is done, the major continuity of the poems begins to appear in fresh light and the prophet achieves a stature commensurate with his stature as Israel's profoundest theologian and supreme master in the art of literary composition.

AUTELS ET INSTALLATIONS CULTUELLES A MARI

PAR

ANDRÉ PARROT

Paris

C'est à la suggestion de Monsieur l'Abbé Cazelles que le titre de cette communication a été choisi et je suis très sensible à l'honneur qui m'a été fait par les organisateurs de ce Congrès, désireux d'associer ainsi archéologie mésopotamienne et certaines conceptions rituelles de l'Ancien Testament. Je leur en exprime toute ma sincère gratitude.

Quelques mots légitimeront, si nécessaire, et mon acceptation et le choix du sujet. L'exploration de Mari, commencée en 1933 et actuellement toujours en cours, après vingt ans, a révélé un habitat sémite, de première importance, fixé sur les bords du Moyen-Euphrate et dont l'histoire peut dès maintenant être retracée et illustrée, de l'an 3 000 av. J.C. à la ruine de cette ville, sous les coups de Hammurabi, roi de Babylone, au XVIIIe s. av. J.C. Des milliers de textes, en cours de déchiffrement, ont fait connaître ce que Goetze a pu appeler „l'âge de Mari" et tous les orientalistes préoccupés d'exégèse d'Ancien Testament ont rapidement entrevu quelle lumière cette documentation épigraphique peut en particulier jeter sur la période patriarcale. Je n'en veux pour preuve que ce qu'en ont déjà écrit, entre autres, nos collègues Albright, Rowley, Schmökel, Böhl, Noth et si j'en ai oublié, je les prie de m'excuser. Tous puisent ou ont puisé dans la bibliothèque de Zimri-Lim qui n'a pas encore révélé tous ses secrets, malgré toute l'activité des déchiffreurs que dirige M. le professeur G. Dossin. Mais Mari ne nous a pas livré que des textes. Nombreux sont les monuments ramenés au jour et parmi eux plusieurs sanctuaires, avec des installations cultuelles dont l'intérêt est tout aussi évident non seulement pour l'étude de la religion mésopotamienne, mais aussi puisqu'il s'agit de Sémites, pour la meilleure connaissance et peut-être la plus exacte compréhension, de certains traits cultuels et rituels des plus hautes époques de l'Ancien Testament. Comment étaient aménagés les sanctuaires sémitiques de Mari, de quelles installations étaient-ils pourvus? C'est ce que maintenant je me propose de préciser sommairement.

Les sanctuaires dégagés à Mari appartiennent à la grande période de la ville, celle qui s'étend du début du IIIe millénaire au XVIIIe siècle av. J.C. Tous avaient plus ou moins souffert des ravages et des destructions, résultat des guerres nombreuses, soutenues par la cité contre des ennemis successifs. Rien n'a jamais pu être retrouvé intact, mais l'architecture peut cependant être appréciée à sa juste valeur et la plupart du temps être interprétée avec la plus grande probabilité, sinon bien souvent avec certitude.

On sait, d'après une tablette de l'époque de Zimri-Lim (XVIIIe s. av. J.C.) qu'il y avait à Mari, 25 temples (G. Dossin, *Le panthéon de Mari*, dans *Studia Mariana*, pp. 40-50). Jusqu'ici, nous n'en avons identifié avec certitude que quatre: ceux dédiés respectivement à Ishtar, Dagan, Ninhursag et Ishtarat; avec probabilité, qu'un seul: celui consacré à Shamash. Il en reste donc vingt et si les divinités de l'époque de Hammurabi n'ont fait que prendre la succession de celles qui les précédaient, localement et nommément, aux divers emplacements de la ville, plusieurs peuvent s'abriter dans des sanctuaires, demeurés jusqu'ici „anonymes", mais déjà dégagés et riches d'enseignement. Il va de soi que nous nous en servirons pour le présent exposé qui s'appuie donc sur les constations faites dans une dizaine des sanctuaires de la ville royale.

Nous constatons tout d'abord, une certaine permanence dans la localisation, nous voulons dire que la divinité peut être adorée pendant quelque mille ans au moins, au même emplacement. Cette permanence du lieu saint ne saurait étonner. Elle est courante en histoire des religions où les saints ont remplacé les dieux. Nous notons ensuite que les rites sont reproduits, pendant des siècles en tout cas, sinon des millénaires, à ce qu'il apparaît sans modifications sensibles, car, à travers les niveaux superposés les installations rituelles se recouvrent, inchangées. Ceci aussi n'étonne pas, car il n'y a rien de plus conservatrice que la liturgie. Cette double constation a été faite au cours du déblaiement du temple d'Ishtar, découvert en 1934 et où nous avons travaillé pendant quatre ans.

Dès l'époque des premiers rois de Mari, à celle de Zimri-Lim, nous avons pu à cet endroit compter cinq sanctuaires superposés. Si, du dernier, il restait trop peu pour qu'on puisse avoir une idée suffisamment nette de ses installations rituelles, il n'en était pas de même de ceux qui le précédaient dans le temps. Remarquons tout d'abord cette distribution essentielle entre cour et cella. Dans la première, à ciel ouvert, on trouve tous les éléments du culte: autel à combustion, vasque à libation, table d'offrande, puits (ou réserve d'eau) (*Syria*, 1936, pp. 15-17). Dans la seconde, il semble qu'on n'ait jamais immolé, mais seulement déposé les statuettes en ex-voto sur les banquettes. En outre, un rite essentiel est documenté par l'enfouissement de réceptacles (que nous avons appelé "Barcasses" pour tenir compte de leur forme curieuse), soit dans le sous-sol, soit à l'intérieur d'une table de terre recouverte d'un revêtement de plâtre. C'est ainsi que dans la cella 17 du temple d'Ishtar, 3 tables retrouvées superposées (et correspondant à trois périodes différentes), contenaient 7 barcasses de terre cuite, cependant que 10 autres récipients identiques, affleuraient au niveau des sols. Ce rite était considéré comme d'une extrême importance car les barcasses réapparurent dans la cella 18 comme aussi à un certain niveau de la cour du temple (niveau C), où la porte donnant accès à la salle, s'encadrait de 7 récipients, cinq à droite, deux à gauche. Immolation d'une part, libation de l'autre, ces deux rites sont ainsi attestés, dans le sanctuaire d'Ishtar au IIIe millénaire av. J.C. et l'on peut ajouter que l'immolation s'accompagne de combustion, dans la cour du même temple.

Le même rite de l'enfouissement des barcasses se trouve ailleurs à Mari. Tout au moins, nous avons constaté à la base d'un autel (dans un temple proche de la ziggurat archaïque („Massif rouge"), l'aménagement d'une petite vasque. De même aussi à la base d'un portail du sanctuaire présargonique de Shamash (P. 25) découvert en novembre 1952, deux cavités allongées avaient été aussi creusées. Ici et là, nous estimons qu'il s'agit toujours de libation, forme bien connue du rite sacrificiel dans le culte sémitique. Est-il nécessaire de rappeler en Israël la libation faite à Mitspa, devant Yahvé? (I Samuel vii 6).

Le deuxième sanctuaire riche en observations fut à Mari, celui dédié à Dagan. L'identification a été établie grâce à trois dépôts de fondation retrouvés *in situ*, consacrés au „dieu, roi du pays". Cette périphrase caractérise ainsi que l'a reconnu M. Dossin, Dagan, dieu majeur de toute la région du Moyen-Euphrate, dont le sanctuaire principal se trouvait cependant à Tirqa, ainsi que l'indiquent explicitement les Archives Royales. Ce sanctuaire était célèbre (la correspondance de Kibri-Dagan est précise à cet égard, qui a été publiée par M. Kupper, *ARM*, III [1]). Le temple de Dagan à Mari était

[1]) Voir aussi la tablette commentée par M. Dossin, dans *RA*, XLII (1948), pp. 125-134 et l'étude de Dhorme, dans *Recueil Edouard Dhorme*, pp. 745-754.

lui aussi en grande vénération. D'après les dépôts, il date du début du IIe millénaire av. J.C. et toutes ses installations lui confèrent une très grande originalité.

Distinguons pour la description des aménagements, extérieur et intérieur. Le temple de Dagan était précédé par une importante esplanade divisée en deux parties par un muret transversal. Dans le secteur le plus éloigné du sanctuaire et sous une sorte de portique, dix bases de pierre étaient disposées, où l'on perçoit une sorte d'alignement. Deux des bases étaient creusées, ce qui leur donnait au premier abord un aspect de cuve, mais après examen nous avons considéré que chacune des bases évidées, risquaient fort d'être le support d'une *masseba*. En effet, nous avons ramassé en grande quantité, tout alentour, les morceaux de gigantesques blocs de pierre basaltique, qui furent travaillés et même polis, mais où l'on ne retrouve jamais trace de sculpture figurée. Une autre base, avec une double mortaise, apparaît avoir elle aussi supporté une stèle ou une statue monumentale. Une dernière, enfin, était ornementée sur ses quatre faces, du thème bien connu des imbrications figurant deux montagnes, avec au centre et comme au coeur d'une vallée, le palmier planté.

La deuxième partie de l'esplanade, celle toute proche du sanctuaire, présentait toute une série d'aménagements d'une extrême importance pour l'histoire du culte. De part et d'autre de la porte du temple, nous avons retrouvé *in situ*, de grands blocs de pierre, creusés de larges cupules et de trous rectangulaires qui contenaient encore des débris de bois décomposé. Nous pensons que nous avons là une indication très nette: il y aurait eu deux *asherîm* dressés de part et d'autre du portail du sanctuaire et sur des autels de pierre, réservés aux libations (les cupules l'expliquent nettement). Ce trait est, à notre sens, d'importance, car on retrouve cette même indication dans le rituel cananéen, à l'époque des Juges. Il nous est en effet raconté que Gédéon abattit l'*ashera* qui était *sur* l'autel consacré à Baal (*Juges* vi 25). Nous estimons donc que c'est à tort que la Bible du Centenaire a traduit par „à côté" de l'autel, l'indication formelle (*'al*) du texte hébraïque. A proximité immédiate des autels, nous avons relevé des tables, faites soit de dalles de gypse sensiblement carrées, soit de matériaux disparates (pierres et briques cuites) recouverts d'une couche de bitume. Tables d'offrandes, lieux d'immolation des victimes, sans nul doute, car sur une de ces tables, nous avons ramassé une énorme cuve en céramique, ornée de deux magnifiques serpents aux corps enroulés. Cette cuve était pleine à déborder, d'ossements d'animaux. Il est difficile de trouver une illustration plus suggestive du sacrifice d'immolation que plusieurs monuments viennent encore confirmer. En effet, dans ce secteur de la fouille, nous avons ramassé plusieurs sculptures, certaines d'un très grand art, représentant le fidèle ou le prêtre, tenant des deux mains plaquées sur sa poitrine, l'animal, bélier ou chevreau, qu'il apportait à l'autel. La tablette du Palais à laquelle nous faisions allusion précédemment, détaillant les sacrifices offerts dans „la totalité des temples" de Mari, indiquait le chiffre de 87 moutons indispensables pour satisfaire les 25 divinités du panthéon mariote. L'intérieur du temple de Dagan, gardé on le sait par une meute de lions en bronze, était fait d'une salle oblongue, avec, adossés à certaines parois, des lits ou des autels. Il est difficile de proposer une interprétation sûre, en face de ces aménagements en briques crues, qui s'ornementent par devant, de pilastres en légère saillie. Les dimensions considérables (3, 25 × 1, 15 × 1, 13; 3, 10 × 1, 52 × 1, 15; 5, 55 × 1, 70 × 1, 35), le fait que des installations sacrificielles très complètes ont été, nous l'avons dit, reconnues à l'extérieur, tout nous incite à proposer plutôt de reconnaître des lits, soit pour l'hiérogamie, soit pour l'incubation. Pour l'une et l'autre formes cultuelles, nous disposons, on le sait, d'une base épigraphique solide et éprouvée et il nous apparaît très vraisemblable que le temple de Dagan fut spécialement affecté à l'un ou à l'autre, voire même à l'un et à l'autre de ces rites. En ce qui concerne l'incubation, rappelons simplement, le récit bien connu de Samuel dans le temple de Silo (I *Samuel* iii).

La troisième source d'information nous est, à Mari, fournie par ce que nous avons dû, faute de documents écrits, appeler jusqu'ici les „temples anonymes" (*Syria*, 1940, p. 8 et sq.) ou „inférieurs", car ils sont apparus sous l'esplanade du sanctuaire de Dagan. Il s'agit d'un complexe architectural, encore imposant malgré sa mutilation où des aménagements nouveaux apparaissent. Un majestueux portail à redents multiples, est encadré d'autels de terre — ici il ne semble pas y avoir de doute — ornementés en façade, de pilastres et de rentrants teintés en bitume. Dans la cour qui précédait le sanctuaire et adossé au mur d'une chapelle, d'autres autels étaient encore disposés, avec ce détail caractéristique que leur face supérieure présentait un ressaut, de même qu'aujourd'hui encore sur les autels du culte chrétien, un degré supporte tabernacle, crucifix, croix et cierges.

Il y a plus. A côté de ces autels, deux blocs de briques crues avec décrochement latéral, supportaient certainement des statues. En effet, nous avons retrouvé, encore enchassées, deux bases de statues. La petite base présentait encore, en avant d'un trou de mortaise rectangulaire, deux pieds posés à plat. La statue était donc fixée à part grâce à un tenon. La deuxième base, plus grande, offrait une cavité d'encastrement irrégulière, des coins de pierre scellés au bitume, rétrécissant le logement. Ces deux bases impliquent donc deux statues divines, non retrouvées par nous, mais où l'on peut raisonnablement reconnaître l'image du dieu et de la déesse parèdre (les pieds assez étroits suggèrent en effet une divinité féminine).

D'autres installations furent encore dégagées dans le même complexe, où nous avons pu reconnaître une table à pente très accentuée (pour les immolations?) et à nouveau un foyer (pierre, briques crues et briques cuites). A signaler enfin, tout au long d'une façade, une banquette étroite de part et d'autre d'un nouvel autel d'un style différent du précédent: il est construit en briques crues, posées sur un étroit socle en briques cuites, placé lui-même sur un socle plus développé en briques crues (pour tout ceci, *Syria*, 1940, pp. 8-13).

A ces installations toutes repérées dans une cour à ciel ouvert, qui attestent par conséquent que la divinité recevait un culte à l'extérieur de sa maison, il convient d'ajouter les aménagements intérieurs: ce sont à nouveau des autels en briques crues, à face supérieure lisse et sans ressaut (et ce trait les différencie nettement des autels extérieurs), dont le devant s'ornemente des mêmes pilastres alternant avec des évidements rectangulaires teintés en bitume. Une fois encore une double interprétation se présente: ou autels véritables ou lits d'incubation ou d'hiérogamie.

A cette documentation qui nous est fournie par l'architecture spécifiquement religieuse de Mari, il convient d'ajouter celle que nous avons pu recueillir dans deux salles au moins du Palais de Mari, puisque l'immense résidence royale (détruite vers 1750 av. J.C.) comptait certainement plusieurs chapelles. Le regretté ADOLPHE LODS avait signalé naguère (*La religion d'Israël*, p. 93), qu'à Jérusalem et à l'époque de Salomon „le temple était avant tout, la chapelle du Palais, analogue à celle que les rois de Mari avaient aménagée dans leur demeure". En réalité, le palais de Mari renfermait plus qu'une chapelle.

En effet, dans la salle 64 qui ouvre par un large portail sur la cour 106, on apercevait dans l'axe de la baie, un élégant podium (H: 0,92; long.: 2,23: larg.: 2, 11). On y accédait de chaque côté par un escalier de trois marches. Le tout est en briques crues (sauf la face supérieure qui, en partie, était faite de longues dalles de pierre), avec un revêtement de plâtre, Un baldaquin dont il restait la marque de deux supports antérieurs, recouvrait l'ensemble. Le dit podium était décoré sur sa face supérieure par huit panneaux simulant un faux marbre, avec un encadrement orné des thèmes de la spirale à enroulements multiples et des flammèches. Evoquait-on ainsi les cérémonies cultuelles de l'eau et du feu qu'une peinture (salle 132) figure explicitement (*Syria*, 1937, pl. XL), nous ne savons? De même, doit-on parler ici de podium, ou d'autel), encore une discrimination difficile à faire. Nous rappelons simplement qu'à quelques pas et au pied de cette installation fut ramassé le corps mutilé de la déesse au vase jaillissant et il serait assez plausible de considérer que cette divinité se trouvait ainsi surélevée face aux fidèles, massés dans la cour voisine (*Syria*, 1937, pp. 69-70; p. 328, pl. XXXVII). Toutefois cette localisation n'est pas définitivement assurée.

La deuxième installation cultuelle certaine retrouvée dans le Palais, se situe dans le sanctuaire privé (salles 149-150), qui, d'après les petites statues inscrites, fut dédié à Ishtar ou Inanna (Statue d'Idi-ilum, *Syria*, 1938, p. 17). Cet oratoire se composait de deux pièces, séparées l'une de l'autre par une porte de bois sculptée et incrustée de lamelles d'os. Nous avions naguère à son sujet (*Syria*, 1938, p. 13), parlé de *hekal* et de *debir*. Si l'on n'accepte pas cette terminologie, que nous utilisions, en référence avec le sanctuaire de Jérusalem, on constatera au moins la distribution bi-partie, en cella et ante-cella. Dans la cella (salle 150), on remarquait un podium bas (h.: 0,40), placé en angle et revêtu de plâtre. Ce podium en recouvrait un autre, appartenant à un état antérieur et beaucoup plus haut (h.: 0, 15). L'un et l'autre étaient en briques crues, avec revêtement de plâtre.

Telles sont les constations sommairement exposées, qu'il nous a été donné de faire à Mari, au cours de huit campagnes de fouilles. Nous allons à leur propos faire quelques brèves remarques. Dans un pays où la pierre est abondante (des carrières peuvent être ouvertes dans les falaises toutes proches), l'architecture est presque totalement en briques crues. Les pavements, les drains, les canalisations, sont généralement en briques cuites. Par contre, les fondations d'importants monuments peuvent être en dalles de gypse, de même que les tombeaux royaux ou princiers du début du IIIe millénaire (*Syria*,

1937, pl. VII, 2; 1938, pl. II, 1-2). Il n'en est que plus important de constater que la plupart des autels identifiés avec certitude, sont en briques crues, c'est-à-dire „en terre". Or précisément le livre de l'Alliance, indique explicitement que les Israélites doivent élever en terre leurs autels, pour y offrir à Yahvé holocaustes et sacrifices de paix, en menu et gros bétail (*Exode* xx 24). Quand des installations sacrificielles font intervenir la pierre (extérieur du temple de Dagan par exemple), il s'agit toujours de blocs soigneusement taillés. Ce qui expliquerait, en sens contraire cette fois, l'interdiction tout aussi explicite d'*Exode* xx 25, de ne pas porter le ciseau sur les pierres de l'autel. Il est assez curieux de constater aussi que dans l'unique cas où un podium-autel se présente avec escaliers (salle 64 du palais), ceux-ci sont sur le côté, comme si l'on avait voulu sauvegarder la pudeur des prêtres, à laquelle se réfère de même explicitement *Exode*, xx 26, qui interdit de monter à l'autel par des degrés.

Si le rituel retrouvé dans le Palais et qui se rapporte au culte d'Ishtar (*RA*, XXXV, pp. 1-13), mentionne des libations d'eau à côté de l'offrande en fine fleur de farine, tout ce qui a été recueilli sur l'esplanade du temple de Dagan, atteste des immolations et des sacrifices sanglants. La cuve pleine d'ossements, les nombreuses représentations de l'offrande du chevreau ou de la brebis, documentent tout aussi parfaitement „le menu et gros bétail" du même Livre de l'Alliance (*Exode* xx 24).

Tout aussi important à notre sens est la constatation faite que dans la capitale du Moyen-Euphrate, *masseba* et *ashera* sont dressés sur l'esplanade d'un sanctuaire où très vraisemblablement la divinité avait dû être adorée aussi sous une apparence humaine. La coexistence de cette double figuration de la divinité, ici sous les traits d'une statue, là sous l'aspect sommaire d'un poteau de bois ou d'un bloc de pierre, confirme s'il en était besoin tout ce que nous connaissons de la religion cananéenne, mais avec des monuments plus récents.

Il nous apparaît donc que la documentation archéologique recueillie à Mari, tout autant que la documentation épigraphique en cours de déchiffrement (Publications en traductions, sous le titre *Archives royales de Mari*, Paris, Imprimerie Nationale) est susceptible d'apporter une contribution intéressante dans l'étude religieuse du monde ouest-sémitique ancien, Canaan y compris. Ainsi aussi, certains textes de l'Ancien Testament, sans doute fixés littérairement à des dates tardives, se réfèrent à des réalités de beaucoup antérieures, réalités que l'archéologie permet désormais d'atteindre avec exactitude et de détailler avec les plus minutieuses garanties de certitude.

JOSEPHSGESCHICHTE UND ÄLTERE CHOKMA

VON

GERHARD VON RAD
Heidelberg

Die Josephsgeschichte ist in jeder Hinsicht von den Vätergeschichten, die sie fortsetzt, zu unterscheiden. Während sich die Abrahams- oder Jakobsgeschichten nahezu alle in den Grenzen eines Umfangs von 20 bis 30 Versen halten, erweist sich die Josephsgeschichte mit ihren nahezu 400 Versen schon äusserlich als ein Dokument, das gattungsgeschichtlich ganz anders zu beurteilen ist; denn ein „Sagenkranz", d.h. eine Aufreihung ehedem selbständiger Erzählungseinheiten, ist sie keinesfalls [1]). Erweitert man den Vergleich auf die inneren Wesensmerkmale, so werden die Unterschiede noch deutlicher: die Abrahams-, Isaaks- und Jakobsgeschichten sind orts- und kultgebundenes Sagengut, thematisch vom Jahwisten (oder schon früher) durch die Erzväterverheissung (Land, Nachkommenschaft) miteinander verklammert. Die Josephsgeschichte ist durch und durch novellistisch, ihr Erzählungsstoff ermangelt durchaus solcher genuiner Bindungen an lokale Haftpunkte [2]). Auch hinsichtlich ihrer literarischen Technik — etwa in der Schilderung komplizierter psychologischer Situationen, oder in der Einlage eines blitzenden Wortes in eine Szene — verfügt die Josephsgeschichte über Möglichkeiten, die über die der älteren Sage weit hinausgehen. In dieser Hinsicht steht sie der Geschichte von der Thronnachfolge Davids nahe (2 Sam. vi bis 1 Kön. ii), wie es denn keines Beweises bedarf, dass auch die Josephsgeschichte literaturgeschichtlich nicht vor der älteren Königszeit angesetzt werden kann.

Aber es lassen sich noch viel engere Verbindungslinien von der Josephsgeschichte zu der spezifischen Geistigkeit gerade dieser

---

[1]) Gegen GUNKEL, der bei der Analyse der Josephsgeschichte viel zu sehr von ihrem vermeintlichen Sagencharakter ausgegangen ist. Genesis pg. 395 ff.

[2]) Nur ganz am Rande in Gen. l 24 konnte die Verklammerung der Josephsgeschichte mit der Erzväterverheissung vollzogen werden. Diese Verklammerung ist in überlieferungsgeschichtlicher Hinsicht (nicht in literarischer!) sekundär. Die ursprünglich selbständige Josephsgeschichte kannte sie noch nicht.

Epoche ziehen. Schon GUNKEL hat an der Josephsgeschichte eine Freude am Fremdartigen wahrgenommen [1]), jenes aufgeklärte Interesse an den Bräuchen und Verhältnissen eines fernen Volkes, an dem Glanz des Pharaonenhofes, an der Installation eines Wesirs, an der Speicherung des Getreides, an der Mumifizierung der Leichen usw. Jene frühe Königszeit war eine Zeit des Abbruches vieler patriarchalischer Traditionen, aber zugleich die Zeit eines ganz neuen geistigen Aufbruches, eine Art Aufklärung, d.h. die Zeit eines Aufwachens des geistigen Selbstbewusstseins. Der Mensch wurde sich seiner geistigen Kräfte und seines ordnenden Verstandes bewusst, und ganz neue Dimensionen seiner Umwelt — äussere und innere! —, die der Glaube der Älteren noch gar nicht wahrgenommen hatte, traten in sein Blickfeld [2]).

Eine dieser neu ins Blickfeld getretenen Dimensionen, die uns aus der Literatur dieser Epoche besonders entgegentritt, ist das, was wir das Anthropologische nennen würden, d.h. eine Konzentration auf das Phänomen des Humanum im weitesten Sinne, auf seine Möglichkeiten und seine Grenzen, seine psychologische Kompliziertheit und seine Abgründigkeit. Ein Weiteres, das sich sofort damit verband, war die Erkenntnis, dass dieses Humanum gebildet und erzogen werden könne und müsse. Das war das grosse Anliegen, mit dem die ältere Weisheit hervortrat [3]). Solch eine Erziehung ist aber nicht möglich ohne ein vorhandenes Leitbild vom Menschen, ohne ein ganz bestimmtes Bildungsideal. Die ältere israelitische Weisheit hatte ein solches und hat es mit Emphase gelehrt. Wir wollen einige Züge davon nennen, denn unsere erste These ist, dass schon hinsichtlich dieses Bildungsideales zwischen der Josephsgeschichte und der älteren Weisheit enge Beziehungen bestehen.

Dass der ursprüngliche Sitz im Leben dieser älteren Weisheit der Hof ist und dass sie ihre vornehmlichste Aufgabe in der Heranziehung eines tüchtigen Beamtennachwuchses gesehen hat, bedarf keiner Erörterung. Auch Joseph ist Beamter, und er ist es geworden, indem er vor dem Pharao eine doppelte Kunst bewies, nämlich

---

[1]) H. GUNKEL, Gen. 397.

[2]) Auch rationale naturkundliche Interessen sind in dieser Zeit aufgewacht, A. ALT, *Die Weisheit Salomos*, ThLz. 1951, p. 139 ff.

[3]) Unter der älteren Weisheit sind die Sammlungen von Sentenzen zu verstehen, die aus der vorexilischen Königszeit stammen, also Prov. x 1 bis xxii 16; xxii 17 bis xxiv 22; xxv-xxix.

die der öffentlichen Rede und die des Ratgebens. Das aber ist genau das, worauf die Weisheitslehrer unablässig gedrungen haben. In entscheidenden Augenblicken gut reden zu können und in irgendwelchen Staatsangelegenheiten einen Rat geben zu können, womöglich seinen Platz in der Nähe des Königs zu bekommen, das war eines der Hauptziele dieser Erziehung.

„Siehst du einen behend in seinem Geschäft,
vor Könige kann er hintreten." Prov. xxii 29.

Und was Sirach sagt, könnte ebenso schon zur Zeit Salomos gesagt sein.

„Vernachlässige nicht die Rede der Weisen . . .
denn dadurch wirst du Bildung lernen,
dass du vor Fürsten treten kannst." Sir. viii 8.

Aus der Fülle der ägyptischen Beispiele sei nur eines herangezogen:

„Wenn du ein erprobter Mann bist, der in der Halle seines Herrn sitzt, so nimm deinen Verstand aufs äusserste zusammen. Wenn du schweigst, ist es besser als Teftefblumen. Wenn du redest, musst du wissen, wie du loskommst. Ein Kunstfertiger ists, der im Rate spricht; schwieriger ist Reden als alle Arbeiten." [1])

Es wäre sicher falsch, in diesen und vielen anderen Mahnungen nur eine äusserliche Dressur sehen zu wollen, die den jungen Mann zu einem raschen Avancieren befähigen sollte. Von einem Bildungsideal zu reden, wäre ja dann gewiss kein Recht. Aber jene Weisen hatten doch ein sehr imponierendes und innerlich gegründetes Leitbild vom Menschen, das sich in einigen Zügen auffallend berührt mit unserem antik-humanistischen, aber auch mit dem der mittelalterlichen mâze [2]). Es ist das Bild eines Menschen, der seinem Wesen durch Zucht, Bescheidenheit, Kenntnisse, Freundlichkeit und Selbstbeherrschung eine edle Form gegeben hat, und — möchten wir gleich hinzusetzen: es ist das Bild Josephs! In Joseph hat der Erzähler das Bild eines solchen jungen Mannes entworfen von bester Bildung und Zucht, von Gläubigkeit und Weltgewandtheit. Das Fundament und der Ausgangspunkt dieses Bildungsstrebens ist die „Gottesfurcht", zu der sich auch Joseph bekennt; und Gottesfurcht ist ganz einfach Gehorsam Gottes Geboten gegenüber

---

[1]) Ptahhotep 24, Übersetzung von H. Kees.

[2]) H. Kees, *Ägypten (Hdb. d. Altertumswiss.* III. Abt., 1, Teil. 3. Band, Kulturgeschichte des alten Orients) p. 268, 283.

(Prov. i 7; xv 33; Gen. xlii 18) [1]. Theologisch ist an diesem Bildungsideal diese Fundamentierung wohl das Wichtigste. Die Weisheit erzieht also nicht auf Kultus und Offenbarung hin, sondern von ihr her. Weil ihm jedes Erlösungspathos fehlt, behält dieses Bildungsstreben etwas Unstarres, Undoktrinäres, und es hat in seiner Bedachtheit auf das Mögliche etwas ausgesprochen Realistisches. Diese Bindung an das absolute Gebot tritt in der Josephsgeschichte besonders deutlich in der Versuchungserzählung (Gen. xxxix) zutage. Damit stehen wir wieder vor einem weitläufigen Feld der weisheitlichen Mahnungen, nämlich denen vor der „fremden Frau" (נָכְרִיָּה) [2]. Die Erzählung Gen. xxxix liest sich doch geradezu wie eine ad hoc verfasste Beispielerzählung zu den Mahnungen der Weisen [3]). Eine andere Warnung der Weisen ist die vor dem „Hitzigen", d.h. vor dem Unbeherrschten, Aufbrausenden. Das positive Gegenbild ist der קַר רוּחַ, der Kaltblütige oder der Langmütige [4]).

„Der Langmütige ist reich an Einsicht,
aber der Jähzornige trägt Narrheit davon." Prov. xiv 29.

Ist nicht Joseph in seinem Verhältnis zu seinen Brüdern auf und ab der „rechte Schweiger", wie ihn die ägyptische Weisheit nennt? Er ist doch „der Kluge, der Erkenntnis zu verbergen weiss" (Prov. xii 23), der seine Lippen „schont" (Prov. x 19). Vor allem lässt sich der „Langmütige" nicht von seinen Affekten treiben. Der Leser soll darüber staunen, bis zu welchem äussersten Grade Joseph imstande war, seine Aufwallungen niederzuhalten [5]). Es ist doch nicht zu verkennen, dass dieses Gebot aller Gefühlsentäusserung, das dieses Bildungsideal aufstellte [6]), der Wesensart des hebräischen Menschen im Grunde recht fremd war. Solche Selbstbeherrschung nennt auch die israelitische Weisheit מֹשֵׁל בְּרוּחוֹ (Prov. xvi 32); solch ein „gelassener Sinn" (Prov. xiv 30) bringt in das Zusammenleben der Menschen etwas Wohltätiges, Aufbauendes.

„Der Langmütige stillt Hader" (Prov. xv 18),

---

[1]) L. Köhler, *Theologie des Alten Testaments*, p. 94.

[2]) G. Boström, *Proverbiastudien* 15 ff.

[3]) Prov. xxii 14; xxiii 27 f. vgl. Weisheit des Anii: Eine Frau, die von ihrem Mann fern ist, „ich bin hübsch" sagt sie alle Tage zu dir, wenn sie keine Zeugen hat. Erman, *Literatur d. Ägypter*, p. 296.

[4]) Prov. xvii 27; xv 18; xvi 32. Über das Ideal des „Schweigenden" vgl. H. O. Lange, *Die Weisheit des Amen em ope*, p. 20 f.

[5]) Gen. xlii 24; xliii 30 f.; xlv 1.

[6]) H. Kees, l.c., p. 284.

von wem gilt denn diese Sentenz, wenn nicht von Joseph? Ja, mehr noch: auch Josephs Verzicht auf Vergeltung, seine zudeckende Güte hat ihre schlagenden Parallelen in den weisheitlichen Sentenzen:

> „Sprich nicht: wie er mir getan, so will ich ihm tun;
> Ich will vergelten dem Mann nach seiner Tat." Prov. xxiv 29
> „Alle Vergehungen deckt Liebe zu." Prov. x 12.

Eine solche Formung des ganzen Menschen gewinnt einer freilich nicht über Nacht; er lernt sie erst in einer schweren Schule, nämlich in der der Demut (עֲנָוָה). Dass „vor der Ehre die Demut stehe", dass „der Lohn der Demut Reichtum und Ehre seien" (Prov. xv 33; xxii 4), das ist wiederum eine Lehre, die die Josephsgeschichte in ihrem ersten Teil breit illustriert.

Soweit von dem Bildungsideal und dem Menschenbild der Josephsgeschichte einerseits und der älteren Weisheit andererseits. Nun aber zu dem theologischen Grundgedanken; unsere These könnte ja nicht als bewiesen gelten, wenn Josephsgeschichte und Weisheit in diesem wichtigsten Punkt eigene Wege gingen. Nun ist die ältere Weisheit bekanntlich sparsam mit direkt theologischen Aussagen, aber die Josephsgeschichte ist es auch. Nur an zwei Stellen spricht sie programmatisch von Gott. Zuerst geschieht das beim Erkennen, wo Joseph den Schleier lüftet und auf die Führung Gottes hinweist, die alle Wirrnisse zu einem guten Ende brachte (Gen. xlv 5ff). Am Ende ist dieser theologische Hinweis noch gewichtiger in dem „Ihr gedachtet mir Böses zu tun, aber Gott gedachte es zum Guten zu wenden" (Gen. l 20). Hier wird das Rätsel des Ineinanders von göttlichem Führen und menschlichem Handeln noch schärfer betont. Gott hat auch da, wo es kein Mensch mehr annehmen konnte, alle Fäden in Händen gehalten. Aber das wird nur behauptet. Das Wie dieses Ineinanderwirkens bleibt ganz Geheimnis. So stehen sich dieses „Ihr gedachtet" und dieses „Gott gedachte" letztlich doch sehr spröde gegenüber. Und nun vergleiche man mit diesem Satz Josephs, auch mit dem in Gen. xlv 8, die Sentenz:

> „Des Menschen Herz denkt sich einen Weg aus,
> aber Jahwe lenkt seinen Schritt". (Prov. xvi 9).

Auch hier geht es 1) um jene alles bestimmende Führung Jahwes und 2) um jene schroffe, verbindungslose Gegenüberstellung von göttlichem Führen und menschlichem Planen. Diese Entsprechung ist frappierend und sie ist nicht zufällig, wie die Sentenz Prov. xix 21 zeigt:

„Viel sind der Pläne im Herzen eines Mannes,
aber Jahwes Rat bleibt bestehen."

Genau wie in der Josephssentenz werden hier die Absichten der Menschen und die Gottes konfrontiert, aber Jahwes Absichten gehen über die der Menschen hinweg. Dass wir es bei diesem schroffen Auseinanderhalten von göttlichem und menschlichem Handeln mit einem zentral weisheitlich-theologischen Thema zu tun haben, zeigt endlich der ägyptische Amen em ope:

„Anders ist das, was die Menschen sich denken,
Anders das, was der Gott tut." (xix 16). [1]

Angesichts der formalen und inhaltlichen Aehnlichkeit dieses Spruches mit dem Satz Josephs — jedesmal wird das Tun der Menschen im ersten, dem Tun Gottes im zweiten Satz konfrontiert — kann man fragen, ob Josephs „Ihr gedachtet . . ." nicht geradezu ein für die Erzählung umstilisierter Weisheitsspruch war. Aufs engste berührt sich mit diesem Thema der Josephsgeschichte ferner die Sentenz Prov. xx 24:

„Jahwe lenkt die Schritte des Mannes,
aber der Mensch, — wie könnte er seinen Weg verstehen!"

In dieses Staunen mischt sich freilich ein Moment der Resignation, das nicht übersehen werden sollte. Es wäre hier ein weites Feld, das auszuführen, wie die Kehrseite dieses imponierenden Glaubens an die Allgenugsamkeit der sich gegen alles durchsetzenden Führung doch eine offenkundige Skepsis gegenüber allem menschlichen Tun und Planen ist. Es lässt sich ja nicht leugnen, dass schon in der Josephsgeschichte eine völlige Zerreissung des göttlichen und des menschlichen Handelns droht und dass das menschliche Handeln unter der Last der Allgenugsamkeit der göttlichen Führung zu einer Bedeutungslosigkeit herabgedrückt wird, die gefährlich ist.

„Es gibt keine Weisheit und keine Einsicht
und keinen Rat gegenüber Jahwe.
Das Ross wird gerüstet für den Tag der Schlacht,
aber Jahwes ist der Sieg." Prov. xxi 30f.

In dieser wundervollen Sentenz ist noch einmal alles ausgesprochen: Jahwe ist in seinem Lenken und Schenken ganz frei.

---

[1]) Übersetzung von H. KEES, *Lesebuch*, p. 46; vgl. dazu K. SETHE, „*Der Mensch denkt, Gott lenkt*" *bei den alten Ägyptern*. Nachr. der Ges. d. Wiss. zu Göttingen, Phil. hist. Kl. 1925, p. 141 ff.

Aber was bleibt für den Menschen? Er kann, ja er muss handeln und rüsten, um dann doch mit all seinen Plänen an eine absolute Grenze zu stossen, um mit seiner Weisheit an Jahwe zu scheitern.

Alles irdische Geschehen ist nach dieser Lehre einer Gesetzlichkeit unterworfen, die sich menschlichem Begreifen völlig entzieht. „Der Gott lebt im Erfolg, während der Mensch im Versagen lebt", sagt Amen em ope (xix 14). Das also ist der Josephsgeschichte wie den eben genannten Sentenzen der älteren Weisheit gemeinsam: sie verweisen das Handeln Gottes in eine radikale Verborgenheit, Ferne und Unerkennbarkeit. Solange der charismatische Deuter da war, wie in der Josephsgeschichte, war keine Gefahr. Aber wie es aussah, wenn der Mensch mit dieser radikalen Glaubenserkenntnis als solcher allein gelassen war, das zeigt uns das Buch Kohelet, in dem die Frage „wie könnte der Mensch seinen Weg verstehen?" schon den Unterton der Verzweiflung angenommen hat (Koh. iii 11; vii 24; viii 17). Die Skepsis Kohelets hat weit zurückliegende Wurzeln! [1])

Wir sind der Frage nachgegangen, in welchen geistigen oder traditionsgeschichtlichen Raum die Josephsgeschichte einzuordnen ist. Sie hat keinerlei historisch-politische Anliegen, ebenso fehlt ihr eine kultätiologische Tendenz, endlich vermissen wir eine spezifisch heilsgeschichtlich-theologische Ausrichtung. Unsere Antwort lautet: Die Josephsgeschichte mit ihrer deutlichen didaktischen Tendenz gehört der älteren Weisheitslehre zu. Daraus ergeben sich Folgerungen, die nur noch thesenartig angedeutet werden können. Zunächst für die Weisheit, und zwar in dem Sinne, dass man sie nicht nur in einigen Sentenzensammlungen greifen kann, sondern dass sie von Anfang an als ein sehr viel umfassenderes geistiges Phänomen auf den Plan getreten ist. Wenn in Ägypten der Einfluss der Weisheit auf das weite Feld der Literatur ein bedeutender war [2]), so müsste man sich wundern, wenn in Israel die Dinge anders gelaufen wären. Hinsichtlich der Josephsgeschichte aber müsste nun aufs neue mit engen Beziehungen zur gleichzeitigen ägyptischen Literatur ge-

---

[1]) Das Thema dieser einbrechenden Skepsis liesse sich bei Amen em ope unschwer weiter verfolgen. Dieser Gläubigkeit, diesem „Sich in die Arme Gottes setzen" (xxii 7) ist eine recht bittere Resignation benachbart: In Gottes Hand gibt es keinen Erfolg und vor ihm gibt es kein Versagen. Wer sich anstrengt, den Erfolg zu suchen, der verdirbt ihn im nächsten Augenblick (xix 22 bis xx 2), Übers. von H. Kees, *Lesebuch*, p. 46.

[2]) H. Brunner, *Ägyptologie (Hdb. d. Orientalistik*, 2. Abschnitt) p. 109.

rechnet werden. Nicht dass sie auch nur in ihrer ungefähren Jetztgestalt eine ägyptische Erzählung wäre, sie ist zu deutlich von einem Nichtägypter und für Nichtägypter erzählt; aber dass sich von Ägypten aus literarische Anregungen, Vorbilder, ja auch unmittelbare literarische Stoffe auf die Entstehung der Josephsgeschichte ausgewirkt haben, ist bestimmt anzunehmen. Es wird kein Zufall sein, dass gerade die Weisheit des Amen em ope von jener persönlichen Führung des Lebens durch „den Gott" spricht [1]), unter gleichzeitiger Betonung ihrer Verborgenheit vor dem Menschen, also genau das, wovon die Josephsgeschichte handelt. Auch Amen em opes Ideal ist das des Diskreten, Bescheidenen, Ruhigen, Überlegenen [2]). Und fragt man ganz allgemein nach den nächtstverwandten Beispielen jener Erzählungskunst, wie sie die Josephsgeschichte übt, so wären wieder in erster Linie ägyptische Erzählungen zu nennen von ganz ähnlich realistisch-psychologistischer Art, wie etwa die Klage des Bauern [3]). Von der Voraussetzung einer Beeinflussung von Ägypten her müsste endlich die Frage nach etwaigen mythologischen Hintergründen der Josephsgeschichte neu gestellt werden [4]). Dass solche in einer sehr fernen Vorstufe des jetzigen Erzählungsstoffes in Rechnung zu setzen sind, ist nicht ausgeschlossen. Auch hier fügt es sich überraschend, dass das Märchen von den beiden Brüdern, das man ja schon lange stoffgeschichtlich mit der Josephserzählung in Verbindung gebracht hat, neuerdings eine überzeugende mythengeschichtliche Deutung erfahren hat [5]). Zusammenfassend sei behauptet: die Josepsgeschichte ist eine weisheitlich-didaktische Erzählung, die hinsichtlich ihres Bildungsideales ebenso wie hinsichtlich ihres theologischen Grundgedankens von starken Anregungen abhängig ist, die von Ägypten ausgegangen waren.

---

[1]) H. Brunner, l.c., p. 107 f.

[2]) H. O. Lange, *Das Weisheitsbuch des Amen em ope*, p. 21.

[3]) J. Spiegel, *Ägyptologie* p. 117, 131.

[4]) B. Reicke, *Analogier mellan Josefsberättelsen i Genesis och Ras Shamra-Texterna*, *Svensk Exegetisk Årsbok* X, 1945, S. 5 f.).

[5]) Jacobsohn, *Die dogmatische Stellung des Königs in der Theologie der alten Ägypter*, *Ägyptol. Forsch.* VIII p. 13 ff.

HEBREW POETIC FORM: THE ENGLISH TRADITION

BY

T. H. ROBINSON

From ancient times students of the Bible have realised that the Old Testament includes a kind of verse anthology, in which we have selections from the poetic literature of a great people. It can be only a small selection, preserved for a special purpose. It is difficult to believe that the Book of Job was the only specimen of its class; though it is unique in quality its form seems too well developed to be a first experiment. A great work of art can appear only in an age where deep thought and lofty expression are common to large numbers of men. Lovely erotic lyrics such as those enshrined in Canticles come to the surface only among a people which had a song in its heart and on its lips. Dante and Shakespeare are at once unique and representative.

From the first (and especially in earlier days) students of Hebrew poetry have been handicapped by their familiarity with the literature of Greece and of Rome. It needs a strong mental effort to convince ourselves that the categories of classical verse may not apply to Hebrew or some other ancient poetic forms. Statements—we could almost say boasts—made by writers like PHILO[1]), JOSEPHUS[2]), and early Christian scholars, seem to have been intended as propaganda. Unless the system of vocalisation handed down to us is grossly misleading the greater number of Hebrew syllables would be counted as 'long'. One or two attempts were made in the seventeenth century to analyse Hebrew poetry on a classical basis, sometimes by applying an Arabic system of vocalisation. LOWTH has an amusing essay in which he parodies one of these, the work of HARE, by offering another, but similar, scheme. He concludes with the words: *hoc*

---

1) Cf. *De Vita Contemplativa*, 10, where various terms are used to describe poetic forms.

2) Cf. *Ant.* II. 16.4, where "hexameters" are mentioned; IV.8.4, Moses composes Deut. xxxii in "hexameters"; VII.12.3, David writes poems in trimeters and pentameters. Though the terms are such as would be used by modern students of Hebrew prosody Josephus was probably thinking of the Greek quantitative metres.

certe me facile impetraturum confido, ut utramque eodem in loco habeat, utrique parem tribuat auctoritatem; hoc est omnino NULLAM[1]).

LOWTH's own views are familiar to every student of the Old Testament. His lectures on the subject were published in 1753 under the title *De Sacra Poesi Hebraeorum*. A second edition appeared ten years later; LOWTH claims to have revised his work thoroughly and to have made many additions and modifications. These, however, did not affect his main position, and were largely confined to the footnotes. He was sufficiently steeped in the classical tradition to believe that there must have been a genuine 'metre' in the strict sense of the term, i.e. a phonetic rhythm based on the alternation of long and short syllables. Our ignorance of the way in which classical Hebrew was pronounced makes it impossible to recover the actual sound and rhythm of its poetry. We can only note that the lines varied considerably in the number of syllables they contained[2]). Many students would agree with LOWTH here, and would go even further, remarking that only a few can imagine what classical Greek poetry conveyed to the ear, for when we read it our rhythm is essentially accentual and not quantitative. One peculiarity of Hebrew verse, however, is obvious: the relation of the sentences, or rather the parts of the line, to one another, '*cujus ea ratio est, ut plena comprehensio in suas partes fere aequaliter distribuatur, atque integra ejus membra integros versus conficiant*[3]). Just as a whole poem falls naturally into periods, so the period falls into versicles, most commonly in pairs but often in slightly larger groups. He goes on to add: '*Hoc iis in maxime locis cernitur, qui apud Hebraeos vates ubique fere occurrunt, ubi rem unam multis modis versant, et in eadem sententia commorantur, ubi idem saepius diversis exprimunt, aut diversa eadem verborum forma includunt; cum paria paribus referuntur, adversis opponuntur contraria* .... It is to be noted that this is not stated as a universal and rigid law, though LOWTH does suggest that the term *mizmôr* necessarily indicated a structure of this kind.

Here we have the famous *parallelismus membrorum*, of which LOWTH has more to say later. Indeed, it is not till we come to ch. XIX that the feature suggested thus in ch. III is fully developed. Here

---

1) *De Sacra Poesi Hebraeorum*, 2nd Ed., 1763, p. 466. Throughout this paper it is this edition which will be quoted, since it represents a more mature view than that of the 1753 edition.

2) Op. cit., pp. 36 ff.

3) Op. cit., p. 39.

we meet with the significant sentence: '*Poetica sententiarum compositio maximam partem constat in aequalitate, ac similitudine quadam, sive parallelismo membrorum ejusdem periodi, ita ut in duobus plerumque membris res rebus verbis verba, quasi demensa et paria, respondeant* [1]). Then follow the three familiar types of parallelism, synonymous, antithetic and synthetic. Each type, especially the first, is copiously illustrated, chiefly from the Psalter, and it is clear that even the class which receives the name 'synonymous' does not consist in mere slavish repetition of an idea.

Lowth goes on to quote [2]) opinions expressed by 'Azariah, a Jew', not, indeed, an ancient Jew, but still a man of recognised authority. He had stated [3]) that Hebrew rhythm does not consist in the number of syllables but in the number of substantial ideas. Every line of verse falls into two parts, and may have one or two similar lines attached to it, making a total of four or six parts; it is not the sound but the sense which has to be considered in the enumeration of verse-units. Lowth himself regards this statement with approval, though he does not develop it further. Probably, like so many scholars since his day, he found that to carry it through to all Hebrew poetry would entail a large number of changes in the traditional text, and did not realise how, especially in some books, the necessary omissions or additions had the support of the Egyptian textual tradition on which the LXX is based. If he had been accustomed to the ideas of textual criticism current today, and to the freedom with which scholars emend conjecturally, he might well have adopted the theories of Azariah with little modification.

Parallelism, as Lowth stated it, involves a rhythm of thought. But he insisted that there must have been also a rhythm of sound in primitive Hebrew poetry: *Hebraeorum scripta quaedam non modo spiritu poetico animata esse, sed numeris etiam et metro aliquo adstricta . . . satis . . . clare opinor constabit* [4]).

In support of this position he noted:

(i) The verses are of different lengths, the shortest containing six or seven syllables, and the longest about twice that number.

[1]) Op. cit. p. 237.

[2]) Op. cit. pp. 258-260.

[3]) *Mantiss. Dissert. ad librum COSRI*, p. 418. Selections from the Hebrew text of Azariah's *Meor Enayim*, ch. XL, are quoted by Saalschütz, *Von der Form der hebräischen Poesie*, 1825, Pt. II, ch. iii, Sect. 53. Lowth quotes from the latter part of one selection, op. cit. pp. 258 f.

[4]) Op. cit. p. 32.

(ii) In any given poem the variation is not usually very great.

(iii) The '*clausulae*' of the verses generally coincide with the divisions of the '*sententiarum membra*' [1]). These features he has noted especially in the alphabetic acrostics, but illustrations are drawn from other books as well, including a number of passages in the prophetic books. To these signs of special poetic form may be added the fairly common occurrence of archaic and other unusual words.

So LOWTH would have assented to the prevalent view that the term *metre* should be limited to a rhythm of sound. He believed that Hebrew poetry was originally metrical, but that the metre could no longer be recovered. His actual words are worth quoting: *Quod .... ad veros horum versuum numeros, ad rhythmum et modulationem attinet, id omne et penitus ignotum esse, et nulla unquam arte aut industria humana investigari posse, ex ipsa rei natura satis apparet. Manifestum est antiquam et veram Hebraica pronuntiandi rationem omnino esse ignotam* [2]).

It has been generally recognised that LOWTH's third type, 'synthetic' parallelism is not strictly parallelism at all. Yet it has been generally accepted as a result of that same impulse which led to the more obvious forms, and for over a century there was little advance on LOWTH's theory as applied to the individual poetic line. Other types were added to his three; BRIGGS [3]) mentions three others. An 'introverted' type (we should probably call it 'chiastic' today) had been observed by JEBB in 1820, and other scholars had added a 'stairlike' and an 'emblematic' form. But the attention of students in the field of poetic structure was mainly concentrated on the verse-paragraph, to which the name 'strophe' was given[4]). It appears to have originated in the work of F. B. KÖSTERS [5]), was modified by MERX, who based his calculations on the line and not on the verse [6]), and reached a climax in the theories of D. H. MÜLLER [7]). It is not necessary to spend time on the subject here; it is enough

[1]) Op. cit., pp. 36 f.

[2]) Op. cit., p. 37.

[3]) See, e.g. Comm. on Psalms, 1907, pp. xxxv. ff.

[4]) It is extraordinary how difficult it is for any of us to escape from the categories and the terminology of ancient Greece, especially as laid down by ARISTOTLE and his colleague ARISTOXENUS. Yet it is at least possible that Hebrew prosody, indeed, Semitic prosody in general, is as little amenable to such treatment as is much of its grammar.

[5]) Cf. *Die Strophen*, TSK, 1831, pp. 40-114.

[6]) See *Das Gedicht von Hiob*, 1871.

[7]) See esp. *Strophenbau und Responsion*, 1898.

to remark that scholars differed widely in their application of the theory, some demanding absolute uniformity in the length of the strophes of each individual poem, others being satisfied with a symmetrical arrangement, while, again, there were those who laid down no rules at all for their length, but made them simply verse-paragraphs. One scholar [1]) found in the number of lines contained in each strophe a symbolic and even a mystical significance. The drastic surgery exercised by writers like BRIGGS in the interests of strophic regularity has led to some reaction against the theory as a whole, but it seems clear that it does appear as an element in the form of some poems, though certainly not of all.

Strophic arrangement is obvious in certain cases. It is usual in alphabetic acrostics, though there are points in Lam. iii where it seems open to challenge. It is, however, unmistakable in Lam. i, ii, iv, and in Ps. cxix. A refrain like that which is found in Pss. xlii-xliii and xlvi seems to be a clear indication of regular stanza structure, though the present text of the former does not give us an exact numerical balance between the three sections. There are other poems in which the sense suggests that the writer had something like this in mind. We can, however, recognise a formal strophic arrangement only when certain conditions are fulfilled. There must be a real division in sense between the sections, and they must shew some regularity, either uniformity or at least symmetry, in the length of the 'strophes'. In other cases we must assume that we have merely verse paragraphs, which are inevitable excerpt in short poems, and are no part of the formal structure. Thus we can divide Job iii into three nearly equal parts: vv. 3-10 ('Why was I born at all?), 11-19 ('Why did I not perish at birth?), and 20-26 ('Why can I not die now?) but we can hardly secure regularity in length without the sacrifice of something we could ill spare. We must rest content with the fact that while a stanza arrangement may be found in a number of Hebrew poems, it is not an essential element in poetic form.

LOWTH's dictum that the metrical structure of Hebrew poetry is no longer ascertainable seems to have been accepted for over a hundred years, but a number of scholars in Europe and America took up the challenge in the last quarter of the nineteenth century. Two names stand out as contributing, each in his own way, to

---

[1]) HENGSTENBERG, whose commentary on the Psalms was published in 1842, see Vol. III, pp. xxxii ff., at the end of the book.

further advance in the study of Hebrew poetic form. The first name is that of J. LEY, whose importance and influence hardly receives sufficient notice from more recent investigators, though, consciously or unconsciously, most build on foundations which he laid. He may have owed something to SAALSCHÜTZ, but his contemporaries seized on his suggestions as offering a totally new approach to the problem of Hebrew metrics. His views have undergone considerable modification, but the principles on which they were based have held good for practically all students of Hebrew poetic form [1]). To him the unit—the individual 'brick' with which the whole structure is built up—is the significant word, and it is the strong accentuation of such words which gives to the Hebrew poetry its rhythm of sound. Thus metre, in the strict sense of the term becomes possible.

Seven years after the appearance of LEY's *Grundzüge* BUDDE published his epoch-making article on the Hebrew dirge [2]). Till very near the end of his long life he was suspicious of all other forms of metre, especially of that which we commonly call the 3: 3. But in *Lamentations* (which has always had a fascination for the 'Metriker') he found a regular arrangement which involved a break in each line, the part of the line which preceded the break being always heavier than that which followed it. In the first part there are usually three but sometimes four 'independent' or 'significant' [3]) terms and two or sometimes three in the second. In certain cases BUDDE had to admit the presence of only two units in the first part, but he maintained that in such cases they were always heavier than the two which formed the second.

The skill with which BUDDE presented his case, together with his personal prestige, secured immediate reception of his views in circles which were not prepared to follow LEY. Even in conservative England at the end of the nineteenth century, the matter was regarded as being at least open, when other types of poetic form (always excepting LOWTH's 'parallelism') were under suspicion. But it was

---

1) See especially *Grundzüge des Rhythmus, des Vers- und Strophenbaues in der hebräischen Poesie*, 1875, and *Leitfaden der Metrik der hebräischen Poesie*, 1887. The latter work shews the effect of much criticism Ley received on details, and is thus a marked advance on the former, but is based on the same essential principles.

2) *ZAW*, 1882, pp. 1-52.

3) BUDDE's term is 'selbständige'; suffixes and short words which merely modify the main terms or shew the relation between them do not form 'independent' ideas.

unfortunate that BUDDE confined his new theory to the dirge. His influence has led many scholars to attempt a distinction between this form and others which appear to resemble it so closely that they differ from it only in the subject matter. To the eye and ear, for example, it is difficult to recognise any essential difference between the poetic form of a verse in Lam.i-iv and that of Ps. xxiii. It may well be that the mourner, improvising over the body of a loved friend, found this echoing rhythm most suitable for his plaint, but it need not be confined to outbursts of sorrow. In English literature the two best known of classical dirges are *Lycidas* and *In Memoriam*. Both are much longer than any known Hebrew Qinah, but neither Milton nor Tennyson would have claimed that his chosen metre was unsuitable for the expression of other emotions.

Nevertheless, BUDDE did make possible the recognition of a genuine metre for many readers who would otherwise have denied its existence. Neither he nor LEY went deeply into the subject, or tried to analyse it from the philological or from the prosodic point of view. BICKELL, it is true, had propounded his theory first in 1878 [1]), but adapted his results to BUDDE's views as soon as the latter appeared. GRIMME, followed to some extent by younger students such as ROTHSTEIN [2]), SCHLÖGL [3]) and VETTER [4]), laid stress on the importance of the time element in the definition of verse-units, going back to the old classical conception of the *mora* as the shortest time-unit.

It was SIEVERS who first gave us a thorough and scientific study of metre in general and applied general phonetic principles to the analysis of Hebrew poetic forms in particular. It is unnecessary to describe a theory and a system so well known to every Old Testament student. It has been subjected to severe criticism from many quarters, but even those who have had most fault to find with it have built on foundations which SIEVERS laid. The publication of his *Metrische Studien* in 1902 is as much a landmark in this special study as are the appearance of LOWTH's *Praelectiones* and of LEY's *Grundzüge*.

SIEVERS was primarily an expert in Indo-European language and

---

[1]) *Die Metrik der alttestamentlichen Poesie*, *ZKT*, pp. 791-796, and *Metrices Biblicae*, 1879.

[2]) See, e.g. *Grundzüge des hebräischen Rhythmus und seine Formenbildung*, 1909.

[3]) *De re metrica veterum Hebraeorum Disputatio*, 1900.

[4]) *Die Metrik des Buches Hiob*, Biblische Studien, 1897.

literature; while he contributed materially to our understanding of rhythm in general, he could not, in the nature of the case, go deeply into the special phonetics of a Semitic language, and it was left to others to carry on this side of the work. Among them the name of SCHLÖGL stands out as that of the first scholar to relate SIEVERS' views to the more intimate and detailed structure of the Hebrew language [1]). Later studies also linked closely together philology and phonetics; we may note in particular the work of W. R. ARNOLD [2]), HÖLSCHER [3]), BIRKELAND [4]) and MOWINCKEL [5]); the two latter pay special attention to the accentuation of Hebrew and, indeed, of the Semitic languages in general.

It is a striking fact that in this brief list of the more important contributions to Hebrew metrical studies in the present century, no English work can be quoted. Even the results of LOWTH's work failed to receive the recognition due to them, and at the end of the nineteenth century one of his really important contributions was still under suspicion. He had insisted that a large part of the prophetic literature was poetry, and constantly drew illustrations from the Prophets. But when the English Bible was revised in the last quarter of the nineteenth century, it was admitted that the Psalms, Job, and Proverbs should be printed in such a way as to shew the poetic lines, but it was still felt that the prophetic books could be regarded only as rhetorical prose [6]). Today no British Hebraist would deny that a large part, perhaps the greater part, of surviving prophetic utterances should be regarded as poetical in form.

No serious contribution to the subject was made by an English

---

[1]) See especially *Die echte biblisch-hebräische Metrik*, 1914, which goes far beyond the earlier essay of 1900.

[2]) *Rhythms of the Ancient Hebrews*, Old Testament and Semitic Studies in memory of William Rainey Harper, 1908, pp. 167-204.

[3]) *Elemente arabischer, syrischer und hebräischer Metrik*, Beiheft zu *ZAW*, 34, 1920 pp. 93-101. HÖLSCHER gives most of his space to the Arabic forms of poetry, with special reference to the *sağʿ*, but makes interesting suggestions on Hebrew poetic form.

[4]) *Akzent und Vokalismus im Althebräischen*, Det Norske Videnskaps-Akademis Skrifter, 1940, No. 3.

[5]) *Zum Problem der hebräischen Metrik*, Festschrift für ALFRED BERTHOLET, 1950, pp. 379-394.

[6]) It may be remarked in passing that the English revisers were not alone in failing to do complete justice to prophetic poetry. Even BH^3 prints Jer. vi 22-24 as poetry and l 41-43 as prose, though the two differ only in a single detail which does not affect the form; the former passage is applied to Zion and the latter to Babylon.

scholar till the publication of GRAY's *Forms of Hebrew Poetry*. Appearing first as a series of articles in the *Expositor*, it was issued in book form early in the first world war, and very soon remaindered. It is, thus, less well known than it deserves to be. GRAY went back to LOWTH, and restated the phenomena of 'parallelism'. He pointed out that the parallels are exact in comparatively few cases; it is but seldom that the terms in the second part of a line correspond completely to those in the first. This form, however, does occur in sufficient numbers to be regarded as a definite type, and to it GRAY gave the name 'Complete Parallelism'. It may be seen in such lines as Ps. xci. 6 or ciii 3. More often the correspondence is only partial; the parallelism is 'incomplete'. Here two forms are possible; one or more elements may correspond exactly, while a third, or even a second and a third, add something to what has already been said. An obvious example may be seen in Is. i 3a, where there is nothing in the second part to balance the verb in the first, and the object of the verb is expanded into two units in the second part. In the following line, on the other hand, we have an example of complete parallelism, subject, negative and verb appearing in both parts. The first of these two lines GRAY would describe as having 'Incomplete Parallelism with Compensation'. There is also another, and a very common type, in which the parallelism is incomplete, but no additional appears to give an exact correspondence in the number of units. This GRAY described as 'Incomplete Parallelism without Compensation'. Examples are too numerous to mention; the most obvious illustration is to be seen in the familiar Qinah.

GRAY also noted those cases in which there is no true parallelism at all, in other words those which exhibit LOWTH's 'synthetic parallelism'. To these he gave the name 'formal parallelism'; perhaps a better term still would be simply 'numerical parallelism'. Other points raised by him may be noted later. He made a really important contribution to the study of parallelism, and it is a matter for regret that his position has not been more fully studied by his successors.

Two more additions to the study of parallelism may be noted. One is the recognition of anacrusis [1]), especially in cases where the poet wishes to emphasise a contrast or to strike a keynote for his poem. Broadly speaking four classes of expressions are to be found at times in this category:

---

[1]) Cf. T. H. ROBINSON, *Werden und Wesen des alten Testaments*, 1936, pp. 37-40.

(a) Merely introductory (words of saying and the like) [1]).
(b) Interjectional [2]).
(c) Adverbial [3]).
(d) Pronominal [4]).

On this point it is enough to say that criticisms passed on the theory have served to shew its author that our reading of Hebrew is apt to be subjective, and that none of us has the right to lay down the law for the rest on such a matter.

More important is the distinction between what we may call internal and external parallelism. Most of the cases which we have in mind are passages in which one part of a line balances the other. This is strictly internal, but it not infrequently happens that the process is carried further, and the whole of one line balances its immediate predecessor. A good example may be seen in the opening verse of Ps. xxvii. In each of the two lines there is genuine parallelism within the line, though the verbal correspondence is not close. But the whole of the second line is very nearly a complete parallel to the first. A similar case may be seen in Ps. xci 5, 6, where again we have internal parallelism in each verse and the two verses are nearly complete parallels. Looser types of external parallelism are not uncommon; it naturally occurs most frequently with the shorter lines. Other examples may be seen in Is. i 4, 8 and 10, xl 3 and 4. So marked is the external parallelism in some cases that scholars have at times run the two lines together and called them fours and fives instead of 2 + 2 and 3 + 2.

Since the appearance of LEY's *Grundzüge* the attention of European and American scholars has been mainly directed towards the elucidation of a true 'metre' of sound in Hebrew poetry, and the work of SIEVERS has been the basis of all later research. In England the tendency has been simply to accept what others have done, without close scrutiny. The reason is probably that English attention during the last half century has been directed rather to philology and theology, with some regard to exegesis. The last named has, indeed, been affected by metrical study, but the others depend on it less. In general, the views of LOWTH and GRAY as to parallelism have been accepted, and there has been no challenge to the general con-

1) E.g. Jer. iv 10.
2) E.g. Jer. iii 21.
3) E.g. Jer. ii 18.
4) E.g. Ps. lxxiii 2.

clusions reached by SIEVERS and his successors. The position of LOWTH and GRAY, in the main, has been supported by comparison with the literatures known in other Semitic languages.

We now have examples of Semitic poetry which were unknown to LOWTH, and one conspicuous instance which came to light only some years after GRAY's death in 1922. In all these other literatures we find phenomena similar to those which we meet in Hebrew, though there are usually minor variations. We have, for example, the old Arabic *sağ*ʿ sometimes described as rhymed prose and sometimes as unmetrical poetry [1]; the latter name will be regarded by many students as a contradiction in terms. There seem to be grounds for holding that this is the source from which the later Arabic poetry sprang; originally it appears to have been used for magic spells [2]. Though there is no kind of metre discernible, there are clear signs of parallelism to be seen in it.

A few examples of ancient Aramaic poetry are known; the most familiar is probably that epitaph on a female devotee of Osiris which is sometimes called the stele of Carpentras [3]. The resemblance in general form to Hebrew poetry is unmistakable.

Accadian literature has presented us with a large corpus of poetic compositions. The best known are the two epics of Creation and of the Flood; both have attracted interest mainly on the ground of the parallels they offer to certain passages in the Old Testament. Accadian has one characteristic which is of great value for Semitic philology: we have the original vowels, while in every other case only the consonantal sounds are represented in writing until comparatively modern times. The general opinion among Assyriologists seems to be that every line of Accadian poetry falls into two parts, of which the first contains normally two main stresses, i.e. significant words, though three stresses are sometimes found. The second half

---

1) Cf. Gray, op. cit., pp. 44 f.

2) Cf. HÖLSCHER, op. cit., p. 93.

3) CIS II. 141; see also SCHLOTTMANN, *ZDMG*, 1879, pp. 187-197. SCHLOTTMANN's translation (which involves some reconstruction at the end) runs:

Blessed be Taba, daughter of Taḥpi,
  The consecrated of the god Osiris.
Nought did she that was evil,
  Nor spoke slander of any, the pure one.
Before Osiris be blessed,
  Before Osiris receive water;
Pray before him, O my delight,
  And among the righteous be in peace.

nearly always has two such units; where a third appears there is usually some further explanation. There may even be cases where a line contains six units, probably to be arranged as 2 + 2 + 2 [1]). Here again we have a close parallel to certain phenomena which we find in Hebrew poetry.

Attempts have been made to find a true accentual rhythm in Ugaritic poetry, but a recent writer, G. D. YOUNG [2]), comes to the conclusion that no such metre is to be found in the surviving Ugaritic poems.

There has been a tendency in recent years to deny that parallelism is an essential element in Hebrew poetic form. Thus HÖLSCHER [3]), speaks of it as being only a matter of style. Others may agree, but it is possible that these scholars have failed to note that what may be a matter only of style in one literature is an essential element in poetic form in another. Rhyme is indispensable in French poetry (except in *vers libre*), but is certainly optional in English and German. The invariable and outstanding feature of Anglo-Saxon poetry is alliteration; this is certainly not essential in later English, though it is frequently, sometimes extravagantly, used by modern poets. A much sounder view is that stated by MOWINCKEL [4]), who follows VEDEL in holding that the original rhythm of poetry is a *Sinnrhythmus*, and that the original metres are *Sinn-metra*. Many scholars, it is true, would define poetry as 'rhythmical speech', implying a rhythm of sound. It may be that the term 'metre' should be confined to rhythmical sounds, and if that is so, some kinds of poetry should be regarded as non-metrical. But this is simply a matter of words; it is almost universally recognised that Hebrew poetry had a definite form, even if that form does not strictly come under the head of 'metre'.

One constant feature emerges in all the forms of early Semitic poetry as known to us, with the possible exception of primitive

---

[1]) Cf., e.g. FRIEDRICH DELITZSCH, *Das babylonische Weltschöpfungsepos*, 1896, H. GUNKEL, *Schöpfung und Chaos*, 1895, p. 30, n. 2, p. 401, n. 1., H. ZIMMERN, ZA, 1893, pp. 121-124, 1895, pp. 1-24, 1898, pp. 382-392. Under the influence of SIEVERS, ZIMMERN attempted to work out a more detailed phonetic scheme, based on the accentuation of Accadian. To the outsider his conclusions are not wholly convincing, but only a specialist in Assyriology is competent to pronounce a definite opinion on this part of his work.

[2]) *Ugaritic Prosody*, *JNES* IX (1950), pp. 124-133.

[3]) Op. cit., p. 93.

[4]) Op. cit., p. 380.

Arabic. Every line is divided into two parts; unable to escape from our classical training, we commonly call this a caesura. It often happens that each part is a complete sentence in itself, e.g. in Is. i 2b, 3b. In the latter case it will be noted that we have what Gray called 'complete parallelism', and it is evidently lines of this kind which led to LOWTH's adoption of the term. In some ways this is unfortunate, for it suggests to the casual reader or hearer that there is always some more or less exact correspondence in thought between the two parts of the line; indeed the second may be taken to be a simple repetition of the first. It is, however, comparatively seldom that we meet with so perfect a correspondence, and some word like 'balance' might more accurately describe the fact. It is the essence of poetic form in every language that it should first create an expectation in the mind of the hearer, and then more or less completely satisfy that expectation. In the forms of poetry best known to us the mind normally fastens on the sound, but in a *Sinnrhythmus* the thought will most impress the listener. It may or may not be a reproduction of ideas in other words, though this is probably the most elementary form; it may be simply the *number* of significant ('selbständige') ideas which serves to satisfy the mind of the listener. That is why the term 'numerical' [1]) has been suggested as an alternative to LOWTH's 'synthetic' and GRAY's 'formal' parallelism.

In any case, the outstanding fact is that the caesura is a real break, both in the sense and in the sound. The last word in the first part is always to be read more closely with that which precedes than with that which follows. There are apparent exceptions; it happens from time to time that where a line contains five significant terms the third seems to belong to the second part rather than to the first. GRAY has suggested [2]) that this may be a deliberate effort to emphasise a word by holding it, as it were, in suspense. Thus in Ps. xlii 5a the verb *'eśpekhā* gains greatly in force if there is a slight pause after it, and at the same time there is additional emphasis on those which follow in the second part of the line: 'Let me remember these things and pour out—my soul upon me' [3]).

It seems to have been the importance of the caesura which first attracted the attention of LEY and BUDDE and formed the basis of

---

[1]) See above, p. 136.

[2]) Op. cit., pp. 177-182, esp. p. 179.

[3]) GRAY, however, realised that this explanation will not apply to every case of this kind; we have to allow for a 2 : 3 as well as for a 3 : 2.

their further study. Quite often the general sense runs straight on, but even so there is a pause between the two parts of the line. The poet may keep the hearer waiting before he satisfies the expectation which he has aroused. The caesura, then, may appear in the middle of a sentence, but a division is always possible; the final test is that the first part can never end with a construct depending on the first word of the second part.

The number of words on each side of the caesura may vary as between two and three. We sometimes find a line which appears to have four significant words in one part or in both; it may be followed by a 3, as in the great Chaos vision of Jeremiah [1]). But as a rule it will be found that there is a lesser break within the 4, and it is, in fact a 2: 2 [2]).

It would seem, then, that both the sense and the sound played a part in Hebrew verse-form. The analogy of the Arabic *sağʿ* gives some ground (so far as analogy ever can) to the view that primitive Hebrew poetry relied rather on the sense than on the sound for its structure. But, through their very nature, the Semitic languages make possible a close connection between the two. We need not go so far as G. Douglas Young does when he says 'The illusion of meter in the poetry of Ugarit is created by the accident of Semitic morphology and parallelism of thought' [3]), but we feel that the statement is on the right lines, though the illusion may not be complete. It is worth noting that nearly every student of Hebrew poetic form has recognised that there must have been some regularity of sound in Hebrew verse; Lowth certainly held that view, and Gray's work includes a careful study of Sievers. The difference between Lowth and Sievers lies in the fact that the older man believed the original sounds to be irrecoverable; the latter accepted the traditional vocalisation with occasional changes.

The loss of the original sounds, however, does not affect the

---

[1]) Jer. iv 23-26.

[2]) Mowinkel, op. cit., has found it possible to arrange the whole of Lam. i-iv as 4 : 3; often he gives the value of two units to a single significant word by counting a secondary accent near the beginning of the word. The *possibility* of such an arrangement in certain cases will be generally admitted, but not all will follow Mowinckel in assuming that Metheg is invariably intended to indicate an accent of such strength. Further, to the reader his reconstruction may imply a complete abandonment of the 'sinnrhythmus', which might be accepted in cases where a word is reinforced by a preposition or other addition, but is hardly valid for forms like the 3rd sing. fem. of the perfect Qal in a verb.

[3]) Op. cit., p. 132.

indisputable fact of the caesura. That break in the line is clearly based on thought and meaning, and makes the criterion of sense-rhythm (if we accept its existence at all) more reliable than that of sound. At the same time, since the great majority of scholars are agreed that sound did play a part in poetic form, we cannot ignore it.

It is generally accepted that the sound element in Hebrew poetic form must have been accentual rather than quantitative. Further, it must have been anapaestic, in the sense given to that term by SIEVERS; this is inevitable if we accept the principles which appear in our present vocalisation, since the whole language is marked by a rising rhythm. The acute analysis carried out by scholars like SCHLÖGL, ARNOLD and BIRKELAND shews that the accent was originally in many cases on the penultimate syllable, but this was due to the presence of a final vowel which has largely disappeared in the Hebrew of our texts. Most Hebrew words contained a series of sounds which led up to a strongly accented syllable; the only exceptions are short words which have nothing preceding that syllable. Unless the traditional pronunciation grossly misrepresents the original, that accent was so strong that it dominated the accidence of the language.

From this fact it results that a thought-rhythm and an accent-rhythm will largely coincide, and the same enumeration of units can be adopted, whether we are counting 'stresses or 'significant words'. But it still remains a question as to which of the two was more prominent in the mind of the poet and of his hearers, and here we have to fall back on grounds of probability. We may suppose that a poet who aimed at 'metre' in the strict sense would tend to be more exact in balancing the length of his verse-members than one who was concerned primarily with the ideas which he wished to express. If, as some of our greatest scholars hold, the thought-rhythm preceded the recognition of a sound-rhythm, we should expect to find that later poets were more regular in their arrangement of sounds than their predecessors had been. Now it is a striking fact that some of our later Psalms, e.g., Pss. lxxiii and cxxxix, shew very little variation in the structure of their lines, while others, more ancient, seem to admit frequent changes from one number of units to another. It is not easy to find any regular system in Jud. v, which, by common consent, is one of the oldest poems in the Bible, perhaps the oldest. No doubt a partial explanation may be found in the length of the tradition and the hazards to which all ancient literature is exposed in the process of tradition, whether that be oral or written. But this can hardly be the whole explanation, for the rhythm helps in accurate transmission so long as a poem is handed down from mouth to mouth. Accadian poetry seems to be comparatively uniform in this respect, while that which has come down to us in Ugaritic shews considerable variation. We should guess that the former is the result of a long process of development, while the latter, though the surviving documents are some centuries later than our earlier Mesopotamian poetry, is still at a less developed stage. In Hebrew poetry we seem to have examples both of the older, and less regular type, and also of the later and more uniform rhythms.

Our instinct, however, is to find regularity where we can, and at once we are faced with two problems. Are there words which, either in sound or in thought or in both, do not form verse units by themselves? And, again, are there words which sometimes can and do form more than one verse unit? These questions have been faced by all students of Hebrew poetic form since LEY, and there is a large measure of agreement, at least in principle.

It has generally been conceded that there are small words which seldom appear as independent units of thought. LEY and his successors drew up lists of them, and though these lists do not agree in every detail, they nearly all include such forms as negatives and monosyllabic prepositions, together with a few other monosyllables which may be used as proclitics or enclitics. If one of these has to carry the weight of a full unit in any line, we are justified in assuming that the poet laid great emphasis on it, since it must be regarded as a single concept. It will be sufficient to cite the familiar instance of Is. i 2b and 3b where the pronouns in v 2 and the negatives in v 3 seem to have unusual importance. In most cases we have to judge by the general rhythm of the poem as a whole, and it is interesting to note that in some of our later pieces there seems to be a tendency to give full rhythm-value to small words which are usually treated as proclitics. Thus in Ps. lxxiii 14 *kol* may have to be read as *kōl* and regarded as a full unit [1]), and in Ps. cxxxix 15 and 20 we seem to need a full unit for *ʾ^{a}šer*. In determining the rhythm-value of these

[1]) The prevailing rhythm in this Psalm is 3: 3, but we are always liable to find 2 : 2 : 2 in such poems; in these cases the second 2 is usually more closely linked with the first, sometimes with the third, but seldom forms a member of equal independence with the other two. This variation is not uncommon in the prophets, and occurs at times in the Psalms, cf., e.g., Ps. xci 3.

short words we must allow the poet a certain elasticity, and try to judge his intentions from the normal rhythm of the whole piece.

We are met with far more difficulty when we try to decide cases in which the rhythm seems to demand two units from a single word. We may regard the problem either as one of sense or as one of sound. On the one hand we may ask whether a particular word is so heavily loaded with meaning as to permit, or even demand, twice as much importance as that which is usually given to a single term. It will be generally admitted that when a word is used in the plural it carries more weight of meaning than it does in the singular, and this principle appears even in the formation of Semitic plurals. If a suffix is added we have a further enhancement, and a prefixed preposition or particle makes it still easier to suppose that the poet meant the whole complex term to be equivalent to two lighter words. Few students today would deny that *'et-môsᵉrôtêmô* (Ps. ii 3) is worth twice as much, in sense as in sound, as a normal Hebrew word.

At this point we may note the emergence of a new term in at least one recent publication. Older students spoke of the 'independent' or 'significant" word that which, in itself, can be regarded as a complete unit by the Hebrew mind. We must remember that the Semite always tended to concentrate on the whole rather than on the parts [1]). Our most recent contributor to the subject of Hebrew poetic form employs the term 'sense-giving' [2]), which is far from being the same thing as 'independent' of 'significant'. It will hardly be denied that there are cases in which the additions to a word *permit* us to regard the composite term as equivalent to two normal words, but it does not follow that they *demand* that treatment from us. Each case must be judged on its merits in relation to its own rhythmic context. If comparison with other lines of the piece suggests that we should treat the addition as a full unit, then it will assume more importance than we should scribe to it in other circumstances.

The modern tendency in dealing with these possible two-unit

---

[1]) Cf. PEDERSEN, *Israel* I-II, Eng. Ed., 1926, pp. 108 ff., esp. pp. 113-4; T. H. ROBINSON, *Genius of Hebrew Grammar*, 1928, p. 12.

[2]) MOWINCKEL, op. cit., p. 385: 'Prädikat mit Suffix und Nomen mit Suffix sind je zwei logische Einheiten; das Suffix ist in dem Satz sinngebend, mitunter auch logisch *betont*.' The use of this principle has helped Professor MOWINCKEL considerably in his reconstruction of Lam. i-iv as 4 : 3 instead of the normal 3 : 2. Some students, however, will be doubtful as to whether it accords with the principle laid down by PEDERSEN and long recognised by others.

forms is to base conclusions on the accentuation of the Hebrew language. LEY himself employed this criterion; he found that different syllables were marked by different strengths of accent, the accent to some extent depending on the length of the vowels. He noted five grades of accent, and believed that a strong stress preceding weaker stresses should count as a full unit. A time factor was introduced by GRIMME; two units must be admitted in the same word if there is a sufficient number of *morae* (the number varying with the strength of the earlier accent) between two accented syllables. Various forms of accent-gradation are recognised by SIEVERS, ROTHSTEIN and SCHLÖGL, while among more recent writers mention may be made of ARNOLD, BIRKELAND and MOWINCKEL. It is generally, and rightly, assumed that the number of weak syllables between two strong accents is necessarily limited; the human ear will not tolerate more than a limited space between two full stresses.

In all these cases two assumptions are necessarily made. The first is that the pronunciation (including the accentuation) indicated in in our Bibles is reliable, at least in general. In recent years doubt has been thrown on the system represented in our printed text, and we have to allow for a certain amount of error. But not all of us would wish to cast doubt on the substantial accuracy of the tradition as it has come down to us.

The second assumption has hardly received the consideration it deserves. The human ear is always subject to an unconscious process of training in its appreciation of sounds, and may learn to derive satisfaction from a sound or series of sounds which had previously been unpleasant. Conversely, it may grow dissatisfied with sounds which had hitherto been unobjectionable. Both to the classical and to the modern European ear, the number of unstressed syllables between two strong accents is strictly limited, but a primitive listener may have accepted a rather longer interval. Such tolerance would be more likely when the attention of speaker and hearer was concentrated more on the sense than on the sound. We may add that the Semitic mind did not produce words of such length as those which we find from time to time in Indo-European tongues. In a language like Hebrew, with its strong accents, it was inevitable that in course of time both sense and sound should play a part in creating and fulfilling that expectation which is the psychological basis of all poetic form.

These remarks lead us naturally to the actual rhythms we find in

Hebrew poetry, whether those rhythms are based on sense or on sound. There are wide differences as to the earliest form. In the *Grundzüge* LEY posited an eight-unit line, but this was generally felt to be too long. Later scholars, e.g. GRIMME, SIEVERS, SCHLÖGL, GRAY and HÖLSCHER, appear to hold that each line is really a combination of twos and threes, with sometimes a four. But which is the earliest form? There has been a tendency in recent years to regard the three-unit verse-member as the original basis from which all later forms have developed [1]). On the other hand there seems to be evidence for the view that the two-unit member is still earlier. The natural form of the simplest sentence is subject + predicate. If we may regard the sense-rhythm as earlier than the sound-rhythm the simplest verse-member will be the 2: 2, which actually occurs in a few poems, e.g. Pss. xxix and xlvi. It also appears in Jud. v, by common consent our oldest substantial Hebrew poem, and seems to be the dominant rhythm, though complete regularity can be secured only by the most drastic surgery. Further, there is ground for believing that it was the earliest form in Accadian, and GRAY [2]) suggested that it was the rhythm of the ancient Hebrew epic. This, however, must be largely a matter of conjecture, since we have no extensive remains of such poetry.

It is fairly easy to see that there might be some extension, especially in the first part of the line. Thus a 3: 2 would be produced, and its greater flexibility would lead to its predominance over the shorter form. There is evidence to suggest that a combination of 2: 2 and 3: 2 was not felt to be objectionable. A further extension takes place by triplication. This takes two or three forms. There are instances where the whole verse-member occurs three times, yielding 2: 2: 2. This, however, is comparatively rare outside the prophets, though we find single lines of this type in a few Psalms, e.g. Ps. xci 3. Much more often we get a third unit in each of the two verse-members, producing the familiar 3: 3. There is even a further triplication to 3: 3: 3, which actually appears to be the rhythm of several Psalms, e.g. Ps. xxiv 7-10 and Ps. c were intended to be 3: 3: 3.

But are we to expect regularity in Hebrew poems, assuming that the same rhythm was preserved through the whole of every poem?

---

[1]) So MOWINCKEL, op. cit., pp. 393 f.
[2]) Op. cit., pp. 221 ff.

If not, to what extent can variation be admitted? In many types of poetry alternative forms appear. The classical metres, except those employed in short lyrics, always had room for alternative feet, though their use was generally restricted to certain parts of the line. The common hexameter, for example, gave free choice between dactyl and spondee in the first four feet, and the iambic trimeter, fairly rigid in Greek tragedy, becomes so free in the Latin of Plautus that it is sometimes difficult to convince ourselves that we are not reading simple prose. We must distinguish between regularity and rigidity, and if a variation occurs with sufficient frequency, we must be prepared to accept it as regular, even though it is not a rigid example of the prevailing rhythm.

We may take examples from *Jeremiah*, a book whose poetic forms have not been the subject of any extended monograph published in recent years [1]). There appear to be some 230 separate poetical pieces in the book [2]). Only ten of these can be regarded as pure 2: 2, and among the ten eight contain no more than four lines. Most of them, then, may be fragments of longer poems which, as so often happens in our prophetic books, have been incompletely preserved. We have however, a few instances in other books where this rhythm appears as the dominant type in a poem [3]). On the other hand 3: 2 is one of the commonest forms; indeed, DUHM thought it was the only rhythm used by the prophet himself. In the Book of Jeremiah there are roughly 130 separate pieces in which 3: 2 is dominant, and between them they include about 700 lines. About 80 of the 130 include one or more 2: 2 lines, and of the remaining 50 only eight contain more than four lines. These short pieces, often fragments, may be regarded as negligible from our present point of view. 200 lines out of a total of over 600 is clearly a large enough proportion to justify us in regarding it as a legitimate variation; it is regular, even if it is not rigid. All told there are 40 other variants, of which the 3: 3 appears sixteen times, distributed among twelve pieces, and

---

[1]) GIESEBRECHT printed a small volume entitled *Jeremias Metrik* in 1905 as a companion to his commentary. Like DUHM he demanded absolute rigidity in the prophetic 'metres' and was thus driven to extensive modification of the text.

[2]) In such a case as this the figures are not to be taken as definitive or final. It is inevitable that students should differ both as to their reading of individual lines and as to the division of the poetical sections into their original units. But there will be a fair measure of agreement on most of the points, and the figures given may be regarded as giving a fair general impression.

[3]) E.g. Is. i 4-9, Pss. xxix, xlvi. and others.

ten may be regarded as 4: 2 or 2: 2: 2. The other fourteen variants include no less than six different schemes. None is frequent enough to justify its inclusion as a regular variation of the 3: 2.

In a large number of cases the rhythmical analysis of 3: 2 poems would be greatly simplified if it were generally admitted that to the ancient Hebrew ear there was no essential lack of harmony between the 3: 2 and the 2: 2. An obvious case is that of Ps. xxiii, where many commentators have attempted to emend v 4; these are all unnecessary when it is realised that this verse is 2: 2.

In the Book of Jeremiah there are some eighty pieces in which the dominant rhythm is 3: 3. In more than half of these we find lines which we can regard only as 2: 2: 2; and of the remainder only eight pieces include more than four lines; we may neglect the other thirty [1]). That is to say that four fifths of the 3: 3 pieces in this book include also lines which are best 'scanned' as 2: 2: 2. Again we are justified in holding this to be a 'regular' variation. Nine other variant forms occur; 3: 2 or 2: 3 in eight pieces (only in one oftener than once) and in seven we find 4: 3 or 3: 4. The other seven variant forms are found only once each. None of these is sufficiently numerous to justify us in regarding it as a 'regular' variation.

The 4: 3 (2: 2: 3) occurs in three poems in the Book of Jeremiah; the best known is the great Chaos vision in iv 23-26 [2]).

It is impossible here to go into details with other books. Suffice it to say that the general conclusions drawn from the Book of Jeremiah can be supported by careful study of poetic form elsewhere. English scholarship will not claim that it is always right or that others are always wrong, even when the latter do not fully recognise parallelism as our best guide to the determination of Hebrew poetic form. At the same time, it does seem at present as if the principles laid down by Lowth, followed up and modified in the light of later research and increasing knowledge of Hebrew and other literatures,

---

[1]) Thirteen are single lines, ten are couplets, and only five reach a length of four lines.

[2]) It should be remarked that the figures are based on a text which has been emended with the help of the LXX. The MT contains about 230 'irregular' lines, but in 170 of these the Greek is translated from a 'regular' text. While there may be strong objection to conjectural emendation *metri causa*, we can feel justified in accepting the Egyptian tradition where it gives us regularity. In rather less than fifty places the Greek text implies a reading which is 'irregular' against the 'regular' form of the MT—a ratio of about 7 to 2 in favour of the Greek.

will lead us to a reasonably consistent system, and help us to read Hebrew poetry as the poets meant it to be read. It will hardly be claimed that the last word has been said on the phonetic laws of Hebrew metre; while they are still a matter for discussion we have a firm and undeniable basis in the balance of words and ideas which appears in all Hebrew poems. Even if an agreed phonetic system is never attained, we can accept the dictum of an American scholar and say 'Where one finds parallelism as a regular feature in a Semitic composition, there one finds poetry' [1]).

---

[1]) G. DOUGLAS YOUNG, op. cit., p. 133.

VORAUSSETZUNGEN DER MIDRASCHEXEGESE

VON

I. L. SEELIGMANN
Jerusalem

Dem heutigen Philologen, der einen Text interpretieren will, gilt meistens das Objekt seines Bemühens als das Produkt einer Welt, die sich von seiner eigenen unterscheidet. Er bestimmt den historischen Hintergrund, die Gefühlsatmosphäre, die semantischen und aesthetischen Ausdrucksmittel des betreffenden Textes und versucht dann dessen Sinn zu verstehen, eben durch sich in die Gefühlswelt des Textes — das heisst manchmal eine ihm gar fremde und weitentfernte Welt — einzuleben. Wenn sich die moderne, historische Exegese Rechenschaft gibt von dem Wesen ihrer Tätigkeit, so stellt sich heraus, dass sie mit bestimmten Mitteln eine Distanz schafft zwischen sich und ihrem Objekt; gewissermassen in der vorgefassten Absicht, diese Distanz mit den gleichen Mitteln zu überwinden.

Wie anders die alte Exegese! Jedem, der einmal einen mittelalterlichen christlichen Bibelkommentar oder eine exegetische arabische Legende gelesen hat, ist gewärtig, wie dieselben mit einer Selbstverständlichkeit, die uns naiv anmutet, die Welt der Bibel mit ihrer eigenen identifizieren. Immerhin, der Umstand, dass für diese Exegese der Bibeltext ein gegebenes, fertiges Ganzes darstellt schafft eine Entfernung zwischen Interpretation und Objekt. Bei den alten Midraschim dagegen — als deren Erbin alle mittelalterliche Exegese, in gewisser Hinsicht, zu betrachten ist — hat man das Empfinden, dass sie dem biblischen Text noch mit einer schöpferischen Freiheit gegenüber stehen. Manchmal scheint es, als ob sie nicht so sehr einen festen, fixierten Text interpretieren, wie einen noch flüssigen, nicht abgeschlossenen, fortsetzen und mit ihren Gedanken umspielen.

Zweck der nachfolgenden Ausführungen ist es, diese Eindrücke zu erhärten durch eine nähere Betrachtung von einigen Aspekten aus der Vorgeschichte des Midrasch, oder richtiger: durch eine Anzahl vorläufiger Bemerkungen zu dem Übergang des biblischen Denkens in das des Midrasch. Wir wollen das Verhältnis darlegen zwischen den Ursprüngen der Midraschexegese und der biblischen Literatur und dadurch einen Beitrag liefern zum besseren Verständnis von beiden. Es wird sich — um das vorweg zu nehmen — ergeben, dass sich die älteste Midraschexegese organisch aus der Eigenart der biblischen Literatur entwickelt hat. Diese Formulierung enthält einen Hinweis auf zwei Erscheinungen, eine literargeschichtliche und eine mehr psychologische. Es ist nicht leicht, den Abschluss fest zu stellen von dem komplizierten und langwierigen Prozess des Werdens biblischer Literatur; in manchen Fällen lassen sich die Anfänge der Exegese geradezu bezeichnen als Ausläufer des Wachstums von biblischen Texten. Zudem aber lebt und webt das biblische Denken weiter in dem des Midraschs: viele psychologische Züge, ja wichtige Elemente des ganzen Denkstils, sind der Bibel und dem Midrasch gemeinsam.

Im Obigen deutete ich hin auf den vorläufigen und skizzenhaften Charakter der diesmaligen Erörterungen. Derselbe ist auch bedingt durch den Umfang des Materials, dessen Durchmusterung für unsere Problemstellung erforderlich ist. Ausser dem Midrasch (namentlich in seinen ältesten Schichten) kommen als Vorstadien in Betracht: die Schriften des Neuen Testaments (manchmal ist auch die sonstige urchristliche Literatur heranzuziehen); die apokryphen und pseudepigraphischen Bücher der beiden Testamente, zu denen sich jetzt die Texte gesellen, deren Bekanntschaft wir erst den Dead Sea Scrolls verdanken. Die alten Versionen, voran die Septuaginta, bewahren nicht wenige Spuren von Interpretation und Interpretationseigenart. Doch lassen sich dieselben noch weiter zurückverfolgen. Einmal ist der Ertrag an Exegese zu werten, der in etwaigen Glossen zum alttestamentlichen Text erhalten ist [1]). Über diesen hinaus sind diejenigen Stellen im Alten Testament zu berücksichtigen, wo ältere Stellen zitiert sind, oder auf solche angespielt wird. Manche derartige Zitate und Anspielungen enthalten eine Abwandlung oder Umdeutung, in gewissem Sinne also eine Exegese, der ursprünglichen Stelle. Nicht wenigen Stellen im Alten Testament ist eine ältere Form vorangegangen, als deren Umformung, Interpretation, (in Sonderfällen durch Missverständnis?) der uns vorliegende Text anzusehen ist. Hier werden wir mit der Tatsache konfrontiert, dass die Anfänge des Interpretierens hinaufreichen bis in das Werden der biblischen Texte selber.

---

[1]) H. W. Hertzberg, „Die Nachgeschichte alttestamentlicher Texte innerhalb des Alten Testaments, in Werden und Wesen des AT", *BZAW* 66, 1936, S. 110-121.

Es lassen sich, wenn ich richtig sehe, verschiedene Elemente und Kategorien nachweisen, die konstitutiv sind für den ältesten Midrasch und seinen Denkstil, das heisst für den Übergang von literarischem Wachsen in beginnende Interpretation. Wie erwähnen zuerst die ausserordentliche Geschmeidigkeit von Erzählung und literarischem Motiv in der Bibel, dazu das Spielelement des semitischen bzw. hebräischen Geistes, sodann eine ausgeprägte Neigung sich Gedanken und Vorstellungen, die einer fremden Umgebung oder anderen Zeit entstammen, durch Umgestaltung der eigenen Atmosphäre bzw. Epoche anzupassen [1]) und schliesslich das Aufkommen eines Kanonbewusstseins: der wandelbare Strom der Überlieferung gerinnt und wird zum heiligen Wort; speziell der Begriff Thorah wird beladen mit einem Inhalt, der Interpretation geradezu herausfordert. Die aufgestellten Kategorien sind verschiedener Wesensart, doch treten sie des öfteren in Kombination auf, sodass scharfe Grenzlinien in den folgenden Austührungen nicht immer gezogen werden können. Der Stufengang unserer Einteilung wird uns aber ermöglichen, von mehr allgemeinen Voraussetzungen fortzuschreiten zu rein exegetischen Elementen und letztere in jedem folgenden Paragraphen stärker hervortreten zu lassen.

I

Grundlage für unsere weiteren Betrachtungen bildet das im Vorstehenden angedeutete Phaenomen der weitgehenden Beweglichkeit [2]) von Erzählungen und literarischen Motiven in der Bibel. Die Erscheinung beschränkt sich keineswegs auf das Alte Testament, sie ist allen alten semitischen und überhaupt den volkstümlich-primitiven Literaturen eigen. Die Methoden der vergleichenden Literaturgeschichte, der Gattungsforschung und der Traditionskritik haben sie in neues und helles Licht gerückt. Dieselben haben uns gelehrt, die biblischen Erzählungen (und zahlreiche Motive in

[1]) J. Fichtner: „Zum Problem Glaube und Geschichte in der israëlitisch-jüdischen Weisheitsliteratur" *ThLZ* 76. 1951, 148 spricht von „der Kraft der Einbewaltigung".

[2]) J. L. Palache, *Het karakter van het Oud-Testamentische Verhaal*, Amsterdam 1925, S. 23 spricht von „een onbeperkte soepelheid en bewegelijkheid" der semitischen Erzählung; für die Betrachtungsweise im hier Folgenden vgl. dort speziell S. 16-21; die exegetischen Arbeiten von M. D. (U.) Cassuto (cf. *Bi Or* IX, 1952, 195 ff.) seit *La questione della Genesi*, Firenze 1934, S. 394; L. Baeck, *Das Evangelium als Urkunde der jüdischen Glaubensgeschichte* (1938) in *Aus drei Jahrtausenden*, Berlin 1939, speziell S. 246-248. Mehr noch als Gunkel versucht Gressmann „vor-biblische" Formen zu rekonstruieren, zu nennen wäre hier besonders: I. Hylander, *Der literarische Samuel-Saul Komplex*, Uppsala 1932, der wohl machmal über das Ziel hinausschiessen dürfte.

Prophetie und Poesie) zu betrachten als mehr oder wenig zufällig erhaltene Glieder einer, auf langen Strecken mündlich überlieferten Traditionskette. Ältere Formen sind diesen Gliedern vorangegangen und ihre Fortsetzung finden sie in jüngeren Stadien und Umbildungen. Der Stoff befindet sich in einem *moto perpetuo*, dem auch die Kanonisierung keinen endgültigen Abschluss bereitet. Ein bestimmtes Motiv kann gleichsam eine Reihe von Abwandlungen durchlaufen, die vor unserem biblischen Text anfängt und in den apokryphen und der talmudischen Literatur weitergeführt wird. Ein Teil der Midraschim trägt somit nicht den Charakter einer Interpretation, sondern vielmehr den von selbständigen Varianten aus der Überlieferungsgeschichte des Stoffes. Es kann auch vorkommen, dass eine erst in einem späten Zusammenhang auftretende Form in Wirklichkeit ein frühes Stadium der betreffenden Tradition darstellt: manchmal enthalten junge Midraschwerke Varianten und Motive, die in der Bibel — zufällig — nicht begegnen, aber gleichaltrig sind mit der dort bewahrten Überlieferung oder sogar älter als dieselbe [1]).

Die Tatsache der Biegsamkeit der biblischen Erzählung braucht hier kaum belegt zu werden. Ein gemeinsames Motiv bildet den Kern für gar ungleichartige Gestaltungen. Bisweilen wollen zwei verschiedene ätiologische Erzählungen einen gleichen Tatbestand erklären: berühmt ist die doppelte Überlieferung über das Sprichwort: Ist auch Saul unter den Propheten? in 1 Sam. x und xix. Die Erzählung von Davids Grossmut gegen Saul hat sich in doppelter Fassung erhalten (1 S. xxiv und xxvi), das Motiv vom Erzvater der am Königshof in der Fremde seine Frau für seine Schwester ausgibt, in dreifacher (Gen. xii, xx, xxvi). Verlockender ist es, die Spuren zu ermitteln von sonst verlorenen Überlieferungen. CASSUTO glaubt bekanntlich in den Büchern Genesis und Exodus Nachklänge hören zu können von altisraelitischen Epen — nach dem Vorbild der kanaänäischen — die den biblischen Prosa-Erzählungen vorangegangen wären [2]). In Am. iv 11 weist das: הפכתי בכם כמהפכת אלהים את סדם ואת עמרה —wo אלהים zu dem Gott Israels im Gegensatz steht— unverkennbar darauf hin, dass die Berichte der Bibel über die Verwüstung von Sodom und Gomorra eine Bearbeitung von einer alten Kanaänaischen Sage darstellen [3]). Unter den vielen Anspielungen

[1]) Als literarische Erscheinung verwandt sind die Agrapha, J. JEREMIAS: *Unbekannte Jesusworte*[2] Gütersloh 1951.

[2]) Vor allem: *Das Epos in Israel* (Hebräisch, Keneseth 8) 1944, S. 121-142.

[3]) J. WELLHAUSEN, *Die kleinen Propheten*[3], Berlin 1898, S. 80; fur אלהים vgl. Ex. xxii 19; Ps. viii 6, lxxxii 1, s. auch H. KRUSE, „Elohim non Deus", *VD* 27, 1949, 278-287

auf den Rahab-Mythus in der Bibel gibt es eine, die die ראשי לויתן erwähnt (Ps lxxiv 14), also einen Kampf gegen ein vielköpfiges Ungeheuer voraussetzt. Dieses Motiv fehlt in den uns erhaltenen babylonischen Versionen des Marduk-Tiamat Kampfes, doch findet sich ein Drache mit sieben Köpfen auf einem Siegel aus Ešnunna, ein solches Untier wird auch erwähnt in altbabylonischen Listen und im Ras Shamra Epos [1]). Im talmudischen Residuum von dem Marduk-Tiamat-Kampf begegnen Züge, die uns aus der babylonischen Überlieferung bekannt sind, jedoch an allen betreffenden Bibelstellen fehlen; eindeutiger als in der Bibel wird hier erwähnt, dass der Kampf stattfindet בשעה שביקש הקב״ה לבראות את העולם und das von Gott umgebrachte Ungetüm wird ausdrücklich als weiblich bezeichnet [2]). Die biblische Überlieferung weiss nichts von einem doppelten Auszug aus Ägypten; mehrere Stellen in späten Midraschim enthalten eine Tradition darüber, in verschiedenen Varianten [3]).

In besonderem Masse gilt das oben Gesagte in Bezug auf die Gestalten der Bibel. Die — uneinheitlichen — Bilder, die die Bibel von ihren Helden entwirft, gelten einer literarhistorischen Betrachtungsweise nicht als Porträts einer historischen Wirklichkeit, sondern gleichsam schon als verschiedene Interpretationen von derselben, bzw. von älteren aus der Überlieferung verschwundenen oder gar absichtlich ausgemerzten Darstellungen, von denen sich trümmerhafte Reste in späten Quellen durch Zufall erhalten haben können. Ezekiël (xiv 14 xxviii 3) sowie die apokryphe Susanna Erzählung bewahren unerwartete Reminiszensen an den ugaritischen Heros Danel [4]) Die kargen Mitteilungen der Bibel über Henoch, den siebenten Ahnherrn von Adam an, dessen dreihundertfünfundsechzig Jahre genau der Zahl der Tage eines Sonnenjahres entsprechen, der mit Gott wandelte und entrückt wurde (Gen v 23-24), werden heute von vielen Forschern als ein Auszug aus einem Kranz von Legenden angesehen, die schon vor der Abfassung der Priesterquelle in Umlauf waren. Jedenfalls weist das μετέθηκεν αὐτὸν ὁ θεός der Septuaginta wohl

---

[1]) A. Heidel, *The Babylonian Genesis*², Chicago 1951, S. 107-108.

[2]) b Baba Bathra 74 b. Die Stelle beeinträchtigt die Argumentation von J. Kaufmann, *Geschichte der israelitischen Religion* (hebräisch) I, Tel Aviv 1938, S. 424: das Rahab Motiv weise in seiner biblischen Form keine Verbindung auf mit der Schöpfung der Welt; des Weiteren siehe S. 169.

[3]) S. Krauss, „Ein Exodus vor dem biblischen Exodus", *WZKM* 38, 1931, S. 76-90.

[4]) B. Mariani, *Danel "Il Patriarca Sapiente"*, Roma 1945.

darauf hin, dass dem Übersetzer im dritten vorchristlichen Jahrhundert Spekulationen bekannt waren über die Himmelfahrt Henochs [1]). Die Qualifikation Gottes bei Jesaiah (xxix 22) als derjenige, der Abraham erlöst hat, setzt eine Überlieferung über die Errettung Abrahams voraus (aus Ur der Chaldäer, aus dem brennenden Feuerofen?) [2]), die sich sonst in der Bibel nicht erhalten hat, deren Spuren aber vielleicht in der späteren Literatur wiederkehren. Flavius Josephus (A.J. II, 9, 2 und 3 §§ 205 und 215) bewahrt bekanntlich von der Geburtssage Moses' eine Rezension, die — auch in Hinsicht auf die Parallelen über die Geburt Sargons, Cyrus', Jesus' u.a. — ursprünglicher sein dürfte als die entsprechende Erzählung in Exodus [3]). In anderem Zusammenhang habe ich darzulegen versucht, dass späte Midraschim noch Bruchstücke enthalten von uralten Legenden über Sauls Geburt, die vom biblischen Text (in 1 Sam. i) zwar vorausgesetzt, jedoch gar nicht erwähnt werden [4]).

Deutlich sichtbar werden nun die hier in Rede stehenden Biegsamkeit und Geschmeidigkeit in der Abwandlung einzelner Motive. Eigentlich will unter Motivabwandlung in diesem Zusammenhang ein Doppeltes verstanden sein, sowohl eine materielle, wie eine formelle Erscheinung. Es kann sein, dass ein bestimmter Gedanke, uns als τόπος von mehreren Stellen bekannt, an einer Stelle anders abgetönt und wie mit einem neuen Inhalt gefüllt erscheint. BULTMANN hat darauf hingewiesen, wie (namentlich bei ben Sira) von Haus aus profane Gnomen einen religiösen Charakter erhalten können [5]). Daneben ist speziell Qoheleth zu nennen. Seine Gewohnheit ist es, Worte der alten Weisheit aufzugreifen, mit dem Zweck ihre Nichtigkeit darzutun; manchmal aber begnügt er sich damit, einen uns bekannten oder unbekannten Satz zu zitieren, während seine Ironie den ursprünglichen Inhalt des Zitats in dessen Gegenteil verkehrt. Volks-

[1]) H. ODEBERG, *Th Wb NT* II, Stuttgart 1935, S. 553 ff.; L. GINZBERG, *The Legends of the Jews*, V, Philadelphia 1925 (1947), speziell S. 157.

[2]) Diese beiden Motive werden Gen. Rabba xlvi 13 in Anlehnung an Gen. xv 7 vgl. Neh ix 7, miteinander verquickt; s. THEODOR, z.St.; s. auch: B. BEER, *Das Leben Abrahams nach Auffassung der jüdischen Sage*, Leipzig 1859; speziell S. 112-116; L. GINZBERG, o.c. I, 1909, (1947), S. 198 ff.; V, 212.

[3]) H. GRESSMANN, *Mose und seine Zeit*, Göttingen 1913, der übrigens seinen Zweifel „ob hier noch alte Überlieferung vorliegt" nicht verhehlt; vgl. id. *ZAW*, NF 3, 1926, S. 307 (und GRESSMANNS scharfes Urteil über den Chronisten *ZATW*, 42, 1924, S. 315 und 43, 1925, S. 151 !).

[4]) *Bi Or*, l.c., S. 199-200.

[5]) R. BULTMANN, *Geschichte der synoptischen Tradition*², Göttingen 1931, S. 102-103.

märchen und Weisheitsspruch erzählen oft davon, dass in Unrecht und mit Gewalt angehäufter Reichtum schliesslich einem Gerechten und Braven zufällt (Spr. xiii 22, xxviii 8, Iob xxvii 16-17). Qoheleth macht daraus: Wer ihm (Gott) missfällt, gibt er das Geschäft zu sammeln und zu häufen, um es dem zu geben der Gott gefällt — auch das ist eitel und Haschen nach Wind [1])! Hier ist ein inhaltliches Motiv abgewandelt, es ist aber bezeichnend, dass Qoheleth festhält an den alten Terminis der Weisheit טוב לפני האלהים und חוטא, deren sittlichen Gehalt er gänzlich aushöhlt! Dies führt uns zu der zweiten, weit häufigeren und auch für unsere Problemstellung noch wichtigeren Erscheinung. Es kommt oft vor, dass jede materielle Übereinstimmung fehlt und dass eine rein-äusserliche Gleichheit von Worten um so stärker die Verschiedenheit des Inhalts hervortreten lässt. Im Hymnus Ps viii wird der Dichter angesichts der Grösse Gottes, die sich in der Schöpfung offenbart, der Nichtigkeit der menschlichen Kreatur inne. In einer merkwürdigen Ambivalenz [2]) weiss er aber zugleich um ihre Herrscherstellung in der Welt und er fragt: Was ist der Mensch, dass Du seiner gedenkst, der Sterbliche, dass Du Dich seiner annimmst (תפקדנו)? Du hast ihn den Engeln nur wenig nachgestellt ... (5, 6). (Ein Echo des Motivs hören wir Ps cxliv 3-4). Iob nimmt den Gedanken in fast denselben Worten auf: Was ist der Mensch, dass Du ihn gross ziehest und ihn Deiner Teilnahme würdig erachtest? Dass Du ihn heimsucht (ותפקדנו) jeden Morgen, jeden Augenblick ihn prüfst? (vii 17-18). Ein hymnisches Motiv ist unter Beibehaltung der Worte verwandelt in ein empörerisches, ein Vorgang der durch den Doppelsinn des Wurzels פקד nahegelegt — und nuanciert wird! Im vierten Esrabuch erscheinen die gleichen Ausdrücke im Gebet des Sehers (viii 34-35): Wirklich [3]), was ist der Mensch, dass Du ihn zürnen solltest, was das sterbliche Geschlecht, dass Du ihm so grollst? Gibt es doch niemand der Weibgeborenen, der nicht gesündigt .... Der semitische Urtext lässt sich kaum rekonstruieren, das Motiv aber hat hier die Funktion erhalten, die ihm im Klagelied

---

[1]) ben Sira xiv 3-4 beklagt und verurteilt den Geizhals, der seinen Reichtum nicht zu geniessen weiss und ihn Fremden hinterlässt. Er setzt, wie auch sonst, Qoheleth voraus.

[2]) Dazu jetzt: G. Lindeskog, *Studien zum neutestamentlichen Schöpfungsgedanken*, Uppsala-Wiesbaden 1952, S. 63; s. auch Anmerkung 2 auf S. 174.

[3]) Die Änderung von: enim, in: autem (Gunkel, nach dem Beispiel Bensley's: an anderen Stellen!) leuchtet mir nicht ein. Eher scheint 33 ein späterer (christlicher?) Einschub zu sein.

zukommt: die eines Appells an Gottes Barmherzigkeit. In den Büchern der Propheten kommen derartige Anlehnungen, Umbildungen und Paraphrasen des öfteren vor: Hosea‘ greift Exodus-Worte auf; Jeremiah lehnt an Hosea‘ an, Ezechiel an Zephanjah und Jeremiah [1]). Den meisten Fällen ist eine Form gemeinsam, die uns die Mehrdeutigkeit des Satzes auf den angespielt wird und der hebräischen Worte überhaupt zum Bewusstsein bringt. Vor kurzem hat ZIMMERLI schön dargetan, wie Tritojesajah Worte aus Deuterojesajah aufgreift und abwandelt. Er hat damit zugleich gezeigt, wie wichtig derartige Untersuchungen für Fragen von Autorschaft und vom Verhältnis biblischer Autoren zueinander sein können [2]).

II

Auf die bis jetzt besprochene Wandelbarkeit von Erzählung und Motiv haben nun zwei verschiedenartige Kategorien eingewirkt, die beide fruchtbar geworden sind für die Entwicklung der exegetischen Denkart und deshalb hier eine etwas eingehendere Erörterung erfordern. In erster Linie, die assoziative Bedeutung, die Doppelsinn des Wortes, Gleichklang und Wortspiel zukommt im biblischen und talmudischen Sprachbewusstsein. Selbstverständlich handelt es sich hierbei um Erscheinungen, die ausserhalb der hebräischen Literatur ihre Parallelen haben; wenden wir unsere Aufmerksamkeit den Formen ihres Auftretens im Alten Testament zu.

Das biblische Hebräisch ist bestrebt, bei der Benennung von Sachen deren charakteristische Eigenschaften — innere, vornehmlich aber äussere — zum Ausdruck zu bringen [3]). Name und Wesen der Sache fliessen also ineinander über und Gleichklang von Namen gilt als eine innere Wesensübereinkunft: Amos sieht Obst קיץ und das genügt dazu, bei ihm die Vorstellung des Endes קץ aufsteigen zu

---

[1]) M. D. (U.) CASSUTO, *Der Prophet Hosea‘ und die Bücher der Thorah* (Hebräisch), *Abhandlungen zur Erinnerung an H. P. Chajes*, Wien 1933, II, S. 262 ff. K. GROSZ, *Die literarische Verwandtschaft Jeremias mit Hosea*, 1930; D. H. MÜLLER, *Ezechielstudien*, Wien 1894, S. 9-10; *Komposition und Strophenbau*, Wien 1907, S. 30 ff.; J. N. SIMCHONI, „Der Prophet Ezechiel" (hebräisch), *He‘atid* IV, 1912, S. 220.

[2]) W. ZIMMERLI, *Die Sprache Tritojesajas*, *Festschrift L. Köhler*, *Schw. Theol. Rundschau*, 1950; vgl. id. „Das Gotteswort des Ezekiel", *ZThK*, 48, 1951, 249 ff.

[3]) Vgl. etwa J. KOEBERLE: *Natur und Geist nach der Auffassung des AT.* München 1801 S. 49 ff.; J. PEDERSEN, *Israel* I-II, London 1926, S. 168 bringt den Zusammenhang zwischen Namen und Sache mit Recht in Verbindung mit der Bedeutung des gesprochenen Wortes und dem Zusammenhang zwischen Wort und Ding.

lassen; das Bild des Mandelbaums שָׁקֵד ruft bei Jeremiah unmittelbar die Vorstellung hervor von Gottes Wachsamkeit שֹׁקֵד [1]). Es ist deutlich, dass hier Voraussetzungen gegeben sind, die der auch sonst verbreiteten Vorliebe für das Wortspiel ein eigenes Gewicht verleihen müssen. In der Bibel eignet dem Spielelement der Sprache überall ein Untergrund von vielleicht primitivem doch unleugbarem Ernst. Wie diese psychologischen Voraussetzungen ihren Ausdruck finden in den Namengebungen z.B. der Genesis-Erzählungen hat Böhl schon dargelegt [2]). Ein zweiter, verwandter Faktor kommt hinzu. Der Jerusalemer Hebraist und Orientalist David Yellin hat vor Jahren [3]) darauf aufmerksam gemacht, dass der Hebräer der ein Wort von doppelter Bedeutung gebraucht, sich im selben Augenblick von beiden Bedeutungen bewusst sein kann. Aus seinen etwa dreissig Beispielen seien hier zwei angeführt: In Jes. v 11 הוי משכימי בבקר שכר ירדפו, מאחרי בנשף יין ידליקם: Wehe denen, die früh morgens schon dem Rauschtrank nachgehen, und die spätabends noch der Wein erhitzt, ist der parallelismus membrorum durchgeführt bis in den Soloecismus der Kontaminationen משכימי בבקר und מאחרי בנשף. So erwartet man denn auch parallel dem שכר ירדפו ein יין ידלקו. Schon ist der Prophet im Begriff dieses דל״ק = רד״ף= verfolgen, zu verwenden, da verfällt er auf die Bedeutung: brennen, יין wird statt Objekt zum Subjekt des in seiner Coniugationsform umgestalteten Verbums יין ידליקם. In Iob ix 30-31 sagt Iob: Wenn ich mich mit Schnee waschen würde und meine Hände reinigen würde mit Lauge בבר, so würdest du mich in die Pfuhl בשחת eintauchen; während des Gebrauchs von בר im Sinne von Lauge ist im Bewusstsein die Bedeutung: Grube mit gewärtig und diese ruft die Assoziation שחת = Abgrund, Pfuhl hervor. Tatsachen wie diese machen verständlich, dass die schriftstellerische Persönlichkeit in der Bibel — sei er als Autor oder als Redaktor zu werten — keinen Anstoss nimmt an

[1]) Die Erscheinung ist oft behandelt worden. Hier sei verwiesen auf G. Boström, *Paronomasi i den äldre hebreiska Maschallitteraturen*, Lund 1928, der in seiner Einleitung 1-21, reiches Vergleichsmaterial beibringt; J. Schmidt, *B.D.* 1938, S. 1 sqq.

[2]) F. M. Th. Böhl, *Volksetymologie en Woordspeling in de Genesisverhalen*, Amsterdam 1925, vgl. *JPOS*, 6, 1926. Der gleiche Zug war auch der griechischen Sprache in einem bestimmten Stadium nicht fremd, L. Lersch, *Die Sprachphilosophie der Alten*, III, Bonn 1841, S. 3 ff.

[3]) D. Yellin, *Doppelbedeutung in der Bibel* (Hebräisch) Tarbiz. 5. 1934, S. 1 ff.; ausführlicher: *Ausgewählte Schriften* II, Jerusalem 1939, S. 86-106 (mit Erwähnung von E. König, *Stilistik etc.*, Leipzig 1900, S. 10 ff. und Heranziehung von der Funktion der Doppeldeutigkeit im griechischen Orakelwesen).

einer doppelten Etymologie: Josef wird so genannt, weil Gott die Schande der Kinderlosigkeit von Rahel wegnimmt אסף, ùnd weil sie betet Gott möge ihr einen Sohn hinzufügen יוסף (Gen. xxx 23-24): wie die Assoziation auf Grund von Gleichklang, so gehört ein Bewusstsein von der Doppeldeutigkeit des Wortes zu den psychologischen Zügen des biblischen Hebräisch.

Ohne Zweifel bildet das Prinzip der Assoziation auch einen wichtigen Faktor bei der Redaktion der biblischen Erzählungen und Prophetien — dieser typischen Übergangsstufe zwischen dem biblischen und dem talmudischen Denken! In diesem Zusammenhang möge hier der Neigung der rabbinischen Auslegung gedacht werden, aus dem Aufeinanderfolgen bestimmter Perikopen auch das inhaltliche Aufeinander bezogen sein derselben zu folgern: דרישת סמוכים [1]).

In der Tat dürfen das Bewusstsein von der Mehrdeutigkeit der Worte und die Vorliebe für das Wortspiel, sowie die Bedeutung, die beiden beigelegt wird, als hervorstehende Merkmale des Midrasch gelten. Dieselben machen sich einigermassen bemerkbar in der halachischen, gesetzlichen, viel stärker jedoch in der aggadischen poetischen und homiletischen Exegese [2]). Es hat keinen Zweck aus der Fülle des Stoffes ein paar Einzelbeispiele herauszugreifen [3]), nur ein paar allgemeine Erscheinungen seien hier vermerkt. Dabei darf eine Erscheinung nicht unerwähnt bleiben, die eben wegen ihres merkwürdigen, uns sogar fremdartig anmutenden, Charakters bezeichnend ist. WIJNKOOP hat vor Jahren, in einem wenig beachteten Aufsatz, behauptet und nach meiner Ansicht bewiesen, dass in der rabbinischen Literatur in sehr vielen Fällen eine Assonanz vorliegt zwischen dem

---

[1]) W. BACHER, *Die exegetische Terminologie der jüdischen Traditionsliteratur*, Leipzig 1899-1905, I, S. 133, II, S. 142-143.

[2]) Das Spielelement ist weit weniger entwickelt in der halachischen Kategorie der גזרה שוה als in der aggadischen der אל תקרי. I. HEINEMANN beschliesst sein klassisches Buch *Wege der Aggadah* (Hebräisch) Jerusalem 1950, mit einer Betrachtung über das Verhältnis von Ernst und Spiel in der aggadischen Auslegung, S. 187-194. Aber den Unterschied zwischen halachischer und aggadischer Exegese: M. KADUSCHIN, *The Rabbinic mind*, NY 1952, S. 122 ff.

[3]) BOSTRÖM, *o.c.*, S. 8-9 bringt Beispiele aus dem Midrasch zu Proverbia (ed. BUBER 1893). Doch sei hier ein Beispiel zitiert, weil es eine direkte Illustration bildet zu den oben erwähnten Stellen aus Amos (קץ) und Jeremiah (שקד). In dem späten Jalqut Schim'oni zu Jes xi 1 wird in einer langen Reihe von Beispielen auseinandergesetzt, dass Israel mit jedem einzelnen Organ gesündigt hat, in jedem bestraft worden ist und dereinst in jedem vertröstet werden wird. Dort heist es u.a. חטאו באף והנם שולחים את הזמורה אל אפם (Ez. viii 17) ולקו באף: אף אני אעשה זאת לכם (Lev. xxvi 16) ומתנחמים באף: ואף גם זאת בהיותם בארץ איביהם לא מאסתים (ib. ib. 44).

des Wortes, den wir oben für das biblische Denken feststellten. Inhalt eines aggadischen Satzes und dem Namen dessen der ihn tradiert [1]). Der Name des Messias z.B. heisst שילה in der Schule von רבי שילא, in der von רבי ינאי dagegen ינון und חנינה in der von רבי חנינה [2]). WIJNKOOP geht so weit auf Grund von der Frequenz dieser Erscheinung, berechtigten Zweifel zu äussern an der Richtigkeit der für die betreffenden Tradenten überlieferten Namen. Von mehr direkter Wichtigkeit für unseren Zusammenhang ist Folgendes. Der übergrossen Mehrheit der mit der Formel אל תקרי eingeleiteten Deutungen liegt jede Absicht fern auf etwaige abweichende Lesarten hinzuweisen; es wird nur eine ansprechende Exegese erzielt durch ein Spiel mit lautlich verwandten Formen, das um so leichter war als die Texte ja unvokalisiert überliefert wurden [3]). Dem sterbenden Mose ist nicht nur das ganze Land gezeigt worden bis an das Westliche Meer הים האחרון, sondern alle Ereignisse der Weltgeschichte bis den jüngsten Tag היום האחרון [4]). Dass es sich bei dieser Erklärungsart nicht um variae lectiones handelt, sondern um ein Spiel mit den verschiedenen Formen und Bedeutungen, geht auch aus dem Umstand hervor, dass die Formel אל תקרי auch gebraucht wird zur Einführung von vom einfachen Wortsinn abweichenden Erklärungen, bei denen der überlieferte Wortlaut absolut keine Veränderung erfährt, z.B. wenn das ממנו Nm xiii 31 erklärt wird, die Kundschafter wollen besagen, die Einwohner Palästinas seien stärker, nicht nur „als wir" d.h. als Israel, sondern auch „als Er" als Gott [5]). Diese Deutungsart hängt ihrem Wesen nach zusammen mit dem Grundsatz: מקרא אחד יוצא לכמה טעמים, sie gründet sich auf dem Prinzip der Mehrdeutigkeit des biblischen Textes [6]), fast identisch mit dem der Mehrdeutigkeit

---

[1]) J. D. WIJNKOOP, „A peculiar kind of paronomasia in the Talmud and Midrash", *JQR*, NS II, S. 1 ff.

[2]) b. Sanh. 98 b. Interessanterweise liegt in manchen Fällen an Parallelstellen eine Nebenüberlieferung vor, in der dann der Ausspruch einem anderen Tradenten (dessen Namen kein Wortspiel bildet) zugeschrieben oder anonym tradiert wird.

[3]) A. ROSENZWEIG, *Die Al-tikri-Deutungen*, *Festschrift Israel Lewy*, Breslau 1911, S. 204 ff., I. HEINEMANN, *o.c.*, S. 127-129; M. KADUSHIN *o.c.* S. 118.

[4]) Sifrê ad Deut. xxxiv 2. Das Beispiel ist bezeichnend, weil eine für die Aggadah typische Historisierung vorliegt, s. des Näheren § III.

[5]) b. Sotah 35a und Parallelstellen. Eine parallele Deutung von Hos vi 2 Er wird ihn auferstehen lassen, statt: er wird uns aufstehen lassen, könnte von Einfluss gewesen sein auf die ältesten christlichen Vorstellungen von der Auferstehung (?)

[6]) In dieser Möglichkeit einer Pluralität der Deutungen sieht M. KADUSHIN, *o.c.* S. 104 ff. ein wesentliches Merkmal aller aggadischen im Gegensatz zur philosophischen oder wissenschaftlichen Interpretation.

Beispiele von solcher Midrasch-Deutung auf Grund von Assoziation und Gleichklang begegnen nun schon innerhalb der Bibel selbst. In seiner Prophetie über Ammon kündigt Amos an (i 15), dass ihr König ins Exil gehen wird, zusammen mit seinen Fürsten: die feststehende Verbindung מלך ושרים erhebt die Tatsache über jeden Zweifel, dass Amos denkt an den König der Ammoniter. Für das israelitische Bewusstsein jedoch, lag in dem Wort מלכם eine Doppeldeutigkeit, es löst Assoziationen aus nicht nur an den König, sondern auch an die Gottheit, die den gleichen Namen trägt. Eine Verbindung der beiden Assoziationen bzw. eine Anspielung auf diejenige Bedeutung, die im Text nicht gemeint war, — ganz im Geist der Midraschexegese! — liegt schon vor in Jer. xlix 3, wo der Vers aus Amos zitiert wird in einer abgewandelten Form: „Malkām wird ins Exil gehen samt seinen Priestern und Fürsten". Hier kann nur gedacht sein an den Gott Milkom, genau wie es xlviii 7 lautet: Kemosch von Moab geht ins Exil samt seinen Priestern und Fürsten.

Es entspricht der Natur der Sache, dass sich das Spielelement besonders gelten lässt in den — oben dargelegten — Fällen, wo es sich bei einer Anspielung auf eine ältere Stelle um eine rein-formelle Gleichheit handelt, in der jede materielle Übereinstimmung fehlt. Ein interessantes Beispiel liefern uns die literarischen Schicksale von Iob xxviii 25. Wir lesen dort, dass Gott unter dem ganzen Himmel schaut לעשות לרוח משקל und das Gewicht, d.h. die Kraft, der Winde bestimmt. Dem Inhalt nach schwebt diese Stelle dem Autor des vierten Esra Buchs vor, wenn er iv 5 seine adynata formuliert: Wiege mir das Gewicht des Feuers, oder messe mir die Maasse des Windes, etc. Doch hatte die Stelle aus Iob schon früher ihre Spur hinterlassen in ben Sira xvi 25 אביעה במשקל רוחי ובהצנע אחוה דעי: ich will behutsam meinen Geist d.h. meine Gedanken äussern und mit umsichtiger Zurückhaltung meine Meinung verkündigen. Dass ben Sira hier von der Stelle in Iob beeinflusst ist, ist gewährleistet, nicht nur durch die weitgehende Ähnlichkeit im Ausdruck, sondern auch durch den Zusammenhang. Bildet doch der Kontext in ben Sira eine Einleitung zu einer Betrachtung über die Schöpfung, die stark erinnert an den Schluss von Iob xxviii. Die Bedeutung der Worte bei ben Sira aber hat nichts mehr mit der an der Iob-Stelle gemein: sie werden rein-spielerisch verwendet [1]).

---

[1]) Der spätere Midrasch z.B. Numeri Rabba xxi 1 fasst רוח an der Iob-Stelle auf als die Meinungen und Eigenschaften der verschiedenen Menschen.

Eben bei ben Sira führt die besondere, spielhafte Aufmerksamkeit für das Wort und für die verschiedenen Möglichkeiten die es enthält schon zu einer richtigen Midrasch-exegese. In Ps lxxxix 20 heisst es: הרימתי בחור מעם מצאתי דוד עבדי: Ich habe einen Jüngling (?) aus dem Volke erhoben, in David Meinen Knecht gefunden. In ben Sira's Lob von den Helden der Vorzeit wird der Inhalt von **בחור**, namentlich aber von **הרימותי** vertieft und es heisst dort (xlvii 2) **כחלב מורם מקדש כן דוד מישראל**: Wie das Köstlichste, das von den heiligen Gaben abgesondert wird, so ward David aus Israel erhoben — die der Bibel noch fremde Form **מורם** hat hier fast die in der Mischnah übliche, technische Bedeutung [1]) !

Ein Beispiel möchte ich dieser Reihe noch hinzufügen, das ich Père Barthelemy verdanke. Das Wochen-Pfingst-Fest gilt bekanntlich im Alten Testament ausnahmslos als das landwirtschaftliche Fest der Erstlinge, im rabbinischen Schrifttum dagegen als Fest der Gesetzgebung. Den Übergang bildet die interessante im sechsten Kapitel des Jubiläenbuchs, wo Gott mit Noah den doppelten Bund schliesst, der das Essen von Blut für ewig verbietet und ein Zeichen stellt, dass es nie wieder eine Sündflut auf Erden geben wird. Deswegen — so fährt der Text (xvii 21) dann fort — ist angeordnet und aufgeschrieben in den himmlischen Tafeln, dass sie in diesem Monat das Wochenfest begehen sollten einmal des Jahrs, zur Erneuerung des Bundes ... denn es ist das Fest der Wochen und es ist das Fest der Erstlingsfrucht; zweifach und von zweierlei Art ist dieses Fest... Offenbar will diese zweifache Art des Festes besagen, dass es den doppelten Charakter hat (bzw. bekommt) von Fest der Erstlinge und von Fest der Gesetzgebung [2]). In diesem Fall aber ist **חג השבועות** Wochenfest (in der Thorah immer Bezeichnung für das landwirtschaftliche Fest) hier gedeutet als **חַג הַשְּׁבוּעוֹת** Fest der Eide und des Bundesschlusses [3]) — ein wichtiges und äusserst

[1]) Wie bedeutsam die Art der Verwendung von älteren alttestamentlichen Texten durch ben Sira ist für die Anfänge der Midrasch-Exegese hat schon S. Schechter gesehen, in seiner *Prefatory Note to the Wisdom of ben Sira*, Cambridge 1899, II, S. 12-38.

[2]) Befremdlich ist die Bemerkung von Charles: *The book of Jubilees*, London 1902, S. 53 ad vi 21: Why this festival should be said to be „of a double nature" I do not see.

[3]) Es stellt sich heraus, dass diese mir von Père Barthelemy in Mai 1953 vorgetragene Erklärung mir schon einmal in 1939 von M. J. Perath mitgeteilt wurde. **ברית** und **שבועה** sind in der Tat synonyme Begriffe; jemand für den der Bundesschluss am Sinai Gültigkeit hat, heisst in der Mischnah (Schebûʿoth III 6) **מושבע . . מהר סיני**.

instruktives Beispiel eines alten Midrasch auf Grund von Assonanz [1]).

Es gibt nun ein Gebiet, wo wir dem Spielelement im hebräischen Geist und seiner Fruchtbarkeit für die Entstehung und die ersten Anfänge eines exegetischen Denkstils noch weiter zurückverfolgen können. Gemeint ist die Entwicklung des Sprichworts — wohl in jeder Literatur das zentrale Betätigungsfeld für die Spielereien der Sprache [2]) — der ich hier in Hinblick auf ihre Wichtigkeit für unsere Problemstellung noch einige Betrachtungen widmen möchte.

Das alte Sprichwort המשל הקדמוני (1 S. xxiv 14) war monostichisch. Die Entwicklung zum Distichon erfolgte mittels einer Ergänzung durch einen zweiten Stichos der wechseln konnte [3]). Infolge dieser Wandelbarkeit kann das zweite Glied gewissermassen die Funktion eines exegetischen Kontextes annehmen, indem es die verschiedenen Bedeutungsinhalte aufdeckt, die potentiell in dem ursprünglichen Monostichon enthalten waren. In diesen Prozess ist uns mancher Einblick vergönnt, so dass wir die Bedeutung ermessen können, die dem Spielelement zukommt, an den nicht so seltenen Stellen im Buch der Sprüche, wo das gleiche Monostichon in der Tat in Kombination mit ungleichen zweiten Gliedern erscheint. Instruktiv dürfte der Vergleich sein von xiii 1 und xiii 8. „Der vernünftige Sohn lässt sich (von seinem Vater) gerne belehren [4]) ולץ לא שמע גערה der liederliche aber hört nicht auf Verweise". Dagegen in 8: Manch-

---

[1]) Eine neue Bedeutung und eine ästhetische Würdigung bekommt — darauf möge im Vorübergehen hingewiesen werden — das Spielelement, wenn in der späteren hebräischen Poesie und Prosaliteratur Bibelverse kunstvoll angewandt werden in einem, von der ursprünglichen Bedeutung abweichenden, Sinn. Die Erscheinung ist so verbreitet und beliebt, dass das Belegen durch Beispiele unnötig — und auch unmöglich ist. Nur als Illustration sei erinnert an מדע לא בא בן ישי (1 S. xx 27): Warum kommt der Erlöser des jüdischen Volkes nicht? (ibn Gebirol) oder לא נגרע שיחה לפני אל (vgl. Iob xv 4) Wir hören nicht auf, zu Gott zu beten (Jehudah ha Levi) s. auch Anmerkung 3 auf S. 170.

[2]) G. Boström, *o.c.* und die dort aufgeführte Literatur. Man bedenke auch die Verwandtschaft zwischen Sprichwort und Rätsel, auf die für die biblische Literatur Tur Sinai immer wieder hingewiesen hat, u.a. „The Riddle in the Bible" *HUCA* I, 1927; „Sitir Šamē Die Himmelschrift", *Arch Or.* 17, 1949, S. 125 ff.

[3]) J. Schmidt, *Studien zur Stilistik der alttestamentlichen Spruchliteratur*, Münster 1936; B. Gemser, *Die Sprüche*, Tübingen 1937, S. 45. Unschätzbares Material zur Entwicklung der Spruchliteratur bei R. Bultmann, *Geschichte der synoptischen Tradition*², Göttingen 1931, S. 84-113; s. auch L. Köhler, *OLZ*, 32. 1929. 32; viele scharfsinnige Vermutungen zu den Umbildungen einzelner Sprüche bei Tur Sinai, *Die Sprüche Salomoh's* (Hebräisch), Jesuralem 1947.

[4]) Von den vielen Vermutungen zu xiii 1a leuchtet mir am meisten ein, zu lesen: בן חכם מוסר אהב.

mal muss Reichtum herhalten als Lösegeld für eines Mannes Leben ורש לא שמע גערה der Arme aber hört nimmer Drohungen. Die gleichen Worte לא שמע גערה geben zwei völlig verschiedenen Gedanken Ausdruck, anders formuliert: die beiden Kontexte erhalten zwei völlig verschiedene Interpretationen des לא שמע גערה. Eine gleichartige Erscheinung weisen x 6 und 11 auf. Die ältere Bedenkung scheint in 11 erhalten: Der Mund der Gerechten ist ein Quell des Lebens ופי רשעים יכסה חמס der Mund des Bösen hingegen ist voll Gewalttat [1]): sie sprechen von nichts Anderem, als von dem Raub, den sie verüben wollen. Lesen wir aber 6: Segnungen (Gottes oder der Menschen) werden dem Gerechten zuteil ופי רשעים יכסה חמס Gewalt aber stopft den Bösen das Maul, d.h. Gottes Strafe macht die Bösen verstummen [2]), so sehen wir, wie der monostichische Spruch einen ganz anderen Sinn bekommt, durch Verbindung mit einem verschiedenen Stichos.

Die Möglichkeit ist nicht ausgeschlossen, dass im letztgenannten Beispiel der Text ursprünglich lautete ופני רשעים יכסה חמס [3]). Auf jedem Fall fehlen die Beispiele nicht, in denen Schicksale und Umdeutung des ursprünglichen monostichischen Sprichworts sich verschlingen mit und teilweise sich gründen auf Textvarianten; gelegentlich dürften dieselben aus alten Missverständnissen hervorgegangen sein. In xx 2 lesen wir נהם ככפיר אימת מלך מתעברו חוטא נפשו Brüllen wie eines Löwen ist des Königs Schrecken, wer sich seinen Zorn zuzieht, verwirkt das Leben. In xix 12 heisst es: נהם ככפיר אימת מלך וכטל על עשב רצונו (vgl. xvi 15b). Auf Grund des Parallelismus postuliert Ehrlich für die erste Hälfte des Spruches die Form: ככפֹר אימת מלך : Wie Reif ist der Groll des Königs, sein Wohlgefallen aber, wie Tau auf Pflanzen. Wäre aus dieser ansprechenden Vermutung zu folgern, dass die Form ככפֹר אימת מלך primär ist und dass die Vorliebe des hebräischen Geistes für das Wortspiel schon in alter Zeit eine Nebenform zeitigte: נהם ככפיר אימת מלך? Der Fall ist extra schwierig zu beurteilen, weil Fragen von etwaigem Missverständnis und von schriftlicher Überlieferung mit im Spiele sind.

Ein noch komplizierteres Beispiel verwandter Natur bietet der Spruch xviii 20 in Vergleich mit seinen Parallelen. So wie wir ihn lesen lautet er: מפרי פי איש תשבע בטנו תבואת שפתיו ישבע [4]), was of-

---

[1]) Vgl. כסה in Parallelismus zu מלא Jes. xi 9 Hb. ii 14; iii 3.

[2]) Vgl. Ps lxiii 12.

[3]) Jr li 51; Ps xliv 16, lxix 8; Job ix 24.

[4]) Muss die Wiederholung des Wurzels שבע aus der Kombination von zwei

fenbar heissen soll, dass jedem vergolten wird nach den Meinungen, die er hegt und verbreitet. Doch lässt der Parallelismus in der Variante xii 14 מפרי פי איש ישבע טוב וגמול ידי אדם ישיב לו kaum Zweifel daran bestehen, dass die ursprüngliche, monostichische Form dieses Sprichworts lautete: מפרי כפי איש ישבע: Wie eines jeden Arbeit, so auch sein Lohn, ein Spruch, der sowohl sprachlich [1]) als gedanklich vor dem MT. den Vorzug haben dürfte. Das טוב in xii 14 will offenbar mit ישבע verbunden und adverbial aufgefasst sein: sättigt sich reichlich, doch scheint das Wort hier sekundär und einer Variantform zu entstammen, wo es eine andere Funktion im Satz hatte, wie noch durchblickt in xiii 2 מפרי פי איש יאכל טוב ונפש בוגדים חמס. Hier weist die Kontrastparallele בוגדים darauf hin, dass טוב Subjekt des ersten Satzes ist, doch ist dessen gegenwärtige Form aus kontaminierender Angleichung an xii 14 (xviii 20) entstanden und er mag ursprünglich etwa gelautet haben: מפרי כפיו יאכל טוב ein anständiger Mann ernährt sich von seiner Arbeit, das Begehren der Raubsüchtigen [2]) geht aus auf Gewalttat. Wenn diese Rekonstruktionen richtig sind, so ist ein ursprüngliches Monostichon מפרי כפי איש ישבע (vgl. xii 14!) (a) variiert zu מפרי כפיו יאכל טוב, das durch eine Kontrastparallele ausgebaut wurde (xiii 2), (b) korrumpiert zu מפרי פי איש ישבע was einen Parellelstichos תבואת שפתיו ישבע ins Dasein rief (xviii 20), der die fehlerhafte Form gewissermassen durch eine interpretatorische Ergänzung bestätigte. Das Aufkommen der Korruption פי anstatt כפי lässt sich am leichtesten vorstellen in schriftlicher Überlieferung, ein Umstand, der jedoch mein Zutrauen zu der hier versuchten Rekonstruktion nicht erschüttert. Ein merkwürdiges Argument zu ihrer Gunsten liegt noch darin, dass der vorausgesetzte Umbildungsprozess „von den Händen zu dem Munde" in der Septuaginta zu xii 14b ἀνταπόδομα δὲ χειλέων αὐτοῦ δοθήσεται αὐτῷ seine Fortsetzung finden würde [3]) !

Auf ein überzeugendes besonders interessantes Beispiel von doppelter Überlieferung eines Sprichworts hat (nach RAHMER und

ursprünglich selbständigen Spruchteilen erklärt werden oder ist sie durch Angleichung veranlasst? Der Parallelismus in Job xv 2 würde eine Lesart תמלא בטנו stützen.

[1]) פרי כפים u.a. xxxi 16, 31. In Deut. xxviii 33 ist פרי = יגיע vgl. dann noch Ps cxxviii 2, Job x 3.

[2]) בוגד auch Js. xxxiii 1 und xxi 2 Parallele zu שדד raubsüchtig, nicht: treulos (was zwar die genuine Bedeutung !).

[3]) Muss hier vielleicht der Möglichkeit eines innergriechischen Fehlers χειρῶν > χειλέων, unter Einfluss der Parallelstellen Rechnung getragen werden?

Früheren) TUR SINAÏ hingewiesen. In Spr xxii 28 אל תסג גבול עולם אשר עשו אבותיך — mit der Parallele Deut. xix 14 werden wir uns sogleich befassen! — wird sichtlich gewarnt gegen das Verrücken von uralten Grenzen, schon von früheren Geschlechtern abgesteckt. In Spr. xxiii 10-11 dagegen אל תשג גבול עולם ובשדי יתומים אל תבא, כי גואלם חזק הוא יריב את ריבם אתך haben wir sozialethische Ermahnungen vor uns, die sich stützen auf einen Appell an den Gott des Rechts, der sich für die sozial Schwachen einsetzt. Die erste Hälfte des Spruchs lautete hier ursprünglich: Verrücke die Grenzen des Ackers der schutzlosen Kinder nicht! אל תסג גבול עוּלים und mache keinen Eingriff in der Waisen Feld. Für diese Koniektur GEIGERS spricht der Parallelismus (identisch mit dem in Iob xxiv 9 [1]) und auch die Übersetzung der Vulgata: Ne attingas parvulorum terminos. Dass Hieronymus in dieser von den anderen alten Versionen abweichenden Wiedergabe beeinflusst sein dürfte von einer zeitgenössischen jüdischen Tradition, wird auch nahegelegt durch die Behandlung, die unsere Stelle in Mischnah und Talmud erfährt. Die Mischnah (Peah v . 6) zitiert אל תסג גבול עולים zur Umschreibung einer Form des Armenraubs גוזל את העניים. Dass hier eine Lesart עולים vorlag — und sie liefert das dritte und stärkste Argument für GEIGERS Vermutung — wird zu Gewissheit erhoben durch die Meinungsverschiedenheit im palästinensischen Talmud, ob das עולים zu erklären sei als עולי מצרים „israelitische Volksgenossen" oder als Euphemismus für אלה שירדו מנכסיהם Leute, die um Habe und Gut gekommen sind. In Zusammenhang mit der Frage, ob jemand eine schwangere Frau heiraten darf, ist in pal. Sotah 4.8 sogar die Lesart אל תסג גבול עוֹלים vorausgesetzt. Es kann kein Zweifel daran bestehen, dass אל תסג גבול עולים und אל תסג גבול עולם zwei Formen darstellen von einem Sprichwort, die schon in biblischer Zeit nebeneinander hergingen [2]). In diesem Falle aber — und dieser Umstand verleiht unserem Beispiel einen besonderen Reiz — können wir die literarische Entwicklung des Spruchs noch näher verfolgen. Man hat schon festgestellt, dass die Vermahnung in xxiii 10 die wehrlosen Kinder zu schonen, mit der Begründung, dass Gott sie sonst rächen wird, ägyptischem Denken

---

[1]) Wo man seit SCHULTENS liest ועול עני.

[2]) Sehr nahe kam dieser Deutung schon im siebzehnten Jahrhundert R. JOMTOV LIPPMAN HELLER in seinem Mischnahkommentar zur Stelle in Peah vgl. auch A. GEIGER in *he-Haluz*, V, 1860, 26; M. RAHMER, *Die hebräischen Traditionen in den Werken des Hieronymus*, I, Breslau 1861, S. 64-67; N. H. TUR SINAI, *Sprüche Salomoh's*, S. 52.

entstammt [1]), während das Festhalten an den von den Vätern abgesteckten Grenzen dem israelitischen historischen Bewusstsein entspricht. Wir hätten es also in אל תסג גבול עולים mit einem ursprünglich ägyptischen Spruch zu tun und in אל תסג גבול עולם (obwohl diese Form in xxii 28 in einer stark ägyptisch gefärbten Umgebung erscheint) mit einer ins Israelitische umbiegende Adaptation — den Begriff wird das dritte Kapitel näher erläutern. Vielleicht dürfen wir noch einen Schritt weiter gehen. In Deut. xix 14 heisst es: אל תסג גבול רעך, אשר גבלו ראשונים Verrücke die Grenzen deines Nächsten nicht, welche die Vorfahren gezogen haben. Mir scheint nun diese gesetzliche Formulierung des Deuteronomiums eine Zwischenstufe darzustellen zwischen den beiden Formen unseres Spruchs. Nicht entscheiden will ich, ob sie ihrerseits entstanden ist aus einer Umbildung des ägyptischen Mahnworts, die aus den schutzlosen Kindern den Volksgenossen machte — wahrscheinlich ist es mir immerhin. Sicher glaube ich, dass sie den Anlass gab, das ältere Sprichwort אל תסג גבול עולים spielerisch zu modulieren zu der dem israelitischen historischen Bewusstsein mehr zusagenden Form: אל תסג גבול עולם. Spr. xxii 28 steht in seiner Formulierung unter Einfluss von Deut. xix 14, wie Spr. xx 10 unter dem von Deut. xxv 13-16 [2]).

III

Bei der Erörterung des Beispiels, mit dem wir den Paragraphen über das Spielelement als interpretationsbildenden Faktor beschlossen, sind wir schon konfrontiert worden mit einer bedeutsamen Erscheinung völlig anderer Art, die noch stärker dazu beiträgt den vorher besprochenen Prozess der Motivübernahme und Motivabwandlung in eine wirkliche Midraschexegese zu verwandeln auch dadurch dass sie ein Element der Bewusstheit in die Vorgänge anbringt bzw. verstärkt. Ich möchte diese Kategorie — teilweise nach dem Vorgang Solomon Schechters [3]) — als Adaptation bezeichnen. Ein späteres

---

[1]) Die Herübernahme in Jr I 34 bietet ein schönes Beispiel von Nationalisierung und Historisierung eines ursprünglich individuell karitativen Gedankens.

[2]) Vgl. J. Fichtner, *Die altorientalische Weisheit in ihrer israelitisch-jüdischen Ausprägung*, Giessen 1933, S. 26-27.

[3]) S. Schechter, *o.c.*, S. 26, doch bezieht er den Ausdruck mehr auf äussere Umbildung; für den inner-alttestamentlichen Prozess s. Anm. 1 auf S. 152 und vgl. noch: L. Venard in *Su. DB* II, Paris 1934, S. 43 s.v. Citations: der in Bezug auf die Zitate im N.T. spricht von accommodation figurative .. par application d'autres personnes, d'autres événements d'autres circonstances que ceux qui sont visés directement dans l'original.

Geschlecht begnügt sich nicht mit der Übernahme des alten Wortes, sondern ändert den Sinn — seltener auch den Wortlaut — desselben, um es dem Denken und Fühlen einer neuen Zeit an zu passen. Die Erscheinung ist alt und verbreitet. In babylonischen Rezensionen von sumerischen Epen werden alte sumerische Götternamen durch babylonische ersetzt, in jüngeren assyrischen Rezensionen treten dafür assyrische Benennungen ein. Profetien von Amos und Hosea' über Nord-Israel sind stellenweise offenbar durch kurze Zusätze auf judaeische Verhältnisse zugeschnitten worden. Interessant ist, wie in der Apostelgeschichte (vii 42) die Drohung Amos' (v 27): Und Ich verbanne euch über Damaskus hinaus, zitiert wird in der aktualisierten Form: Und ich verbanne euch über Babylon hinaus. Im Bibeltext von Rabbi Meir, so erzählt uns der palästinensische Talmud hiess es, anstatt משא דומה (Jes xxi 1) משא רומי [1]); doch nahm man im allgemeinen eine solche Änderung nicht vor, der sah darin vonselbst das dischen Zeit, der in seinem Text אדום fand, Bibelleser der talmurömische Reich oder die christliche Kirche vorgezeichnet.

Es braucht nicht vieler Worte um darzulegen, dass die Adaptation eine wichtige Kategorie bildet für das biblische Denken und nicht weniger ein Hilfsmittel für die moderne Exegese (soweit dieselbe wahrhaft historisch und religionsvergleichend sein will), ermöglicht sie doch dem Ausleger fest zu stellen, inwieweit Gesetzgeber, Dichter und Propheten bei Übernahme fremder, gemeinorientalischer Stoffe dieselben umbilden um sie dem religiösen Denken Israels anzupassen. Beschränken wir uns auf zwei bekannte Beispiele. In den Sprüchen des Amenemope (Kap. IV) wird der Hitzige dem Baum im Walde verglichen, der sein Ende findet in dem Feuer, der wahre Schweigende dagegen dem Baum, der im Garten blüht und dort verbleibt im Angesicht seines Herrn. Von Jeremiah wird das gleiche Bild verwendet, jedoch botanisch-klimatologisch abgewandelt, es ist die Rede von dem Strauch der Steppe und dem Baum gepflanzt an Wasserbächen. Wichtiger ist, dass anstatt des Hitzigen derjenige erscheint, der sich auf Menschen verlässt und anstatt des Schweigenden der Mann der auf Gott vertraut. Letzterer ist dann in Ps i, infolge der weiteren Entwicklung der Frömmigkeitsideale, umgebildet zu dem Frommen der sich in das heilige Buch vertieft: das übernommene Bild des Baumes wird zum Träger von einer Folge typisch-israelitischer

[1]) pal. Taänith I, 1.

Gestalten [1]). Instruktiv ist auch die Entwicklung des Rahab-Motivs. An drei Stellen, wo es auftritt (Ps lxxxix 11, Iob ix 13, xxvi 12) hören wir ohne Zweifel einen Nachhall des babylonisch-mythologischen Motivs von dem göttlichen Ungeheuer [2]), das bei der Schöpfung der Welt vom Schöpfergott bekämpft und besiegt wird, nur dass in der Bibel — wie KAUFMANN mit Recht betont — der Schöpfergott seine Herrschaft keineswegs diesem Sieg verdankt, sondern nur die Mächte bestraft, die sich gegen ihn empören [3]). Das gleiche Motiv begegnet nun Jes. li 9-10: Hervor! Hervor! Leg' Kraft an Du Arm des Herrn, Hervor wie in den Tagen der Vorzeit, den uralten Geschlechtern, Warst Du es nicht, der Rahab zerhieb [4]), das Ungeheuer durchbohrte? Warst nicht Du es, der das Meer ausgetrocknet, die Wasser der grossen Tiefe, der die Gründe des Meeres zum Weg gewandelt, dass die Erlösten durchzogen? Hier fliessen die Wundertaten Gottes bei der Schöpfung und beim Auszug aus Ägypten, beim Durchzug durch das Rote Meer ineinander; die Möglichkeit eines solchen Ineinanderfliessens war gegeben durch die hervorgehende Identifikation von dem Meeresungeheuer Rahab mit Ägypten [5]). Von Deuterojesajah wird das kosmisch-mythologische Motiv historisiert und so endgültig aufgenommen in die israelitische Religion.

Diese für den israelitischen Denkstil bezeichnende historisierende Adaptation der Motive bekommt nun da ihren Platz in der Geschichte der Exegese, wo sie verbunden wird mit der Ausdeutung eines alten Textworts, so z.B. wenn wir bei ben Sira lesen: (l 26-27 [37-38]) בשני גוים קצה נפשי והשלישית איננו עם ישבי שעיר ופלשת וגוי נבל הדר בשכם Zwei Völker sind mir in der Seele verhasst, das dritte ist kein Volk; die Bewohner von Edom und Philistea und das unwürdige Volk,

---

[1]) H. GRESSMANN, *Israels Spruchweisheit im Rahmen der Weltliteratur*, Berlin 1925, S. 30-33.

[2]) So nach den grundlegenden Ausführungen von H. GUNKEL, *Schöpfung und Chaos*, Göttingen 1894, S. 29-90 gegen HERTLEIN *ZAW* 38, 1920. Beachtenswert ist, dass רגע in Job xxvi 12 noch die ursprüngliche, von der Septuaginta mannigfach bezeugte Bedeutung: vernichten, hat; רגע הים ist eben abgeschwächte Nachwirkung der früheren mythischen Vorstellung.

[3]) J. KAUFMANN, *l.c.* (Anm. 3 auf S. 154).

[4]) המחצבת stellt wohl eine kontaminierte Form da von החצבת zerschlagen (wie im Ugaritischen auch Hos vi 5) und einem späteren המחצת, derartige Kontaminationen (Zch x 2 נסעו aus נסו und נעו u.s.w.) sind bekanntlich zahlreich im masoretischen Text, einstweilen: R. GORDIS *The biblical text in the making*, Philadelphia 1937, S. 41-43.

[5]) Jes. xxx 7, Ps lxxxvii 4 genau so wie der Pharao Ez. xxix 3 (vgl. xxxii 2) der Drache gennant wird, der inmitte seines Nils lagert.

das in Schechem wohnt. Deutlich wird hier Deut xxxii 21 aufgenommen und ausgedeutet. Wenn die Schrift dort sagt, dass Gott Israels Eifersucht und Zorn erwecken will durch ein Nicht-Volk, das nichtwürdig ist (לא עם, גוי נבל), so weiss ben Sira, wie offenbar auch seine Zeitgenossen, dass damit die verhassten Eindringlinge dunkler Herkunft, die Samaritaner von Schechem gemeint sind [1]). Wir haben hier einen richtigen aktualisierenden Midrasch vor uns, was noch eindrücklicher wird durch den merkwürdigen Umstand, dass die gleiche Auffassung, die von ben Sira implicite vorausgesetzt wird, sich als explizierte Auslegung erhalten hat in einer Version eines späten Midraschwerkes ad Deut. xxxii 21: durch ein Nicht-Volk, hiermit sind die Kuthäer (Samaritaner) gemeint [2]). Aufmerksamkeit verdient die Tatsache, dass der gleiche Deuteronomium-Vers an einer berühmten Stelle im Römerbrief (x 19) von Paulus in einer anders gerichteten Adaptation verwendet wird: die Nicht-Völker d.h. die Heiden — so hat es Moses gesagt — werden einst Israel seinen Platz bei Gott strittig machen ! Beiden Deutungen gemeinsam ist der Zug, dass die Exegese bedingt ist von den Erfahrungen des Auslegers in der Geschichte.

Anderswo habe ich ausgeführt, wie sehr das historische Erlebnis bestimmend ist für die alt-jüdische Exegese; das Gleiche gilt auch für die alt-christliche. Die jüdische Exegese wurzelt im Midrasch und das Ziel des Midrasch ist, den Bibeltext zu aktualisieren, d.h. zu zeigen, dass das alte Bibelwort sich bezieht auf geschichtliche Ereignisse in der Zeit des Erklärers. Der griechische Übersetzer von Jes. ix 11 ארם מקדם ופלשתים מאחור findet in den Aramäern und Philistäern von Jesajah's Zeit die Syrier und Hellenen seiner eigenen zurück [3]). Dieses Bestreben zu aktualisieren erhält seine besondere Ausprägung in Zeiten von Krisis und Religionsverfolgung, wenn das Ende aller Dinge bevorzustehen scheint. Der Augenblick, da Antiochus Epiphanes sich am heiligen Tempel in Jerusalem vergriff und die jüdische Religion mit seinen Massnahmen bedrohte, wurde die Geburtsstunde der jüdischen Apokalyptik. Man glaubte zu erleben, was die Propheten vorhergesagt hatten; der Feind wurde von der Volksphantasie aus-

[1]) S. Schlesinger, *MGWJ*, 83, 1939. 277.

[2]) *Midrasch Tannaim zum Deuteronomium* ed. D. Hoffmann, Berlin 1909, S. 196. Freilich bezweifelt der Herausgeber die Echtheit des Passus an unserer Stelle.

[3]) In einem Sabbathlied von Jehudah ha Levie ist der gleiche Text transponiert auf die Christen und Araber, in der Zeit der Reconquista אדום מקדם ליום ראשון, ערב מאחור ליום ששי ed. H. Brody, IV, Berlin 1930 S. 3; ein schönes Beispiel dafür, wie die Aktualisierung durch die Jahrhunderte geht !

gestattet mit allen Zügen des grossen Bedrückers, den Jesajah in klassischer Weise gezeichnet hatte. Eine Reihe von Danielstellen (ix 27; xi 10, 27, 30, 36, 40) an denen die markantesten Ausdrücke aus Jesajah mit Anspielungen auf Numeri- und Habakuk-Texte verweben sind, liest sich wie ein aktualisierender Kommentar zu Jesajah's Prophetie über Assur (sie bildet wohl das schönste Beispiel von Bibelerklärung innerhalb der Bibel). Zudem weisen auch die Jesajah-Septuaginta und die Bücher der Makkabäer Spuren davon auf, wiesehr die Erlebnisse der Zeit die Auslegung des Jesajahtextes bestimmt und gefärbt haben. Einen klassischen Ausdruck findet das Wesen dieser apokalyptisch-aktualisierenden Exegese in dem Pescher Habakuk (DSH), wo die Rede ist von denjenigen, „welche den Bund Gottes dadurch brechen, dass sie nicht glauben, wenn sie all' das, was über das letzte Geschlecht kommen wird, hören aus dem Mund des gerechten Priesters, dem Gott [Weisheit ins Herz] gelegt hat, so dass er alle Worte auszulegen weiss von Gottes Dienern den Propheten, durch die Gott all', was über sein Volk und Land kommen würde, angekündigt hat". Wir stossen hier auf die apokalyptische Stimmung derer, die glauben das letzte Geschlecht zu bilden; diese Stimmung verbindet sich mit einer Würdigung der Prophetie (die uns im nächsten Paragraphen noch beschäftigen wird) und auch mit einer Auffassung vom Wesen der Exegese. Dieselbe ist um so bezeichnender, weil das Wort פשר, das gebraucht wird um die technisch-exegetische Tätigkeit des gerechten Priesters anzudeuten, bekanntlich Mal über Mal wiederkehrt, um jedes Stückchen Einzelexegese einzuleiten; die Bestandteile des Bibeltextes werden zitiert und dann durch ein פשרו: dies bezieht sich auf angewandt auf die Ereignisse und Figuren aus der Gegenwart des Erklärers [1]).

Sicher bewirken das sektarische Milieu [2]) und das apokalyptische

[1]) Für diesen Absatz vgl. I. L. Seeligmann, *The Septuagint Version of Isaiah*, Leiden 1948, S. 82 ff. Der Pescher Habakuk wurde kurz nach Abschluss dieser Arbeit bekannt; es scheint derartige Pescharim zu mehreren Prophetenbüchern gegeben zu haben (einstweilen vgl. C. J. Milik, *RB*, 59, 1952 412 ff). Dass der Pescher Habakuk, wohl im ersten nachchristlichen Jh. entstanden, meine früheren Darlegungen bestätigte, wurde hervorgehoben von Eiszfeldt, *ThLZ*, 1949, S. 478, vgl. auch *Bi Or* 6, 1949, 5. Für die Bezeichnung des Pescher Habakuk als Midrasch scheint mir nach wie vor mehr die Art seiner Aktualisierung als seine Technik bestimmend; etwas anders (an sich sicher beachtenswert Brownlee, *BA*, 14, 1951, S.76). Für פשר in der Bedeutung der aus DSH zitierten Stelle vgl. noch Numeri Rabba xix ומי יודע פשר דבר זה הקב"ה שפירש את התורה למשה.

[2]) Der Ausdruck bei M. A. Beek, *Inleiding tot de Joodsche Apocalyptiek*, Haarlem 1950, Kap. IV.

Bewusstsein am Ende der Zeiten zu leben, eine Steigerung des Bestrebens das Prophetenwort auf die eigene Zeit zu übertragen und damit des Motivs der Adaptation. Doch ist dieses Motiv auch sonst im israelitischen historisch-gerichteten Denken von besonderer Bedeutung geworden für die älteste jüdische und christliche Exegese; es lässt sich über dieselbe hinaus lange zurückverfolgen im Alten Testament selbst; ich möchte das an zwei Beispielreihen zeigen.

In der Entwicklung des Verhältnisses von Individuum und Gemeinschaft in Israel begegnen sich zwei verschiedene und fast gegensätzliche Tendenzen. Wir sehen, wie sich das Individuum aus den Bindungen der Stammesgemeinschaft löst; umgekehrt ist das historische Bewusstsein so stark dass ursprünglich individuelle Äusserungen übertragen werden auf die Erlebnisse der Gemeinschaft. Die Dank und Klagelieder des Einzelnen erfahren dadurch in der volkstümlichen Exegese schon früh eine Umbiegung. Psalm xxx lässt sich kaum anders erklären als das Danklied eines Einzelnen, der von einer schweren Krankheit genesen ist. Die Überschrift, die ihn als Lied bei der Einweihung des Tempels bezeichnet, weist wohl darauf hin, dass die Generation, die nach dem Babylonischen Exil den Tempel von neuem aufbaute und einweihte, den Inhalt des Psalms auf die Leiden des Volkes Israel bezog [1]). In der ergreifenden Klage von Jeremiah (xx 17-18): Warum bin ich nicht am Mutterleib gestorben, warum aus der Mutter Schoss hervorgekommen Mühsal und Kummer zu sehen (d.h. zu erleben)? — ist mit: Mühsal und Kummer, sicher das eigene persönliche Schicksal des Propheten gemeint. Das vierte Esra-Buch aber legt den Vers seinem Seher in den Mund (v 35) in der ausdrücklich erweiterten Form: „Wäre mir doch meine Mutter zum Grab geworden, damit ich Jakobs Mühsal nicht hätte sehen müssen und nicht den Kummer des Geschlechtes Israel?" Überaus zahlreich sind die Beispiele dieser Erscheinung im Midrasch zu den Psalmen; ich zitiere nur das zu Ps xiii 6: Ich aber vertraue auf Deine Treue, mein Herz jubelt, weil Du mir geholfen, ich singe dem Herrn weil Er mir wohlgetan. Der Midrasch liest und deutet diese Äusserung eines Individuums als das Zeugnis der Gemeinschaft von Israel während der Bedrückung in den vier Weltreichen: Ich vertraue auf Deine Treue in Babel, mein Herz jubelt weil Du mir geholfen, während der Herrschaft der Meder, ich singe dem Herrn in der Zeit der Griechen (hellenistischen Könige), weil Er mir wohlgetan

---

[1]) H. Ludin Jansen, *Die spätjüdische Psalmendichtung usw.*, Oslo 1937, S. 99.

angesichts der Gewalt der Römer [1]). Die Leiden von Exil und Bedrückung, zu denen sich später der Anspruch der Christen gesellt, sie hätten den wahren Glauben und das jüdische Volk sei von Gott verworfen, vertiefen die israelitische Überzeugung, das auserwählte Volk zu sein, bis zu der dreisten Behauptung, die Welt wäre nur um Israels willen erschaffen worden. Eine Praefiguration dieses Ausspruchs treffen wir an einer Stelle in vierten Esra Buch, wo ein Zitat aus Deuterojesajah eine merkwürdige Umdeutung erfährt. In einer begeisterten Verherrlichung Gottes lesen wir bei Deuterojesajah (xl 15): Sieh, alle Völker sind wie der Tropfen am Eimer und gelten Ihm wie das Stäubchen an der Wage; sieh die Inseln wiegen Ihm wie ein Sandkorn. Einziges Ziel dieser Verse ist es die souveräne Allmacht Gottes, so eindrucksvoll wie möglich darzustellen. Der Seher im vierten Esra Buch dagegen spricht (vi 55-56): Du hast gesagt, dass Du unseretwillen diese Welt geschaffen habest, die übrigen Völker, die von Adam abstammen, hast Du für nichts erklärt: sie seien dem Speichel gleich, mit dem Tropfen am Eimer hast Du ihren Überschwang verglichen. Das deuterojesajanische Motiv von der Majestät Gottes hat sich hier verwandelt in das von der Nichtswürdigkeit der heidnischen Völker. Nahegelegt wurde diese weitgehende Verschiebung der Exegese durch eine, schon in der Septuaginta bezeugte Textvariante, die anstatt כדק: wie ein Sandkorn, las כרק und so die Völker dem Speichel gleichstellte. Es verdient Beachtung, dass sich die gleiche Auslegung wie im vierten Esra-Buch — offenbar ohne dass eine Abweichung vom masoretischen Text vorausgesetzt wäre — auch im späten Midrasch Numeri Rabba findet, sogar in zwei Formen [2]).

Eine gleichartig adaptative Auswirkung auf die Textdeutung hat auch das Verlangen nach dem Messias. Für die ganze nachexilische Zeit — vielleicht schon früher — lässt sich das Streben verfolgen in Texten, die im ursprünglichen Zusammenhang von dem König reden, den Messias zurück zu finden. So heisst es Ps. lxxii 8 vom König in einer dem babylonischen Hofstil entlehnten Formulierung, Er herrsche vom Meer zu Meer, vom grossen Strom bis zu den Enden der Erde; die Aussage wird Zach ix 10 wortwörtlich auf den Messias übertragen. In Ps. ii 8-9 wird der israelitische oder judäische König

---

[1]) I. L. Seeligmann, „Phasen uit de geschiedenis van het Joodsch historisch bewustzijn", *MVEOL* VII, Leiden 1947, S. 66-69.

[2]) Num R. i 4; iv 2. Die Midraschim lehnen sich an Jes. xl 17 (nicht: xl 15) an, der Gegensatz ist beide Male אֲבָל ישראל.

dadurch gefeiert, dass der Hofdichter Gott zu ihm sprechen lässt: Verlange von Mir, so geb' Ich dir Völker zum Erbe, die Enden der Welt zum Besitz. Du wirst sie mit eiserner Keule zerschmettern, wie Töpfergeschirr zertrümmern. Das vielleicht berühmteste Dokument der Messiaserwartung der hasmonäischen Zeit, der siebzehnte der Psalmen Salomoh's klagt über die Könige die Davids Thron entweihen, über den heidnischen Feind, über das Volk in Sünde und fährt dann fort: Schau Herr, und lass' ihnen ihren König erstehen, den Sohn Davids ... und gürte ihn mit Kraft, dass er unrechtmässige Herrscher fälle. Dass er Jerusalem reinige von den Heiden, ... die Sünder aus dem Erbe austreibe und ihren Übermut zertrümmere wie Töpfergeschirr, mit eiserner Keule zerschmettere all' ihren Bestand. Die späteren hasmonaäischen Könige, Usurpatoren auf Davids Thron [1]) freuten sich keiner besonderen Beliebtheit bei den Frommen ihres Volkes: die Ausrottung der Heiden kann nicht ihre Aufgabe sein. So rüstet die polemische, im Grunde anti-königliche Literatur der Zeit, den Messias, den idealen Sohn Davids aus mit den Zügen, die im biblischen Psalm dem innerweltlichen König eigen waren: die Spannung zwischen Ideal und Wirklichkeit — deren schöpferische Bedeutung z.B. MOWINCKEL erkannt hat — macht hier ihren Einfluss geltend in der adaptativen Exegese. Etwas anderer Art scheint, auf dem ersten Blick unser nächstes Beispiel. Der Dichter des Ps. viii staunt darüber, wie von Gott der Sterbliche und das Menschenkind [2]) mit Macht über die Schöpfung bekleidet worden und alles, die Tiere des Feldes, die Vögel des Himmels und die Fische des Meeres seinen Füssen unterstellt ist: Diese Aussage wird im Neuen Testament auf den Christus bezogen, mit solcher Selbstverständlichkeit, dass diese Deutung im Hebräerbrief zwar ausgeführt ist (ii 6-9), im Epheserbrief (i 22) und im ersten Korintherbrief (xv 27) aber ohne Weiteres vorausgesetzt. Mit Rücksicht auf die messianischen Assoziationen, die seit Daniel in der apokalyptischen Literatur mit dem Begriff Menschensohn verbunden wurden, lag es auf der Hand, den Menschensohn dessen Füssen alles unterstellt war, mit dem Christus zu identifizieren [3]).

[1]) V. APTOWITZER, *Hasmonäische und anti-Hasmonäische Parteipolitik im rabbinischen und pseudepigraphischen Schrifttum*, Wien 1927; I. L. SEELIGMANN, *Historisch bewustzijn*, S. 62.[18]).

[2]) Es fällt schwer erwähnen zu müssen, dass heute (wieder) mit Nachdruck die Meinung vertreten wird, an Stellen wie Ps viii sei בן אדם a royal title, *Bi Or*, 8, 1951, S. 188 u. 192.

[3]) Zum ganzen Problem cf. A. VIS, *An inquiry into the rise of Christianity out of Judaism*, Amsterdam 1936.

Doch sei im Lichte der soeben gegebenen Beispiele, wo die Attribute des Königs auf den Messias übertragen worden sind, die Frage gestattet, ob vielleicht der Gedanke von Ps. viii, bevor er auf den Messias gedeutet wurde, auf den König angewandt worden war und ob uns eine Spur sieder hypothetischen Zwischenstufe in der Auslegungsgeschichte erhalten wäre in Dan ii 37-39, wo Daniel zu Nebukadretsar spricht: Du, o König, König der Könige — dem der Gott des Himmels das Königtum, die Macht und die Kraft und die Ehre gegeben hat und dem Er in der ganzen bewohnten Welt die Menschen, die Tiere des Feldes und die Vogel des Himmels in die Hand gegeben und den Er über sie alle zum Herrscher gemacht hat — du bist das Haupt von Gold!

Durch die zentrale, allbeherrschende Stellung, die der Christus im neutestamentlichen Denken innehat, werden alle mögliche Figuren und Ereignisse der alttestamentlichen Welt auf ihn und sein Leben bezogen. Hier geht die adaptative Auslegung über in die typologische, die in mancher Hinsicht auch für die rabbinische Aggadah bezeichnend ist, doch kann sie uns hier nicht weiter beschäftigen [1]). Nur sei zum Abschluss dieses Paragraphen — einigermassen auch als Überleitung zum folgenden — auf eine nicht so leicht durchsichtige, aber äusserst merkwürdige Stelle im Römerbrief (x 6-8) aufmerksam gemacht, die in einer kühnen Adaptation eine Deuteronomiumstelle (xxx 12-13), in der von der Thorah die Rede ist auf den Christus anwendet. Wer will hinauf gen Himmel fahren den Christum herabzuholen, wer wird hinab in die Tiefe fahren den Christum von den Toten heraufzuholen. Die Transposition, durch die jüdische Aussagen über die Thorah auf den Christus übertragen werden, begegnet auch sonst im paulinischen Denken [2]).

Unsere Ausführungen in den beiden letzten Paragraphen dürften dazu beitragen den Unterschied klar zu stellen, zwischen den Anfängen der jüdischen und christlichen Exegese und der interpretatorischen Tätigkeit der ersten hellenistischen Philologen. Zwar trug zur Ent-

[1]) Vielleicht noch bezeichnender als Röm. v 14 ist 1 Kor. x 11; vgl. L. Goppelt: *Typos*, Gütersloh 1939; vor allein aber die lichtvollen Ausführungen R. Bultmanns *ThLZ* 75. 1950. 206 ff. Wohl kennt die Aggadah das exegetische Prinzip מעשה אבות סימן לבנים (σημεῖον nicht τύπος) doch ist das mehr eine Neigung an späteren Stellen in der Bibel eine Wiederholung zu finden von dem was den Erzvätern wiederfuhr, eine Neigung, die gelegentlich (Genesis Rabba xl 5 ad Gn. xii 16) begünstigt wird durch Dupletten.

[2]) W. Schmauch, *In Christus*, Leipzig 1935, hält sogar das ἐν χριστῷ für eine Ablösung eines jüdisch-hellenistischen ἐν νόμῳ vgl. meine Bemerkungen ad LXX Jes xxxiii 6, *Septuagint Version* 107.

stehung derselben eine Wertschätzung Homers als Inbegriff aller Schönheit und Weisheit bei, die sich vielleicht der Wertschätzung der Bibel vergleichen liesse, doch ist das gelehrte Interesse an schwierigen und dialektischen Wörtern (glossographie) und Lauterscheinungen (Prosodie)[1]) sehr verschieden von der nachhaltigen Wirkung des Spielelements und vor allem von dem erlebnismässigen Charakter der ältesten Midraschexegese.

IV

In den bisherigen Ausführungen war die Rede von Gestaltungen und Umbildungen, die eine Auslegung zwar anbahnen, aber noch nicht als Auslegung im eigentlichen Sinne gelten können. Das Spielelement färbt die Motivabwandlung, das Zitat wird durch Adaptation transponiert, doch betreffen all' diese Erscheinungen eine sich noch im Fluss befindliche, nicht „geronnene", zum Abschluss gekommene Literatur. Richtige Exegese tritt erst da auf, wo sich den bisher genannten Elementen noch ein anderartiges hinzugesellt: das Erklären-wollen einer abgeschlossenen Schrift, der überdies eine besondere Bedeutung beigelegt wird, weil sie als Wort Gottes aufgefasst wird. Hier kann nicht daran gedacht werden, den Stadien der Kanonisierung der Heiligen Schrift nachzugehen; wie dieselbe sich vollzogen hat, ist keineswegs so sicher, wie man wünschen möchte und wohl mancher zu meinen scheint [2]). Doch interessiert uns hier nicht der äussere Prozess der Kanonisierung, sondern der Wandel im Bewusstsein, der dem alten Wort eine neue Bedeutung und Autorität beilegt.

Dieser psychologischen Umwertung wurde von zwei Seiten her Vorschub geleistet: Einerseits kam das Gefühl auf, dass das Zeitalter der Prophetie vorüber sei. Im jüdischen Volksbewusstsein scheint das Ende der Prophetie ungefähr mit dem Abschluss der persischen Periode in Palästina zusammen zu fallen : so wollen es die einstimmigen Zeugnisse von Josephus und der talmudischen Literatur, Malachi gilt der Tradition als der letzte der Propheten und seit der zweiten Hälfte des Buches Daniel tritt die (unter parsistischem Einfluss stehende !) Apokalyptik als pseudepigraphisches

---

[1]) F. Susemihl, *Geschichte der griechischen Literatur in der Alexandrinerzeit* II Leipzig 1892 S. 663-665, Nachtrag zu I 327-329.

[2]) Einstweilen vgl. etwa: Strack-Billerbeck, *Kommentar zum NT aus Talmud und Midrasch*, IV, München 1928, S. 415-434 und R. Meyer in *ThWbNT.* III, Stuttgart 1938, S. 979-987.

Schrifttum auf [1]). Nun hatte man in Israel von jeher all' was geschah betrachtet als die Verwirklichung eines vorhergehenden Gotteswortes und auch der klassischen ethischen Prophetie blieb immer ein Element der Zukunftsverkündigung anhaften [2]). So waren seit der griechischen Zeit zwei Voraussetzungen dafür gegeben, die nunmehr vorliegende Schriften der Propheten aufzufassen von Gottes Ankündigung von dem was sich in der Gegenwart begab, oder auch als Vorhersagung einer noch bevorstehenden Zukunft. Wir streiften oben diese Einstellung in Bezug auf das Buch Daniel und die Entstehung der Apokalyptik, sie ist aber auch bezeichnend für die ganze neutestamentliche Denkart. Diese Wertschätzung gab Anlass, sich immer wieder in die prophetischen Schriften zu vertiefen und für jedes Detail derselben Erklärungen zu versuchen: in der Tat wird im Pescher Habakuk (DSH vii 4-5 vgl. II 8-9) der priesterliche Lehrer der Gerechtigkeit als derjenige bezeichnet, dem Gott alle Geheimnisse in den Worten Seiner Diener der Propheten kundgetan hat.

Noch stärkere Antriebe erhielt das Bedürfnis anderer Kreise, das Heilige Wort zu erklären, von den gesetzlichen Schriften her, Thorah im engeren Sinn. Von alters her bildeten die Gesetze Objekt der Ausdeutung und Erweiterung, namentlich durch die Priester [3]), die einzelne priesterliche Entscheidung, der einzelne richterliche Ausspruch, die einzelne Belehrung der Weisen hatten schon immer als Gottes Wort gegolten [4]). Eine wichtige Neuerung bedeutet es, wenn der ganze Komplex von Vorschriften samt dem historischen Rahmen,

---

[1]) Jos. contra Apionem I. 8.40 vgl. b. Sanh 11b; Canticum Rabba ad viii 10 Seder 'Olam Rabba xxx; neben R. Meyer, *l.c.*; vgl. vor allem: E. Urbach, Wann hat die Prophetie aufgehört? (hebräisch) *Tarbiz* 17, 1946, S. 1 ff.

[2]) J. Kaufmann, *Geschichte der israelitischen Religion* (hebräisch), IV, Tel Aviv 1942, S. 153 ff. leitet bekanntlich den Ursprung der biblischen Historiographie aus der israelitischen Anschauung her, die die Geschichte als Verwirklichung des Gotteswortes betrachtet, vgl. heute etwa: G. Östborn, *Yhwh's Words and Deeds*, Uppsala 1951; und W. Zimmerli, Verheissung und Erfüllung, *Evang. Theologie* 12, 1952, S. 48. Die Bestimmung des „mantischen" Elements in der klassischen Prophetie bleibe einem anderen Zusammenhang vorbehalten.

[3]) Ein Vergleich von der Formensprache in Hagg. ii. 12 הן ישא איש mit der in Jer. iii 1 הן ישלח איש legt die Vermutung nahe, dass uns hier Beispiele bewahrt sind eines schon in der vorexilischen Zeit fest ausgeprägten Stils der priesterlichen Kasuistik.

[4]) J. Begrich, „Die priesterliche Tōrā, *BZAW*, 66, 1936, S. 63 ff.; daneben G. Östborn, *Tōrā in the OT*, Lund 1945; das schöne Buch hätte überzeugender gewirkt, bei einer anderen Formulierung des Ch. III The king as the emparter of Tōrā.

in den er hineingestellt ist, mit dem Anspruch auftritt, Thorah zu sein. Wir können diesen Übergang noch genau erfassen durch einen Vergleich vom alttestamentlichen Buch Proverbia mit den späteren Sprüchen des ben Sira. In dem berühmten, leider nur griechisch erhaltenen, Kapitel ben Sira xxiv werden die Züge der kosmischen Weisheit (Prov. viii 22 ff.) auf die an Israel offenbarte Thorah übertragen. Diese Übertragung legt den Grund zu der Anschauung von der Präexistenz und der Überzeitlichkeit der Thorah, die das gesamte rabbinische Denken während Jahrhunderte beherrschen wird. Zudem aber — und das ist für unseren Zusammenhang von besonderer Wichtigkeit — tritt die Thorah hier auf, nicht als vereinzelte Weisung, sondern als das abgeschlossene Gesetzbuch: Das alles ist das Bundesbuch Gottes, das Gesetz, das uns Mose gebot als Erbteil für die Gemeinde Jakobs (23; mit Entlehnung aus Deut xxxiii 4 !). Diese Erscheinung beschränkt sich keineswegs auf den locus classicus in Kap. xxiv; sie ist typisch für das ganze Buch. In Proverbia ist Thorah noch die Ermahnung von Vater, Mutter oder Lehrer [1]), in ben Sira ist sie das Gesetzbuch Gottes: ein Vergleich von Spr. xxviii 7 נוצר תורה בן מבין, ורועה זוללים מכלים אביו mit Sir. xxxv 24 נוצר תורה שומר נפשו ובוטח בה̆ לא יבוש macht das besonders eindrücklich. In Sir. xiv 20 heisst es: Selig der Mann, der über Weisheit nachsinnt, dazu die Fortsetzung xv 1: Wer den Herrn fürchtet tut das und wer am Gesetz festhält erlangt sie. Der Gottesfürchtige ist zu demjenigen geworden der an dem Gesetz festhält; genau so: ii 16; xix 19. 20; xxi 11, xxxviii 34 [2]). Auch der Prozess, in dem sich das Gesetz b u c h Gottes die Stellung erringt, die es auf Jahrhunderte innehalten wird, vollzieht sich am Ausgang der persischen Zeit.

Mit diesem Übergang aus dem Begriff der vereinzelten Weisung in den des ganzen Komplexes der Lehre kommt auch — so dürfen wir annehmen — die Neigung auf, sich in die Thorah zu vertiefen und ihren Sinn zu verstehen. Schon der Dichter des wohl in der hellenistischen Zeit entstandenen Thorahpsalms cxix (18) betet: Öffne mir die Augen, dass ich die Verborgenheiten Deiner Lehre schauen möge [3]). Wie stark sich diese Neigung zur Vertiefung und

[1]) Man vergleiche die überzeugenden Ausführungen bei J. Fichtner, *Die altorientalische Weisheit usw.*, Giessen 1933, S. 83-85.

[2]) Die Beispiele sind dem griechischen Text entnommen, der den in Rede stehenden Gedanken auch ix 15 (vgl. 16 !) zum Ausdruck bringt, wo der hebräische Text verderbt zu sein scheint.

[3]) Auf die Tatsache, dass hier der Midrasch als Exegese vorausgesetzt ist, machte mich Z. Mossel (jetzt Ramath Gan) vor Jahren aufmerksam.

Ausdeutung ausprägte, erfahren wir an unerwarteter Stelle in einer Dublette der Septuaginta zu Prov. xiii 15 שכל טוב יתן חן σύνεσις ἀγαθὴ δίδωσιν χάριν, τὸ δὲ γνῶναι νόμον διανοίας ἐστίν ἀγαθῆς. Hier finden wir neben einer buchstäblichen Übersetzung: ein guter Verstand verleiht Anmut, eine andere: es ist Sache eines guten Verstandes das Gesetz (= die Thorah) zu kennen, d.h. nur eine gute Begabung vermag das Gesetz zu verstehen. Man hat auf Grund des Kontextes der Übersetzung den Eindruck, dass die zuletzt erwähnte Wiedergabe die ältere ist [1]). Sie setzt — und darauf kommt es hier an — die Entwicklung eines Thorahstudiums im jüdisch-alexandrinischen Milieu voraus. Nebenbei verdient die Tatsache Beachtung, dass der Übersetzer das Wort חן ohne weiteres als Thorah deuten kann, offenbar setzt er eine Gleichsetzung voraus wie אין חן אלא תורה „wenn die Schrift von חן redet, so meint sie immer Thorah", die es ihm gestattet, wo er das Wort חן vorfindet den Begriff Thorah zu substituieren [2]). M.a.W. im jüdisch-hellenistischen Denken von Alexandrien konnte die Thorah — schon früh? — durch figürliche Begriffe angedeutet werden, ein Umstand, der uns vielleicht einen Einblick in die Art der dortigen Exegese gestattet.

Wir haben die Schwelle erreicht, wo Motivabwandlung, Spielelement und Adaptation in richtige Auslegung übergehen. Man vertieft sich in alle Einzelheiten des Schriftwortes, vor allem auf dem Gebiet der Halachah, der gesetzlichen Bestimmungen, das uns hier nicht weiter beschäftigen soll. Doch tritt auch die freiere, dichterische Aggadah mit wirklichen Fragen an den Text heran. Sie will z.B. die in der Thorah bzw. in der Bibel anonym auftretenden Personen identifizieren, eine Erscheinung, die während der ganzen Geschichte des Midrasch überaus häufig ist und sehr alt sein dürfte. Die Aggadah denkt sich auch die Situationen aus, die den Hinter-

---

[1]) Nur zu ihr, der zweiten, Wiedergabe (und nicht zu der ersten) passt die Fortsetzung : die es gering schätzen geraten ins Verderben, hier ist als Objekt sicher an νόμος gedacht; in der Tat findet sich LXX Jes. xxvi 14 als Wiedergabe von בג"ד: ἀθετεῖν τὸν νόμον. U.a. aus diesem Grunde scheint mir das τὸ δὲ γνῶναι νόμον διανοίας ἐστίν ἀγαθῆς ursprünglich der Stelle xiii 15 an zu gehören und von dort aus in ix 10 sekundär zitiert wird nach der Wiedergabe von תחלת חכמה יראת ה̆ ודעת קדושים בינה.

[2]) Zu dem Vers Spr. xiii 15 ist die hier vorgetragene Deutung der LXX in palästinensischen Quellen nicht bekannt. Wohl wird sie in Betrachtungen zu anderen Versen des Spruchbuchs vorausgesetzt, so z.B. in Sifrê Numeri xiv zum Priestersegen (vi 25; ed. Horovitz, Leipzig 1917, S. 44) wo es heisst: „Er verleihe Dir Gnade (חן) durch das Studium der Lehre, wie es heisst: Die Thorah (so der Midrasch) verleiht einen Gnadenkranz (Spr. iv 9 und vgl. i 9) usw.

grund bilden sollen zu den literarischen Erzeugnissen der Bibel. Hier sind die Psalmenüberschriften zu nennen, die manche Psalmen einer bestimmten Situation zuweisen, wie denn der ganze Prozess der Redaktion der Bibel als eine alte Schicht der Aggadah zu werten ist. In diesen Psalmenüberschriften lässt sich — so wenig übrigens wie in der Halachah und Aggadah überhaupt — nicht immer entscheiden, wo alte Tradition vorliegt und wo die historischen Daten der Bibel von der Phantasie Späterer ergänzt und ausgeschmückt worden sind [1]). Den Anfang der Worterklärung bilden die Stellen in der Bibel, wo seltene Wörter durch mehr gebräuchliche glossiert (b.z.w. ersetzt !) worden sind. Doch geht auch die spätere Aggadah nicht selten von regelrechten Worterklärungen aus. Denselben kommt besonderes Gewicht zu, weil die Midraschim mitunter anknüpfen an Wortbedeutungen, die in ihrer Zeit noch im Sprachgebrauch lebendig waren (wie sich gelegentlich erhärten lässt aus den alten Versionen und den Dead Sea Scrolls) später aber verloren gegangen sind [2]). Die älteste Form der fortlaufenden Texterklärung dürfte diejenigen sein, in der eine zusammenhangende Bibelstelle zergliedert, so zu sagen in ihre einzelnen Bestandteile zerlegt wird und sodann jedes Textelement mit Hilfe eines aus anderen Zusammenhang stammenden Bibelverses verdeutlicht wird [3]). Daneben finden sich schon frühzeitig Fälle, in denen mehrere Sätze frei paraphrasiert, gewissermassen zu einem neuen Kontext verarbeitet werden. Zwei derartige alte Beispiele seien hier — zum Abschluss — erwähnt. In DSD II 1 ff. [4]) segnen die Priester alle diejenigen, die zu

---

[1]) Nach der Ansicht TORCZYNERS, seit: Das literarische Problem der Bibel, *ZDMG* 85, 1931, S. 297 ff. jetzt TUR SINAI, „The literary character of the Book of Psalms", *OTS* VIII, 1950, S. 263 ff. (vgl. *Die Sprache und das Buch* (Hebräisch), II, Jerusalem 1951, S. 3-58) gehören umgekehrt die Psalmen und Prophetien ursprünglich einer historischen Rahmenerzählung an, und hat man die Überschriften als Reste des alten sonst verloren gegangenen Rahmens zu betrachten.

[2]) Einstweilen vgl. etwa meine Bemerkungen: *The Septuagint Version of Isaiah*, Leiden 1948, 51-54, die sehr der Ergänzung bedürfen. Eine verwandte Erscheinung bildet die Tatsache, dass die Midraschim oft Formen des at.lichen Textes aufbewahren, die vom MT. abweichen, sei es dass sie dieselben ausdrücklich zitieren, sei es — und das sind die wichtigeren Fälle — dass sie sie einfach voraussetzen. Auch die Frage in wie weit die Konstituierung des MT schon eine Exegese darstellt — vgl. das Parallelproblem in den meisterhaften Ausführungen von I. GOLDZIHER, *Die Richtungen in der Koranauslegung*, Leiden 1920, Kap. 1 — muss einem anderen Zusammenhang vorbehalten bleiben.

[3]) So in der Pesach Haggadah (L. FINKELSTEIN, „The oldest Midrash", *HThK*, 31, 1938, S. 291 ff.) und an vielen Stellen der halachischen Midraschim, Mechilta usw.

[4]) Wohl älter als DSH (vgl. S. 171[1])

Gottes Teil gehören ... und sprechen: Er segne Dich mit allem Guten, behüte Dich vor allem Bösen, Er erleuchte dein Herz mit Einsicht, die (ewiges?) Leben schenkt, Er sei dir gnädig mit Kenntnis der Ewigkeit, Er wende dir das Angesicht Seiner Gnade zu zum ewigen Frieden. Hier ist der Priestersegen in Nm. vi 24-26 als Textwort benutzt und ausgedeutet [1]). Im weiteren Verlauf wird das Schicksal derer, die dem Teil Belials angehören dargestellt in einer Mischung von paraphrastischen Ausführungen zu Versen aus Deut. xxviii und xxix mit einer Umkehrung des eben zitierten Priestersegens: Gott sei dir nicht gnädig, wenn du zu Ihm rufst, ... Er wende dir das Angesicht Seines Zorns zu und Friede sei dir nicht beschieden! In formal ähnlicher Weise flehet der Seher Esra (II Esra vii 132-138) Gottes Gnade für die Sünder in einer erweiternden Paraphrase zu Ex. xxxiv 6: Der Barmherzige, weil Er sich derer erbarmt, die noch nicht in die Welt gekommen sind, der Gütige, weil Er gütig ist, gegen die, die sich zu Seinem Gesetz bekehren, der Langmütige weil Er den Sündern als Seinen Geschöpfen Langmut erweist, usw. usw. [2]). Wir sehen, wie eben Grundsätze des biblischen Glaubens die Grundlage bilden für eine erweiterende Auslegung!

Aus dem Ganzen der vorstehenden Erörterungen dürfte hervorgehen, dass es nicht leicht fällt die komplizierte Erscheinung zu definieren, die wir gewöhnt sind als Midrasch zu bezeichnen. Sie beruht eben auf sehr verschiedenartigen Voraussetzungen. In der Tat wohnt ihr die Spannung eines gewissen Paradoxes inne. Auch nachdem der Midrasch zur richtigen Auslegung eines festen und fertigen Textgebildes geworden ist, bleiben ihm Elemente der Beweglichkeit, des Spiels und der Aktualisierung anhaften; einerseits will er einen abgeschlossenen Text erklären, der eben in dieser Gestalt die höchste Autorität besitzt, andererseits ist er bestrebt denselben — wie das gerade unsere letzten Beispiele noch einmal gezeigt haben — offenzuhalten, vor Versteinerung zu behüten und mit immer neuen Leben zu erfüllen — fur jede neue Situation und für jeden neuen Tag!

---

[1]) W. H. Brownlee bringt dieses Beispiel *o.c.* 60. Es verdient hinzugefügt zu werden, dass והבדילו ה̆ (Deut. xxix 20) in DSD II 16 zitiert wird ויבדילהו אל ganz in Übereinstimmung mit der sonstigen religiösen Ausdrucksweise der Sekte (vgl. vor allem: S. Lieberman, „Light on the case scrolls from rabbinic sources", *PAAJR* 20, 1951, S. 400), die für Fragen wie die der Elohistischen Bearbeitung eines Teils der Psalmen von Interesse sein dürfte.

[2]) D. Simonsen, Ein Midrasch im IV. Buch Esra, *Festschrift I. Lewy*, Breslau 1911, S. 270 ff.

A PROPOS DU SECOND CENTENAIRE D'ASTRUC RÉFLEXIONS SUR L'ÉTAT ACTUEL DE LA CRITIQUE DU PENTATEUQUE

PAR

R. DE VAUX

Jerusalem

En 1753, parut un volume intitulé *Conjectures sur les mémoires originaux dont il paroit que Moyse s'est servi pour composer le Livre de la Genèse. Avec des Remarques, qui appuient ou qui eclaircissent ces conjectures* [1]). L'ouvrage portait la marque d'un libraire de Bruxelles, en réalité il avait été imprimé à Paris. Il était anonyme, mais on sut bientôt qu'il avait pour auteur JEAN ASTRUC.

Ce passager clandestin, embarqué avec les Argonautes de l'exégèse, était le fils d'un pasteur protestant de la région nimoise, qui était passé au catholicisme au moment de la révocation de l'Edit de Nantes [2]). Après avoir fait ses études de médecine puis enseigné à Montpellier, il était à Paris depuis 1730, médecin consultant du roi Louis XV et professeur au Collège Royal. Il avait publié un gros traité *De Morbis Venereis*, traduit bientôt en français, des *Mémoires pour servir à l'histoire naturelle du Languedoc* et il allait donner deux ans plus tard des *Dissertations sur l'immatérialité et l'immortalité de l'âme*. Mais cet homme dont les curiosités si variées étaient servies par une érudition étendue, n'avait pas l'esprit des „encyclopédistes" de son époque. Si ce laïc, introduit à la Bible par les leçons de son père, se lançait dans l'exégèse, c'était avec la persuasion que ses recherches confirmeraient l'authenticité, ou comme on disait joliment alors la génuinité des livres attribués à Moïse.

En lisant la Genèse et les deux premiers chapitres de l'Exode, il avait remarqué que, dans certains passages, Dieu était appelé

---

[1]) „Bruxelles, chez Fricx, Imprimeur de Sa Majesté, vis-à-vis l'Eglise de la Madelaine, MDCCLIII". C'est un volume in-12° de 525 pages.

[2]) Sur la vie de JEAN ASTRUC, voir la notice biographique de P. ALPHANDÉRY, en tête du livre d'A. Lods, *Jean Astruc et la critique biblique au xviiie siècle* (Cahiers de la Revue d'Histoire et de Philosophie Religieuse, n° 11), Strasbourg et Paris, 1924.

Elohim tandis que d'autres passages le nommaient *Jéhovah*. En mettant bout à bout les éléments de chaque série, il obtenait deux récits suivis et parallèles, dans lesquels disparaissaient les répétitions et le désordre chronologique qui gênent le lecteur du livre actuel. En dehors de ces deux grands documents, ASTRUC isolait les textes où Dieu ne paraît pas (cela fait très peu de chose), puis ceux qui concernent les peuples étrangers; cette dernière source pouvait se distinguer en huit petits documents, ainsi un document pour l'expédition des quatre rois, ch. xiv, un autre pour la descendance d'Ismaël, ch. xxii, 12-18, deux pour les listes édomites, ch. xxxvi, etc. ... Moïse avait rassemblé ces onze mémoires originaux et les avait transcrits sur trois ou quatre colonnes. Mais les copistes ultérieurs avaient fait de cette synopse un texte continu, en se trompant dans l'ordre des parties. Et cela suffisait, aux yeux d'ASTRUC, pour résoudre les difficultés et expliquer la composition du livre.

On peut sourire aujourd'hui de cette solution: elle ouvrait néanmoins la voie à deux siècles de recherches critiques sur le Pentateuque, car elle offrait un premier essai consistant d'une théorie „documentaire". Plus que cela; la répartition des sources que propose ASTRUC pour les quatorze premiers chapitres de la Genèse est déjà très voisine de celle que WELLHAUSEN rendra classique et, en donnant l'alternance des noms divins comme critère de la distinction, il a posé une règle dont on ne s'est guère écarté.

Cependant l'accueil fait aux *Conjectures* fut d'abord assez froid [1]). En France, le livre reçut des approbations mitigées et des critiques superficielles, mais il ne causa pas de scandale ni ne stimula l'étude. En Allemagne, on prit à son égard des positions plus tranchées. Les traditionalistes le jugèrent sévèrement, cependant EICHHORN adopta le système d'ASTRUC et, après avoir hésité à reconnaître sa dette, rendit justice au médecin français dans le second volume de son *Introduction à l'Ancien Testament*, qui parut en 1781 [2]). Et ce n'est sans doute pas un hasard si, deux années après, paraissait une traduction allemande de *Conjectures* d'ASTRUC [3]). Mais EICHHORN donnait à la

---

[1]) Les jugements portés sur les *Conjectures*, en France et ailleurs, ont été rassemblés par A. LODS, *Jean Astruc* ..., p. 62-79.

[2]) J. G. EICHHORN, *Einleitung in das Alte Testament*, II § 416.

[3]) *Mutmassungen in betreff der Originalberichte, deren sich Moses wahrscheinlicherweise bei Verfertigung des ersten seiner Bücher bedient hat, nebst Anmerkungen, wodurch diese Mutmassungen teils unterstützt, teils erläutert werden.* Aus dem Französischen übersetzt. Frankf. a. M. 1783. In-8° de vii-556 p.

théorie une précision plus grande et tentait d'apprécier ce qui, en dehors de l'alternance des noms divins, caractérisait les sources, leur genre littéraire, leur sens religieux. C'est lui qui assura le succès de l'hypothèse documentaire.

On chercha ensuite d'autres voies: on dissocia le texte en une multitude de fragments ou, au contraire, on admit simplement un écrit fondamental qui n'aurait reçu que des compléments. Mais on revint enfin aux documents. En 1853, juste un siècle après les *Conjectures* d'ASTRUC, HUPFELD publia un recueil d'études sur les sources de la Genèse [1]). Il y établit que le mémoire à d'ASTRUC, qui emploie *Elohim* comme nom divin, représentait en réalité deux documents, différents de style et de pensée, le *Premier Elohiste*, qu'on appela ensuite le *Code Sacerdotal*, et le *Second Elohiste*, qui est devenu l'*Elohiste* tout court. Si l'on ajoute le *Deutéronome*, auquel RIEHM consacra l'année suivante un livre important [2]), la théorie des quatre Documents était lancée et, spécialement sous la forme qu'imposa le talent de WELLHAUSEN, elle domina désormais la critique du Pentateuque.

En 1753, ASTRUC; en 1853, HUPFELD. Il ne semble pas que l'année 1953 doive être aussi décisive pour la critique. Mais l'histoire la retiendra peut-être comme la date moyenne d'un tournant de nos études. Cette orientation nouvelle est, pour une bonne part, l'oeuvre des exégètes scandinaves et il m'est agréable, ici à Copenhague, de rendre hommage à leur travail, même si j'hésite devant certaines de leurs conclusions.

La théorie documentaire ne satisfait plus beaucoup de nos contemporains. Ceux même qui lui restent fidèles ne l'adoptent pas sans des modifications notables. Appliquant les mêmes principes de distinction, on a depuis longtemps poussé plus avant l'analyse des sources, au risque de volatiliser les „Quatre Documents". On met en question l'existence autonome d'un *Elohiste* ou d'un *Ecrit Sacerdotal*. On se dispute sur l'étendue, la date, le milieu d'origine des Documents. Surtout, en reconnaissant que tous ces Documents intégraient des éléments anciens et en faisant porter davantage la recherche sur ces éléments, on détache la théorie documentaire de la construction historique et religieuse à laquelle elle était liée depuis WELLHAUSEN. Mais, du même coup, la confiance dans les Docu-

---

1) H. HUPFELD, *Die Quellen der Genesis und die Art ihrer Zusammensetzung*, Berlin, 1853.

2) E. RIEHM, *Die Gesetzgebung Mosis im Lande Moab*, Gotha 1854.

ments est ébranlée, car la distinction de ces Documents, leur étendue, leur date, leurs tendances sont déterminées autant par des critères historiques et religieux que par des indices purement littéraires.

Aussi bien, ce ne sont pas seulement les conclusions de la théorie documentaire que l'on refuse maintenant d'accepter, c'est la méthode elle-même que l'on déclare erronée. Ce rejet s'exprime de la manière la plus franche dans les travaux récents d'IVAN ENGNELL. Comme tout l'Ancien Testament, le Pentateuque, même étant admis que certaines parties, spécialement des textes législatifs, ont été mises assez tôt par écrit, est le résultat d'une longue transmission orale, d'une tradition vivante, inséparable des conditions de vie du peuple. Il faut donc le juger en fonction de cette tradition orale, il faut remplacer la méthode de critique littéraire par une méthode d'histoire de la tradition [1]). Imaginer la composition du Pentateuque comme un travail de cabinet, où des scribes ont découpé, collé, combiné, interpolé des textes écrits préexistants, c'est aux yeux d'ENGNELL une conception livresque, occidentale, anachronique, une *interpretatio europeica moderna* [2]), qui est radicalement fausse.

Un tel mode de composition littéraire n'est cependant pas si „européen" qu'on le dit et il a été largement pratiqué par les Orientaux. Les historiens et les géographes arabes copient, combinent, glosent à plaisir les écrits de leurs devanciers: le grand ouvrage d'Ibn al-Athir est une mosaïque d'emprunts à Tabarî, Mubarrad, Baladhuri, etc. ... [3]). On trouve les mêmes procédés chez les auteurs syriaques. Ainsi, dans une Chronique anonyme du xiiie siècle, tout le début jusqu'à Moïse suit de très près tantôt le *Livre des Jubilés*, tantôt la *Caverne des Trésors* [4]). Si ces témoins sont récusés comme trop „modernes", on rappellera que TATIEN est un Oriental et un ancien et que son *Diatessaron* est le modèle d'une compilation à laquelle peut s'appliquer la critique des sources. Si cette analogie est écartée

---

[1]) Cf. le dernier exposé d'ensemble donné par ENGNELL dans *Svensk biblisk uppslagsverk* (SBU), II, 1952, s.v. Traditionshistorik metod. col. 1429-1437.

[2]) L'expression revient souvent sous la plume d'ENGNELL, ainsi *Gamla Testamentet. En traditionshistorisk inledning*, I, Uppsala et Stockholm, 1945, p. 185; *The Call of Isaiah* (Uppsala Universitets Årsskrift, 1949, 4), p. 56 en note; *SBU* II, col. 90 et 327.

[3]) I. GUIDI, *L'historiographie chez les Sémites*, dans Revue Biblique, 1906, p. 509-519.

[4]) *Chronicon ad annum Christi* 1234 *pertinens*, ed. I. B. CHABOT, Corpus Scriptiorum Christianorum Orientalium, Syri, series III, xiv-xv. Cf. E. TISSERANT, *Fragments syriaques du Livre des Jubilés*, dans *Revue Biblique*, 1921, p. 55-86; 206-232.

parce que l'oeuvre provient d'un milieu littéraire différent de celui de l'Ancien Testament [1]), on notera que, dans la Bible elle-même, les Chroniques utilisent les Livres de Samuel et des Rois, que les Livres d'Esdras et de Néhémie sont des recueils de documents. Pour en revenir au Pentateuque, si le Deutéronome a quelque rapport avec le „livre" trouvé dans le Temple sous Josias, nous nous retrouvons en face d'un problème de critique littéraire.

Si ces exemples sont encore jugés trop récents, on peut invoquer de très anciennes analogies sémitiques. On découvre aujourd'hui que l'Épopée de Gilgamesh a été composée à partir de sources sumériennes indépendantes et fortement remaniées [2]). Le Récit du Déluge, la Tablette XI, n'avait primitivement rien à faire avec Gilgamesh et toute la Tablette XII n'est qu'une traduction servile d'un texte sumérien, que les scribes babyloniens ont ajoutée artificiellement à l'Épopée. Il est d'ailleurs évident que les problèmes de critique littéraire se posent dès qu'existe une littérature écrite. Or les textes de Râs Shamra nous ont appris qu'une littérature religieuse, épique et cultuelle, existait dès le milieu du IIe millénaire avant notre ère chez les proches voisins d'Israël. On objecte que la Phénicie n'est pas la Palestine israélite et que ce n'est pas seulement un pur hasard si rien de semblable à ces textes n'est sorti du sol, si bien fouillé, de la Palestine [3]). Ce n'est pas un hasard, c'est la conséquence du matériel d'écriture, peau ou papyrus, qui était employé et des conditions climatiques qui empêchaient sa conservation, sauf dans des circonstances exceptionnelles. Ces circonstances se sont trouvées réalisées dans les grottes du Désert de Juda, d'où sortent en ce moment les restes d'une littérature qu'on croyait à jamais perdue, ainsi les originaux des livres apocryphes, ou qu'on ne soupçonnait même pas, ainsi les commentaires bibliques et les règles de la secte de Qumrân. On ne peut donc rien conclure de l'absence de textes littéraires dans les grandes fouilles palestiniennes et, lorsque la Bible se réfère à d'anciens „livres", comme le Livre des Guerres de Yahvé, Num. xxi, 14, ou le Livre du Yashar, Jos. x, 13; 2 Sam. i, 18, il n'y a aucune raison de mettre ce témoignage en doute.

---

[1]) I. ENGNELL, dans *Gamla Testamentet*, I, p. 208; *SBU.*, II, col. 1436, contre HAMMERSHAIMB et MOWINCKEL

[2]) S. N. KRAMER, *The Epic of Gilgameš and its sumerian sources*, dans *Journal of the American Oriental Society*, — 1944, p. 7-23; H. RANKE, *Zur Vorgeschichte des Gilgamesch-Epos*, dans *Zeitschrift für Assyriologie*, N. F. xv, 1949, p. 45-49.

[3]) I. ENGNELL, *The Call of Isaiah*, p. 58.

L'application au Pentateuque des méthodes de la critique littéraire se justifie encore par d'autres raisons. Notre étude ne peut prendre d'autre point de départ que les „livres" qui nous ont été transmis et c'est finalement la composition de ces „livres" et leur histoire qu'il faut expliquer. On nous concède d'autre part, que des éléments de ces livres ont existé séparément en tradition écrite et l'on ajoute que la mise par écrit de l'ensemble ne constitua rien d'essentiellement nouveau, la tradition ayant déjà reçu sa forme définitive et fixe au stage orale [1]). On insiste d'ailleurs sur la fidélité remarquable de cette tradition orale. Est-il alors tout à fait illégitime de lui appliquer la même critique des sources qu'à des textes écrits [2])?

Toutes ces réserves étant faites, le bénéfice incontestable des travaux de NYBERG, BIRKELAND et ENGNELL [3]) a été de mettre en lumière le rôle prépondérant de la tradition orale dans la composition de beaucoup de livres de l'Ancien Testament, le maintien d'une transmission orale à côté de la transmission écrite et la réaction de l'une sur l'autre. En dehors des analogies qu'on a invoquées et qui ne sont pas toutes valables, la raison profonde est que l'Ancien Testament n'est pas un livre mort, mais qu'il a été le trésor d'Israël, qui en a vécu et qui l'a gardé vivant, une Parole, la Parole toujours présente de Dieu à son peuple. Regardant au delà des livres du Pentateuque tels qu'ils nous sont parvenus, on cherchera moins, ou on ne cherchera plus, des documents écrits que des scribes ont tronqués et raccordés et que nous pouvons isoler et reconstruire. On renoncera à répartir entre des sources écrites toutes les péricopes, tous les versets ou les demi-versets du texte. On ne publiera plus guère de Bibles polychromes, ou dans lesquelles des artifices de typographie remplacent l'arc-en-ciel des couleurs, ou dans lesquelles des sigles marginaux distinguent entre plusieurs documents et de multiples rédacteurs. Il faut sans doute renoncer à se référer à des „documents" et parler de „traditions", écrites ou orales, avec tout ce que cela implique de vivant, mais aussi de plus vague et de plus fluent.

Car les partisans de la tradition orale insistent beaucoup sur sa

---

[1]) *Ibid.*, p. 57.

[2]) Cf. les bonnes réflexions de C. R. NORTH, *Pentateuchal Criticism*, dans *The Old Testament and Modern Study*, ed. H. H. ROWLEY, 1951, p. 78.

[3]) H. S. NYBERG, *Studien zum Hoseabuche*, Uppsala, 1935; H. BIRKELAND, *Zum hebräischen Traditionswesen*, Oslo, 1938; I. ENGNELL, les ouvrages déjà cités et *Profetia och Tradition*, dans *Svensk Exegetisk Årsbok*, XII, 1947.

stabilité. Mais des objections sérieuses ont été faites à cette affirmation [1]) et il ne suffit peut-être pas de répondre [2]) que cette fidélité est assurée, pour l'Ancien Testament, par son caractère de littérature sacrée et ses attaches avec le culte. Il faut ajouter que cette fidélité, qui est réelle sans être absolue ne se vérifie que dans un même milieu de transmission et que la tradition y reste plastique, parce qu'elle reste vivante.

Nous avons dans le Pentateuque des narrations qui se répètent, ainsi l'aventure d'Abraham et de Sara chez le Pharaon, Gen. xii, 10-20, et chez Abimélek, roi de Gérar, Gen. xx, 1-18, et une histoire semblable est racontée d'Isaac et de Rébecca, encore chez Abimélek, Gen. xxvi, 7-11. Il y a aussi des narrations qui se combinent: à travers les ch. vi-viii de la Genèse, on distingue deux récits du Déluge, où le cataclysme est produit par des agents différents, où il a une durée différente, où Noé embarque dans l'arche un nombre différent d'animaux. Dans l'histoire de Joseph, se mêlent deux manières d'expliquer son enlèvement: Ruben veut sauver Joseph mais celui-ci est pris par les Madianites, ou Juda, pour sauver Joseph, le fait vendre aux Ismaélites, Gen. xxxvii, 18-35; deux manières de présenter ses débuts en Égypte: chez Potiphar qui lui confie des prisonniers, ou chez un anonyme qui le jette en prison, Gen. xxxix; deux manières de raconter le second voyage des fils de Jacob en Égypte: Ruben ou Juda se portent garants pour Benjamin, Gen. xlii, 37 et xliii, 9.

On pourrait naturellement multiplier ces exemples. Il est très vrai que l'ancien esprit oriental était moins sensible que nous à ces répétitions et à ces dissonances; la preuve en est qu'elles ont été conservées dans la rédaction finale du Pentateuque. Il est possible que certaines d'entre elles aient coexisté à un stade de la transmission orale. Mais on ne peut guère échapper à la conclusion qu'elles dénotent des traditions parallèles, qui ont d'abord été indépendantes.

Ayant reconnu leur existence, la critique doit chercher à les distinguer. C'est en se fondant sur l'alternance des noms divins, Elohim et Yahvé, qu'Astruc avait essayé de reconstituer les deux grands

---

[1]) J. van der Ploeg, *Le rôle de la tradition orale dans la transmission du texte de l'Ancien Testament*, dans *Revue Biblique*, 1947, p. 5-41 (la tradition orale n'est fixe que lorsqu'elle s'appuye sur un texte écrit); G. Widengren, *Literary and Psychological Aspects of the Hebrew Prophets* (*Uppsala Universitets Årsskrift*, 1948, 10).

[2]) I. Engnell, *The Call of Isaiah*, p. 59; *SBU.*, II, col. 1433.

„Mémoires" A et B, qu'il mettait à l'origine de la Genèse [1]). Ce critère a été généralement accepté et a déterminé le choix des sigles donnés à deux des „documents", l'Elohiste et le Yahviste. Mais il y eut des oppositions. La validité de l'argument a été attaquée du point de vue de la critique textuelle, spécialement par DAHSE [2]): les variantes de certains manuscrits hébreux et celles, beaucoup plus nombreuses, de la Septante prouveraient que, sur ce point, le Texte Massorétique a été retouché en bien des endroits et ne peut pas servir de base à cette distinction des sources. Mais ceux qui se réfèrent encore à l'ouvrage de Dahse omettent de signaler qu'il a été l'objet d'une réfutation serrée et, semble-t-il, décisive de SKINNER [3]). Les rares leçons aberrantes de certains manuscrits hébreux ne méritent pas considération en face de l'accord général de la tradition. Quant aux variantes de la Septante et de ses recensions, il faudrait prouver qu'elles ne sont pas des accidents de la version grecque et qu'elles remontent à un texte hébreu plus pur que celui de la Massore. Ici, le témoignage du Pentateuque samaritain est concluant: pour la Genèse, contre plus de 300 cas où le samaritain s'accorde avec le Texte Massorétique, on ne relève que 9 variantes, dont trois seulement sont appuyées par tel ou tel manuscrit hébreu, trois sont attestées par des témoins grecs secondaires et une seule se retrouve dans la forme commune de la Septante. Encore ne s'agit-il que de la répétition du nom d'Elohim dans un passage „élohiste", Gen. xxxv, 9b. La fidélité du Texte Massorétique dans la transmission des noms divins est confirmée par tous les fragments du Pentateuque qui ont déjà été lus dans les manuscrits prémassorétiques de Qumrân [4]).

On a tenté aussi d'expliquer l'alternance des noms divins sans recourir à une diversité de sources. Que cela puisse répondre parfois au désir que l'auteur ou le narrateur avait de varier son style ne doit pas être exclu *a priori*: dans les textes de Râs Shamra, le nom de Baal

---

[1]) Il avait été devancé, en 1711, par WITTER, mais celui-ci ne s'était occupé que des récits de la création, cf. A. LODS, *Un précurseur allemand d'*ASTRUC, HENNING BERNHARD WITTER, dans *Zeitschr. f. d. Altt. Wissenschaft*, xlii 1925, p. 134-135.

[2]) J. DAHSE, *Textkritische Materialen zur Hexateuchfrage*, I, 1912, p. 1-121.

[3]) J. SKINNER, *The Divine Names in Genesis*, dans *The Expositor*, 8e serie, april-august 1913; reimprimé en volume, Londres, 1914.

[4]) On peut s'étonner de la méthode de MOWINCKEL qui, reconnaissant la valeur des noms divins comme critère de la distinction des sources mais voulant retrouver la source élohiste dans l'histoire primitive, suppose que les noms divins ont été modifiés dans de longs passages, *The two sources of the predeuteronomic primeval history (JE) in Gen.* 1-11, 1937, p. 50-58.

alterne avec celui d'Hadad ou avec une épithète divine. Mais l'explication ne vaut pas lorsque de longs passages n'employant que Yahvé sont suivis par de longs passages n'employant qu'Elohim, et c'est de là qu'ASTRUC était parti. On a donc suggéré que chacun des noms avait une qualification particulière. L'hypothèse est très ancienne. TERTULLIEN considérait que le nom de *Dieu* (Elohim) était atemporel et employé pour cette raison au premier chapitre de la Genèse, mais qu'au ch. ii, après la création de l'homme dont il est le maître, Dieu était appelé le *Seigneur* (κύριος, par quoi la Bible grecque traduit Yahvé). Certains rabbins imaginaient qu'*Elohim* était un nom de justice et *Yahvé* un nom de clémence. Plusieurs modernes [1]) pensent qu'*Elohim* est employé quand l'accent est mis sur l'aspect „théologique" ou „cosmique", *Yahvé* quand on insiste sur l'aspect „moral" ou „personnel", sur les rapports de Dieu avec l'homme et spécialement avec son peuple élu. Il est bien évident qu'*Elohim* est le nom commun de Dieu, sans égard aux incidences de la Révélation, et que *Yahvé* est le nom propre sous lequel Dieu s'est révélé à Israël. Mais il faudrait prouver que l'emploi des deux noms se conforme à cette distinction, et cela parait bien difficile. Reprenons des exemples déjà donnés. Dans Gen. xii, Abraham en Égypte fait passer Sara pour sa soeur; elle est prise pour le harem de Pharaon. Dans Gen. xx, Abraham à Gérar fait passer Sara pour sa soeur; elle est enlevée par Abimélek. Il est difficile d'imaginer deux situations plus semblables; mais à Gen xii, 17, „*Yahvé* frappa Pharaon de grandes plaies", tandis qu'à Gen. xx, 3, c'est „*Elohim* qui visita Abimélek en songe". Où serait l'opposition entre une conception „morale" et une conception „théologique", entre un Dieu „personnel" et un Dieu „cosmique"? [2]). Si l'on prend un récit composite comme celui du Déluge, aucune différence de point de vue ou d'intention n'explique pourquoi on lit à Gen. vi, 5 „*Yahvé* vit que la méchanceté de l'homme était grande sur la terre" et à vi, 9" *Elohim* regarda la terre: elle était pervertie"; à vi, 13 „*Elohim* dit à Noé: ... Fais-toi une arche" et à vii, 1 „*Yahvé* dit à Noé: Entre dans l'arche".

Le critère des noms divins reste valable, mais il ne doit pas être appliqué mécaniquement et il est insuffisant. C'est pour l'avoir employé seul qu'ASTRUC avait confondu dans son Mémoire A deux

---

[1]) F. BAUMGÄRTEL; *Elohim ausserhalb des Pentateuch*, 1914; *U. Cassuto*, *La questione della Genesi*, 1934; I. ENGNELL, *SBU.*, II, 330, s.v. Moseböckerna.

[2]) Les explications que donne CASSUTO, *La questione della Genesi*, p. 51, sont peu satisfaisantes.

quantités aussi différentes que la tradition élohiste et la tradition sacerdotale. Mais cette alternance des noms divins coïncide avec des variations de vocabulaire, de forme littéraire, d'intention, de doctrine. Pour reprendre une expression d'HUMBERT, qui a été adoptée par BENTZEN [1]), ce sont de telles „constantes" qui permettent de démêler l'écheveau des traditions. On distingue et on suit assez facilement tout au long de la Genèse le fil des trois traditions yahviste, élohiste et sacerdotale. Il est très significatif que les deux fondateurs de la théorie documentaire, ASTRUC et HUPFELD, soient partis de l'étude de ce livre. Après la Genèse, le courant sacerdotal s'isole sans peine dans la fin de l'Exode, tout le Lévitique et une grande partie des Nombres, mais il est plus difficile de répartir le reste entre les courants yahviste et élohiste. Si, en dehors de cette particularité littéraire, on considère que le contenu de la Genèse, histoire primitive puis histoire patriarcale, la distingue des trois livres suivants qui traitent tous de Moïse et de la sortie d'Égypte, on se demandera si la composition de la Genèse n'a pas été régie par des circonstances un peu particulières. Après les Nombres, ces courants disparaissent au profit du Deutéronomiste. Leur résurgence au sortir du Pentateuque, dans le Livre de Josué, qui était communément admise — la critique documentaire parlait plus volontiers d'un Hexateuque que d'un Pentateuque —, est aujourd'hui mise en doute. Elle est formellement niée par NOTH [2]) et il semble en effet qu'on ne peut retrouver ces trois courants en dehors du Pentateuque qu'en modifiant les critères qui servent à les distinguer. Il est alors loisible de poursuivre l'analyse au delà de Josué et HÖLSCHER est dans la logique du système lorsqu'il reconstruit un document yahviste qui va jusqu'à la séparation des royaumes d'Israel et de Juda, 1 Rois xii, et un document élohiste qui continue jusqu'à la fin des Livres des Rois [3]).

D'autre part, du Deutéronome jusqu'aux Rois, se retrouve une parenté de forme et d'esprit qui est plus ou moins accusée selon les livres mais qui est certaine. Inversement, l'influence deutéronomiste sur les premiers livres du Pentateuque se réduit à quelques touches,

---

[1]) P. HUMBERT, dans sa recension de W. RUDOLPH, *Der „Elohist" von Exodus bis Josua*, dans *Theologische Literaturzeitung*, 1938, col. 417; A. BENTZEN, *Introduction to the Old Testament*, II, 1948, p. 26.

[2]) Déjà dans *Das Buch Josua*, 1938, puis *dans Überlieferungs-geschichtliche Studien*, I, 1943, p. 180 s.; *Überlieferungsgeschichte des Pentateuch*, 1948, p. 5.

[3]) G. HÖLSCHER, *Geschichtsschreibung in Israel. Untersuchungen zum Yahvisten und Elohisten*, 1952.

qui peuvent n'être que des retouches ou s'expliquer autrement. On est conduit ainsi à séparer le Deutéronome du Pentateuque et à le joindre aux livres suivants, pour constituer un grand ouvrage deutéronomiste, et c'est ce que font résolument NOTH et ENGNELL [1]). Les quatre premiers livres forment alors un autre ouvrage, un „Tétrateuque". On peut objecter [2]) que ce Tétrateuque serait un torse sans tête: il est centré sur la promesse faite aux Pères, puis à Moïse et au peuple de leur donner la Terre Sainte en héritage, mais il s'arrête avant la conquête de Canaan, c'est-à-dire avant l'accomplissement de la promesse. Cependant, si l'on admet — ce que d'autres considérations favorisent — que les quatre premiers livres du Pentateuque ont été unifiés dans le cadre de la tradition sacerdotale à la fin de l'Exil, ne peut-on pas concevoir que le Tétrateuque reste ouvert comme une espérance: l'espérance dans les promesses que l'ancienne conquête de Canaan avait paru accomplir, que les péchés du peuple avaient compromises, que les exilés de Babylone se rappelaient et que le Retour réaliserait.

Si l'on refuse un Tétrateuque parce que ce serait une oeuvre tronquée, il ne suffit pas d'y ajouter le Deutéronome, qui se clôt lui-aussi avant l'accomplissement de la promesse, il faut aller au moins jusqu'à Josué: on n'a de choix qu'entre un Tétrateuque ou un Hexateuque. De toute manière, pour qu'il y eût un Pentateuque, il a fallu que le Deutéronome fût séparé de sa suite, lorsqu'on voulut isoler et rassembler ce qui concernait l'oeuvre de Moïse, les Cinq Livres de la Loi.

Ce stade livresque n'est plus celui des traditions, auxquelles il faut revenir. Celles-ci contiennent toutes, dans une proportion variable, des narrations et des lois. De l'une à l'autre, certains faits se retrouvent, certaines prescriptions sont reprises, mais avec d'autres détails, d'autres associations et dans un autre esprit. Ces contacts sont assez nombreux et ces différences sont assez fortes pour qu'on doive conclure à des traditions d'abord indépendantes et en partie parallèles. Lorsque VOLZ et RUDOLPH [3]), et d'autres après eux, nient l'existence autonome d'un „Elohiste", ils négligent ou minimisent les constantes qui rapprochent les divers éléments „élohistes"

---

[1]) NOTH, dans toute la première partie de ses *Überlieferungs-geschichtliche Studien*, p. 3-110. ENGNELL en dernier lieu dans *SBU.*, II, art. Moseböckerna.

[2]) Ainsi A. BENTZEN, *Introduction to the Old Testament*, II, 1948, p. 74 s.

[3]) P. VOLZ et W. RUDOLPH, *Der Elohist als Erzähler: Ein Irrweg der Pentateuchkritik?*, 1933; W. RUDOLPH, *Der 'Elohist' von Exodus bis Josua*, 1938.

et donnent à cette tradition sa physionomie propre. Il est vrai que, dans la fusion qui s'est opérée, la tradition élohiste a été sacrifiée au profit de la yahviste, peut-être parce que celle-ci avait reçu plus tôt une forme écrite, qui lui assura la prépondérance. Lorsqu'ENGNELL ne reconnait dans le travail „sacerdotal" que la dernière aventure de la transmission du Pentateuque [1]), il n'explique pas comment un même milieu de tradition a pu admettre des éléments aussi disparates ou les assumer sans les transformer davantage. Car une tradition ne se maintient vivante que si elle assimile. Il a dû y avoir une tradition sacerdotale d'abord indépendante et la composition finale du Tétrateuque, ou du Pentateuque, ne se conçoit guère autrement que comme un travail rédactionnel.

Les quatre grands courants de la tradition se sont formés, développés et maintenus dans des milieux différents. Ils se rattachent vraisemblablement aux sanctuaires où se rassemblait Israël. Des conteurs y rappelaient les aventures et les hauts faits des ancêtres, y exaltaient les actions puissantes de Dieu et ses bienveillances pour le peuple qu'il s'était choisi. Ces récits épiques servaient de commentaire aux fêtes où l'on commémorait les interventions de Dieu dans l'histoire du peuple. Sans qu'il soit nécessaire d'admettre un récit proprement cultuel, une liturgie, c'est la vérité qu'on retiendra de la thèse de PEDERSEN sur la „légende pascale" d'Ex. i-xv [2]). Plus sûrement encore, les recueils législatifs se sont formés dans les sanctuaires: ceux-ci avaient nécessairement leurs lois sacrées, qui réglaient l'ordonnance du culte, le statut des prêtres, les devoirs des fidèles. Davantage encore, car c'est auprès des sanctuaires et de la bouche des prêtres qu'on venait chercher les décisions juridiques et les directives morales, tout ce qu'incluait, pour un esprit hébreu, le concept de *tôrâ*, la Loi.

L'histoire des anciens sanctuaires nous est trop mal connue pour qu'on puisse beaucoup préciser. Il apparait certain, au moins, que la tradition yahviste est d'origine judéenne. On n'expliquerait pas autrement la part qu'elle fait aux événements d'Hébron et de ses environs dans l'histoire des Patriarches, le rôle qu'elle donne à Juda dans l'histoire de Joseph. Par contraste, on a communément admis que la tradition élohiste proveneit du Nord [3]). Cette origine est

---

[1]) En dernier lieu, *SBU.*, II, s.v. Moseböckerna.

[2]) J. PEDERSEN, *Passafest und Passalegende*, dans *Zeitschr. f. d. Altt. Wissenschaft*, N. F. II, 1934, p. 161-175; Id., *Israel, its Life and Culture*, III-IV, 1947, p. 728-737.

[3]) En particulier O. PROCKSCH, *Das nordhebräische Sagenbuch. Die Elohimquelle*, 1906.

contestée aujourd'hui par des exégètes aussi différents de tendances que le sont NOTH et HÖLSCHER [1]). On peut hésiter, mais il semble bien que les meilleurs arguments soient encore en faveur d'une origine éphraïmite pour le fond de la tradition élohiste. Quant au Deutéronome, plusieurs travaux récents, depuis WELCH [2]) jusqu'à tout dernièrement VON RAD [3]), ont rendu vraisemblable qu'il rassemble des traditions du Nord, apportées en Juda par les Lévites après la chute du royaume d'Israël, mais c'est à Jérusalem qu'elles furent organisées et animées d'un esprit nouveau. La tradition sacerdotale se rattache au milieu du Temple et aux prêtres de Jérusalem.

Dans ces milieux, les traditions ne sont pas restées figées. Elles se sont développées, se sont adaptées aux conditions changeantes des époques. Les dispositions législatives ont été réunies en codes, les narrations ont été organisées en cycles, les lois ont été mises en rapport avec les histoires. Assez tôt, certaines parties ont été écrites, non seulement des textes législatifs ou institutionnels, mais aussi des récits. La tradition orale a d'ailleurs continué parallèlement à cette tradition écrite et l'a influencée. Tout cela se fit dans les divers milieux et fut le travail de plusieurs siècles. Faut-il alors renoncer à dater les traditions et dire, avec PEDERSEN, que „toutes les sources du Pentateuque sont aussi bien préexiliques que postexiliques" [4])? Sans doute on ne peut plus, en termes de traditions, proposer des dates aussi précises qu'on le fait quand on parle de documents fixés par écrit. On peut cependant chercher à déterminer l'époque où la tradition s'organisa avec ses traits essentiels. Cette époque est différente à la fois de celle de la rédaction finale et de celle des éléments anciens qui sont assumés. Cette mise en forme des traditions peut sans doute résulter de la pression anonyme du milieu, cependant lorsqu'elle révèle un plan voulu, une intention, elle s'explique mieux par l'intervention d'une personnalité qui non seulement rassemble les éléments mais les fait servir à son but; cela suppose un „auteur", qu'il soit simple narrateur ou écrivain. Il est difficile de ne pas reconnaître l'oeuvre d'un auteur, et j'ajouterai: la main d'un auteur écrivain, dans les grands récits yahvistes de la Genèse.

---

[1]) M. NOTH, *Überlieferungsgeschichte des Pentateuch*, 1948, p. 249; G HÖLSCHER, *Geschichtsschreibung in Israel*, 1952, p. 179 s.

[2]) A. C. WELCH, *The Code of Deuteronomy*, 1924.

[3]) G. VON RAD, *Deuteronomium-Studien*, 1948, p. 48.

[4]) J. PEDERSEN, dans *Zeitschrift f. d. Altt. Wissenschaft*, 1931, p. 179. La même expression dans A. BENTZEN, *Introduction to the Old Testament*, II, 1948, p. 64.

On peut au moins déterminer la date relative des diverses traditions: le courant sacerdotal, qui s'affirme pendant l'Exil, est postérieur à celui du Deutéronome, qui prend naissance à la fin de la monarchie. Les courants yahviste et élohiste sont antérieurs: la tradition yahviste a pris corps, et a peut-être été mise par écrit pour l'essentiel, dès le règne de Salomon; on ne peut pas assurer que la tradition élohiste soit beaucoup plus jeune.

Ces conclusions rejoignent, pour l'essentiel, les positions classiques de la théorie documentaire. Mais elles sont moins affirmatives et surtout elles sont accompagnées d'une double réserve: d'une part ces traditions, même formées, ont continué de vivre et d'assimiler des éléments nouveaux, d'autre part elles ont eu une préhistoire qu'il est important de considérer.

La théorie documentaire avait été liée, depuis WELLHAUSEN, à un schéma évolutionniste de l'histoire religieuse et institutionnelle d'Israël. Cette construction avait été ébranlée avant même qu'on ne mît en question les méthodes de critique littéraire sur lesquelles elle s'appuyait. Ce fut la conséquence des progrès de l'archéologie orientale. Les fouilles faites en Asie Antérieure, la découverte et la lecture de nombreux textes qu'on pouvait dater ont fait sortir la Bible de son isolement et ont éclairé la nuit qui l'enveloppait. En même temps que se révélaient les conditions concrètes de la vie d'Israël en Palestine, la connaissance des civilisations voisines permettait des comparaisons avec ses coutumes, ses institutions, ses modes de pensée et d'expression. La Bible retrouvait son milieu culturel, son *Sitz im Leben.*

Le résultat de ces recherches est que beaucoup des récits du Pentateuque et pas mal de ses dispositions législatives supposent une situation historique, un état social, une mentalité juridique qui ne sont pas ceux de l'époque où l'on place leur rédaction finale, qui sont même antérieurs à l'époque où l'on présume que le corps des traditions se forma. Par exemple, les narrations de la Genèse sur les Patriarches [1]) les présentent comme des semi-nomades; ils se déplacent précisément dans la zone où le climat favorise ce genre de vie et où la géographie politique indique que cet état social existait au IIe millénaire avant notre ère. Ce qui est dit de leurs attaches

[1]) Je me permets de renvoyer à mes articles *Les Patriarches hébreux et les découvertes modernes*, dans *Revue Biblique*, 1946, p. 321-368; 1948, p. 321-347; 1949, p. 5-36. Voir tout récemment, C. H. GORDON, *Introduction to the Old Testament Times*, 1953, p. 100 s.

ethniques correspond à la répartition des peuples à la même époque. Certains de leurs usages trouvent des parallèles dans les textes juridiques du milieu du IIe millénaire, spécialement ceux de Nuzi. Tout cela avait changé après la sédentarisation d'Israel et au temps de la monarchie. Le fond des traditions patriarcales est donc antérieur. Or elles sont conservées dans des courants qui émanent de milieux différents mais qui sont parallèles et qui proviennent donc d'une source commune. Il ne s'agit pas d'un document primitif, d'une *Grundschrift* [1]), mais d'un trésor de souvenirs communs à toute la nation, avant que les milieux ne se soient diversifiés. Cela, qui s'établit d'une manière assez probante pour les récits patriarcaux, vaut également pour les traditions sur la sortie d'Égypte, dans la mesure où on peut les distinguer.

La question ne se pose pas tout à fait de la même manière pour les sections législative. Parce qu'elles contiennent des prescriptions qui s'imposent et qui doivent être appliquées, il était recommandé de les fixer par écrit, par contre il était nécessaire de les adapter non seulement aux conditions des milieux qui les recevaient mais aussi aux circonstances et aux idées, qui changent avec le temps. Cela explique qu'on rencontre dans des ensembles récents à la fois des éléments antiques, qui paraissent comme sclérosés, et des formules ou des dispositions qui témoignent de préoccupations nouvelles. Cela explique qu'entre deux corps de lois il y ait une sorte de continuité ou d'emboîtement, comme on le remarque entre le Code de l'Alliance d'Ex. xxi-xxiii et le Code du Deutéronome. Quant à l'ancienneté du Code de l'Alliance, elle est assurée par les contacts frappants qu'il a avec les vieilles législations de l'Orient, non pas seulement le Code d'Hammurabi ou les lois assyriennes, mais les autres textes que les archéologues et les philologues ramènent à la lumière, hier les codes de Lipit-Ishtar et de Bilalama, aujourd'hui celui d'Urnammu.

Cela vaut pour les lois cultuelles autant que pour le droit civil. Le Lévitique n'a reçu sa forme définitive que dans le Second Temple, après l'Exil, mais il incorpore des éléments très antiques. La Loide Sainteté de Lev. xvii-xxv remonte à la Monarchie, les prohibitions alimentaires de Lev. xi ou les règles de pureté de Lev. xv sont cer-

---

[1]) M. Noth, qui admet cette origine commune de J et de E, ne veut pas décider s'il s'agit d'une source orale ou écrite et emploie le terme de *Grundlage*, cf. *Überlieferungsgeschichte des Pentateuch*, 1948, p. 403.

tainement héritées d'un âge primitif. La liste des fêtes d'Ex. xxiii, 14-19 et xxxiv, 18-24 se retrouve dans Deut. xvi et dans Lev. xxiii, mais elle est précisée et enrichie. Les grands types de sacrifices sont anciens, mais leur importance relative et leurs circonstances varient avant d'être fiées par le rituel de Lev. i-vii. Ce sont les expressions d'une foi vivante et d'un culte qui se modèle sur la situation changeante des fidèles et des sanctuaires. Cela reste une même foi et un même culte.

Ainsi, par une longue tradition orale et écrite, les narrations et les lois du Pentateuque remontent au temps où Israël se constitua en peuple. Or cette époque est dominée par la figure de Moïse: il a inspiré à Israel le sentiment de son unité, il lui a donné sa religion et ses premières lois. C'est là un fait essentiel, qui est commun à toutes les traditions et qu'on ne peut mettre en doute sans rendre inexplicable toute la suite de l'histoire. Les traditions antérieures à lui et le souvenir des événements qu'il a conduits sont devenus l'épopée nationale, la religion de Moïse a marqué pour toujours la foi et la pratique du peuple, la loi de Moïse a continué de le régir. Les adaptations que commanda le changement des temps se firent selon son esprit et se couvrirent de son autorité.

C'est ce rôle historique que la tradition exprime en attachant au Pentateuque le nom de Moïse et l'on vient de dire que sur ce point elle est très ferme. Mais elle est beaucoup moins explicite, jusqu'à la période juive, pour attribuer à Moïse lui-même la rédaction des livres. Lorsqu'elle dit que „Moïse a écrit" elle s'exprime en termes généraux; jamais elle ne se réfère sous cette forme à l'ensemble du Pentateuque et quand le Pentateuque lui-même emploie, très rarement, cette formule, il l'applique à un passage particulier [1]). L'intérêt que tous les travaux récents portent soit à la tradition orale soit à l'histoire prélittéraire des livres souligne que cette question de la rédaction est beaucoup moins importante que celle du fond. Or les apports nouveaux de l'archéologie et de l'histoire orientales et les études comparatives qui sont ainsi rendues possibles permettent de conclure à l'origine mosaïque première des traditions qui composent le Pentateuque. Elles restèrent des traditions vivantes et, parce qu'elles étaient vivantes, elles maintinrent l'élan que Moïse avait donné.

---

[1]) Voir à ce propos A. van Hoonacker, *De compositione litteraria et de origine mosaica Hexateuchi*, édité par J. Coppens dans les *Verhandelingen van de Koninklijke Vlaamse Academie voor wetenschappen, letteren en schone kunsten van België*, 1949, p. 19 s.

Tout ce qui précède n'est point donné comme la solution d'un problème qui, sans doute, occupera toujours les exégètes. Notre temps remet en question beaucoup de points que l'on considérait comme acquis. Certaines des conclusions de nos devanciers résisteront à cet assaut, d'autre seront modifiées. Il est trop tôt pour apprécier les résultats de cette crise, mais on s'oriente certainement vers une théorie plus souple, moins livresque que n'était la théorie documentaire classique, une théorie moins simple aussi. Sur cet état actuel de la recherche, on a voulu seulement faire ici quelques réflexions, imitant la modestie d'ASTRUC, qui ne proposait que des *Conjectures*.

PROPHECY AND ESCHATOLOGY

BY

TH. C. VRIEZEN

Groningen

INTRODUCTION

No agreement has been reached as yet on the question of the eschatological character of the classical prophets of Israel. This is due partly to differences of terminology, partly also to the divergence of opinions on the contents of the prophetical message. Some scholars refuse to ascribe eschatological ideas to the Israelitic prophets because they deny that these prophets had any expectation of salvation (WELLHAUSEN); others do attribute such hope of salvation to the Israelitic prophets, but will not use the word "eschatology" to denote this hope, because the definite content which they ascribe to the word eschatology does not warrant its application to the preaching of the prophets (EERDMANS) [1]. Other again ascribe to these prophets both the expectation of salvation and eschatology, because they think the preaching of doom and salvation typical of eschatology. Lastly, there are also those who look upon the hope of salvation as such a common ancient-oriental phenomenon that they would consider it ridiculous not to credit the Israelites, *a fortiori* the prophets, with eschatology.

Some time ago J. LINDBLOM [2]) raised the matter expressly by drawing attention to the unsatisfactory situation which is the result of the "vague notions of the term eschatology and the lack of clear definitions in O.T. studies". He thinks "the whole question of the eschatology one of the most urgent tasks incumbent upon O.T. scholarship to-day". In a later paper [3]) he himself gave the answer by distinguishing "between an historical eschatology and a cosmolo-

---

[1]) *Godsdienst van Israel*, I, 1930, p. 186 ff.; *The Religion of Israel*, 1947, p. 140.

[2]) *The Servant Songs in Deutero-Isaiah*, 1951, pp. 96, 104.

[3]) In an unpublished paper read during the session of the Society for O.T. Study at Rome, April 1952; cf. Ordo Lectionum, Eighth Paper: *The Problem of Eschatology in the O.T.*

gical eschatology, the former typical of the classical prophets, the latter of a later date and reaching its ripeness in the apocalyptic literature" [1]).

It seems to me that the matter is so important that it is desirable to raise the problem here too, even if the answer I have arrived at does not differ much from Prof. LINDBLOM's. There are, as we said, two sides to this question: on the one hand it is a matter of form or terminology: in what sense must or may the word eschatology be used?, on the other it is a matter of content: what is the characteristic content of the prophetical hope, and does this permit the qualification eschatological?

Of course these questions bring with them many others, viz. about the origin and background of the prophetical message, about its development in the various prophetical figures, about the connection between the eschatological hope of the Scriptural prophets and that of the later apocalyptic writings. Of course these questions can only be touched upon, as the two principal questions will occupy all the time at our disposal.

I. SOME REMARKS ON THE TERM ESCHATOLOGY

In Old-Testamentary scholarship the terminology very often is a most difficult problem, which must always be considered with understanding, but also in a critical spirit. The terms that are employed are by no means always derived from the O.T. itself, and very often words have to be used that were borrowed from our Western range of ideas, even if they do not sufficiently reflect their Semitic equivalents.

In our scholarly research we stand, partially at least, committed to certain terms borrowed from other branches of scholarship. In studying the O.T. one has to employ again and again ideas borrowed mainly from systematic Christian theology. Of course this often causes difficulties, and creates short-circuits, because these ideas do not always match with those of the O.T. Though the Christian theological ideas are often derived from the Bible, they have also frequently undergone the influence of Greek or Western thought. It is not possible, however, to leave this existing terminology without more ado, and to attempt a complete modification by introducing a separate new terminology; the phenomena of the humanities do not allow of classification so easily as those of science, where an unlimited number

---

[1]) *The Problem of Eschatology in the O.T.*

of formulae and sigla is available, for the spiritual phenomena with which the humanities are concerned are of a far more complex and organic nature than those of science, and cannot be denoted adequately by sigla and formulae. Moreover, besides words that give an analytic juxtaposition of things, the humanities in particular also need words that, as general notions, comprise certain complex groups of ideas and that characterize these groups in their complexity.

The term eschatology is one of those that have always denoted a complex of ideas; though the origin of the word is not clear (it has apparently not yet been in use a long time [1])), it has always comprised all that was taught about the "Endschicksal des Einzelnen und die Zukunft des Weltganzen" [2]); it is not only used in dogmatics, but also in the phenomenology of religion, in the history of religion and in Biblical Theology, and has therefore become a fairly general idea. The term may have originated in the dogmatic field, and may have to be looked upon simply as a translation of the dogmatic term *De Novissimis*. It may also have been introduced by the nascent Biblical Theology, in which case it might have been used as a more general term in connection with the historical nature of this branch of scholarship. On this point I have not been able to reach certainty [3]).

The question with which we are concerned here is especially this: in which sense must and may the word eschatology be used scientifically, what is its import? There are some who think that, on account of the traditional use of this word, it can only be employed in connection with that notion of the last things that arises from "die Vorstellung von jenem grossen Drama der Endzeit mit dem die Weltzeit endet und eine neue ewige Zeit des Heils anbricht" [4]), while

---

[1]) Cf. B. A. van Groningen, *In the Grip of the Past*, 1953, p. 115; *Enciclopedia Italiana*, XIV, 1932, p. 287; s.v. Escatologia; *Dictionnaire de Theologie Catholique*, V 1, 1912, p. 456, s.v. Eschatologie.

[2]) A. Bertholet, "Eschatologie", *R.G.G.*, II, p. 320 (2nd edition).

[3]) At any rate it is clear that Roman-Catholic theology has adopted this word only gradually and at a late date (cf. the two encyclopaedias mentioned above), and that the strictly orthodox Reformed theology has also for a long time abstained from using this word. Especially in Germany and England it seems to have been used at an early date. It was already employed by D. Fr. Strauss in his *Glaubenslehre*, II, 1841, the last chapter of which is called: *Die Lehre von den letzten Dingen*, but in this chapter we find a separate section on: *Die biblische Eschatologie*, in which among other things the questions of life and death are also dealt with.

[4]) G. Hölscher, *Die Ursprünge der jüdischen Eschatologie*, 1925, p. 3; J. Lindblom is also inclined to subscribe to this view: *The Servant Songs in Deutero-Isaiah*, 1951,

others, on account of the phenomenological use, are of the opinion that the term can also be employed as an indication of certain expectations concerning the end in which the destruction and renovation of the kosmos are left out of account but which keep within the framework of history [1]. In any case we may be certain that formally eschatology means nothing but: the doctrine of the last things, and that this word in itself does not imply a definite content.

The O.T. gives some indication of a more extended use of the word eschatology so as to include parts of the prophetic message, for again and again the formula *'aḫarit haiiamīm* is used in the prophecies, and this expression has both a more general and a more restricted meaning: it may denote the future in general as well as the last days [2]. In Israel no fundamental distinction was made between things to come (without any further definition), indicating the limit of the speaker's horizon, and the future taken absolutely [3].

On the ground of the various reasons mentioned above the use of the word eschatology in a wider sense must be considered not only completely admissable but even advisable [4]. If it should have to be restricted to the specific group of data that taught a cosmic-dramatic destruction of the world, this would mean that not only all pre-exilic prophetic ideas would be excluded *a priori*, but also all post-exilic prophetic ideas, except possibly a few apocalyptic pieces within the writings of the prophets. In that case all these older data would have to been looked upon as having no connection with a last decisive moment in the world. Because this tendency has dominated a long time, a mistaken notion about the prophetic ideas on salvation

---

p. 96, n. 1. He thinks that "essential to all eschatology is the distinction between the two "αἰωνες", and: "the eschatological ideas are supra-historical and supra-natural; they are essentially of a mythical nature".

[1]) J. LINDBLOM also considers this possible; esp. in his paper read at Rome, see p. 199, n. 3.

[2]) Cf. p. 199, n. 1. EERDMANS' definition of the meaning of the term as "in future" is one-sided; in Is. ii 2, Mi. iv 1, Jer. xxiii 20, xxx 24, xlviii 47, xlix 39, the eschatological meaning cannot be denied. Cf. KÖHLER, *Lexicon in Veteris Testamenti Libros*, s.v.

[3]) See p. 223 f.

[4]) The use of the word in a sense that comprises "the extreme stages in the development of things in the past as well as in the future" is not advisable; cf. B. A. VAN GRONINGEN, *op. cit.*, p. 115, n. 6., versus G. VAN DER LEEUW, *Phaenomenologie der Religion*, Tübingen, 1933, p. 549 f. and "Urzeit und Endzeit", *Eranos-Jahrbuch* 1949, Sonderdruck 1950, p. 31. A. M. BROUWER, *Wereldeinde en wereldgericht*, 1928, p. 2 f. mentions the use of the word in an axiological meaning, in the works of TROELTSCH and P. ALTHAUS (*Die letzten Dinge*).

and doom could spring up. But as it is the facts that must decide this question, it will be necessary to inquire into the actual import of the prophetic preaching concerning the future. Only thus is it possible to arrive at an objective decision.

We now pass, therefore, to what is certainly the most important point: the inquiry into the import of the prophetic message concerning the future. Is it possible to discover here any elements in which a definite, decisive expectation regarding the future of the world is expressed?

II. THE MATERIAL

It is impossible to deal with the expectations of the future among the classical prophets without giving a short general description of the appearance of the prophets themselves. For their preaching cannot be divorced from their appearance. I cannot refrain from quoting JACOB [1]): "il n'y a pas un prophétisme, il y a des prophètes", following this up, however, with "il n'y a pas des prophètes, il y a un mouvement prophétique". The prophets were independent but not solitary. There is a double relation: they stand in the midst of their people, and also, as it were, side by side. The relation between some of them can still be made out clearly, e.g. between Jeremiah and Hosea, Jeremiah and Micah, Deutero-Isaiah and Isaiah, to mention only a few striking examples [2]). But they also stand in the midst of their people and share the religion with this people; they are no solitary figures, as the O.T. scholars of the last century would have it who looked upon them as a new phase of the religion of Israel and even attributed the creation of Yahwism to them. To counterbalance this tendency it was a salutary influence that JOH. PEDERSEN represented the prophets as the reactionaries among their people [3]). This attitude may, of course, lead to a different kind of one-sideness, for the prophets are certainly not men who wanted the old spiritual life to continue as it was because it was old; else they would not have caused so much opposition in all walks of life as they did, one by one and from first to last (Amos, Micah, Isaiah viii 11 f., Jeremiah); but PEDERSEN's idea is correct in so far that the prophets continue the message of ancient Israel! Their attitude towards the religion of

---

[1]) *Revue d'histoire et de philosophie religieuses*, 32, 1952, 59-69; E. JACOB, *Le prophétisme israélite d'après les recherches récentes*.

[2]) There must also be connections between Isaiah and Amos, Isaiah and Micah, Zephaniah and Amos, Ezekiel and Jeremiah.

[3]) *Israel* III-IV *passim*.

their people is absolutely positive, and for that very reason their attitude towards the people itself is as absolutely critical. The great secret of their life was that they had heard Yahweh speak of doom; this caused them to take up such a radically critical attitude [1]), absolute realists as they were in all matters of faith. On the basis of the purest Israelitic faith and called by the Word of God they come to their people and level their most radical criticism against it. It is not accidental that Amos' great collection of prophecies against the people begins with Israel's creed: *rak 'etkem jada'ti mikkol mišpeḥot ha'adama*, linking up with the words of Gen. xii 3 and preceded by a mention of the deliverance from Egypt; and for that reason Amos' conclusion that God announces judgment on Israel in particular is not accidental either.

Amos also shares the belief in the future *jom Jahwe*; he does not blame the people for believing in that day which again and again was given a central position by the cult [2]) but because it does not take the day seriously as the day of Yahwe and will not think of judgment [3]). By virtue of his vocation (the visions in ch. vii-ix) he has to announce the judgment to Israel; but on account of his religion which he has in common with the people there are also other elements in his faith; characteristic of this is v 14 f., where he refers with approval to the people's faith that rests on the fact that God is near; he also thinks it possible for the people to save its life by repentance, although this applies only to a remnant and though he speaks here with great hesitation: "*it may be* that the LORD God of hosts will be gracious unto the remnant of Joseph" (v 15); the "*it may be*", so characteristic of Amos and of Zephaniah (ii 3).

In spite of his message of doom Amos has always felt that there is a relation between God and the people—he always speaks of *'ammi* in his prophecies (vii 8, 15; viii 2; ix 10, cf. 14), and he nowhere arrives at the verdict that God has rejected Israel, even if he prophesies

---

[1]) Hos. vi 5; Is. vi 8-13, xlix 2; Mi. iii 8; Jer. i 10-19; xxviii; Ez. iii 4-9.

[2]) The literary connection between the *jom Jahwe* and the cult, in Amos and Zephaniah (i 7), is not accidental. Cf. on the whole of this problem: S. Mowinckel, *Psalmenstudien*, II, and the literature that has sprung up around his book. I am still not convinced that it is possible to reason as integrally as Mowinckel does and to reconstruct a New-Year festival by combining non-Israelitic data with data from the Psalms; cf. also p. 226, n. 2, 3.

[3]) E. Würthwein, *Z.f. Th. u. K.*, 49, 1952, 1 ff., may be right in saying that the element of judgment was not lacking in the cult, but this does not explain the radicalism of Amos' preaching, for this can only be understood from the special calling of the prophet (Amos vii 7 ff.).

that the people shall fall and rise no more (v 2). The same thing applies to the doctrine of election in later times: in spite of the judgment and even in spite of the preaching of rejection the election is not abandoned. That is why the prophets (and not Deutero-Isaiah alone) distinguish between two Israel-types: Israel as the empirical people that perishes, and Israel as the people of God, which exists and remains, visible only to the eye of faith. The same idea is found in the prophecies of Amos. That may be the reason why in the last prophecy of judgment recorded in his book, he says that God will sift the house of Israel among all nations (i.e. that He will send them into exile everywhere), but also that all the sinners of the people shall die by the sword (ix 9-10). Here a distinction is drawn between the people as a whole and a part of the people.

In Amos we find an expectation of salvation as well as the preaching of judgment, but it is not closely connected with the latter, his real message, so that it has always aroused doubts, for obvious reasons, but nevertheless it is not impossible that the words are authentic [1]). There is another similar case: what Amos says in ix 7 about Yahweh's care of other nations than Israel does not seem quite in agreement with iii 2, yet the tension between the two texts should not be exaggerated and accentuated needlessly, so as to make it appear a contradiction. It seems quite acceptable to me, therefore, (apart from the question whether the words of Amos ix 11-15 as we have them are altogether authentic) that the prophet believed in the salvation of his people, in the restoration of the Davidic rule [2]). But this hope of salvation brings harldy anything new that cannot have formed part of the hopes that the people of Judah cherished already and of which it had always sung in its psalms. The only difference is, perhaps, that it is more sober and matter-of-fact than the hopes of the people, and that the decline of the house of David is viewed with great realism. It was Amos' life-task to proclaim the imminence of the absolute judgment to Israel at a time when nobody expected it; he was a man with only one string to his bow, and his shot went home!

His task was the destruction of expectations that were seized too eagerly and were tainted by sin, but without creating new hopes.

---

1) The authenticity was also defended by MAAG, *Text, Wortschatz und Begriffswelt des Buches Amos*, 1951, p. 246 ff.

2) B. DUHM, *Das kommende Reich Gottes*, 1910, p. 16, thinks: "Psychologisch sollte man es freilich für fast undenkbar halten dass er geglaubt habe, es komme nichts mehr nach". But the prophecy itself he refers to the spurious later additions.

But because of this radical destruction he has been the man who has done more than anyone else to make the restoration possible.

It is difficult to say in how far Hosea's work builds on that of Amos. He probably lived somewhere near the Southern border of his country, so in the vicinity of Bethel where Amos' appearance caused such a stir, and it is hardly conceivable that Hosea should have remained unaware of Amos' proclamation of judgment. The appearance of Amos cannot have been forgotten after about ten years if Micah's appearance was still remembered after a century. At any rate, an immediate connection is not demonstrable, for Hosea has a style that is all his own and has wrestled in his own way with the problem of the judgment he, too, had to announce. For him the problem is that Yahweh abandons His people to destruction; he pictured Yahweh as the God of wrath and at the same time as the loving God, far more so than Amos did, who knew Him as the mighty Yahweh Sebaoth, the God of justice; words as *ḥesed* and *'ahaba* for the relation to God are lacking in Amos, and so are images in which God is depicted as a ferocious panther or bear acting in fierce anger [1]); images so dear to Hosea's passionate mind. But God says: "mine heart is turned within me" (xi 8 ff.), and Hosea cannot stop at the judgment: the other side, the communion between God and the people [2]), must also be brought out in Hosea's message; an element of which we catch only a glimpse here and there in the preaching of Amos. For Hosea the judgment cannot be the end, but through it salvation is obtained [3]). It could hardly be otherwise in Hosea's preaching. It is incredible that the passages in which Hosea's hopes of salvation manifest themselves should have been declared spurious [4]). Hosea states emphatically that it is God in His love who does all this; it is grace, but it also seems to Hosea that in fact God cannot act otherwise. It is true that Hosea rejects the hope of the people that God will accept an act of penitence immediately (vi 1 ff.), but this alone does not satisfy Hosea, and he is convinced that ultimately God will grant

---

1) A comparative study of the vocabulary and imagery employed by the prophets would be most valuable. If the above-mentioned work by MAAG were supplemented with other, preferably comparative studies, the figures of the prophets would stand out more clearly.

2) In Hosea we find a much more intimate (almost a mystical) relation to God than in Amos; on Hosea cf. SELLIN, *Das Zwölfprophetenbuch*, 1929, p. 19.

3) See also W. COSSMANN, *Die Entwicklung des Gerichtsgedankens bei den alttestamentlichen Propheten*, 1915; cf. also Hosea ii, xiv.

4) The ease with which DUHM (*loc. cit.*) comes to this conclusion is striking.

restoration. There exists a close connection between the pathetic words of xi 8 ff. and ii 16 ff. and xiv 2 ff.

The hope of salvation depicted by Hosea shows traits of his own surroundings; the people is blessed in its agricultural life [1]). The peace among the animals and the expectation of the destruction of the implements of war in Israel (ii 20) may also be connected with it, although from a literary point of view these themes break the connection between ii 19 and 21 to some extent. The word *le'olam* of ii 21 implies the idea that the salvation will be permanent; this is also implicit in his expectation that the heavens will hear the earth in aid of Israel. In spite of all this it is difficult to say in how far we may speak of a real renewal of the old hopes in Hosea's preaching. The principal new element are the positiveness with which God's judgment is announced and the absoluteness of the necessity of conversion; it is only through this judgment and this conversion that the restoration can break through, and this can only come to pass by a miracle of God. At any rate Hosea has two strings to his bow, and is quite a different man from the great one-sided farmer from the border of the Judean desert.

With Isaiah we reach a new stage in the development of the hope of salvation. On the one hand he resembles Amos, for in his prophecies judgment and salvation are not linked together so closely as in Hosea but on the other hand the expectation of salvation has a special place in his mind as also in the case of Hosea, though in a different way again. Salvation is far more of a miracle in Isaiah's prophecies; salvation and doom are hidden in the counsel of God, and to the prophet's mind the relation between the two can only be paradoxical. Isaiah is as radically positive about the absoluteness of the judgment (ch. vi) as Amos is, but on the other hand there is the certainty that a remnant—the remnant that in Amos *may perhaps* obtain salvation—shall return; and moreover there is a hope of salvation that far exceeds Hosea's in more than one respect and has been of great influence on the spiritual life of his people and, we may even say, of the world. The strong differences of opinion on the exegesis of Isaiah, especially of the chapters vi-ix, can only be solved if one has come to see the paradoxical in Isaiah's ideas. This appears in various texts, e.g. where Isaiah says (xxviii 21) that God who chastises His people does an act strange to Him (paradoxical [2]) *zar ma'asehu*), and even

---

[1]) With HÖLSCHER, *Die Propheten*, p. 209 ff. and SELLIN, *op. cit.*, p. 6.

[2]) PAUL HUMBERT, "Les adjectifs *zar* et *nokri*", *Mélanges Syriens M. R. Dussaud*, p. 261.

the work of a stranger [1]) (*nokrija ʿabodāto*). In this way the act of God's judgment is placed in quite another light than by Hosea, who looks upon it as done in passionate anger, or by Amos, who merely considers God's judgment just. To Isaiah it seems "strange"; we should say: incomprehensible, paradoxical. These words ot Isaiah are, indeed, followed by the well-known passage on the work of the farmer who treats his land and his products in various ways, but does everything wisely. He ends this passage by saying of Yahweh: *hiphlīʾ ʿeṣā, higdīl tušia*, "He is wonderful in counsel and excellent in working" (xxviii 29b). He repeats this word about God's strange work once more and with greater stremgth: *laken hinneni josef behaphliʾet haʿam hazze, haphleʾ wapaleʾ*, "Therefore, behold, I will proceed to do a marvellous work and a wonder" (xxix 14). Such a text as xxx 15 also shows this love of the paradoxical: "In returning and rest shall ye be saved, in quietness and in confidence shall be your strength". When one has discovered this element in Isaiah's general prophecies to the people one need not be astonished on finding it in his hopes of salvation as well, which in their elaborated form as they have been handed down to us (such as viii 23 ff.) were addressed to his disciples rather than to the people; the first great message of salvation: *haʿam haholekim baḥošeq raʾū ʾor gadōl* also contains the paradox, and so does the announcement of the coming of the king of salvation, in which the contrast between the child of ix 5 and the task with which it is charged gives the whole a curious note [2]). It is, therefore, certainly a misjudgment of the personality of this prophet to demand that his prophecies should always form an airtight system. On the contrary, we should be prepared to find the strongest internal contrasts, which, indeed, we do find. We may also expect to find high hopes in the prophecies of one who has such strange ideas about his God; and, again, we do find that his expectations are high-pitched. As to the former, I first of all mention the ambiguous name *šeʾar jašub*: a remnant returns; the real meaning of which is ambiguous in every respect: a remnant that—only or certainly—comes back, i.e. repents or returns [3]). The name *Immanuel* seems to me to be ambiguous, too:

---

[1]) On this text see PROCKSCH in his *Kommentar*.

[2]) Cf. especially viii 23a, see below, p. 211.

[3]) Cf. x 20-22, where the double aspect of the idea is expressed. The three verses, and certainly the last paradoxical words *killaion ḥaruṣ šoṭef ṣedaqa* (*ṣedaqa* in a double sense) are authentic.

precative (God be with us) or positive (God is with us) [1]), as is also shown by the explanatory verses of viii 5-10 [2]).

---

[1]) Cf. A. BENTZEN, *Jesaja*, I, 1944, on this text, and: *Skandinavische Literatur z. A.T.*, 1938-1948, *Theol. Rundschau* N.F., 17, 1948-9, p. 291.

[2]) Ch. vii and viii give an impression of the way in which the word of God comes to the prophet; this appears most clearly from viii 1-4. There the prophet "receives" a word, without explanation; he does not understand it but has it written down in the presense of witnesses. Afterwards follows the explanatory revelation: it is to be the name of the son who will be born to him, and it appears that the name refers to the imminent invasion of Palestine by the Assyrians. So with Isaiah a revelation may consist of two separate parts: first a prophecy without any further qualification, the revelational meaning of which is not made clear until later. The prophecy comes to Isaiah and Amos in different ways. The latter "sees" something, he is of the *ro'e*-type but receives the revelation together with the vision (cf. e.g. what Amos writes on the character of the prophet in iii 7). To the former the prophecy comes more abruptly and is also auditive; it begins as if it were an oracle; the word of revelation proper may remain hidden for some time. (Have we not got here, in fact, two types of prophets: Amos the ancient *ro'e*, and Isaiah who rather represents the type of the cultic oracular prophet, which, again, is not the same as the original *nabi*-type?). This also throws light on the difficulties of interpretation caused by vii 10-17 as well as on the composition of vii 10-viii 10. In vii 10-17 Isaiah records exactly what happened at a second meeting with Ahaz, which presumably took place at the royal palace; cf. the use of the plural form in vs. 13 and 14; the words spoken here by Isaiah are said by Yahwe (Yahwe in vs. 10 is original); this speaking of Yahwe is in itself oracular in many respects; that is why the explanatory revelations about the remarkable words on eating butter and honey and about the connection between the subsequent events, do not come until later in vii 18-25 (+viii 21-23a). The double meaning of Immanuel is explained in viii 5-10; it is possible that viii 6-8 and viii 9-10 date from different periods: the former may date from the time after the revelation received in viii 1-4, and viii 9-10 may be connected with the revelation of vii 1-7. The same opinion is held by BENTZEN, rightly in my opinion. If this view is correct the two passages were put together by Isaiah himself at the time when these pieces were assembled, so as may be the case with x 20-22, cf. p. 208, note 3. The prophecies about the two kingdoms of Damascus and Ephraim are explained in viii 1-4 (cf. that it is the Assyrian king who will invade the country; in vii 18 this had still remained uncertain so that *melek Assur* in vii 17 and 20 must be a gloss.). The chapters are the result of the whole complex of revelations which was granted to Isaiah in the years 734-3. In that period he is constantly occupied with what happens in the world. (cf. also that e.g. viii 10 reminds us again of vii 7 *lo takum* and *lo jakum*). viii 11-15 evidently is a revelation connected with the fact that he was accused of conspiracy during that period. On account of that charge viii 16 contains the decision to retire from politics for the time being and to speak to his disciples only, and to wait for God to speak (vs. 17); there is no need for Isaiah to speak, for his appearance thus far, the simple fact that he is there and his silence, and the names of his sons are signs and omens enough (vs. 18). His disciples need not speak either, except when they are asked to pass on oracles from the dead etc. Then they shall give the *tora* and the *tehuda* (vs. 19, 20). If we are right in assuming that this is the structure of the chapter, two conclusions are justified: this part was written in 734-3, and: this part is absolutely authentic (except for a few glosses and shifted passages).

In ch. vi the prophet describes his calling; he is charged to realize the fall of his people by his preaching: the paradoxical element in his instruction (vi 9b and 10, cf. also xxix 9-16 !) still puzzles those who want not only to hear the words but also to understand them; that this task imposed by God is incomprehensible is, however, expressed most emphatically by this paradox. As appears from this chapter Isaiah knows, like Amos and Hosea, that he is called to proclaim the coming judgment; there is no question here of a positive aspect of the task, as in Jeremiah i 10 [1]).

Isaiah has not by any means told all about his work; in his "confessiones" (vi-viii 23 or ix 6) we do not find, e.g., why he called his first-born son *še'ar jašub*, though this was probably done in accordance with divine instructions [2]). Much attention is paid in Isaiah's memoir to the meetings with the king, the representative of the house of David. One gets the impression that the inclusion of ch. viii 23 ff. may be connected with this. The words addressed to Ahaz in vii 7-9 raise some problems, but the passage has probably not been transmitted to us in quite the correct form. The second text connected with Immanuel (vii 15) is completely enigmatical: it apparently referred to the young queen of whom Isaiah said that she was pregnant and would bear a son whom she would call Immanuel (because of the great distress among the people at the moment of his birth, so in a precative sense?) but that the child would eat butter and honey, the choicest foods the land produced, even before the child himself would be able to choose. Then, in explanation, follow the words: then the country of Damascus and North-Israel, of which you are

---

[1]) The translation: *to graze bare* for בער is to be rejected in spite of BUBER's opinion (so KÖHLER's *Lexicon*). The interpretation of the last words as a promise, advocated by ENGNELL, *The Call of Isaiah*, 1949, is most improbable. Very remarkable is the way in which ENGNELL defends the authenticity of Is. vi 13[end] on the ground of a dogmatic translation in the Septuaginta in which the text in question is not found in the principal mss. On account of the positive translation of vs. 12 (where the reading *'azoeba* is translated in the Septuaginta by: *those who are left*, *remnant*, cf. I. L. SEELIGMANN, *The Septuaginta version of Isaiah*, 1948, p. 63 f.; ENGNELL thinks that the Septuaginta-translation μακρυνει for *riḥaq* may also be taken in a positive sense, but here he evidently mistakes μακρυνει for μακροθυμει; at any rate the translation *will become forbearing* for μακρυνει is not supported by LIDDEL-SCOTT) ENGNELL thinks that the last three words of vs. 13 (*not* found in the Septuaginta) were to be found in the Hebrew text from which the Septuaginta was translated ! In this way it is possible to prove anything; on textual questions the hypercritical "traditionsgeschichtliche" school comes remarkably close to its opposite, the fundamental school.

[2]) Cf. p. 208, note 3.

now afraid, will be a wholly deserted country. After that we come to the enigmatic words of vs. 17, of which we cannot establish with certainty whether they contain a promise or a threat. From the "explanation of his appearance", probably added afterwards by the prophet (vs. 18 ff.), it appears that he originally expected the danger to come from two sides, from Egypt as well as from Assyria (vs. 18) and that he nevertheless entertained hope for those few who had escaped from the catastrophe, and even expected that they would have plenty (vii 21-22). vii 23-25 and viii 21-23a probably belong together. Here the desolateness of the country is depicted after it has been left by the conquerors; there is nothing to be done with it, and anyone who attempts to achieve anything in this waste land will fail miserably, so that in his despair a man may come to curse his God and his king. Only if this great distress is accepted one may be saved from the blackness of despair (vs. 23a: but there is no darkness for him who has borne her anxiety, or: who has been anxious about her; this can only be understood as forming a contrast with the preceding and as a paradox). The picture reminds us of the expectation of Hosea that the people will return to the desert: in Isaiah the land itself becomes waste. While in Hosea's prophecy the people is saved collectively, in Isaiah only individuals survive the judgment. In my opinion viii 6-10 must also be explained in such a paradoxical sense: the first song of Immanuel depicts the distress, which does not even halt at the borders of Judah, and it also mentions the punishment of Ahaz who has called in the aid of the Assyrian—here the name Immanuel is used precatively (vs. 6-8); in the second verse Immanuel is used positively: in this name the prophet also hears a promise of certain salvation (see p. 209, n. 2). No wonder, then, that this prophet with this faith in the God who works miracles could sing the song of salvation and proclaim the message of the saviour-king[1]) when his predictions actually came true and the first part of Israelitic territory had been occupied (viii 23-ix 6). I do not feel certain that Isaiah should have been thinking here of the proclamation of the accession of a historical king (this should have been Hizkiah). It may be considered an established fact, however, that Isaiah expected this hope to be fulfilled soon in this period. It is apparent from the illustrious names given by Isaiah to the future wearer of the crown (rightly seen by PROCKSCH[2]) and BUBER[3]) as the anti-king who is

---

[1]) Cf. A. ALT, "Jes. viii 23-ix 6", *Bertholet Festschrift*, 1950, pp. 29-49.

[2]) *Jesaja*, I, on this text. PROCKSCH speaks of: "geistliche Gegenkönig".

[3]) *Der Glaube der Propheten*, 1950, p. 201; BUBER speaks of a theo-political figure.

opposed to Ahaz) that his hope is not merely historical but also belongs to the religious field of the history of salvation. What else could, indeed, be expected of this prophet? The names of the anti-king are most significant [1]). In these names a new definitive expectation of salvation for Israel as a marvellous token of the grace of God is implied.

In the Immanuel-pericope we have a prophecy of the year 734, in the pericope about the saviour-king (viii 23-ix 6) a prophecy from the time of the occupation of the Northern kingdom and the annexation of the conquered territory to Assyria (so after 732); in ch. xxviii 16 f. we find a later prophecy from the last period of the existence of Samaria (so between 725 and 722) containing the well-known prophecy: "Behold, I lay in Zion for a foundation a stone, a *boḫan*-stone, a precious corner-stone, ...: he that believeth shall not make haste. Judgment also will I lay to the line, and righteousness to the plummet". In the middle of this prophecy which predicts in the first place the fall of Samaria but also the fall of Jeruzalem (vs. 17b-19), Isaiah brings a message that can give intrepidity to the faithful again (it is contrasted emphatically to the seeming contempt of death of the scoffers in Jerusalem), viz. the promise of God that in His destruction of Jerusalem He is working at the rebuilding of a new city, with justice and right as standards. Here destruction and restoration are linked together very closely. If these verses are torn from their context (as is done by PROCKSCH) they lose much of their power. For Isaiah the imminent downfall is no reason for "anxious haste", but a sign of God's work, even of God's work of salvation. For the scoffers a change will come soon—when they see the floods rise morning after morning and all day long, then shall terror strike the inhabitants: "and it shall be a vexation only to understand the report" (xxviii 19c). This is a proof that from the ruins of the old Jerusalem Isaiah expects a new Jerusalem, a new kingdom, a kingdom of justice to arise. From the outset he has never given up hope, although he knows that God has turned away from the house of Jacob (viii 17); now this hope has grown into a firm belief [2]).

---

[1]) The number of names cannot be reduced to three, as BUBER does (*pele* being combined with *šemo*), nor is it possible to extend it to five, the usual number in Egypt (ALT). Neither may the names be looked upon as merely human epithets due to an oriental ruler or to a king of Israel (as BUBER and ALT advocate). Cf. e.g. the first name *pele'jo'es* with Is. xxviii 29, where it is said of Yahwe: *hiphli' 'eṣa*. The second and the third name are also most significant!

[2]) A parallel to the preaching of xxviii 16 f. is to be found in i 26 f. (also iv 2?).

This faith and this hope have created two culminatingpoints: ch. xi 1 ff. and ii 2 ff., placed at the beginning and at the end of the first collection of his prophecies.

The beginning of ch. xi [1]) alludes to the complete destruction of the house of David: a rod out of the stem of Jesse and a branch grown out of his roots shall bring forth new life. It has become clearer and clearer to Isaiah that the house of David, too, is to be destroyed but for a remnant [2]), for this house cannot bring about any improvement no more than Israel. The only thing that can save is the spirit of Yahweh which teaches wisdom and understanding, *ʿesa* and *geboera* (words reminding us of ix 5), knowledge and the fear of God! [3]). That this high hope should end in a picture of the coming kingdom of grace, the images of which are derived from ancient paradise-motifs, need not astonish us in the work of this poet-prophet.

If the honour of having written the song of victory of Yahweh's salvation of the nations (ii 2 ff.) is due to any prophet, this prophet must be Isaiah, in spite of the well-known literary-critical problem. The style is an argument in his favour [4]) and so is his great positive appreciation of Jerusalem which he has never abandoned. The song is more than a mere national song, such as we know from the post-exilic period, and more than a prophecy that the nations shall come to Jerusalem to hear the word of God, it is also a promise of the salvation

---

[1]) The authenticity of xi: 1 ff. is doubted fairly generally, apparently on very vague grounds; cf. HÖLSCHER, *Die Propheten*, 1914, p. 364, who thinks that although little can be said against the Isaianic origin, the affinity with other comparable prophecies of salvation of a more recent date makes it probable that this prophecy should be late, too. In my opinion both the spiritual character of the saviour-king depicted in ch. xi and the picture of the kingdom of grace which reminds us very strongly of mythological paradise-motifs make a great man like Isaiah a more probable author than an unknown post-exilic poet.

[2]) Cf. M. BUBER, *Der Glaube der Propheten*, p. 213, who attributes this poem, too, to a later period of Isaiah's life. BUBER, however, attempts too much to place this prophecy in the light of history, esp. vs. 6 ff., by considering them to be a "Sinnbild des Völkerfriedens" p. 215.

[3]) The link between Isaiah and Micah (ch. v 1 ff.) is here more evident than anywhere else—and we may take it that Micah must have been the one who received. Cf. that Micah, too, in v 1—although in other terms—only expects salvation to come from a new Jesse—from the little town of Bethlehem; and Micah v 3 is also closely related to Is. xi 2 ff. This simplifies the judgment of the duplicate passages of Is. ii and Micah iv a great deal.

[4]) HÖLSCHER, p. 360, thinks e.g. that the theological ideas of the priestly *tora* on Zion and of Zion as the highest of the mountains stand in the way of Isaianic origin; but *tora* need not at all refer especially to the priest, and the idea of Zion as the highest mountain may equally well be ancient as late.

of the whole world. The song is more melodious and more positive in content than any comparable poem. I think, therefore, that this rich and mature song of faith was most probably written by the visionary [1]) who may be called the creator of the expectation of the new kingdom of grace.

Isaiah's greatness [2]) lies in the fact that at the hour of the crisis he delivered his people from "the grip of the past", the longing for the ancient kingdom of David, and that he directed the attention of the people to new vistas in which the eye of faith beheld a new kingdom, a kingdom founded, it is true, on the history of Israel (and especially on the spiritual and universal tendencies of the oldest Israelitic historian, the Yahwist, expressed in Gen. xii 1-3 [3])), but also a kingdom with its zenith not in the past but in the future, because its new kingship, granted by God, would be the bearer of the highest spiritual values. By this deliverance Isaiah has given new life to the great and profound ideas of the religion of Israel—new not only in the sense of "again", but also in the sense of "in a new way", by elevating them to another plane. Owing to the message of judgment which he had to bring, he understood that if anything were to come of the ancient historian's vision, the life of the people from high to low would have to be inspired by right and justice, by the fear of God and by the spirit of God.

It has sometimes been supposed that in his remnant-idea Isaiah had created the idea of the congregation and that he saw the salvation in this idea. The remnant, which for Isaiah may for a moment have been represented by his disciples alone, as a congregation, never was his ultimate ideal [4]). The very fact that ch. xi, as the last form of Isaiah's preaching of the kingdom, depicts the king to such an extent with images derived from true religious life (cf. the *jir'at Jahwe* in xi $2^{b\beta}$ and the demand made upon Isaiah himself in viii 12 f.), shows that for him the new kingdom and the faith are the same [5]).

---

1) Cf. also M. Buber, *Der Glaube der Propheten*, p. 216.

2) Cf. the underlying idea of B. A. van Groningen's work *In the Grip of the Past*, 1953.

3) Cf. also A. Alt, "Gedanken über das Königtum Jahwes", in *Kleine Schriften zur Geschichte des Volkes Israel*, I, p. 357.

4) That Isaiah does *not* mean the congregation apart from the people, becomes clear in ch. xxviii and i 26 f., where he expects a new Jerusalem. For that reason Isaiah may not be represented as the creator of the idea of the congregation.

5) For that reason it is likely that the theocratical idea of the Deuteronomist authors originated with the circle of Isaiah's disciples; it may not be opposed to Isaiah; cf. my: *Die Erwählung Israels nach dem Alten Testament*, 1953, p. 55 ff.

M. Buber has spoken of theopolitics, a good term that may take the place of the over-burdened word theocracy. I should, however, like to maintain, against this scholar, that in Isaiah's theopolitics it is not man but God who is the politician, because it all comes from Him and His spirit (xi 1-3 the *ruach*; ix 5 the special divine epithets; ii 2 ff. the *tora* and the *debar Jahwe* as the dominating factors [1])), and because the Kingdom which he sees is one that transcends the work of man (xi 6-9), a kingdom, moreover, that will last forever (ix 6c: *meʿattā weʿad ʿolām*). Isaiah is the man who on the one hand is certain that Israel (Judah) is no longer of any value as a people in his days and will perish, but who on the other hand firmly believes in the future of his people, because he knows that God is at work on Israel. And therefore his faith gives him the certainty that God will create something new from the coming destruction and chaos: a kingdom of right and justice under a divine kingship, the kingdom of God among mankind, beginning in Israel, but a blessing for the whole world at all times.

After Isaiah little was added to this message until the exile; his contemporary Micah, who lived in a slightly more recent period, and who reminds us very strongly of Isaiah and Amos in his preaching, is in one respect more consistent, at any rate more direct that Isaiah —he announces *expressis verbis* the destruction of the temple (iii 12); his hopes of salvation remind us strongly of Isaiah: v 1-4 might be a compendium of Isaianic teaching. In the other prophets after Isaiah we also find again and again ideas already expressed by one of the three oldest prophets.

Universal ideas are not wholly lacking (Zep. iii 9), but we get the impression that the struggle to save the spiritual life of Israel is so hard that their preaching must grow more and more concentrated and must therefore centre on the judgment (and the salvation) of Israel. Jeremiah does not, probably, express any hope of salvation with respect to the nations [2]). It is true that religious life centres more and more on the inner man; in Micah vi 8 (walking humbly with God), in Zephaniah iii 1 (the remnant is *ʿani* and *dal*) and especially in Jeremiah xxxi 31-34 (the description of the total inward renewal of the religious life of the people and of the individual) this emerges more and more clearly as the destruction of the life of the people is

[1]) This against M. Buber, *Der Glaube der Propheten*, p. 127. The explanation of Is. ii 5 as "Israel muss mit dem 'Gehen' beginnen, damit die Völker folgen können" really cannot be called exegesis !

[2]) It is difficult to decide whether iii 17 is original (cf. xii 14-17).

realized more and more; this has also left its traces on Jeremiah's Messianic hope; the *ṣemach ṣaddiq*, as it is called, bears the name *Jahwe ṣidqenu* (xxiii 5 f.) and reveals essentially the same traits as Isaiah's last expectation in xi 1 ff.

Jeremiah's contemporary, Ezekiel, also emphasizes the inward renewal of the people (by the spirit of God) in xxxvi 26-28; and in his work, too, the expectation of the universal importance of Israel is lacking completely. The nations exist for him only as witnesses in the background of the tragedy of which Israel is the central figure. This concentration on the life of Israel itself and this turning in upon the most profound life of the spirit can be accounted for completely in the work of this prophet by the situation resulting from the absolute annihilation of outward existence,—especially when we compare his attitude with the preaching of Isaiah, for whom, after all, this destruction was still to come, and with the preaching of Deutero-Isaiah and Zechariah, who come or have come to that attitude owing to him. Nevertheless the hope of salvation in Ezekiel is complete; it is expressed especially in the often repeated words (also found in Jeremiah): "Ye shall be my people and I will be your God" (Ezek. xxxvi 28, etc.), in the promise: "My tabernacle also shall be with them" (xxxvii 27), in the name Ezekiel gives to Jerusalem in the last verse of ch. xlviii: *Jahwe šamma*, and no less in the description of the place of the temple in ch. xl-xlviii, and of the living water of the temple-brook that transforms the Judean desert and makes the Dead Sea abound in fish; and already in ch. xxxvi the prophet expresses the expectation that the country that was desolate shall become like the garden of Eden. God Himself shall rule His people and set up one shepherd over them (xxxiv 23; xxxvii 24). All this is a description of a total inward and fundamental renewal of Israel, a renewal which presupposes a clean break with all that had gone before. Although the rôle of the past is more important to Ezekiel than in Isaiah and Jeremiah, that does not mean that Ezekiel lives in the grip of the past. He critisizes, at any rate, the past very severely. Though the renewal is inward it is real. Outward salvation consists of the deliverance of the world and of being taken back to the land of the fathers [1]). All his hope is summed up in the description of the resurrection from the dead and experienced as a miracle, as a new life received from God

---

[1]) In my opinion ch. xxxviiif. should be classed among the younger apocalyptic additions; so also Bertholet, *Hesekiel* (*Handbuch zum A.T.*, 1936).

When we pass from Ezekiel to Deutero-Isaiah it is—in spite of the hope that even Ezekiel has never abandoned—as if we emerge from a dark cave, with only a narrow streak of light before us to show us the way, into the open air full of light and with a wide horizon. Everything has changed here—the prophet with whom he is linked most closely is certainly the first Isaiah, his great namesake or, better perhaps, his great teacher. HÖLSCHER calls him the first great eschatological preacher [1]), VOLZ has spoken of him as the prophet who is inspired wholly by eschatology [2]) and many other scholars agree with that opinion [3]). Some time ago this view was attacked strongly by J. LINDBLOM [4]), who is convinced that "the prophet is conscious that he is witnessing not the end of history, but a new act of a historical drama" [5]).

We shall have to recur to this subject but first we shall bring to the fore a few of Deutero-Isaiah's ideas. From various terms and images used by the prophet it appears that for him the salvation he expected and probably still saw enacted in part, far transcended what may be called a historical event. First of all we point out the use of the verb *bara'*, which he employs more than any other author [6]) which proves that for him the salvation of Israel was no less than a new creation [7]). Therefore he sees new things (*ḥadašot*) come to pass that have never been [8]); what God does in Israel may be compared with the creation in primeval times (li 9 ff.) or with the deliverance from Egypt, it will even surpass this deliverance (Israel left Egypt with haste, Deut. xvi 2, but from Babylon they shall not go out with haste, nor go by flight, Is. lii 12). The whole world shall witness it and is hoping and waiting for it (L 4 f.). Yahwe shall now be glorified in the presence of

---

[1]) HÖLSCHER, *Ursprünge der jüdischen Eschatologie*, 1925, p. 15.

[2]) *Jesaja* II; and "Der Eschatologische Glaube im A.T.", *Festschrift Beer*, 1935, p. 81.

[3]) J. LINDBLOM (*The Servant Songs in Deutero-Isaiah*, 1951, pp. 94, 10, 2) still mentions: BEGRICH, CAUSSE, SELLIN, HEMPEL.

[4]) *Op. cit.*, p. 95 f.; 101, n. 12, where R. H. PFEIFFER, H. H. ROWLEY and A. GUILLAUME are cited or introduced.

[5]) *Op. cit.*, p. 102.

[6]) See P. HUMBERT, "Emploi et portée du verbe *bârâ* (creêr) dans l'Ancien Testament", *Th. Zeitschrift*, 1947, p. 401; F. M. TH. BÖHL, *Bara als terminus der Weltschöpfung im altt. Sprachgebrauch*, *Festschrift Kittel*, 1913, p. 42 ff. Deutero-Isaiah uses the word 16 times; P uses it 12 times; and in the whole of the O.T. it occurs 44 times (HUMBERT).

[7]) HUMBERT, *op. cit.*, p. 420; in HUMBERT's opinion the term has not only a soteriological but also an eschatological meaning, p. 421.

[8]) Is. xlviii 6 f.; xli 20; xliii 7, 19; xlv 8; xlvi 9 f.; xliv 24 ff.

all, unto Him every knee shall bow (xlv 23). The gods of the world are nothing and are mocked. Yahwe reigns in Jerusalem (lii 7 f.); to Israel it is said: Behold your God (xl 9). God shall make an everlasting covenant (*berith ʿolam : ḥasde Dawid hanneʾemanim*) with Israel, so that all the nations shall run unto it (lv 3-5). Israel is called upon to be an *ōr goiim*, a *berith ʿam*, to teach the world the *tora* and the *mišpat* (xlii, xlix).

One can certainly not deny that Deutero-Isaiah is a poet and that he uses many images owing to a desire to express things in an elevated style that is all his own. But the pathos that dominates all this, is also that of the visionary who sees the birth of a new world. The purely historical events are also seen in this light: the rise of the new world-power only happens in order to prepare the way for God's work with Israel, to give Israel freedom so that it may fulfil its function in this world; to him and to his younger contemporary Zechariah (see below) the coming fall of Babylon is a definitely established fact. In what the prophet sees happening a new world is implied. J. Lindblom rightly says that what the prophet expects "belongs to present history", but it seems to me that he does not do justice to the message of this prophet by saying that this is "not the end of history, but a new act of a historical drama". I should like to propose the reading: *the* renewing act of *the* historical drama. In other words, what happens here takes place within the historical framework of the world, but it is something that definitely changes this world, and as such the *ʾaḥarit haiiamim*, though this expression is not used by him [1]).

These high hopes have passed from Deutero-Isaiah to his contemporaries and to the later prophets, to Haggai, Zechariah and the prophets and poets whose words were collected in Trito-Isaiah. In many different keys they sang of the salvation of which their master had spoken to them. From their prophecies it is obvious that the salvation expected by them would mean an absolutely decisive new situation in the world; heaven and earth and all the nations shall be shaken, and all that is precious shall be brought to the temple (Haggai ii 6-9); God shall overthrow the strength of the kingdoms of the heathen, and Zerubbabel shall be made the signet of His glory (Haggai ii 20-23); Jerusalem shall be the City of God (the metropolis

---

[1]) But Yahwe knows the *ʾaḥarit* (xli: 22; xlvi: 10). In itself *ʾaḥarit* need not be an eschatological term, as Köhler, *Lexicon* (s.v.) emphasized too strongly.

of the world, Zech. ii 5-9; 10-17; viii 20-23) when Yahweh has overcome the nations (Zech. ii 1-4). In the notions on salvation found in Trito-Isaiah Jerusalem is, rather one-sidedly, made the centre of interest, while on the other hand these notions also bear universal and supra-historical traits (Is. lxv 17-25; lxvi 5-24). In the first prophecy various traits that are elaborated in later apocalyptic writings (a new heaven and earth, a long term of life, such as men had before the Flood, the Isaianic peace of paradise) are clearly present already; we have here a later period (cf. e.g. Zech. viii 4 f. with Is. lxv 20) in which people revel spiritually in the signs of future salvation. Beside the cosmic element (Is. xxiv 21-23; Joel iii 3 ff.) the salvation of the individual is emphasized more and more in Joel and Is. xxiv-xxvii, so that here the borderline of later apocalyptics is reached. The transcendentalizing elements of later apocalyptics are the next stage. When we consider the transition from prophetic to apocalyptic preaching it strikes us how gradually this transition takes place; it is clear that there are differences, and even very important differences between the older, prophetic, and the younger, apocalyptic ideas, but there is no clear break between these two. We cannot without more ado say: here prophecy ends, there eschatology begins [1]). Even if certain elements (especially the transcendentalizing ones) may be called particularly apocalyptic, they are so closely linked with other, more prophetical elements that a complete separation of the two is never possible.

On the one hand people in the period after Deutero-Isaiah lived in the certainty that their hope of salvation would be fulfilled immediately; besides the expectation of Haggai und Zechariah I think I may point out the well-known words of the Chroniclers which prove that Jerusalem is thought of as the Kingdom of God on earth [2]). But on the other hand people also live in the expectation that salvation will soon be actualized; in support I refer to the elements of calculation that are already found in the Priestly Code, which probably contains an eschatological element in its chronological scheme [3]). This element of calculation is elaborated in the book of Daniel [4]).

[1]) See R. H. Charles, *Religious Development between the Old and New Testament*, reprinted 1948, p. 15 ff. M. A. Beek, *Inleiding in de Joodse apocalyptiek van het Oud- en Nieuw-Testamentisch tijdvak*, Theologia VI, 1950, p. 3 f.

[2]) Cf. 1 Chron. xvii 14, etc.

[3]) See among other works: L. Köhler, *Theologie des A.T.*, 3, 1953, p. 72, 238, N. 70.

[4]) Dan. ix 24-27; cf. also the 390 years of the Damascus writing, and perhaps

Besides these, other ideas develop which take the expectation of salvation more and more in a universal and transcendental sense: on the one hand we find disappointment that the actualisation of salvation should hold off for so long, on the other hand there is a transcendentalising element at work that had sprung up at an earlier period; but probably the dualism of Parseeism also makes its influence felt here to some extent.

IIB. CONCLUSIONS FROM THE MATERIAL

Looking back on Israelitic prophetism after this survey, I see two culminating-points: Isaiah (surrounded by Amos, Hosea and Micah), and Deutero-Isaiah, the one at the entrance to the dark tunnel through which Israel must pass, the other at the end of this tunnel; they are, as it were, the poles on which the prophetical message turns. The former lives in the tension of expectation, the latter in the tension of fulfilment, if I may use these two words which certainly do not exclude each other.

The task of the prophets has been to announce the downfall of the people of God, Israel, as it lived empirically, in order that in this way the people of Israel, which had been chosen by God, should fulfil its calling [1]). The secret of the prophetic activity is the double aspect of Israel: the empirical Israel as the people of God. And the error in many studies on the message of the prophets is that this point is not borne in mind sufficiently. The other day this became clear to me when I looked through one of the older dissertations on the subject [2]), in which the classical thesis of WELLHAUSEN is defended that all hopes of salvation (called eschatological ideas) are post-exilic; this is finally supported by a quotation from KÜCHLER [3]): "When solche gegensätzliche Meinungen (about downfall and renewal) bei demselben Mann in derselben Zeit seines Lebens für möglich gehalten werden dürften, fällt . . . der Charakteridentität einer religiös-

---

of Ez. iv 5; one of the calculations may have been: 2666 (Creation till Exodos), 480 (temple of Salomon), 430 (Kings of Juda after the building of the Temple), 390 (period of doom of Israel), 40 (period of doom of Judah), i.e. 4006 years.

[1]) J. LINDBLOM, "The historical eschatology originates in the belief in the election of Israel and is unique for the Israelite religion" (*Paper for the Society for O.T. study*, Roma 1952); cf. also M. A. BEEK, *op. cit.*, p. 5.

[2]) TH. L. W. VAN RAVESTEYN, *De eenheid der eschatologische voorstellingen van Jesaja* (thesis), 1910, p. 251.

[3]) *Die Stellung Jesajas zur Politik*, p. 55 (quoted by VAN RAVESTEYN).

sittlichen Persönlichkeit"; according to VAN RAVESTEIJN there would be two persons in one individual: a prophet of doom and an idealistic poet. But this older WELLHAUSIAN school did not observe that by virtue of its character the Israelitic faith possessed the possibility to proclaim the destruction of Israel as an empirical people and yet to keep the certainty that the God of Israel could bring His people to new life even through destruction. EERDMANS was one of the critics who remained convinced that the prophets did not only live by moral convictions but believed in the power of God, who would not leave His chosen people without a future [1]). EERDMANS' trend of opinion is more correct than that of the "eschatologians", like GRESSMANN, who accepted, indeed, the hope of salvation, but had to consider it in the writings of the prophets as a remnant of a prophetic, and even pre-Israelitic, general ancient-oriental eschatology [2]). In our opinion MOWINCKEL is right in claiming that there is no question of eschatology proper with the ancient-oriental peoples [3]).

It is not possible here to trace the roots of the expectation of salvation in Israel completely: they are bound up with the whole history of the people and with spiritual life in all its aspects, and therefore also with cultic life, with the place of the king among the people, though none of these elements should receive special emphasis [4]). This much we may, however, consider an established fact that Israel's special religious consciousness of its calling, which is rooted in its history (the history of salvation) and in the structure of its religion, is always present in the background of the prophetical message and that without it neither the critical attitude of the prophets nor their preaching concerning the future can be understood. The famous verse of Amos iii 2 indicates the true starting-point: Israel as the special people of God is punished by God with particular severity for its sins. We may never forget that *everything* that happens to Israel in the course of history is only viewed in religious light; for the prophets there exists, indeed, no such thing as profane history, and practically, but for one or two exceptions, history in its entirety, which is directed by Yahwe, is viewed in connection with Israel.

---

[1]) *Godsdienst van Israel*, I, 1930, p. 186. Cf. also L. DÜRR, *Ursprung und Ausbau der isr. jüd. Heilandserwartung*, 1925).

[2]) H. GRESSMANN, *Der Ursprung der isr. jüd. Eschatologie*, 1905; *Der Messias*, 1928.

[3]) *Thronsbesteigungsfest Jahwäs und Ursprung der Eschatologie*, 1922, p. 221 ff.

[4]) Neither, in my opinion, the cult (MOWINCKEL), nor e.g. the faith in God and the name of God as such (e.g. BLEEKER, *Over inhoud en oorsprong van Israels heilsverwachting*, 1921; and VAN GRONINGEN, *In the grip of the past*, p. 120).

Yahwe calls Assur, and afterwards Nebuchadrezzar and Cyrus, because He wants to punish or to deliver Israel, He sends the nations away again because they have done their duty or have assaulted Israel. The prophets are concerned with Israel as God's people, and as such it is not annihilated, even if it is destroyed empirically. For the prophets the possibility of a separation between God and the empirical people is an incontestable fact; they have cleansed the Israelitic religion of every naturalistic residue and then — because the relation between God and the people is looked upon as starting from the will of God— never abandoned their faith in the people of God. For faith has a logic that is all its own, and in Israel it is absolutely religious-realistic or, we might say, existentialistic, and not intellectual-abstracting. Only if we bear in mind the double meaning of the name Israel can we follow the prophets, especially Deutero-Isaiah [1]).

Thus we see them appear in history side by side: Amos, who was the first to make the terrible discovery of the downfall of the people and can only here and there rise above it in his preaching; Hosea, who on account of his experience (on the ground of divine demands that came to him) could struggle through and reach the certainty that Yahweh was paving the way for the new relation by His judgment, because He is the God who loves Israel, while in the name *šeʿar jašub* Isaiah has from the outset emphasized and borne witness to God's strange work which contains a terrible threat but to the eye of faith a promise as well.

The contrast between God and man is expressed clearly by Isaiah in its two aspects (Is. vi: the contrast between the Holy One and the sinner; Is. xxxi 3: the contrast between the Spirit and the flesh), so that the distance between God and man is brought to the fore, as against the old unity of God, man and world (which PEDERSEN has observed in ancient Israel). For Isaiah the renewal is by no means simply "historical" in our sense of the word (this term can be as misleading as the word "eschatological"): it is historical and at the same time supra-historical, it takes place within the framework of history but is caused by forces that transcend history, so that what is coming is a new order of things in which the glory and the Spirit of God (Is. xi) reveals itself. Already in Hosea's picture of the flowering wilderness, the peace among the animals, the response of the heavens

---

[1]) Even the people upon which the judgment falls is called "my people" by the prophets. A few times Isaiah uses the expression: this people (vi 10; viii 12; ix 15; xxviii 11, 14; xxix 13, 14), but also: my people !

to the earth, there are elements present that afterwards are deepened, spiritualized by Isaiah. The divine names of the Saviour-king are so many pledges for the new Kingdom, the Spirit of God is the source of life that begins to flow, salvation is extended to the world of nations; the earth is given a new aspect. What God is bringing about through the downfall of Israel is: a new Israel in a new world (Is. xi 9).

And the message of Deutero-Isaiah is the answer to this vision of faith; here we hear the cry: the time of salvation has come (Yahweh reigns in Zion); and the miracles commence, the world of nations is rising up and looking out—God gives His new creation.

This expectation that salvation is going to be actualized dominates the prophecies of the first few centuries after the exile. The message of salvation becomes of central importance, the preaching of judgment becomes secondary. Jerusalem is seen as the centre of the new world that is coming and as the throne of the Kingdom of God. Especially in Haggai and Zechariah i-viii these things seem to have come very near; afterwards comes the disappointment at the delay and then the Kingdom of Salvation becomes more and more a thing of the future; it becomes cosmic and transcendental, so that a new form of eschatology appears: the apocalyptic form.

III. FINAL CONCLUSIONS

May we use the word eschatology with regard to the prophetical expectation of salvation? In my opinion there is, indeed, no other word in our vocabulary, phenomenological and theological, to characterize this expectation, though some objections could be urged against the word because of its ambiguousness. Eschatology can be used in a narrower and a wider sense. In a narrower sense the only thing we can understand by it is the apocalyptic form of *ʿolam hazze* as against the *ʿolam habba*, or life in heaven as against life on earth.

But eschatology can also be used in a wider sense, to denote the faith that knows of a *new Kingdom*, a new world, even if there is no question here of the destruction of the kosmos and even if we see that it is all enacted within the framework of this one world of God. For *future* and *end*, for *later* and *last* Hebrew thought has only one word, *ʾaḫarit*, just as it has only one word for *prehistoric time* and *the past* (*qedem*) and for *always* and *eternity* (*ʿolam*) [1]).

[1]) Cf. the different ways in which Hebrew expresses the superlative degree, see D. Winton Thomas, *A Consideration of some Unusual ways of Expressing the Superlative in Hebrew*, *V.T.* III, 1953, 209 ff.

Time is not divided into periods which are given separate names; Hebrew thought does not know our idea of time and so it cannot divide time, for this way of thinking is not analytical but totalizing [1]). Our ideas can never be applied to Hebrew thought without more ado because they express sharper distinctions, and for that reason we cannot say, for instance, that the word eschatology as the doctrine of the eschata (superlative) cannot be employed to denote the doctrine of a renewal that falls within the framework of history, for Hebrew thought does not make such a sharp distinction between the historical and the supra-historical as we do. The Israelitic idea of history, too, differs from ours [2]). Because this language uses so few abstractions and makes so few distinctions [3]) it sometimes seems as if things are not kept apart sufficiently. But that is not true; from a distance this may seem to be the case more than it actually is. Even if for Isaiah things are enacted within the framework of this world there does exist for him an absolute break between that which exists now in order to be destroyed and that which is coming to renew the world [4]).

---

[1]) See JOH. PEDERSEN: *Israel*, I-II and TH. BOMAN, *Das hebräische Denken im Vergleich mit dem Griechischem*, 1952, p. 109 ff.; but *aḥarit* is not "hinter*ste* Seite" (hind*most* part); cf. E. JENNI, "Das Wort *ʿOlam* im A.T.", *Z.A.W.* 64, 1953, 197 ff.

[2]) *Toledoth* is history in the sense of: coming into existence, and the manifestation of what has come into existence; no attention at all is paid to the way in which this happens (immanently or transcendentally). *Haja* is *to become* and *to be*. The statical idea is unknown in ancient Israel, and so is an all-embracing idea of the world as a whole. The whole way of expression that is employed is different, it is concreting instead of abstracting: the "first" is "the one at the head", the "last": "the one at the back". In Gen. i the world is not created out of *nothing*, because there was no word to denote that; this idea does not emerge until the later Jewish world, influenced by Hellenistic thought; before that time *nothingness* was denoted by *tohu wabohu*, the chaos. Israelitic thought, which is practical, total and existential, which does not analyse and abstract strictly, does not permit in the older period the formation of ideas like : *last*, *the end* as such, etc. This must not be neglected in dealing with the problem of eschatology, otherwise things that belong together might be separated. The later eschatology is as closely related to the earlier prophetical eschatology as the later doctrine of the creation *ex nihilo* to that of Gen. i where the world is created by the word from the *tohu wabohu*.

[3]) Owing to this, words are, for instance, given a certain fluid meaning, so that it is not always possible to say with certainty what they mean exactly. A construction with *min*, for instance, may be comparative or separative: I love him above, more than, or: I love him and not the other....; probably the pitch or the word-accent play a part here which could not be expressed in writing.

[4]) Some have made the remark that the prophets did not expect the annihilation of the world, because they only spoke of their own country. I do not think that this is to the point (see p. 221 f: the whole history centres for the

It seems to me that if we are to arrange the data regarding eschatology in a sound objective survey we must distinguish four main periods. This is not to say that a clear historical break between these periods could be indicated exactly, for again and again the ideas of one period run on into another: either they are assimilated into it or they remain side by side with the more recent ideas. In a sense we must take over the remark made by STEUERNAGEL at the beginning of his essay on Jewish eschatology, viz. that there is no method in it but that a series of „Einzellinien" (lines of development) have sprung up [1]), which diverge from and are connected with each other and date from very different periods. In such a "fluid" sense we may arrive at the following classification into periods of the eschatological ideas:

1) pre-eschatological (before the classical prophets),

2) proto-eschatological (Isaiah and his contemporaries),

3) actual-eschatological (the eschatology which is being realized of Deutero-Isaiah and his contemporaries),

4a) transcendentalizing [2]) eschatology (the form of eschatology in which salvation is not expected to come in this world, but either spiritually in heaven or after a cosmic catastrophe in a new world),

4b) beside (and through) this transcendentalizing eschatology the various historical eschatological forms continue to exist in the last stage [3]), in the sense of 1) the pre-eschatological, 2) the proto-eschatological or 3) the actual-eschatological (though the last two occur least frequently). Especially the pre-eschatological ideas with their strong ethnical leanings live on in certain political Messianic expectations and movements. In this period 2) is mostly strongly transcendentalized; cf. on the transcendental form of 2) Daniel vii, etc. [4]). In the religiosity of more mystically-minded sects like the

prophets in Israel); moreover it must be held possible, that the prophecies of doom of the different *goiim* may have the meaning to express the idea that the whole world is to be judged.

[1]) C. STEUERNAGEL, "Die Strukturlinien der Entwicklung der jüdischen Eschatologie", *Bertholet-Festschrift*, 1950, p. 479 ff. Cf. also R. H. CHARLES, *Religious development between the O. and N.T.*, 16 ff.

[2]) In how far this transcendentalizing eschatology springs directly from Hebrew thought as a reaction on the delay in the realization of the eschatological expectations, or from outside Israel, especially from Parseeist or perhaps afterwards also Hellenistic thought, cannot be gone into at greater length here.

[3]) Cf. STEUERNAGEL, *op. cit.*, p. 480 ff.

[4]) STEUERNAGEL, *op. cit.*, p. 481 f.

Essenes [1]) 3) also seems to play a part, though a dualistic element also has influence there. A pure continuation of 3) is to be found especially in the early period of the Christian Church.

We shall now attempt to give a further definition of the characters of the first three periods and of their relation to each other.

The first period which I call pre-eschatological, is the period before the appearance of the classical prophets. In those days there is the expectation of a *jom Jahwe* [2]), which, as appears from Amos, is seen as the day of salvation on which Yahwe shall bring Israel to its full glory. He shall lead it back to the life it once had in the time of David. The future is seen to a great extent in the light of the past, the idealized age of David; people live at least as much in the grip of the past as in the grip of the future, though the latter element was not entirely lacking in Israel even in the days before the classical prophets (the Yahwist in Gen. xii 3). In this pre-eschatological period Israel's hopes are, as far as we can ascertain, mainly political-national (Gen. xix; Numb. xxiv; Deut. xxxiii, Yahweh-King-Psalms (?) [3])), though moral motives were not wanting. This form cannot really be called eschatological [4]), because this expectation is not concerned with the renewal of the world but with Israel's greatness [5]). Its tendency is much rather

[1]) They know themselves to be the holy congregation of God.

[2]) On the explanations of the *jom Jahwe*, on the one hand looked upon by Mowinckel as identical with the New-Year's Day and the Feast of the Ascension to the throne, on the other hand generally looked upon as the day of the victory of Yahwe as warrior, see H. Wheeler Robinson, *Inspiration and Revelation*, 1946, p. 138 ff.

[3]) Using the Psalms as historical data is one of the most difficult problems. This goes especially for the so-called Psalms on the Ascension to the throne. Because of their contents (Abraham, Moses, Aaron are mentioned and there are several things that remind us of the preaching of the prophets), their place in certain groups of Psalms, and also their style, they give the impression of generally belonging to a later period, to the cult of the second temple rather than to that of the first so that one might be inclined to class these Psalms (with Gunkel-Begrich) among the "eschatological" Psalms rather than among the very ancient cultic songs—even though the type may be old and may have belonged to the cult of the ancient New-Year's Feast as the feast of Jahwe-Malak. Here we cannot go into Mowinckel's thesis in his *Psalmenstudien*, II, in detail, where he looks upon eschatology as a psychological reaction (it is not clear in what period this becomes manifest) to a lassitude with regard to the cult of the feast of Yahwe as King: eschatology is an escape into the future as soon as the cult (which is here looked upon as a dramatical and effective rendering of the religious ideas) no longer conveys anything to the people.

[4]) This also with Mowinckel, but according to him for a different reason, viz. because in the cult the faithful already experienced the realization of the *jom Jahwe*.

[5]) On the other hand an idea such as the Yahwist's on the moral-spiritual calling of Abraham and his importance to world-history may not be looked upon as a

expansive-nationalistic than looking out spiritually for a new world created by Yahweh; moreover it is, in fact, directed to the past rather than to the future. Yet I think that this period may be called pre-eschatological, to denote that even in this period there were elements that are found again in the next period and themes on which this next period rests. I especially think of the certainty of Israel that it is God's people, a certainty the background of which lies not only in the cult but especially in history [1]).

The second period is that of Isaiah (Amos to Jeremiah): it is the period in which the vision of a new people and a new kingdom is beginning to play a part, a kingdom that will embrace the whole world and that rests on spiritual forces that spring from God [2]): I should like to call this the period of *awakening eschatology*; this kingdom certainly is an eschaton, *'aḥarit*, though it appears in history.

The third period is that of Deutero-Isaiah; its influence was felt until many centuries afterwards in various movements (see above, p. 225). This period I should like to call: *actualizing eschatology*: the kingdom of God is not only seen coming in *visions* but it is *experienced* as coming. The world is going to be changed: Israel is now called upon to be a light to the world and the nations are called upon to listen, and people feel certain of the glory of Zion, the mountain of God's temple, where every knee shall bow and all kings shall pay true homage to Israel.

Then there is a fourth period, the apocalyptic period of *dualistic eschatology*. Owing to various causes, first and foremost because of the disappointment after those high hopes and owing to the influence of a growing sense of distance in religious life, of a process of transcendentalizing, but also under the influence of the new worldview of Persian dualism [3]) and Hellenistic thought the eternal world of God above and reality on earth below, which is to be destroyed, are separated; the divine is transcendentalized and this implies that the world

---

national hope connected with this; he is rather a precursor of the great prophets (see my: *Die Erwählung Israels nach dem A.T.*, p. 86 ff.).

[1]) MOWINCKEL, *Psalmenstudien*, II, has acknowledged this factor, too, but he has assessed its value too low, at any rate he has not developed it; p. 320 f.

[2]) The opinion of CHARLES, *op. cit.*, p. 19 and *passim*, that "the prophetic expectation of a blessed future for the nation from an ethical stand point was materialistic", is not correct.

[3]) It is very probably that this influence must be admitted; we must bear in mind the remark of H. GRESSMANN, *Der Messias*, p. 352, that this influence was that of the religion of the people; it is, however, most unlikely that is should already have been noticeable at the time of the generation of the exile.

is secularized; God and the world are separated. The difference between this period of eschatology and the preceding is not only that the latter is actualized within the framework of time and the former is not, but there is also a difference in scene of action and in person. We might always say that in the time of the classical prophets (so also in the first period after the exile) there still is unity of place and time (this world) and action (person; it is God who truly works). In the apocalyptic period this unity is broken; the place where the new kingdom is to be realized is different, for the world is to be destroyed and a new world shall come; the time is different, for we enter into eternity here [1]); and the action is different, too: there is not merely the activity of God in behalf of the Messianic figure, but there are many figures who take action, who do preparatory work, while the Messiah (Messiahs) becomes the bringer of salvation.

The eschatological vision is an Israelitic phenomenon which has not really been found outside Israel—as has rightly been maintained by MOWINCKEL against GRESSMANN etc. [2]); but it is not the wishdream of a people that had become tired of its cult (MOWINCKEL), it must be accounted for by a truly genuine Yahwism, purged from nationalistic, worldly and secularized expectations by the religious prophetical criticism.

Eschatology did not arise where people began to doubt the actuality of the cult, but where the prophets were confronted with the actuality of their own faith in God and where this realism of faith was directed critically at the life of the people [3]). As a result the prophets admitted that the divine judgment was coming but also confessed that the Holy God remained unshakeable in His fidelity to and His love of Israel. Thus the life of Israel in history came to have a double aspect: on the one hand judgment is near at hand, on the other hand, however, salvation lies in the future. In this way the classical prophetical religion brings about a tension completely different from the

---

[1]) BUBER, *Der Glaube der Propheten*, p. 216, rightly calls the *Endzeit*: "Stillstehen der Geschichte".

[2]) Cf. in connexion with this, from a quite other side B. A. VAN GRONINGEN, *op. cit.*, p. 120, who shows the sharp contrast of the Israelitic and Christian faith with the Greek philosophy of life; neither philosophy nor religion created here the idea that there was any purpose for the world. „The gods have no leading role notwithstanding their power; they merely manifest themselves. There is no law aiming at a final purpose, but one which determines that everything happens as it does".

[3]) Cf. W. EICHRODT, *Theologie des A. T.* I 205 f.

tension that dominates the cultic religion. People begin to think in terms of a near future and a more distant future [1])—the latter indicates the limits of the horizon and must, therefore, from the point of view of the prophet, be final; for him it is essentially an *'aḫarit* in the sense of an eschaton. Eschatology is not a wish-dream that admits of a psychological explanation, but a religious certainty which springs immediately from the Israelitic faith in God as rooted in the history of its salvation. The eschatological vision was *possible* because Israel knew its God as the active Creator-God, who in His holiness does not abandon this world and goes on working in history; this vision became *reality* because the prophets, penetrating into the knowledge of God's holy Being, more and more experienced the discrepancy between what was and what should be. The final break in the ancient-Israelitic totalitarian philosophy of life which started from the unity of God, the world, the people and the compatriot, is the point where eschatology breaks through; and eschatology is the form in which the critical realism of faith of the prophets maintained its confession of Yahweh, the Lord of the World. The basic-content of eschatology is the prophetical word of God that Jeremiah as well as Ezekiel impress upon their people in their greatest distress: "Ye shall be my people, and I will be your God".

Lastly eschatology is the universal form of the confession of praying faith, that was given a definite personal form by the Psalmist:

Jahwe jigmor ba'adi, Jahwe ḥasdeḵa le'olam, ma'ašē jadeḵa 'al teref!
(Ps. cxxxviii 8)

---

[1]) H. H. Rowley, *The Growth of the O.T.*, 1950, p. 83 f.